UNREVOLUTIONARY ENGLAND

1603 - 1642

UNREVOLUTIONARY ENGLAND, 1603-1642

CONRAD RUSSELL

PROFESSOR OF BRITISH HISTORY
KINGS COLLEGE LONDON

THE HAMBLEDON PRESS
LONDON AND RONCEVERTE

Published by The Hambledon Press, 1990

102 Gloucester Avenue, London NW1 8HX (U.K.)

309 Greenbrier Avenue, Ronceverte WV 24970 (U.S.A.)

ISBN 1 85285 025 6

British Library Cataloguing in Publication Data

Russell, Conrad, *1937-*
Unrevolutionary England, 1603-1642
1. Great Britain, 1603-1649
I. Title
94'06'1

Library of Congress Cataloging-in-Publication Data

Russell, Conrad.
Unrevolutionary England, 1603-1642/ Conrad Russell.
Includes bibliographical references.
1. Great Britain – History – Early Stuarts, 1603-1649.
I. Title.
DA390.R84 1990
941.06'1 – dc20 90-4256 CIP

Printed in Great Britain on acid-free paper and bound
by W.B.C. Ltd., Maesteg.

Contents

Acknowledgements vii

Introduction ix

I. POLITICS

1 The Nature of a Parliament in Early Stuart England 1

2 Parliamentary History in Perspective, 1604-1629 31

3 The Foreign Policy Debate in the House of Commons in 1621 59

4 The Examination of Mr. Mallory after the Parliament of 1621 81

5 The Theory of Treason in the Trial of Strafford 89

6 The Authorship of the Bishop's Diary of the House of Lords in 1641 111

II. MONEY

7 Monarchies, Wars, and Estates in England, France and Spain, *c.* 1580- *c.* 1640 121

8 The Ship Money Judgements of Bramston and Davenport 137

9 The Wardship of John Pym 145

10 Charles I's Financial Estimates for 1642 165

III. RELIGIOUS UNITY

11 Arguments for Religious Unity in England, 1530-1650 179

12 The Parliamentary Career of John Pym, 1621-1629 205

IV. THE ROAD TO CIVIL WAR

13	The British Problem and the English Civil War	231
14	Why did Charles I call the Long Parliament?	253
15	The British Background to the Irish Rebellion of 1641	263
16	The First Army Plot of 1641	281

V. EPILOGUE

17	The Catholic Wind	305
Index		309

Acknowledgements

The articles reprinted here appeared first in the following places and are reprinted by the kind permission of the original publishers.

1 *Before the English Civil War*, edited by Howard Tomlinson (Macmillan, 1983), pp. 23-50, 202-6.

2 *History*, 61 (1976), pp. 1-27.

3 *Historical Journal*, 20 (1977), pp. 289-309.

4 *Bulletin of the Institute of Historical Research*, 50 (1977), pp. 125-32.

5 *English Historical Review*, lxxx (1965), pp. 30-50.

6 *Bulletin of the Institute of Historical Research*, 41 (1968), pp. 229-36.

7 *Legislative Studies Quarterly*, vii no. 2 (May 1982), pp. 205-20.

8 *English Historical Review*, lxxvii (1962), pp. 312-18.

9 *English Historical Review*, lxxxiv (1969), pp. 304-17.
Appendix I: *Notes and Queries* (Jan. 1969), p. 33.
Appendix II (*with Evelyn Gore*): *Bulletin of the Institute of Historical Research*, 46 (1973), pp. 106-7.

10 *Bulletin of the Institute of Historical Research*, 58 (1985), pp. 109-20.

11 *Journal of Ecclesiastical History*, xviii (1967), pp. 201-26.

12 *The English Commonwealth, 1547-1640: Essays in Politics and Society Presented to Joel Hurstfield*, edited by A. Clark, A.G.R. Smith & N. Tyacke (Leicester University Press, 1979), pp. 147-65.

13 *History*, 72 (1987), pp. 395-415.

14 *History*, 69 (1984), pp. 375-83.

15 *Historical Research*, 61 (1988), pp. 166-82.

16 *Transactions of the Royal Historical Society*, 5th Series, 38 (1988), pp. 85-106.

Introduction

These essays, taken together, constitute one expression of the historiographical creed which came to be known in the late 1970s by the general name of 'revisionism'. That creed, of course, had many practitioners, whose positions were never identical, yet it may be claimed that all versions of revisionism, like all brands of whisky, enjoyed certain broad similarities. Perhaps the most important of these was a rejection of a dialectical framework for history, a disinclination to see change as always happening by means of a clash of opposites. To those aware of the strength of Hegel's influence on the philosphy of the nineteenth and early twentieth centuries, it should come as no surprise to realize that the dialectical framework was never confined to the followers of Marx. It influenced Gardiner as much as Tawney, and Notestein as much as Hill, and revisionism has always been directed against the historiographical assumptions Whigs and Marxists held in common. So far, it has been the Whigs who have given us a run for our money.

In particular, as A.F. Pollard's work on *The Evolution of Parliament* illustrated,[1] it was not only Marx who attempted to import into the study of history a body of ideas derived from Darwin. S.R. Gardiner, as a good Victorian, was deeply influenced by the notion of progress, and from this notion developed an attachment to what revisionists have learnt to describe as 'teleological' history: a tendency to use history as a way of explaining why events led to their ultimate conclusion. As a result, or so most revisionists have argued, the story we have been told has been seen through the distorting medium of hindsight. This attempt to evade the influence of hindsight on the story has happened in other fields of historical investigation, including the origins of the English Reformation, and in all of them, historians writing in the 1970s have been attempting to argue that hindsight has grossly distorted the story we have hitherto been told.

There is, of course, nothing wrong with the belief that it is the duty of historians to explain why events turned out as they did. To say, in Professor Elton's phrase, that the Parliaments of the early seventeenth

[1] A.F. Pollard, *The Evolution of Parliament* (1926).

century were not 'A High Road to Civil War'[2] does not absolve us of the need to find out what the causes of the English Civil War were.[3] Somewhere, there was a road, whether high or low, which led to the English Civil War, and it is our duty to find it. The attack on hindsight has not been an attempt to evade the search for causes. It has been an attempt to avoid the pressure to assume, *a priori*, that the result we are investigating was inevitable. We have therefore tried to avoid forming a picture in which only those parts of the story which appear to have led towards the final result were thought worthy of notice.

Revisionism has also been an attempt to restore the study of political narrative history. To let the search for causes or explanations take priority over the establishment of the correct story is to put the cart before the horse. It has throughout been the revisionist creed that we must establish the course of events by treating it as a subject worthy of study in its own right, and then and only then attempt to analyse its causes. This is the point of Dr. Morrill's famous insistence that we should 'look after the pennies and the pounds will look after themselves'.[4] We have been suggesting that the fashionable denigration of *l'histoire événementielle* has been capable of leading to a significant distortion of the *longue durée*. We believe that the logically correct order of proceeding is to establish the correct events first, and to consider their explanation afterwards. We do not believe that it is only errors by previous historians which make the political narrative need revision: we are well aware of the flood of new documents which have become available over the past forty years, and always prepared to consider the possibility that new material may produce some significant change in the story.

These essays are also informed by a reluctance to assume with as much confidence as the Victorians did that England is always a special case. The International Commission for the History of Representative Institutions has now done too much work to make it very easy to assume that there is anything specially English about Parliaments. Still less would we make the potentially offensive assumption that the survival of Parliaments in England is due to any special moral virtue among the English. We would at least entertain the hypothesis that during the Thirty Years' War, as during the Second World War, the survival of our representative institutions owes something to the English Channel.

The pieces here printed have been written over a period of twenty-seven years, and my ideas have inevitably and rightly changed over that

[2] G.R. Elton, 'A High Road to Civil War?', in *Essays in Honour of Garrett Mattingley*, Ed. Charles H. Carter (1966) pp. 325 ff.

[3] On this subject, see my *The Causes of the English Civil War*, Oxford University Press, forthcoming.

[4] *Times Literary Supplement*, 24 Oct. 1980. I would like to thank Dr. Morrill for supplying the date of this reference.

period. Looking back, it appears to me that the article on 'Parliamentary History in Perspective', published in 1976, was the watershed in my own thinking. Yet in reaching that watershed, I was necessarily influenced by the findings of the earlier articles included in this collection, and their contents still provide many of the themes which give this collection such unity as the reader may think it possesses. In deciding to print them as they stand, rather than to pour new wine into old bottles, I have been influenced by this fact. Their factual findings still appear to me to be largely correct, and where they strike me as old is in their use of terminology. In particular, they contain several uses of the terms 'opposition' and 'Puritan' which I would now regard as misleading.[5] Readers may, of course, think that I was right then and am wrong now, but I hope they will not quote this terminology as representing my current thinking. It is because the factual findings still appear to me to be correct, and part of the material on which my present ideas are based, that I have thought these pieces suitable for inclusion.

There is no section here which is specifically devoted to the task of refuting the view that the English Civil War was the result of preceding social change, but readers who wish to pursue that theme will find a good deal of material which may help to explain why I do not see it in that light. The article on Bishop Warner's diary of the House of Lords, and a number of passages in other articles, point to the view that the peers' importance in the politics of the early seventeenth century has been underestimated. This proposition applies, not only to their importance as one of the two Houses of Parliament, but also to the importance many of them enjoyed as individuals, both through their influence at court, and through their contacts in the House of Commons. My biographical work on John Pym has tended to sustain this view, since it is clear that, without patrons among the peerage, he would have stood very little chance of election to the House of Commons. He certainly will not serve for a model of 'the rising gentry', trying to acquire a political influence commensurate with their economic power. Pym's economic power was very small, and the source of his political influence is perhaps illustrated in his employment as draftsman for the document which has become known to history as 'the Petition of the Twelve Peers'. When Clarendon described him as a 'man of business', he may not have meant all the innuendoes Professor Graves has given to the term,[6] but he was clearly using a terminology closer to

[5] See, for example, 'The Wardship of John Pym', p. 149 for a usage I would not now wish to repeat. Nor would I wish to repeat the description of Sir Robert Berkeley as an 'extremist' in 'The Ship Money Judgements of Bramston and Davenport', p. 139. For my reasons for abandoning this belief, see my *The Fall of the British Monarchies, 1637-1642*, Oxford University Press, forthcoming, chapter I.

[6] Michael Graves, 'The Management of the Elizabethan House of Commons: The Council's Men-of-Business', *Parliamentary History*, vol. II (1983), pp. 11-38.

Professor Graves's than, for example, Tawney's.

To say this is not to accept the caricature picture of clientage in which members of the Commons move while lords pull the strings.[7] Members of the Commons had minds of their own, and even when we regard some of them as 'clients' of peers, it does not follow that they were puppets. K.B. McFarlane was undoubtedly right that, in the fifteenth century, influence between lord and retainer was a two-way street. As a minister might sometimes influence his king, so a retainer might sometimes influence his lord.[8] In the seventeenth century, it is also true that they might sometimes take different lines. In many cases, such as Sir Thomas Barrington and the Earl of Warwick, or Richard Knightley and Viscount Saye and Sele, the social and economic standing of peer and gentleman was too nearly equal for it to be possible to treat them as anything but allies. Dr. Adamson's picture of 'bicameral factions' is more accurate than a straight picture of patron and client.[9] Nevertheless, the importance with which peers emerge from my work and from Dr. Adamson's, is so great that an attempt to investigate the economic standing of the aristocracy in order to explain the reduction of their influence over the events of 1640-42 becomes a serious example of putting the cart before the horse.[10] As those events come to be better understood, they look less and less like events which social change could readily explain.

These essays are divided into four sections and an epilogue, dealing in turn with politics, money, religion and the events of 1640-42. Since events have a tiresome tendency to be interrelated, no such division can be complete or watertight. Some repetition is inevitable, but this is the basic principle on which the material is divided. It is only the first section, devoted largely to negative propositions, which can enjoy even a limited claim to express the creed of revisionism as a whole. The unity of revisionists in the 1970s was always built round a series of negative propositions. We always agreed, even then, that if we ever succeeded in establishing these negative propositions, we would be free to disagree quite considerably about what should be put in their place. The three remaining sections represent preliminary sketches towards a new picture, and these make no pretence to speak even in the most limited way for anyone but myself.

The material in this first section questions a creed which, in its broad

[7] It is not clear that any revisionist has ever held this view, but since it is sometimes charged upon us, it is necessary to disown it.

[8] K.B. McFarlane, 'Parliament and "Bastard Feudalism"', *T.R.H.S.* 4th Series (xxvi) (1944), pp. 53-79, reprinted in *England in the Fifteenth Century*, Ed. G.L. Harriss (1981) pp. 1-21, esp. pp. 12 and 19-20.

[9] J.S.A. Adamson, 'Parliamentary Management, Men of Business and the House of Lords 1640-1649', in *A Pillar of the Constitution*, Ed. Clyve Jones (1989), pp. 21-50.

[10] Lawrence Stone, *The Crisis of the Aristocracy*, Oxford (1965) p. 7.

essentials, has been unchanged from 1924 to 1974. It is that expressed in Wallace Notestein's Lecture on *The Winning of the Initiative by the House of Commons*, delivered under the first Ramsay MacDonald government.[11] It must be said, in the first place, that no historical paradigm lasts for fifty years without being rather good; that creed lasted, in part, because it was defended by a large amount of good historical scholarship. In the second place, however, it must be said that when any creed does last fifty years, the ultimate breaking of the dam gives rise to a good deal of historical turbulence. The accumulated small change of fifty years' research builds up a considerable body of material which must be reordered and reclassified. This is a task which is still in its early stages, but it is already possible to see that a new body of small change is being built up.

The central negative propositions are set out in the first two essays, on 'The Nature of a Parliament', and on 'Parliamentary History in Perspective'. They are designed to deny the picture of events which used to be encapsulated in the words 'the struggle for sovereignty'. The first central theme is the denial of a 'two sides' model of politics, in which members of Parliament used to be seen as belonging either to 'the government' or to 'the opposition'. It was assumed that members behaved, or ought to have behaved, in a way consistent with their 'side', that if we knew which side a man was on, we had discovered the first thing necessary to understanding his politics.

This picture was always anachronistic. It is the first characteristic of an opposition that it represents an alternative government, and therefore an alternative power base. Any power an opposition may possess arises from the belief that it might one day be in office, or from the belief that it is necessary to outmanoeuvre it lest one day it might be in office. Under a hereditary monarchy, opposition is a status likely to represent political oblivion, and it is not surprising that able politicians should have devoted considerable effort to avoiding it. There are only two ways in which serious political opposition is possible under a monarchy. One is through possession of a Pretender or a reversionary interest to the throne, who may provide the necessary alternative source of power, and it is one of the peculiarities of the early Stuart period that no Pretender was available. The other way is through the use of an army, and that was not available until August 1640. In the seventeenth century, unlike the fourteenth, opposition had to rely on a foreign army.

It seems to have been the belief of the old school that Parliament constituted such an alternative power base, a sort of collective Pretender. It is this belief, the teleological assumption that we are witnessing a kind of progression towards 'parliamentary government' which is denied in the other central negative proposition of these essays. Throughout this

[11] Wallace Notestein, *The Winning of the Initiative by the House of Commons* (1924).

period, England was and remained a monarchy, and even though that monarchy might sometimes call Parliaments, the King remained the only permanent source of power. Any power a Parliament might possess was its power to persuade the King.

This does not mean that a Parliament was useless as a forum in which to persuade the King. Buckingham, like Burghley, was quite capable of using a Parliament to good effect in the task of persuading an obstinate sovereign, yet the power deployed was that of the individuals who could be arrayed in a Parliament: it was not that of an institution automatically powerful simply because it chose to say 'no'. Nothing in these essays is designed to deny that a Parliament could be useful in persuading a King, especially if he wished, or might wish, to do something for which extraordinary supply was useful. They are designed, however, to deny that a Parliament was in any position to coerce a King, even if it did attempt to withhold supply until it received redress of the grievance which concerned it for the time being. It was, after all, because this was so that in 1649, it proved necessary, in effect, to get rid of the Parliament as well as the King.

Among the individual specific pieces, the study of 'The Foreign Policy Debate in 1621' is directed to one of the showpieces of the old interpretation. It is designed to show that if we assume a 'two sides' model, with government and opposition arrayed on opposite sides, and if we assume long-term constitutional objectives instead of short-term political ones, we simply cannot describe what was happening. If we assume members were concerned with bringing about or preventing parliamentary supremacy, rather than with bringing about or preventing a war with Spain, their actions became unintelligible. Whether the reconstruction suggested here is in fact the correct one is uncertain, and I have sketched a different one in *Parliaments and English Politics, 1621-1629.*[12] Both appear to be compatible with all the known evidence, and only the discovery of new material is likely to decide between them. What both have in common is that they do not appear to be compatible with the old interpretation. Even James's 'tendency to make constitutional issues' seems more likely to be designed to fight off the pressure for war with Spain than to fight off any pressure for parliamentary supremacy. James's 'tendency to make constitutional issues' was because once he could fight on that ground his victory was assured. *Mutatis mutandis*, a similar article could have been written about any of the milestones of the old

[12] For the alternative interpretation, see my *Parliaments and English Politics, 1621-1629*, Oxford (1979), pp. 121-44. The alternative interpretation would start from the hypothesis that Buckingham encouraged the foreign policy debate with James's prior approval. James's objective would then be the result he achieved, of discrediting the pressure for war by tarring it with the brush of constitutional impropriety. In neither interpretation can the debate be seen as an attempt by a Parliamentary opposition to 'win the initiative'.

interpretation. It has been done for the Apology of the Commons of 1604, the Great Contract of 1610, the appropriation of supply in 1624, the impreachment of Buckingham in 1626, the passage of the Petition of Right, and even the impeachment of Strafford in 1641. In all these cases, the use of the old framework led to an inaccurate description of events, and this is the best reason for regarding it as misconceived.[13]

The little article on 'The Examination of Mr. Mallory' is included because, not being a specifically revisionist article, it helps to illustrate some of the points this collection is not intended to argue. It was never my intention to argue that all that happened in the Parliaments of the 1620s was a model of amiability. Revisionists are often accused of believing that the whole period was one of 'consensus'. It was, no doubt, one where the search for it continued in situations where believers in the two-party model would not have sought for it, but it should be clear that between Mallory and Buckingham, there was not even the shadow of consensus in January and February 1622. This article can also illustrate that the proposition that people were not engaged in pursuing long-term constitutional objectives need not mean that they were unconcerned with immediate constitutional issues. Freedom of speech and parliamentary privilege were issues of considerable importance to Mallory, and he was willing to suffer for them.

None of this material was ever designed to argue that the early seventeenth century was immune from the normal disagreements of politics. Such disagreements happened, and on occasion they could be deep and bitter. This was particularly true of issues involving religion or the progressive collapse of the financial system. It was much less true in issues involving constitutional and legal thinking. It is that area, in which Notestein and his followers were particularly tempted to see two rival party programmes, in which disagreements were in fact least deep. There was a very wide measure of agreement on the principles on which the country ought to be governed when the system was working well. The problem was that the system was not working well, and the disagreement was about why it was not working well. Such disagreements were usually derived from different underlying assumptions about one of two things. One, as in the case of Pym, was religion: for Pym, foreign policy was as much a by-product of his religion as his interpretation of the Thirty-Nine Articles. The other, as in the case of Seymour, was money: most of Seymour's legal disagreements with Charles were ultimately derived from

[13] See, for example, G.R. Elton, quoted in n. 2 above; Eric Lindquist, 'The Failure of the Great Contract', *Journal of Modern History*, vol. 57 (1985) pp. 617-51; J.N. Ball, 'The Parliamentary Career of Sir John Eliot 1624-1629', Cambridge Ph.D. thesis (1953) pp. 40-1; J.N. Ball, 'The Impeachment of the Duke of Buckingham in the Parliament of 1626', in *Mélanges Antonio Marongiu*, Ed. Emile Lousse, Brussels (1968) pp. 35-48, and my *Fall of the British Monarchies, 1637-1642*, Oxford University Press (forthcoming), chapter VII.

Seymour's belief that Charles ought to have been able to manage on the sums Seymour saw fit to vote to him, and from Charles's knowledge that he could do no such thing. When I said there was no 'opposition' in early seventeenth-century Parliaments, I did not mean such battles were not fought to win: I meant they were not fought to bring in an alternative government. Charles was a ruler to whom there was no alternative, and the view of Parliaments as an alternative government in waiting was the deepest misapprehension in the traditional view. Under a ruler to whom there is no alternative, political battles are not fought by assembling an 'opposition': they are fought by collecting friends at court. One of the biggest objections to calling disagreements in early seventeenth-century Parliaments 'opposition' is that it makes us lose sight of the rules by which such disagreements had to be resolved. The moment a seventeenth-century cause became an 'opposition', it was reduced to the choice between rebellion and failure. English Parliamentarians were not reduced to that point until after the assembly of the Long Parliament.

Another major point the case of Mallory may illustrate is the discontinuity between the political issues of the 1620s and those of 1640-42. Anyone who still wants to find a 'parliamentary opposition' in the 1620s would be likely to choose William Mallory as one of his best cases. He was an inveterate troublemaker and deeply suspicious of power. Yet Mallory was a Royalist in 1642, and possibly a church-papist as well. He might be used as a representative of an 'opposition', but he would hardly serve for representative of a 'Puritan opposition'. In 1640-42, when the issues were much more strictly religious than they were for most of the 1620s, Mallory did not even enjoy the option of being a Parliamentarian, and it was either he or his son who moved that the Militia Ordinance should be burnt in Palace Yard.

The one issue in the 1620s which most clearly divided people along the sort of lines which were to divide them in 1642 was the issue of war with Spain and the Spanish Match. This issue, which divided Buckingham from James, was never a government versus opposition or court versus country issue, but the ideological approach to foreign policy involved did separate future Royalists from future Parliamentarians with a greater accuracy than any other issue of the period. On this issue, Mallory is no exception. He is one of a considerable body of people, possibly about the same size as the Royalist party in 1642, who did no more to help on the drive to war in 1621 or 1624 than the barest courtesy to official influence demanded. This list includes Sir Thomas Wentworth, John Glanville in 1621, Sir Francis Seymour, Sir Guy Palmes, Sir John Strangeways and William Noy. If we look for the ideas and attitudes which divided them from such men as Pym, Rudyerd, Harley and Wilde, we will be as near understanding the ideas which divided men in the Civil War as we can ever be in the 1620s. Yet we will not have discovered a government versus opposition split: we will have found a test which flushes out most of those, such as Manchester, Holland and Sir John Coke, who combined membership of the government in the 1620s with Parliamentarian sympathies in the Civil War.

The essay on the trial of Strafford is one of only two in this collection which deal specifically with the history of ideas. This is an area in which there is much more work to be done, and in which it is possible that as much revision will need to be done as in the history of the political narrative. This piece is an early one, as much of its terminology illustrates, but it was also the first which created in me a nagging anxiety about whether the received story could be true. It is hard to imagine that those who held the beliefs described in this essay could have formed the intentions which traditional historiography attributed to them.

Again, as in the case of Mallory, we are not dealing with consensus, nor even with the absence of bitter conflict. The notion that consensus existed between Pym and Strafford while they fought each other to the death is somewhat too paradoxical to be taken seriously. Yet it is also striking how far Pym and Strafford fought each other in terms of a common body of ideas, how far they were fighting for control of an ideological high ground which they identified in very similar ways. For both of them, unity was the one thing to be desired, and the destruction of unity the one crime which overrode all others. Each, of course, thought its destruction almost entirely the work of the other, but it is surely clear that two politicians who naturally thought in party terms would not have chosen to fight on this particular ground: there would have been no strategic gain in conquering it.

They agreed, even more obviously, in an ideological rejection of change. These men were not adopting a posture of progressives: their view of change was postlapsarian and fearful. Nor were they people who, like some of the Levellers, concealed a devotion to a brave new world under the cult of a mythical antiquarian past. Both of them needed to look no further back than the reign of James for a past in which they had been at least reasonably content. They seem to me to illustrate my maxim that 'when things cannot continue as they have been, conservatism becomes a force for instability'.[14] One of the things on which Pym and Strafford agreed most deeply was that if unity, balance and harmony were disappearing, someone was to blame and should be punished for it. It was this common conviction, as much as anything else, which drove them to hostilities with each other. In terms of political theory, differences between them were not wide. Everyone had a double-barrelled view on the relations between law and prerogative, one barrel for use when the King was right, and the other for use when he was wrong. They disagreed, of course, about which barrel should be applied to the Bishops' Wars, but

[14] 'The Nature of a Parliament', below, p. 24.

the merest glance at Pym's views on the treatment of recusants or Irishmen should show that, quite as much as Stafford, he possessed the other barrel when he thought it appropriate. Once this double-barrelled effect is allowed for, their views on the relations of law and prerogative are not as far apart as they seem.[15] J.W. Allen's statement that 'there is hardly anywhere to be found any suggestion that the king can make law'[16] seems to me to be correct, and it is hard to reconcile with any attempt to divide seventeenth-century thinkers into absolutists and contractualists. The differences between Pym and Strafford were religious and political, and were encapsulated in the question whether the Bishops' Wars were an attempt to conquer our co-religionists, or to repel an assault by Puritan rebels. Pym and Strafford were divided in 1641 by the same issues which divided them in 1624, and these issues were not primarily constitutional.

After the appearance of my article on 'Parliamentary History in Perspective', one of my senior colleagues said to me: 'after the destruction comes the construction: that's much more difficult'. Parts II, III and IV are attempts to meet that challenge. The second part deals with the proposition that the seventeenth century saw the decline of a political system in part because that system no longer allowed the Crown an adequate revenue.[17] The system by which the Crown tried to live in normal times on its ordinary revenues (including those, like Tonnage and Poundage, which came from a long-term Parliamentary grant), while relying on occasional Parliaments for extraordinary supply, lasted from approximately 1300 to 1689. By 1629, it was a system visibly on its last legs, but which none of the parties concerned were willing to replace.[18] It was because the system's political health was so good that its financial ill-health did not persuade anyone to make serious attempts to replace it.

Here, if not in the political story, there do seem to have been long-term forces at work, leaving politicians at their mercy and unable to control them. Some of these forces were economic, but they were nothing to do with any change in the class structure. The first of these forces was inflation, running through the century from 1510. Its effects were masked for some sixty years by the Dissolution of the Monasteries, and for another thirty or forty by credit, failure to pay debts, and other hand-to-mouth expedients. The Crown's revenues seem to have been exceptionally ill-suited to the task of adaptation to inflation. By 1640, the Crown was far

[15] I owe this point to the Rev. Dr. Daniel Doriani, who originally made it about the views of William Gouge and others on the duties of a husband and the duties of a wife.

[16] Quoted below, 'The Theory of Treason in the Trial of Strafford', p. 94.

[17] I owe the central idea of this section to the late Professor Joel Hurstfield, whom I would like to thank for many kindnesses.

[18] G.L. Harriss, *King, Parliament and Public Finance in Medieval England*, Oxford (1975) p. ...

poorer, and therefore much weaker, than it had been a century earlier.

Inflation was a European, and not just an English, trend. So was the other trend which brought this effect about. It was that series of changes in warfare which have been collectively dubbed 'the military revolution'.[19] These are the changes which began, about the beginning of the sixteenth century, when fortifications caught up with gunpowder. The result was much larger armies, much longer wars, and an increase in the cost of war which outstripped even the general rate of inflation. 'Monarchies, Wars and Estates' investigates the possibility that this trend created a general European threat to the idea of taxation by consent, since the sums required were now too large for consent to be likely to be forthcoming. The length of the new wars was perhaps as serious as their cost, since it meant that it was becoming very hard indeed to finance wars by occasional and extraordinary assemblies.

These points underline the fact that the central problem was not normally Parliamentary refusal of supply in order to secure redress of grievances. It was that the sums Parliaments offered were simply not large enough. This fact much diminished Parliamentary bargaining power, though it did not totally destroy it. The Crown might on occasion make concessions in order to obtain Parliamentary supply, especially since its granting had a political, as well as a financial, value. Yet some concessions which were wanted, especially those which involved giving up sources of revenue members thought illegal, the Crown simply could not afford until its legal sources were big enough to live on. Others the Crown did not find the supply a big enough bait to justify. The Crown did on occasion make concessions in order to obtain urgently needed supply, but such concessions tended, as in 1624 and 1628, to prove to be more cosmetic than substantial.

The English Parliament paid for its power, after 1689, and paid the very heavy price of becoming a permanent assembly. It was probably not until after 1660 that the growth of London had advanced far enough to make this development conceptually, socially or logistically possible. Jacobean London, like twentieth-century Brighton, was better suited to hosting conferences than to housing a permanent assembly.

'The Ship Money Judgements of Bramston and Davenport' pinpoints one way in which these developments in warfare had made the Crown's legal powers obsolete. By 1634, the change from occasional conscription of merchant ships to the building of a permanent Royal Navy was

[19] See, among much else, Michael Roberts, *The Military Revolution*, Belfast (1956), Geoffrey Parker, 'The "Military Revolution" 1560-1660: A Myth?', *Journal of Modern History*, vol. 48 (1976) pp. 195-214 and Michael Howard, *War in European History* (1976). On the naval dimension of these developments, I have had much valuable help from Dr.

substantially complete.[20] This meant that the King's legal power to conscript ships in an emergency was becoming redundant. Instead, he needed to raise a permanent regular tax for the finance of the Royal Navy. Yet, though the King's military needs had changed, his legal powers had not. Charles had the choice of acting arbitrarily and illegally, on the one hand, or of failing to guarantee English security on the other hand. He chose, as any head of state in his position probably would have done, to act arbitrarily and illegally, but it was the defence budget, not absolutist theory, which drove him to do so.

'The Wardship of John Pym' illustrates some of the ways in which it was easy for the Crown's income to fall behind inflation. The most important of these was the Crown's dependence on local servants with roots in the local community. This was both the strength and the weakness of English local government: it was the root, both of government by consent, and of the Crown's power to secure obedience. Yet, because these officials were unpaid or very poorly paid, they held office for the sake of the influence it gave them in their local communities. In the case of the Pym wardship, the Crown's local servant was the feodary, John Colles, and the person he was assessing was his sister. It is not surprising that his sister got better service from him than did the Crown: this local loyalty of officials was not only a root cause of royal poverty, but also a principle which made the whole system work.

The devices Colles used to keep his sister's assessment down were ones which were being used all over the country. Manors were suppressed, or confused with other manors of similar name. Valuations were kept constant in times of rising values, a method which could only be used in time of inflation. The Exchequer and the Court of Wards, institutions which knew records but not lands, were in no position to put a stop to this practice. Above all, the Crown lost from the widespread tendency of cash-hungry landlords to move away from a rental income towards an income from entry fines paid on the signing of a new lease. Entry fines might be regarded, not as income, but as capital gains, and could therefore easily be excluded from an income figure based on rentals. Since entry fines were by their definition occasional, they were very difficult to include in any regular figure for income, even with the best will in the world. Unlike John Colles, I wanted to arrive at a useful figure for Pym's income including entry fines, and I have not succeeded.

The two small notes on administrative reforms illustrate the sisyphean task facing a Crown servant who tried to change these things. Robert Cecil's deliberate attempt to increase revenue from wardship began

[20] On this change, see Andrew Thrush, 'Naval Finance and the Origins and Development of Ship Money', in *War and Government in Britain, 1598-1650*, Ed. Marc C. Fissel, Manchester, forthcoming. I am grateful to Mr. Thrush for letting me see this valuable article in draft.

almost the moment he took over from his father, who had had no such ambition. Since he could not increase the valuations, he set out to increase the rates of charge on these valuations. In this example, he was increasing entry fines for new wardships from two years' rent at the assessed values to three years' rent. As a way of dealing with under-valuation, it was a blunt instrument, and it inevitably led to protests.

The note on Pym and the Queen's Receivership is based on a discovery made by the late Miss Evelyn Gore, who spent much of her life collecting material on the life of Pym.[21] It shows the terms on which he was granted office of Queen's Receiver, and shows that someone in the Crown's service, possibly Robert Cecil, was trying to overcome some of the faults of the Crown's system of paying its servants. Probably few things in the whole system of Crown finance caused more political trouble than the lack of a satisfactory system of paying Crown servants. Crown salaries, like Crown revenues, tended to stay static through a century of inflation. Since it was clear the Crown could not adopt the obvious remedy, there was little pressure for it, and the pay claim of the Navy Officers, in 1638-40, is the first case known to me of a pay claim based on inflation.[22] Instead, Crown servants relied on perquisites, fees and gifts, all of them liable to create political trouble, and all of them hard to induce officials to control or abandon. In setting up the office of Queen's Receiver, however, the Crown had no vested interest or established custom to face: there had been no need for a Queen's Receiver since the death of Katherine Parr, and the past century had added nothing to the traditional rights the office-holder could claim to be his property. Faced with this unusual opportunity, the Crown took the obvious remedy, and instituted an adequate salary without any of the normal perquisites. This seems to suggest that the failure to extricate the Crown from its financial jungle was not because the Crown did not know what should be done, but because the jungle was truly impenetrable. It was not until a very different attitude to public finance had come to prevail among the political nation at large that significant long-term improvement became possible. 'Charles I's Financial Estimates' gives some idea of how serious the political consequences for the Crown were. Charles, like Robert Cecil in 1610, had put his faith in a Parliamentary solution to the Crown's financial difficulties, and found his faith misplaced.[23]

Religion, which is the theme of the third part, is another area in which

[21] I would like to thank Miss Gore's heirs, and especially Mr. John Gore for their kind permission to make use of Miss Gore's typescript. None of the Pym manuscripts she possessed have been seen since her death at Henley-on-Thames in 1952.

[22] Alnwick MSS vol. 15 (British Library Microfilm 286) ff. 156r-159v. I would like to thank His Grace the Duke of Northumberland for permission to use these MSS.

[23] The words are those of my former pupil Mr. Alum Bati, who wrote them when they were much more unconventional than they have since become.

trouble arose because ideas had failed to keep up with facts. From the late sixteenth century onwards, religious division was an established fact: it was never again going to be possible for the power of the state to eradicate all religions of which it did not approve. Yet at the same time, the idea that it was the duty of the state to enforce and defend true religion with the power of the sword continued with almost undiminished vigour. Indeed, for some people, of whom Pym was one, the knowledge of the difficulty of the task was an added spur: if it were not done quickly, it would be too late. This situation in which the conventional wisdom of the times was driving governments to attempt the impossible was always likely to produce trouble: it was not only Laud who felt that 'there is more expected from me than the craziness of these times will give me leave to do'.[24]

The ideals behind such attitudes have been ones to which historians have been very reluctant to bring any sympathetic understanding. As nineteenth-century historians felt the need to testify to their dislike for arbitrary government, so twentieth-century historians have felt the need to testify to their freedom from religious intolerance. This need, however admirable in itself, is a distraction from the task of understanding the societies on which we work, which must remain the historian's primary responsibility. The desire to prohibit something simply because we think it wrong is not extinct in modern society, and we are not entitled to claim a moral superiority to the seventeenth century because they felt it too.

The modern assumption that religion is a private matter is a consequence, not a cause, of the fact that the state no longer attempts to enforce it. Nothing which the state attempts to enforce can remain a private matter, and so long as the state enforced religion, the belief that religious dissidents were disloyal was a self-fulfilling prophecy. For example, so long as the Long Parliament was in session and Pym hoped to eradicate popery in Ireland, no Irishman could possibly afford to treat his religion as a private matter.[25] To many, no doubt, this was a matter for sincere grief but it remained nonetheless true.

Fear of religious division was increased because it was liable to disrupt families, as well as states. The family was a 'little kingdom', and the husband's authority, as much as the King's, depended on the belief that it was ordained by God. At one and the same time, the husband was told he must make his wife come to church, and the wife was told she ought to obey God rather than man. If husband and wife disagreed in religion, it was a prescription for chaos. If Dr. Amussen is right that the period saw a 'crisis of gender relations', the Reformation and the resulting religious

[24] W. Laud, *Works*, Ed. W. Scott and J. Bliss, Oxford (1847) VI ii 311.

[25] See my *Fall of the British Monarchies 1637-1642*, Oxford University Press (forthcoming) chapter X.

division is a probable cause.[26] It is certainly true that male chauvinism was not an insignificant part of the forces pressing for the preservation of religious unity. The fear of religiously mixed marriages was an important part of the fear of the power of popery at the English court.

Tolerance often depends on a willingness to admit that the other party may be right, and this admission is often resisted because it carries an admission that one may oneself be wrong. That admission was particularly difficult for those who, in Archbishop Heath's memorable phrase, were 'leaping out of Peter's shippe'.[27] and found it peculiarly hard to admit that the life-raft on which they had seized might turn out to be no more than a straw. Calvinist emphasis on 'the comfortable certainty of true faith'[28] includes a strong desire to replace the security which they, their parents or their grandparents had given up, and the certainty of election to which many of them clung was hard to combine with an admission that the other party might be right. For many, the need to persecute was an essential part of their psychological security. When this need was combined with a fear of moral relativism which the late twentieth century should be well able to understand, the resulting mixture was very powerful indeed.

The career of John Pym illustrates most of these propositions. He knew his opponents attempted to enforce religion: his stepfather had been sheriff of Cornwall in 1588, and was in the Commons on the Fifth of November 1605. He knew about the need for certainty, since his mother seems to have been one of those pathetic Calvinists who believed they were predestined to damnation. The career of Pym also illustrates that in religion, as in politics, the two-party model for historiography will not work.

We used to believe in a world in which Anglicans and Puritans provided a recognizable two-party scheme: the Anglicans were the government at prayer, and the Puritans were the opposition at prayer. Thanks to the work of Dr. Tyacke, Dr. Lake, Dr. Fincham and others, it is now clear that this was never an accurate picture.[29] We have seriously underrated how Protestant the prevailing orthodoxy of the church of England under Elizabeth and James was, and correspondingly

[26] Susan Amussen, 'Gender, Family and the Social Order 1560-1725', in *Order and Disorder in Early Modern England*, Ed. Anthony Fletcher and John Stevenson, Cambridge (1985) pp. 196-217.

[27] T.E. Hartley (Ed.) *Proceedings in the Parliaments of Elizabeth I*, vol. I 1559-81, Leicester (1981) p. 13. I would like to thank my wife for drawing my attention to this phrase.

[28] H.C. Porter, *Reformation and Reaction in Tudor Cambridge*, Cambridge (1958) p. 281.

[29] Nicholas Tyacke, 'Puritanism, Arminianism and Counter-Revolution', in Russell (Ed.) *The Origins of the English Civil War* (1973) pp. 119-43, and *Anti-Calvinists*, Oxford (1987); Peter Lake, 'Calvinism and the English Church 1570-1635', *Past and Present* no. 114 (1987) pp. 32-76; K.C. Fincham, 'Archbishop Abbot and Protestant Orthodoxy', *Historical Research* vol. lxi (1988) pp. 36-64.

underrated the extent to which that orthodoxy was altered by Charles I. Dr. Lake is surely right that the body of beliefs which has since come to be known as 'Anglican' was invented by Richard Hooker.[30] When Hooker invented it, it was not the creed of the church of England: the first Supreme Head to accept these ideas was Charles I.

For Pym, these ideas were incompatible with his definition of Protestantism, and they therefore changed him from a loyal, if anxious, subject of James I into a passionate and uncompromising opponent of Charles I. What is true of Pym seems to be true of most of the circle which provided the inner ring of the parliamentary leadership in 1642. In religion, as in politics, the absence of a two-party model, and the fact that there was no government-opposition split, does not mean that there was harmony or consensus. Statements about the absence of a Puritan-Anglican conflict are statements on what conflicts were about, or statements on how conflicts were conducted, not statements of the absence of conflict. Dr. Tyacke and I have sometimes been accused of talking of a 'Calvinist consensus', but we are not aware that we have ever used the phrase. Fortunately, the article by Dr. Fincham and Dr. Lake on 'The Ecclesiastical Policy of King James I' will serve for a paradigm of how ecclesiastical conflicts were conducted.[31] Between, for example, Abbot and Neile, differences were wide and deep, and pursued with a relentless determination. How they could usefully be pursued was limited by the fact that they were both members of the same bench of bishops: they were not setting out to oppose it, but to control it. Above all, the form of the contest between them was a contest for the favour of James: if either of them had taken up a position of 'opposition', he would have admitted defeat in the only contest which mattered before he had even begun. To call someone a 'Puritan', for example, was to accuse him of opposition, and therefore of disloyalty. It is hardly surprising that men like Pym insisted that, whoever might be meant by the word 'Puritan', it was not them. The redefinition of the word 'Puritan' under Charles, to cover far more people than it had covered before, was a serious threat to them, and was resisted accordingly. In religion as in politics, the rejection of the two-party model does not assert a belief in some Garden of Eden in which there was no disagreement. It enables us to begin the task of discovering who disagreed about what, and how their disagreements were conducted.

The fourth part, inevitably more preliminary than the other three, tackles the question of what really happened in 1640 to 1642. It is only when this question is properly answered that we can look back and see what long-term developments might have contributed to such events. The two key themes of this part are the British dimension, and the actions of

[30] Peter Lake, *Anglicans and Puritans?* (1988) p. 227.

[31] K.C. Fincham and Peter Lake, 'The Ecclesiastical Policy of King James I', *Journal of British Studies* vol. 24, no. 2 (1985) pp. 169-207.

Charles I. It was the appearance of the Scottish army which created an alternative power base in England, and the Petition of the Twelve Peers, submitted on the same day as the battle of Newburn, which marked the beginning of opposition politics. The extent to which this changed political rules is illustrated by an anxious letter from Pembroke to Charles in November 1641, assuring Charles that he had never thought of coming into office any way but by the King's goodwill.[32] At no time in the 1620s could it have been necessary to write such a letter.

The proposition that the crisis of 1637-42 and after was a British crisis is best illustrated by a narrative, and that story is told in my *Fall of the British Monarchies, 1637-1642*. What appears here is a series of illustrative sketches on that theme.[33] 'Why Did Charles I Call the Long Parliament?' does not only remind us that the Parliament was called to deal with an invading army: it also reminds us that the first deadlock was produced by Charles's entire failure to make common cause with his Parliament against that army. The chapter on the Irish Rebellion illustrates the proposition that in multiple kingdoms, two is company, but three is a crowd. The Irish consequences of any Anglo-Scottish rapprochement were always potentially serious, and a significant contributory cause of the Irish Rebellion. The Irish Rebellion itself is another place where the forces which determined events were British: Charles could not get rid of his English Parliament while it was still in progress. Like all the British material, it also illustrates the fact that belief in unity of religion made the task of governing multiple kingdoms with different religions almost impossible. The proposition that belief in religious unity was a major cause of instability is even truer in a British context than it is in an English one.

The story of the Army Plot is the story of Charles's unsuccessful attempt to fight his way out of some of these troubles. It highlights the fact that Civil Wars, like divorces, take two to make them. We have for too long analysed the final crisis as if Charles were merely a passive figure, someone to whom things were done, rather than an active participant. This assumption is false: England, and the other kingdoms of Britain, were still monarchies, and the King's actions were a vital part of the story. Those actions are part of the story of the coming of Civil War. In threatening his Parliament with armed force, and then failing to make that threat effective, Charles got the worst of all possible worlds.

The epilogue, 'The Catholic Wind', was originally written as a *jeu*

[32] Christ Church Oxford, Evelyn MSS, Nicholas Box no. 27 (my numeration) 29 November 1641. I am grateful to Dr. J.S.A. Adamson for drawing my attention to this collection.

[33] See, for example, Andrew Thrush, 'Naval Finance and the Origins and Development of Ship Money', for the information that Charles had considered trying out Ship Money in a pilot scheme in Scotland.

d'esprit, but it was startling to discover how easy it was to write. If, as is suggested in that piece, the survival of Parliaments and of Protestantism was still an open question in 1688, that belief must cast doubt on the view that any fundamental shift of power had taken place as a result of the English Civil War. In fact, it must cast doubt on the notion that there was ever such a thing as an 'English Revolution'. It is a view incompatible with the teleological view that England was experiencing an inexorable shift towards parliamentary government. It is incompatible with any attempt to argue that James II was in some sense opposing the tide of history, and therefore must imply that the survival of the English Parliament had not been guaranteed by its rather pyrrhic victory in the English Civil War. It also may suggest the view which John Pym and Christopher Haigh have in common, that England's conversion to Protestantism was superficial and incomplete. Though it suggests that view, it need not imply it. That view seems not to give sufficient stress to the existence of a large and committed body of zealous Protestants, yet it rightly reminds us that S.R. Gardiner never had historical warrant for his desire to identify that body as 'the nation'. Catholics were not un-English, however hard John Foxe might try to depict them so, and from the Reformation to Catholic Emancipation, they remained a substantial force in the country. The real point appears to be that England was a country divided by the Reformation, and that division lasted. The central division, after about 1580, seems not to be between Protestants and Catholics: it is between those who were converted to Protestantism, and those who conformed to it. What happened after 1660 is that the conformists got the better of the converts. Whiggery was the converts' attempt to get their own back.

It is too early to discuss the response of other historians to the work in this final section. The major books in which these ideas are developed, *The Fall of the British Monarchies, 1637-1642* and *The Causes of the English Civil War*, are both still in the press and, before the reviews, it is very difficult to guess from which quarter they will be criticized. The bulk of the essays on the 1620s, however, have been in print for eleven years and more, and have been available long enough to give rise to a considerable volume of debate. In particular, we have seen the emergence of a new 'Post-Revisionist' school, for which the collection of essays on *Conflict in Early Stuart England*, edited by Richard Cust and Ann Hughes, may serve as a showpiece. Some response to their findings and arguments would appear to be in order.

One of their central propositions is the one suggested by the title, that 'conflict and division were thus perfectly possible within the intellectual framework of early Stuart England'.[34] This is a proposition I have never

[34] Richard Cust and Ann Hughes (Eds.) *Conflict in Early Stuart England* (1989) (hereafter 'Cust and Hughes') p. 18.

denied, but I am perhaps open to the reproach that I did not assert it as loudly and clearly as, in a perfectly balanced account, I should have done. It is extremely difficult, in the course of polemical writing, to do full justice to the valid points of one's opponents' case, and Richard Cust's account of *The Forced Loan* illustrates some points where, though I tried, I did not fully succeed.[35] A collection designed to achieve perfect balance, rather than to argue a case, would contain more pieces on the lines of 'The Examination of Mr. Mallory' than this one does.

This proposition applies also to the force of attachment to Parliaments, to the rule of law, and to the principle of taxation by consent. I remain aware of the force of all these things, but, in the immediate requirements of arguing a case, did not always say so as loudly and clearly as I should have done. Dr. Cust's account of *The Forced Loan* has drawn attention to one important example in which this was so. My conviction that these were not 'opposition' creeds, however, remains unshaken, and I would regard Dr. Cust's article on 'The Privy Council and the Forced Loan' as one of the finest pieces of 'revisionist' writing known to me.[36] There is here the need for a course correction, but there is also substantial common ground.

There are other points where what is required seems to be explanation, rather than course correction. The contributors to *Conflict in Early Stuart England* have stressed that the Crown was prepared to make concessions and adjustments in order to obtain Parliamentary subsidies, although the subsidies were not enough to meet the Crown's needs.[37] The same was true in the Council Committee which decided to summon the Short Parliament.[38] I was not aware that I had ever denied that this was so. What I was concerned to deny was a proposition they are not advancing, that parliamentary refusal of supply had any *coercive* effect on a Crown determined to stand and fight. Though I have argued that the Crown could not be solvent with Parliaments, I have not argued that it could be solvent without them. Whether the Crown was more insolvent with Parliaments or without them was a question on which two views were possible at any time between 1624 and 1639, and one on which most Councillors remained in doubt. It was therefore one on which trifles might easily make them change their minds. In the Council debate on whether to call the Short Parliament, neither party was claiming that its proposed course could make the Crown solvent, but only that it would make the Crown less insolvent than that advocated by the other party. In this situation, Parliamentary supply could be used for bargaining with a willing opposite number, but not for the coercion of an unwilling one.

[35] R.P. Cust, *The Forced Loan*, Oxford (1987).

[36] R.P. Cust, 'Charles I, The Privy Council and the Forced Loan', *Journal of British Studies* vol. 24, no. 2 (1985) pp. 208-35.

[37] Cust and Hughes, p. 30 and chapters 4 and 6 *passim*.

[38] *The Fall of the British Monarchies, 1637-1642*, chapter III.

There seems here to be no substantial ground for disagreement, once both cases are adequately understood.

I have rather more reservations about Dr. Cust's willingness to revive a court-country dichotomy. I agree with him, of course, that people sometimes portrayed politics in this way: Sir James Bagg and Thomas Scott of Canterbury were both real figures, and the evidence Dr. Cust has drawn from them is genuine. Where he and I are at present inclined to disagree is in how typical we think such figures are. Dr. Cust would see them as speaking for a much more substantial body of opinion than I would. This, however, is the sort of question on which evidential certainty is methodologically almost impossible to come by, and we are both aware of that fact. I am rather more unhappy about the formulation that 'court' and 'country' could operate as an ideological framework within which people viewed politics'.[39] I am more inclined than Dr. Cust to give weight to the fact that a considerable proportion of our expressions of 'country' sentiment come from courtiers, willingly or unwillingly absent from court. When we are told, immediately after the Earl of Pembroke's dismissal from the office of Lord Chamberlain in July 1641, that 'my Lord Pembroke (they say) plays the philosopher, and commends highly the retired country life, to which he will betake himself', I do not take the information very seriously. When I find a man like Lord Chancellor Ellesmere saying that 'it seems to me that heaven is in the country, where there be no rubbish of court nor state affairs to stop', I do not suspect him of intending to retire from office.[40] A very high proportion of utterances on court and country deserve this sort of suspicion. Dr. Cust and Dr. Hughes would not wish to go back to the world of the 1960s, in which the words 'court' and 'country' were used as party labels, and men could be described as 'supporters' of one or the other. For Dr. Cust and Dr. Hughes, 'court' and 'country' are images: they are rhetorical stage props men might use to justify positions in which they found themselves. The images were used in this way, and the quotation from the Earl of Pembroke above will serve to illustrate the fact. They would also want to suggest that the use of such rhetorical images might have a fixing effect, and tend to lock people into positions they had once adopted. This sometimes happened, and the antipathy between Sir John Eliot and Sir James Bagg is perhaps a case in point. How often it happened is a question on which our hunches may differ, but which we can safely leave to be resolved by future research.

A considerable amount of clarification is needed on the issue of localism, but I hope that what is needed amounts to better understanding rather than a course correction. When I look back at my remarks about

[39] Cust and Hughes, p. 14.

[40] S.P. 16/482/94. L. Knafla, *Law and Politics in Jacobean England*, Cambridge (1977) p. 56. Ellesmere disliked London so much that he chose to live in the country at Islington.

localism, they almost always refer to royal demands for money. In this context, they still appear to me to be correct. For men like Sir Francis Seymour and Edward Alford, loyalty to their local communities was often incompatible with voting the sort of sums the Crown needed. For ambitious men like Sir Robert Phelips, the need to secure a local power base was a serious obstacle to voting the sort of sums the Crown needed. There are perhaps more occasions than I then noticed, especially in the resistance to war with Spain, when localism was invoked as a respectable excuse for not financing a policy with which the speaker was out of sympathy, but the basic point stands.

Where I seem to have inadvertently given a wrong impression is in suggesting that the word 'localism' implies a general indifference to national issues. I have no difficulty with the material in *Conflict in Early Stuart England* which is designed to assert the existence of an informed public opinion, nor with the desire to assert the concern of that public opinion with national issues.[41] I would want to stress that the intensity of such concern varied from person to person and from time to time, but would probably not be alone in doing so. I would accept the warnings of Dr. Cust, Dr. Hughes and Dr. Lake about the danger of the *argumentum ex silentio*:[42] we cannot assume that the absence, for example, of a massive body of material attacking the illegality of Ship Money during the 1630s means that opinion was not held. Nor can we assume that the fact that something is recorded apparently neutrally in a letter or a commonplace book means that it was felt neutrally. There are many cases in which we know the writer's mind so well that we can be almost certain of the contrary. My only warning, in accepting this case, is that we should not leap straight to the opposite extreme. We should not shift from the *argumentum ex silentio* which says there was no more discontent than we can discover, to the tip of the iceberg hypothesis, which assumes that every recorded example of discontent is a type of many more. Silence is silence, and can be circumvented only by a persistent search for more sources.

With the religious material in *Conflict in Early Stuart England*, I have little if any disagreement. I would agree with the authors that 'Arminianism did not emerge from nowhere',[43] and also that Calvinist-Arminian debate dealt with fundamental questions left over by the Reformation. To that extent, I agree with them that the developments following Charles's adoption of Arminianism were not 'random accidents'. These issues were almost bound to be argued out, though they could have been discussed with greater safety if they had been postponed for a few years longer. Where I do see a 'random accident', and may be stating a view

[41] Clive Holmes, 'The County Community in Stuart Historiography', *Journal of British Studies*, vol. xi, no. 2 (1980) pp. 54-73.

[42] Cust and Hughes, pp. 31-2 and other refs.

[43] Cust and Hughes, pp. 24 ff.

unacceptable to them, is that I believe that if James had been succeeded by his Calvinist daughter instead of his Arminian son, it is not only possible that the Civil War might never have happened: it is also possible that it could have happened with most of the leading protagonists on opposite sides to those they in the event took.

The one area where I am in fundamental disagreement with *Conflict in Early Stuart England* is Johann Sommerville's chapter on 'Ideology, Property and the Constitution', and with the other contributors to the extent to which they have followed this. This chapter is an attempt, powerfully argued, to go back to a 'two sides' picture of early seventeenth-century political ideas, with King and leading members of Parliament holding fundamentally opposed pictures of the English consititution. If this view were to be accepted, it would imply, either that most men ignored their own ideas when it came to the point of action, or that my own account of the politics of the period is fundamentally wrong. I am naturally reluctant to believe either proposition, and do not find seventeenth-century political ideas nearly as easily categorized as Dr. Sommerville does. This is not the place to begin an argument as large as this,[44] and at this point it is right to say only that, as usual, the debate goes on.

[44] For a brief outline of my reasons for disagreeing with this view, see my *Causes of the English Civil War*, chapter VI.

I

POLITICS

1

The Nature of a Parliament in Early Stuart England

'I am forced a little to begin in general of the parliament and to call to your memories (though I know you know it already) what a parliament is.'[1] A historian starting out on an apparently elementary task of this sort must share James I's misgivings, yet the things we know already, like the things we can do in our sleep, are ones on which we sometimes need refreshing. Inhabitants of the modern English-speaking world, to whom parliaments are as familiar as the air they breathe, have grown up with a number of what James Mill would have called 'indissoluble associations' with the word 'parliament'. Some of these associations, when applied to the world before the English Civil War or even before 1689, are necessarily false, yet, because they are among the images that the word 'parliament' creates in our minds before we have even begun to think, they are very hard to discard. In fact, like James I, I want to call in question some of the things I am sure we know already, because a number of the things we 'know' about parliament are not known historically. Unless we can dismiss these associations from our minds, we risk committing the same anachronism as was committed by Sir Edward Coke, examining parliaments in the time of 'Ina, King of the West Saxons'.[2]

Minds trained on the eleven-plus examination in England, or on multiple choice questions in the United States, are conditioned to thinking in terms of opposites. Given a pair of familiar names, they will set them up as a sort of see-saw, and tell a story in which, as one goes up, the other has to go down.

I would like to thank the Central Research Fund of the University of London, the Twenty-Seven Foundation, the A. Whitney Griswold Fund of Yale University, and the Concilium on International and Area Studies of Yale University for grants towards the cost of reading the MSS used in this essay.

1. NRS, II, p. 3.
2. D'Ewes, *Journals*, p. 465. The fact that Coke supposed that the preamble of Ine's laws, describing how he took counsel of his notables, was evidence that he had called a parliament, should help to shed light on what Coke meant by a parliament.

This sort of unconscious model-making profoundly influences our patterns of thought. When we know, as twentieth-century historians cannot help knowing, that king and parliament later fought a civil war against each other, we risk finding them fixed as opposites in our minds as firmly as Liberal and Conservative, or as Stephen and Matilda. In doing this, we miss the main reason why 'this bloody and unnatural war' of 1642 was such a profound shock to those who took part in it. We thus risk endowing the participants with motives they could not have had. It takes an effort to remind ourselves that the king was a member of parliament, and claimed privilege for his servants just like other members.[3] Indeed, on occasion, he exercised his right as a member to sit in the House of Lords. To us, the body which remained at Westminster during the Civil War was a parliament, yet Lord Montagu was perfectly right to insist that it was not: it was the Lords and Commons, whereas a parliament consisted of the king, Lords and Commons. 'My heart, hand and life shall stand for parliaments, but for no ordinance only by Lords and Commons.'[4]

For those in whom the tendency to think in opposites has been reinforced by the influence of Montesquieu (a conspicuous offender in this respect), it is also easy to think of king and Commons as representing two different branches of government called 'executive' and 'legislative'. However, England has never had the separation of powers (and still does not). When a parliament was assembled, nothing more than a quick change of hats by some of the members was needed to produce an executive. The Privy Council on occasion met in the Palace of Westminster, in order to allow themselves to take part in parliamentary debates at the same place. When the Commons, in 1572, wanted to name a committee to consider a bill about receivers of crown lands, they sent it to a committee of six, including the Chancellor of the Exchequer and the Queen's Remembrancer, which was to meet in the Chancellor of the Exchequer's house.[5] Lords' committees might include a quorum, or even a majority, of the Privy Council. Such people could hardly have a constitutional conflict with themselves.

Today, when we are used to a permanent institution called

3. See *LJ* III, p. 156 for a successful claim of privilege by an outlawed Beefeater called Original Bellamy, on the ground that he was the king's servant.

4. Esther S. Cope, *The Life of a Public Man: Edward, First Baron Montague of Brighton* (Philadelphia, 1981) p. 191. *HMC Buccleuch*, III, pp. 414–15.

5. *CJ*, I, 95.

'parliament', it is easy to forget that there is no such subject as 'parliament in the early seventeenth century': there are irregularly recurring events called Parliaments. This difference of linguistic usage conceals a deep difference between seventeenth- and twentieth-century habits of thought. This is a barrier I have discovered by accident: when I first entitled a book *The Crisis of Parliaments*, I did not realise I was making a point of importance. What has since taught me I had done so is the frequency with which colleagues, otherwise well capable of accurate citation, misquote the title of this and of my subsequent book on *Parliaments and English Politics 1621–1629*, and quote me as writing on a singular *Parliament and English Politics*.[6] A linguistic and conceptual habit which produces such persistent error on so straightforward a fact as the wording of a book title is likely to produce other errors also. This, like the incredulity on the faces of an audience when it is pointed out that there was no parliament in session at any time during 1688, suggests that the impermanence of parliaments during the seventeenth century, though a known fact, requires more absorbing than it has yet received.

In an age when 'parliamentary government' has become both a slogan and a fact, it is easy to suppose that parliaments were in some sense part of the 'government' of seventeenth-century England. Yet the JPs of Herefordshire were right to remind Sir Robert Harley, in April 1642, that 'we send you, not with authorities to govern us or others (for who can give that to another that is not in himself), but with our consent for making or altering laws as to his majesty, the Lords and Commons shall seem good'.[7] Before the works of Henry Parker began to appear, most Englishmen did not identify legislation as a key part of 'government': the word was more likely to apply to executive power in general, or more particularly, to the power of appointment.[8]

6. For example, Derek Hirst in *HJ*, 23, no. 2 (1980), 455. Even if these are all printers' errors, they remain significant: printers have habits of thought too.

7. BL Loan MS 29/173, ff. 239–40. I am grateful to Ms Jacqueline Levy for this reference.

8. This point seems to have been truer in the 1620s than it was in a period of rapid change like the 1530s. Some people held to a Cromwellian notion of legislative sovereignty, while others stressed a notion of fundamental law which was closer to Sir Thomas More than to Thomas Cromwell. For the Cromwellian view see Sir Richard Grosvenor, Cheshire RO Grosvenor MSS 2 February 1624 and Robert Cecil in Elizabeth Read Foster (ed.), *Proceedings in Parliament 1610*, II p. 66. For the other view, see

continued

II

It is worth remembering what a parliament was not, for otherwise we may not approach our sources with the humility necessary to learn what it was. In the first place, each parliament was the king's creation. The only way a parliament could be brought into being was by the king's writ, summoning members of both Houses to Westminster (or elsewhere) at forty days' notice. The Lords were summoned individually, and insisted, against Charles I's occasional incredulity, that they received their summonses as of right.[9] The Commons, on the other hand, were chosen by authority derived from the king, but not chosen by him. In enjoying authority which ultimately came from the king, without being appointed by him, they could be compared (as they sometimes were) with members of juries. An assembly not summoned by the king's writ, like those of 1660 and 1689, was scrupulously not described as a 'parliament', but only enjoyed the status of a convention. Being summoned by the king for his purposes, parliaments legally existed only during the king's pleasure: the words 'the king's majesty doth dissolve this parliament' brought them to a legal end upon the instant. Indeed, so firm was the legal principle that a parliament was the king's parliament and called to advise him that, except in 1649, a parliament ceased to exist immediately upon the death of the sovereign who had called it. A new king had to issue new writs to hold a new election for a new parliament.

The point was well put by John Hooker, member for the city of Exeter in 1571:

> the king who is God's anointed being the head and chief of the whole realm and upon whom the government and estates

continued
the Earl of Leicester: 'there are some things, resolved upon by the common and universal consent of the nation, which are immutable, and cannot be altered by the sovereign power of either king or parliament, or of both together, but must still remain as long as the nation continueth to be a nation, that is until this civil society so united be dissolved'. This is followed by a classic statement of the doctrine of the 'ancient constitution', based on Coke and Lambarde. Kent AO De L'Isle and Dudley MSS, Z 47, unfoliated and undated, ? c. 1641. I am grateful to Viscount De L'Isle and Dudley, VC, KG for permission to quote from his family papers, and to Blair Worden for drawing my attention to this uncalendared portion of the De L'Isle and Dudley collection.

9. On the question of the crown's right or otherwise to withhold a Lord's writ of summons, see Russell, *Parliaments and English Politics*, p. 16 and references there cited.

> therof do wholly and only depend: hath the power and authority to call and assemble his parliament, and therein to seek and ask the advice, counsel and assistance of his whole realm, and without this authority, no parliament can properly be summoned or assembled. And the king having this authority, ought not to summon his parliament: but for weighty and great causes.[10]

James I was quite right to remind the parliament of 1621 that 'a parliament is composed of a head and body. The head is the monarch and the body the three estates. In monarchies only are parliaments held, which were created by monarchs. A strange folly it is in those that would have parliaments to be popular contrary to their own institution'.[11]

Kings had invented parliaments, and made and unmade them as they pleased. Any power parliaments might have was derivative: the king was the source of their existence, and the root cause of their authority. Their power, when it existed, was power to persuade the king to do what he would not otherwise have done. Since it had to be exercised *through* the king, there was a limit to the extent to which it could be exercised against him. Though Coke and others occasionally quoted fourteenth-century statutes saying a king should call a parliament once a year, in practice he called parliaments when he chose. It is then essential, to understand both why parliaments were created and why they continued, to ask what benefit the king derived from their existence. There was a widespread belief that good kings did call parliaments, but it would be carrying *noblesse oblige* too far to suppose they called them simply on grounds of principle. Kings called parliaments for their own advantage or not at all.

The principle that all parliamentary authority was derivative was, though, a principle for settled times. In unsettled times, when there was doubt who the king should be, or who his successor should be, when he was ill, absent or insane, had suffered catastrophic military defeat, was approaching bankruptcy, or had otherwise lost the authority necessary to govern, things could be very different. In such times, responsibility for clearing up the mess devolved, *de facto* if not *de jure*, on influential members of the political

10. John Hooker, *The Order and Usage How to Keep a Parlement in England*, in Vernon F. Snow, (ed.), *Parliament in Elizabethan England* (New Haven, 1977), pp. 145–6.

11. NRS, IV, p. 2.

community. A parliament was an excellent device for sharing the responsibility as widely as possible among them. Periods of exceptional parliamentary influence of this sort had recurred cyclically since Simon de Montfort's days, but they were always temporary: the object of the exercise was not to set up parliamentary government, but to repair the monarchy on a more stable basis.

Why did the king call parliaments? In a sense, the reasons for calling parliaments are as manifold as the individual parliaments themselves, yet all of them are something to do with consent. It had been established in Edward I's reign that members elected to the Commons were deemed, because they represented their communities, to have *plena potestas*: what they decided was binding on those they represented.[12] On some occasions, members tried to refer back to their constituencies for instructions, but they had no need to do so: whatever they decided was binding on their constituents. The advantages of this fact to the king were potentially immense. If a parliament voted a tax, no one could say 'I never agreed to this': every potential protester was legally bound by the act of his representative. If a law was made about some potentially explosive matter such as the succession or a religious settlement, it could be a great advantage to the crown to argue that this law was binding on everyone because it was the act of the whole realm. This was particularly important to the crown because the men who would have to enforce a law, or collect a tax, were often not merely bound, but personally parties to the decision, because they had been in parliament when it was taken. When a subsidy was to be collected, commissioners were named under the Great Seal (not by the Parliament), and the leading figures among them were normally those who had voted the tax. Their proceedings in the counties were normally begun by a speech from a member of parliament among them, and in defending the grant of subsidy, the member would be justifying his own act.[13] When laws were passed, most

12. J. G. Edwards, 'The *Plena Potestas* of English Parliamentary Representatives', in Fryde and Miller (eds.), *Historical Studies of the English Parliament*, vol. I, pp. 136–49.

13. For an example of how much discomfort this might cause, see Sir Thomas Wentworth's Rotherham speech in 1621, J. P. Cooper (ed.), *The Wentworth Papers*, Camden Society, 4th ser., 12 (1973), pp. 152–7. For an example of how far a sense of wartime emergency might be built up in order to justify a grant, see Hants. RO Jervoise MSS 0 21 (?1601). It is remarkable how few people seem to have kept the speeches they made on these occasions: the only other example known to me is Bodl. Lib. MS Rawlinson D723, ff.

members, when they went home, became part of the executive responsible for enforcing the laws they had made. Lord Keeper Nicholas Bacon used to tell members that making laws without executing them was like buying a new set of garden tools, and then never using them. In 1604, James I, in exhorting members to execute the laws they had made, held forth on the divine right of JPs.[14] In both spheres, the requirement of general consent had become established largely because it was to the crown's advantage that it should be so. The king did not create a separation of powers: he put his power in a wider context. It could still be said in the seventeenth century, as Fleta said in the thirteenth, that 'the king has his court in his council in his parliaments'.[15]

More generally, a parliament might be asked about any other business on which the crown thought its interests would be served by a search for general consent. In the words of the writ of summons, they were called '*ad tractandum et consentiendum pro quibusdam arduis et urgentibus negotiis statum et defensionem regni et ecclesiae Anglicanae tangentibus*': to treat and consent about difficult and urgent business concerning the state and defence of the kingdom and the Church of England.[16] The wording specifically authorised debate about both religion and foreign policy. It was a convention that a parliament should always be called at the beginning of a war. This was, in large measure, because a war always created a need for an extraordinary grant of taxation. It was also frequently the crown's reasoning that the grant (and any necessary succeeding grants) was more likely to be forthcoming if a parliament had already been a party to a decision to go to war. From 1323 to 1639, I am aware of only one significant war started without the meeting of a parliament, and that, in the first year of Henry IV, was because the king had promised not to ask for a subsidy for one year.[17] Moreover, the assembly of a parliament provided a

29–30 (anonymous and undated, ?1621).

14. Hartley I, pp. 49, 190; *CJ*, I, p. 145.

15. Quoted by F. W. Maitland in Fryde and Miller, *Historical Studies*, p. 128.

16. PRO C218/1. For an earlier and very similar wording, see S. B. Chrimes and A. L. Brown, *Selected Documents of English Constitutional History 1307–1485* (1961), p. 362.

17. I am grateful to Dr Michael Prestwich and Dr J. R. L. Highfield for advice on this question. *Rot. Parl.* III, pp. 427–8. I am grateful to Dr Highfield for this reference. See also E. B. Fryde, 'Parliament and the French War' in Fryde and Miller, *Historical Studies*, pp. 242–61.

golden opportunity to offer a propaganda justification of a war to most of those who would be responsible for the administrative effort involved in prosecuting it.

The assembly of a parliament was also an extension of the obligation on the sovereign to take counsel. Few things, if anything, were more central in mediaeval political thought than the belief that a good ruler took counsel from a wide variety of sources. A bad ruler, like Rehoboam, would take counsel from an inner ring of flatterers, who would tell him what he wanted to hear. A good ruler would take counsel from a wide circle of experienced people, who would tell him what he needed to know. There was no better way of ensuring that counsel did not come from a closed circle than to take the counsel of the whole realm. In asking for counsel, whether in the Privy Council or in parliament, the sovereign necessarily authorised a degree of freedom of speech: the good counsellor, like Escalus in *Measure for Measure* or Kent in *Lear*, could be recognised by his willingness to give unwelcome advice which was nevertheless for his ruler's good. This was the basis of the parliamentary practice of free speech, which seems to have long ante-dated a formal privilege of free speech.[18]

In the tradition of counsel, there was always a potential ambiguity. Queen Elizabeth, for example, conceded that all the members were counsellors even if only during the parliament, yet she and James I believed that counsel was to be given when the ruler asked for it, and only on subjects on which the ruler asked for it.[19] It was a view which had always tended to commend itself to rulers. Yet the tradition of faithful counsel could include the obligation to give counsel even if the time or subject, as well as the substance, were unwelcome to rulers. Kings, being wilful, needed to be recalled to their own best interests as often as possible.

Parliaments, as far back as the reign of Henry III, had always tried to persuade kings to do things they did not like. There was nothing in the least new about them sometimes opposing the king's will: that is what a faithful counsellor was for. What did have a profound effect on the way parliamentary business was conducted was the fact that the ultimate object of every political manoeuvre had to be to persuade the king to

18. J. S. Roskell, *The Commons and their Speakers 1376–1523* (Manchester, 1965), p. 51.

19. D'Ewes, *Journals* p. 466: NRS, II p. 4. Queen Elizabeth was drawing a contrast between the members who were only counsellors during the parliament and the Privy Councillors, who were counsellors all the time.

change his mind. Seventeenth-century parliaments could not simply overrule a reluctant monarch by the deploying of a bare parliamentary majority. They had to bring him, by whatever inducements, to adopt different counsels. By the very nature of the political methods open to them, parliaments were not a rival power centre: they were one more among the manifold pressures the king reacted to when choosing his course of action. As the Earl of Bedford put it in 1640: 'in a parliament speakers make the premises but the aye or no makes the conclusion, so parliaments make premises or major or minor but it kings [sic] that makes the conclusion by granting or dissolving'. Bedford appreciated that however strong his parliamentary base might be, in the end, only the king's fiat could crown his strategy with success. His epitaph, reputed to have been chosen by himself, claimed that he had been 'trusted by King Charles in his most secret counsels'. The Army Plot, taking place at about the time when this was probably composed, showed that Bedford had been guilty of foolish optimism, but at least he understood the nature of the system within which he had to work.[20]

In return for doing the king's business, members of both Houses were allowed an opportunity to do their own business. Any member of either House could propose a bill, and almost no issue was too small to be made a matter of parliamentary legislation. There is no better way to convey the flavour of business involved in bills than to list the bills considered in one day. On 26 May 1604, the Commons considered a bill for relief of those suffering from the plague,* a bill for deceitful making of cloth, a bill to prohibit heirs from benefiting from reversal of attainders if they did not take the oath of supremacy, a bill for an exchange of lands between Trinity College Cambridge and Sir Thomas Monson, to confirm letters patent to the Earl of Nottingham,* to confirm the Queen's jointure,* for the sale of the lands of Sir Thomas Rowse,* a bill 'against conjuration, witchcraft and dealing with evil and wicked spirits',* for allowing Sir Thomas Throckmorton to sell lands,* for preservation of pheasants,* and the expiring laws continuance bill.*[21] Nothing short of an actual list can convey the mis-

20. Bedford Estate Office, vol. 25 (unfoliated): Fourth Earl, miscellaneous papers. I am grateful to the trustees of the Bedford Settled Estates for permission to quote from these papers.

21. *CJ*, I, pp. 226–7. An asterisk indicates those bills which reached the statute book. The proportion is far higher than it would have been later in the century.

cellaneous quality of business transacted by bill. Some of these bills would be of general concern, and some, including a high proportion of the economic bills, would originate from special interest groups. Many others, such as the bills to break entails to allow people to sell land, would be of desperate concern to a few individuals, but of no great concern to the parliament as a whole.

Beyond the formal business, a parliament also provided, in Professor Elton's phrase, a 'point of contact'.[22] Many gentlemen who spent their lives carrying out the king's commands valued the chance to see in real life the man whose image they were used to seeing on the coinage and the Great Seal. In return, kings expected to use their parliaments to discover any particular issue which was causing concern to their subjects. The Parliament of 1621, in persuading the king that he had been granting patents to the point at which they became a grievance, was doing just the sort of thing parliaments were for. On some issues, the assembly of representatives from all parts of the realm could allow members to discover that what they had taken for a series of particular grievances were in fact parts of one general grievance, calling for a general remedy by legislation.[23]

The function of a parliament as a 'point of contact' did not apply only to contact between members and the king. Bishop Parkhurst of Norwich did not always look forward to parliaments, yet when he tried to look on the bright side of a tiresome upheaval, the chance to see his old friend Bishop Berkeley of Bath and Wells came second only to the chance to try to pass an Act to deal with his defaulting receiver.[24] For many people, a parliament was an ideal chance to renew contact with friends or relations who happened to live in other counties. It was also an ideal chance to compare notes with people from other counties, and to acquire a greater sense of England as a whole. As one Elizabethan MP put it:

22. G. R. Elton, 'Tudor Government: Points of Contact: Parliament', *TRHS* (1974), 183–200.

23. See, for example, the case of Martham parsonage, A. Hassell Smith, *County and Court: Government and Politics in Elizabethan Norfolk*, (Oxford, 1974), pp. 265–76, 335–6. The story which begins here ends with the Concealments Act of 1624. See also Ashton, *English Civil War*, pp. 44, 69 and other refs.

24. R. A. Houlbrooke (ed.), *The Letter Book of John Parkhurst*, Norfolk Record Soc., 43 (1975), pp. 142–3, 163–4, 29.

> We who have never seen Berwick or St. Michael's Mount can but blindly guess at them, albeit we look on the maps that come from thence, or letters of instruction sent from thence: some one whom observation, experience and due consideration of that country hath taught can more perfectly open what shall in question thereof grow, and more effectually reason thereupon, than the skilfullest otherwise whatsoever.[25]

Against this background, it makes sense that the most important symbolism of a parliament was that of unity. It was part of the conventional wisdom of the seventeenth century that the king and his people, like head and body, had no true independent life: their strength was in their interdependence. Properly understood, these ideas of unity were supposed to enhance the king's position, and not to weaken it. As Henry VIII said, 'We be informed by our judges that we at no time stand so highly in our estate royal as in the time of parliament, wherein we as head and you as members are conjoined and knit together into one body politic'.[26] Disagreements between a king and his parliament were often compared to disagreements between husband and wife: there were enough married men in both houses for them to be well enough aware that such things happened. Yet matrimonial disagreements (if not taking place in the Webb household) do not normally lead to the drawing up of a constitution. They are better resolved by other methods.

It had always been a central concern of mediaeval parliaments, and of mediaeval barons before them, that the king should be well advised. In most reigns, an evil or unpopular adviser could be levered out of the king's favour without recourse to a parliament. Under Henry VIII, as Wolsey and Cromwell discovered, advisers risked being eased out of the monarch's favour by the activities of their fellow-advisers. Under Elizabeth, it had proved unnecessary to use a parliament to remove the Earl of Essex: his own behaviour ultimately offered better proof that he was a bad adviser than any parliament could do. On other occasions, monarchs

25. Hartley I, p. 227. I am grateful to Mr David Brentnall for drawing my attention to this reference.

26. James Daly, *Cosmic Harmony and Political Thinking in Early Stuart England*, American Philosophical Society, vol. 69, pt. 7, (Philadelphia, 1979), p. 18; G. R. Elton, *The Tudor Constitution* (Cambridge, 1960), p. 270.

persisted in hanging on to advisers whose existence constituted a grievance. In such cases, there was a tradition pre-dating parliaments, and stretching back to clause 50 of Magna Carta, that an assembly of the king's leading subjects could, in effect, make it a condition of further co-operation that the advisers in question should be removed. In the fourteenth century, this process had become partly formalised as impeachment. The process was rarely needed, and was not used between 1449 and 1621, but it existed. Only two kings before Charles I attempted to make an issue of principle out of the attempt to withstand the removal of their advisers in this manner, and it is perhaps not a coincidence that those two, Edward II and Richard II, had both ended up deposed.

III

Sir John Fortescue, writing during the Hundred Years' War, began a myth, which has been popular ever since, that there was something especially *English* about parliaments and estates. In fact, during the fourteenth century, increasing royal needs for money (among other causes) had led to the development of similar institutions all over, or almost all over, Europe. Many of these had, in 1600, procedural and other advantages the English parliament lacked. In particular, many continental estates enjoyed a legal permanence which English parliaments did not have. The symbol of such permanence is not only recognition as enjoying the legal status of a corporation, but also the existence of permanent officials or standing committees, who could speak in the name of their estates between sessions. The Catalan Cortes chose *Diputats*, who could speak to the king on their behalf between sessions, and often did so to considerable effect. When Sully, in France, wanted to do business with the Agenais, he found the area represented by its Syndic, in whom much of the authority of the estates was vested between sessions.[27]

One of the crucial issues, as Professor Major has recently reminded us, is that of control over the *collection* of taxation. It was because many French provincial estates had control over

27. Elliott, *Revolt of the Catalans*, p. 7 and *passim*; J. Russell Major, *Representative Government in Early Modern France*, (New Haven, 1980), pp. 165–6, 198, 239, 383–8 and other refs. On the significance of control over collection of taxation, see also Charles Jago, 'Habsburg Absolutism and the Cortes of Castile', *AHR*, 86, no. 2 (April 1981) 307–26, especially p. 310.

the collecting of the taxes they voted that they were able to pay their own salaried officials, and thereby to ensure some continuous legal existence. By contrast, in the English parliament all the salaried officers, the Lord Chancellor, the Speaker, the Clerk of the parliaments, the Gentleman Usher of the Black Rod, etc., were paid by the crown. With the theoretical exception of the Speaker, they were also appointed by the crown.

English parliaments, however, enjoyed a clear advantage over most of their continental counterparts in that, at least until 1603, they were clearly *national* assemblies. In France, the estates which mattered in the seventeenth century were, as any reader of Professor Major's new book must appreciate, not Estates General, but estates particular. The heart of French representative institutions was in the provincial estates. By contrast, the crown enjoyed the advantage of being the sole guardian of the *national* interest, and the sole focus for national loyalties.[28] In Spain, it was not at all clear what 'nation' the king's subjects belonged to: was there one nation of Spaniards, or separate nations of Castilians, Aragonese, Catalans, Valencians, Portuguese, etc.?[29] In the Iberian peninsula, there was one king and many cortes, and the cortes, almost necessarily, tended to appear as champions of particularism. In Italy and Germany, estates, like most other institutions, were provincial, and even in the Netherlands, the Estates General were much limited by their labyrinthine relationship with the seven provincial estates. Perhaps only in Sweden did estates share with the king the opportunity to champion the national interest.

In England, on the other hand, it was possible to define a nation as a body which shared a common parliament. Sir Edwin Sandys, in 1607, said that 'it is not *unus grex* [one people] until the whole do join in making laws to govern the whole: for it is fit and just that every man do join in making that which shall bind and govern him; and because every man cannot be personally present, therefore a representative body is made to perform that service'.[30] Yet this conviction, like so many others, was being stated *because* in at least one

28. Richard Bonney, 'The English and French Civil Wars', *History*, 65, no. 215 (October 1980), 380–1.

29. For Olivares' views on this subject, see Elliott, *Revolt of the Catalans*, pp. 204, 400–1.

30. *The Parliamentary Diary of Robert Bowyer*, ed. D. H. Willson (Minneapolis, 1931), pp. 258–9, 256n.

significant respect, it had become out of date. For Sandys was speaking in the English parliament, on the union between England and Scotland, and the drift of his argument was that the English and the Scots could not be one nation, because they did not have one parliament. From 1603 onwards, it was a new cause of instability in relations between crown and parliament that they were relations between a king of Great Britain and a parliament of England. In particular, during the Short Parliament of 1640, the king saw a rebellion by his own Scottish subjects, which he had no choice but to put down, where the English parliament saw an unpopular foreign war, which they were not bound to encourage by any grant of money.

Ireland created similar problems for rather different reasons. The Earl of Leicester, probably about the time of his appointment as Lord Deputy of Ireland in 1641, carefully noted the constitutional position:

> the kingdom of Ireland was conquered by the kings of England, and it may be reckoned among the patrimonials appertaining to the king (of which Grotius speaks) . . . because it was acquired by him out of his patrimony and not by the parliament, therefore it belongs to the king and not to the parliament.[31]

The English parliament periodically made claims to authority over Ireland, but these claims were *ultra vires*: Ireland had its own parliament, which took a very dim view of any suggestion that it was subordinate to the parliament of England.[32] Professor Koenigsberger's suggestion that relations between different parts of multiple kingdoms were a cause of instability in England, as well as on the continent, appears to be abundantly justified.[33] In a sense, then, the Union of the Crowns, in 1603, made it less true than it had been before that English parliaments were truly national assemblies. From a British point of view, they were no such thing.

With the possible exceptions of Francis Bacon and John

31. Kent AO, De L'Isle and Dudley MSS Z 47 (unfoliated). The fact that Leicester's office as Lord Deputy of Ireland was held of the king, but could not be held of the parliament may help to explain his half-hearted excursion into royalism during the Civil War. See also Roland Hutton, 'The Structure of the Royalist Party 1642–1646', *HJ*, 24 no. 3 (September 1981), 561.

32. NRS, IV, pp. 258–60, 278–81, V, 127–8; *HMC De L'Isle and Dudley*, VI, p. 407. *LJ*, IV, p. 339.

33. Koenigsberger, *Dominium Regale*.

Pym, members of parliament seem to have been remarkably little influenced by finding themselves an English parliament advising a British king: indeed, the 'British problem' might have been a less significant cause of instability if it had affected English thinking more than it did.

IV

By contrast, members of the Commons, if not of the Lords, were much more influenced by awareness of their own impermanence. This awareness of impermanence had a profound influence on the ways in which members felt able to pursue political objectives. Members of parliament who came to Westminster normally expected to remain there for three months at most, and then to return to their normal base of operations. Moreover, a considerable proportion of the members were in a hurry to go home. In the summer of 1641, when the summer recess was most unseasonably delayed, Sir Arthur Hesilrige and Zouch Tate set off for home without leave. The Serjeant at Arms was sent after them, and summoned them to return, but they refused. Bishop Parkhurst, shortly before the parliament of 1572, was perturbed about lodging with the only person who had offered him accommodation: 'as well because there is no furniture, as because she is noted to be a great enemy to religion'. It comes as no surprise to find Parkhurst reporting that 'on the 30th [May] the session having finished, we all hastened homewards, thoroughly tired of the City'. In 1629, the Earl of Manchester was unable to provide lodgings for his brother Lord Montagu, because 'my sons, now all at home, take up all the room'.[34]

A realistic member of parliament, however seriously he regarded the service, could not help looking on it merely as a diversion from his normal duties. A permanent post, which continued to exist between parliaments, was a more important source of power than even the most regular election to parliaments. In Somerset in the 1620s, there was no doubt at all that Sir John Poulett, DL, JP (but not a member of any parliament after 1614) was a more important figure than John Pym, member of parliament in all the parliaments of the 1620s, but enjoying no permanent office of more distinction

34. PRO SP 16/483/54; *CJ*, II, p. 263; *Letter Book of John Parkhurst*, ed. R. A. Houlbrooke, Norfolk Record Society, 43 (1975), pp. 171, 69; *HMC Buccleuch*, I, p. 268.

than that of receiver of crown lands. In 1604, Sir Francis Hastings, in disgrace for petitioning against the deprivation of ministers '*in aliena republica*', in a foreign county, was dismissed from all his local posts, Deputy Lieutenant, Justice of the Peace, and captain in the militia. He remained a member of parliament, because that post was not in the king's gift, but he does not seem to have felt that remaining a member of parliament reduced the sense of exclusion of 'a poor old gentleman'. Hastings is now chiefly remembered as a member of parliament, yet his letters give the impression that his sense of his own importance was based on his position as Deputy Lieutenant and Justice of the Peace, with his parliamentary position a very poor third.[35]

For those members who did not own town houses, one of the important social dislocations involved in long sessions of parliament was the expense, and a long parliament was a financial burden for which they were unprepared. Sir Henry Slingsby spent £731 on staying in London as a member of the Long Parliament in 1640–1. Sir Thomas Barrington was more fortunate, yet his household accounts too show the dislocation and the surprise involved in the slow realisation that he was taking part in a long parliament. He began by taking lodgings in Fleet Street on a weekly basis, arriving promptly the day before the parliament opened. After seventeen weeks, these had cost him £254-18s-7d, and he decided he wanted something more permanent. He then took a thirty-one-year lease of a house in Queen Street, at an annual rent of £130. By December 1641, he had realised he was in for a long haul, and apparently began to feel the need for some of the comforts the family were used to in the country. The list of things they brought up to London in December 1641 included '3 pairs of good whole blankets' and a collection of the family's own beds. Perhaps the significant fact is that Barrington did not do these things until the Parliament had been in session more than a year.[36]

For Barrington, however unexpected such a translation might be, it was not unmanageable: he was a prosperous man, of the sort who might have acquired a town house anyway, he was accompanied by his family, and his journey from Essex was

35. M. Claire Cross (ed.), *Letters of Sir Francis Hastings*, Somerset Record Society, 69 (Frome, 1969), pp. 90, 107 and *passim*.

36. J. T. Cliffe, *The Yorkshire Gentry* (1969), pp. 125–6; Essex RO Barrington MSS DD/Ba A 14. In the references to 'good' blankets and beds, it is tempting to place weight on the adjective.

a short one. For others, the dislocation was more unwelcome. During the trial of Strafford, the Earl of Bath was one of the Lords' reporters for many of the conferences with the Commons, and appeared to be taking the trial seriously, yet his letters indicate nothing so powerfully as his longing to leave London and return to the company of his 'wench', whom he assured that she had never been out of his thoughts for an hour except perhaps when he was asleep.[37]

We should not assume that every gentleman automatically wanted to be a member of parliament. In 1624, Sir Robert Phelips, trying to clear the ground for his own candidature, approached Sir Edward Hext to find out whether he wanted to stand, and received the reply that Hext was 'so weak and feeble as I dare not go out of my parlour from the fire, and there am so loaded with clothes as you would admire and yet cannot keep myself from taking of cold, but cough all night long'. Hext's servant encouraged Phelips to take this show of reluctance seriously: 'my master doth desire his friends and well-willers by all means possible to excuse and free him from that place at this time, for that he hath already served twice in the place, and there are many more gentlemen of worth in the county worthy of the place... P.S. My master will not hinder Sir Robert's election, nor any man's else for ought I know so that he may be freed himself'.[38] So long as most members, and even some peers, had their real roots in the country, 'parliamentary government', implying as it did more or less continual parliaments, was likely to be a social, as well as a conceptual impossibility. It is not a coincidence that the rise of parliamentary government, after 1689, comes at a time when the fashion for town houses (and the money for them) had spread sufficiently widely to be likely to include most of the people likely to be elected. So far as I know, no one has maintained that gentlemen who were elected to parliament were interested only in local issues. It is a more accurate formulation to say that whatever issue they were debating, they could not be indifferent to the local repercussions of that issue.[39] This fact is particularly relevant to grants of taxation. Members might on occasion feel that the national interest,

37. Kent AO U 269/C267 (Sackville MSS). The *Lords' Journals* show Bath as one of the most conscientious members.

38. Somerset RO Phelips MSS 224/12 and 219/32. Hext's remarks about the cold are the more credible for being dated 19 January.

39. Clive Holmes, 'The County Community', *JBS*, 19 (1980), 54–73, has done a useful service by pointing to the limits beyond which revisionist stress

continued

their own interest and their political beliefs could be served by a grant of taxation, and yet feel that the hostility to such a grant in their own communities might be more than, as representatives, they could safely override. In 1604, private approaches were made on the king's behalf to Sir Francis Hastings, to suggest that the Commons might vote a subsidy. Hastings expressed doubts because

> The remainder of an whole subsidy lying still on his people to be paid, the continuing of them long in payments of late years without small intermission, and the poverty the country is generally grown into thereby causeth the Commons to be loath to hear of a subsidy yet, and fearful to grant any at this time, lest the people generally should distaste, whose feelings are not least in matters of this nature.

It is of course possible to interpret such passages cynically, and to suggest that they make a good cloak for a reluctance which was personal. Yet in this case Hastings did, in spite of his misgivings, raise the possibility of a subsidy on the floor of the Commons. Perhaps, then, his hesitations deserve to be taken at face value.[40]

It was this sort of hesitation which led Queen Elizabeth to complain, in 1593, that some members regarded the necessity of their counties more than the necessity of the state.[41] Yet, however infuriating such concern with local reactions might appear to the crown in time of war, it was part of the necessary price for the existence of anything approaching a genuinely representative assembly. One of the reasons for the summons of a representative assembly was to tell the Crown about this sort of local feeling.

Some members of the Commons were not representatives in any sense recognisable today. John Pym's constituency of Tavistock was controlled by the Earl of Bedford, and I know no evidence that he ever set foot in it. He could well afford to say,

continued
on localism should not be allowed to go. It is, however, a moot point who, if anyone, holds the ideas he is attacking. I am grateful to him for not suggesting that I do so.

40. M. Claire Cross, *Hastings' Letters*, pp. 85–6; *CJ*, pp. 242, 994–5. Hastings appears to have predicted with painful accuracy the arguments employed by Hoskins and Sir Richard Spencer against his proposal.

41. D'Ewes, *Journals*, 466.

42. A. H. A. Hamilton, (ed.), (1877), *Notebook of Sir John Northcote*, p. 107.

in 1640, that they should consider the present necessity and not the satisfaction of the country.[42] On the other hand, those who represented populous constituencies such as Somerset, Yorkshire or Kent had genuinely been chosen by a substantial electorate, and could not be indifferent to the effect of their doings on those who returned them.[43] In between these extremes, there were a variety of degrees of influence. There were many cases of boroughs returning a member recommended by a powerful man, yet not many of these pressures were absolutely irresistible. A patron's chance of returning his nominee depended in part on his care in selecting a nominee who would be congenial to those who were asked to return him. There is thus no absolute antithesis between elected members and those returned by patronage. It was the easier for boroughs to reject patrons' nominees because there was a law still in force which said that all members had to be resident in their constituencies. This seems to have been a classic case of a law being honoured in the breach: the 1571 parliament spent a long time considering a bill to repeal it, and chose not to because, so long as the law was on the books, it was always possible for a borough to refuse a nominee on the ground that he was not a resident, and therefore it would be illegal to return him.[44] There is, then, a possibility that local sentiment influenced even those which appear to be nomination returns.

If we concede that Professor Hirst is right that a number of members of the Commons were representing substantial numbers of electors, and that their political behaviour might be influenced by pressure, instructions or other electoral considerations, we still have to decide how this evidence ought to be used. There are two ways it may be fitted into the general story. One is to assume that electoral pressure confers considerable extra strength on members of parliament: to assume that, as 'representatives of the people', they were in a position to wrest more power from the Crown than they could have done without it. The other way of interpreting this evidence would be to regard it as a considerable political embarrassment to many of the Commons. In a case like the Oxford session of 1625, electoral pressure then could open up a gap between the minimum that would satisfy the crown and the maximum that could be explained away in the country, leaving members in the position of embarrassed pig-in-the-middle. In this way,

43. Hirst, *The Representative of the People?*
44. Hartley I, pp. 225–31.

electoral pressure may have diminished members' freedom of choice, and thereby reduced their usefulness to the king. In 1629, a Welshman was in trouble for saying that the king was the 'pollingest' king that ever was, and he would be chased out in favour of the Elector Palatine. He said that the king would lose the hearts of his subjects by charging them so deep with loan money *and subsidies*.[45] Any former member of parliament who heard this may have felt some alarm: it may have been axiomatic in law that the consent of a parliament would be taken for the consent of the whole realm, but members could not be sure that it would always be axiomatic in fact.

V

Indeed, this sensitivity to local pressure contributed a good deal to bringing the whole parliamentary system to the verge of extinction. This collapse, between 1625 and 1640, is the more striking for the fact that the system which was proving inadequate had been in regular use for some three hundred years. During that time, it had survived numerous crises. impeachments, power struggles, unpopular wars, and even three depositions of kings. Why, when the system had proved so tough in the face of many strains, did it prove so inadequate in the middle of the seventeenth century?[46]

It does not appear that the system by which the king relied on frequent parliaments for legislation and extraordinary supply had lost any of its hold on the emotional loyalties of Englishmen. To people like Lord Keeper Coventry or Sir Robert Phelips, parliaments symbolised the unity of the King with his people. They were thus important evidence that he was not a tyrant. For those involved in local government, it was also important that the king occasionally wanted their advice. Many of them undertook a backbreaking load of work, for reasons in which loyalty, as well as self-importance, played a part. In return for this body of work, they expected an occasional hearing. Moreover, if the principle of consent to taxation were ever formally abandoned, many believed the crown's appetite for money might prove insatiable.

On the other hand, there is very little evidence to suggest that, before November 1640, many members wanted parlia-

45. *CSPD 1628–9*, vol. 146, no. 27.

46. G. L. Harriss, 'Mediaeval Doctrines in the Debates on Supply 1610–1629', in *Faction*, pp. 73–103.

ments to do more than they had. In particular, there is no sign during the 1620s of any change in the idea that parliaments were occasional and short-term assemblies. Without a change in this point, parliaments could not enjoy much more status than they already did. Charles I's continental wars offered the prospect of very frequent parliaments, but the reaction of members was not to cry out for annual parliaments: it was to cry out against annual subsidies.[47]

Nor is there much sign, early in Charles I's reign, of any conscious attachment to a programme of unparliamentary government. Those who billed Charles, in 1625, as a prince 'bred in parliaments' were making a fair point. Charles, as Prince of Wales, had been a regular attender in the House of Lords in two consecutive parliaments. The help he gave to the passage of such measures as the Monopolies Act of 1624 did not suggest that he came to the throne handicapped by any unparliamentary outlook. Even more, many of Charles's councillors, such as Manchester, Coventry or Secretary Coke, shared many of the same principles which informed a man like Sir Robert Phelips. Whatever brought the system to the verge of collapse, it does not appear to be the clash of two rival constitutional ideologies. Strongly held beliefs there certainly were, but these were not two rival bodies of beliefs. They were one shared body of beliefs, whose application was frequently in dispute. There was nothing new about this, and it was hard to see why it should have brought the system to a halt.[48]

Just as it is necessary to see what uses parliaments had for the king in order to understand why they were created, so it is necessary to understand what they were no longer offering to the king in order to see why they came so near extinction. In essence, the problem was that, from the 1590s onwards, parliaments were not offering the crown enough to live on, while at the same time insisting that the crown should take nothing but what they gave to it. For example, the parliament of 1628 voted five subsidies, amounting to approximately £275,000. This appeared to them to be an act of unparalleled generosity, and they insisted, in turn, that the king should raise no revenues but the ones he was legally entitled to. The king, then, was given £275,000 towards needs that were near a million, on condition that he did not try to get anything else.

47. Russell, *Parliaments and English Politics*, pp. 251, 283n, 284, 426–7.

48. See G. L. Harriss in *Faction*, p. 98: 'it would be difficult to claim that any of the disputes over supply during these twenty years (1610–29) either raised new constitutional principles or resulted in more politically damaging conflicts than those of earlier centuries'.

No wonder that the king, in the end, tried to wriggle out of the financial straitjacket, and raise money by means he was not entitled to. What is remarkable is not that the king did this, but that he did not do it sooner. In November 1640, Sir Benjamin Rudyerd reported a widespread opinion that parliaments would take more from the king than they gave to him. Rudyerd's answer, that the hearts of his subjects were the greatest treasure the king could have, was good political theory, and good English constitutional convention, but set against the abolition of ship money, it was remarkably poor financial arithmetic.[49]

How did this gulf open up between the income the king derived from parliaments and the income he needed to live on? A great deal of it happened because of events in the country, not at Westminster. English parliaments did not control the assessment of the taxes they voted, and the fall in the yield per subsidy, from £130,000 in the middle of Elizabeth's reign to £55,000 in 1628, cannot be blamed on members of parliament: it must indicate a considerable resistance to taxation in the country at large. In 1628, the Privy Council was reduced to sending out circular letters asking that the yield of the subsidies should not be less than it had been in 1563, and this over a period in which the value of money had fallen substantially.[50]

Why so intense a reluctance to pay taxes? Reluctance to pay taxes is normal, but in this period, it was either exceptionally strong or exceptionally effective. Part of this is the result of inflation, and of the pressure of growing population on food resources. The war taxation of 1597–1601 had come during a period of what George Abbot called 'great cleanness of teeth', when taxpayers might reasonably feel that the purchase of food (if available) had first claim on their resources. The years c.1600–30 were, in most of Europe, the period when the population curve reached a peak, and therefore times of considerable economic hardship. It is also possible that population mobility, combined with the engrossing of land into fewer hands, had the effect of narrowing the country's taxable base. There were certainly fewer taxpayers on the subsidy books, and the decline may not have been entirely due

49. PRO SP 16/471/38.

50. Hants. RO Jervoise MSS 0.21: I am grateful to Dr Kevin Sharpe for this reference. *APC 1628–9*, pp. 516–17. See D'Ewes, *Journals*, 458, for Lord Keeper Puckering, in 1593, quoting the queen to the effect that the problem was largely caused by the wealthy turning the tax on the weaker. This problem was in large measure a legacy of the Elizabethan war with Spain.

to evasion.[51]

At the same time as the country's capacity to pay was going down, the crown's needs were going up. Inflation, in part, explains both phenomena, but it is not the whole explanation. In 1559, Lord Keeper Nicholas Bacon, opening Queen Elizabeth's first parliament, asked his hearers to

> consider the huge and wonderful charge newly grown to the crown, more than ever before hath been wont, and now of necessity to be continued – as first the maintenance of garrison in certain places on the sea coasts, as Portsmouth and others, with new munition and artillery, besides the new increased charge for the continual maintenance of the English navy to be ever in readiness against all evil haps, the strongest wall and defence that can be against the enemies of this island . . . in mine opinion, this doth exceed the ancient yearly revenues of the crown.[52]

Sixteenth- and seventeenth-century warfare was not only more expensive than that of the Hundred Years' War: it also demanded that a far greater proportion of the sinews of war be provided, on a regular basis, out of the crown's budget. In 1610, Robert Cecil, setting out the cost of garrisoning Ireland, again reminded his hearers of the novel point that much of the expense of war now went on in peacetime.[53] This was why the crown now needed what it requested in 1610: not occasional supply from parliaments when needed, but regular and permanent additions to its revenue. Such a request necessarily disturbed the whole basis for co-operation between crown and parliaments: the use of an occasional body for regular supply was likely to be an unstable system. These growing needs created a pressure for parliaments either to become much more important, or to become obsolete. Either they had to give the crown what they had never done before, or they had to let the crown raise the money without their consent. It is because such a choice went clean against everyone's inclinations that it

51. A. B. Appleby, *Famine in Tudor and Stuart England* (Stanford, 1978), p. 141. See Keith Wrightson and David Levine, *Poverty and Piety in an Essex Village Terling 1525–1700* (1979), pp. 29–36. If other parishes, like Terling, 'filled up at the bottom', the number of taxpayers would not have risen in proportion to population. I am grateful to Dr Wrightson for some helpful correspondence about this very tentative suggestion, for which he should not be held responsible.

52. Hartley, I, p. 37.

53. Foster, *Proceedings*, II, pp. 14–21.

was evaded for so long. When things cannot continue as they have been, conservatism becomes a force for instability.

What drove Charles I to do without parliaments for eleven years was his need for money. Among the things which particularly scarred Charles were the refusal of supply in time of war, in 1626, and the refusal to grant Tonnage and Poundage in 1628 and 1629. Yet taxation had never been the only thing which required general consent: new laws did also. It is striking how little the crown appears to have been handicapped during the 1630s by the lack of ability to make new and clearly binding laws. Here, the general conservatism of the early seventeenth century is relevant: the law-making power appears crucial in periods of rapid change, like the 1530s, when new laws are urgently needed. During the early seventeenth century, there appears rather to have been a feeling that there were too many laws already. Sir Edward Coke, as Speaker of the Parliament of 1593 'came to speak of laws, that were so great and so many already, that they were fit to be termed *elephantinae leges*, therefore to make more laws it might seem superfluous'. The view was often expressed that what was needed was rather a codification of laws, to make them more intelligible. James I, in 1610, even expressed the view that the laws should be in English. This, like many other utterances about laws during the early seventeenth century, shows that the law reform movement of the interregnum had a prehistory. An amateur parliament, busily legislating about any item that takes its fancy, can cause considerable legal confusion.[54]

If the crown did not want parliaments to make new laws, and get more money without them than it had done with them, it is no wonder it did not call them for some time. Neither of the reasons which had led the crown to see advantage in calling parliaments ever since the reign of Edward I appeared to be valid any longer.

Yet it soon appeared that the importance of parliaments to Englishmen could not be measured by what they did in settled times. In settled times all parliamentary authority was derivative: parliaments were the moon to the royal sun. Yet in unsettled times, many people would instinctively turn to a parliament to put the stamp of general authority, and of

54. D'Ewes, *Journals*, p. 459; Foster, *Proceedings*, II p. 60. I am indebted for this paragraph to David Lieberman, 'The Province of Legislation Determined', (University of London, Ph.D., 1980). The questions he has asked about the eighteenth century should also be asked about the seventeenth.

respectability, upon whatever emergency measures the situation demanded. The more startling the emergency character of these measures, the more important it was that as many people as possible should share the responsibility by being parties to them. There can be few better examples of this way of thought than Lord Burghley's Interregnum Bill of 1584. Burghley's draft recounts that, in the event of the Queen's assassination, there would be an 'interregnum', and the realm would want a lawful sovereign. He provided that the Privy Council, whose places would normally cease on the death of the sovereign who appointed them, should remain in office 'by authority of this parliament', 'until by a greater assembly in a parliament of the three estates of the realm further order shall be published'. The parliament which had last met was then to reassemble, to reappoint the Councillors or to appoint new ones, to try titles to the crown, and 'declare their decision in the form of an Act of parliament'. Any who resisted this determination were to be proclaimed traitors to the crown by the authority of the three estates. They were to authorise *some* members of the Council to spend public money. There is very little this bill does not allow to a parliament, but the arrangement is, in its essence, temporary: it is to hold the fort until a new king can be put securely on the throne.[55] It is worth comparing this with the argument of Serjeant Manwood, in 1571, that whoever denied the authority of a parliament to determine the succession thereby denied the queen's title.[56] By contrast, after 1603, when the throne was securely settled, Sir Edward Coke vehemently denied that such a thing as an interregnum could exist, and even so devoted a parliamentarian as Edward Alford was prepared to say that an Act of parliament could do anything *except* alter the succession to the crown.[57]

The two ideas most people seem to have been unwilling to give up were the attachment to parliaments as an expression of unity, and the belief in their necessity as an emergency remedy in unsettled times. Beyond this, there remained a deep attachment to the principle of consent, which Charles I was too in-

55. Sir John Neale, *Elizabeth I and Her Parliaments*, vol. II (1957), pp. 45–6; PRO SP 12/176/22 and 30. It is to be hoped that Burghley may be allowed to have had parliamentary principles (which differed from the queen's) without being a member of an 'opposition'.

56. Hartley, I pp. 217–18. As a gloss on Henry VIII's Succession Acts, Manwood's view was surely correct.

57. Hawarde, *Les Reportes del Cases in Camera Stellata*, p. 164; NRS, V, p. 20.

articulate to answer, like Cromwell, by asking 'where shall we find that consent?'.

VI

Though this attachment to parliaments was intense, it was not yet in any sense an 'opposition' creed. Indeed, in 1640, some of the people who were expressing it most intensely were a faction within Charles I's Privy Council. Charles, if the term had been available to him, might have chosen to describe them as 'the wets', but he still employed them. So long as he did, they could continue to believe that their principles were compatible with the crown's service. Among these people, one of those whose views are best documented is Secretary Vane. On 30 September 1640, he wrote to his fellow-Secretary Windebank, saying the Danish Ambassador had hoped to mediate between the king and the Scots, but this was now unnecessary, 'the king being now resolved to proceed therein with advice of his peers and kingdom, which is but high time'. In May 1641, he sent his fellow-Councillor Sir Thomas Roe a horrified report of the Army Plot, concluding: 'I hope my next will tell you that his Majesty is resolved to reconcile himself with his people, and to rely upon their counsels, there being now no other left'.[58] The Earl of Leicester, who succeeded Strafford as Lord Deputy of Ireland, made notes about 'alteration of government by settled parliaments, or sovereign courts or counsels . . . in vain is the net laid in sight of any bird, *Prov.*'[59] The Earl of Northumberland, Lord Admiral, reported during the Bishops' Wars that 'it grieves my soul to be involved in these counsels'.[60] Those who thought this way probably included Manchester, Salisbury, Holland, Leicester, Northumberland, Vane, Roe, Pembroke, Saville and, among those no longer in office, Secretary Coke and Lord Keeper Coventry. It is to be hoped that such a list can show that strongly held parliamentary convictions did not have to be opposition convictions. The

58. PRO SP 16/468/116; SP 16/480/20. Roe's reply to Vane suggests that he shared the same political outlook. He said that if he did not find Vane better than he left him: 'I shall envy those that perish with honour than they that outlive the honour and peace of their country'. SP 16/480/26. Roe was writing with some of the Army plotters aboard his ship. I hope this note may show that 'the place of principle' might still be in the king's service.

59. Kent AO De L'Isle and Dudley MSS Z 47. His source, *Proverbs* 1:17, is worth reading in context.

60. Kent AO U1475 C 2/42, 7 May 1640.

parting of the ways, for this group, did not come in the 1630s: it came between the Army Plot of May 1641, which advertised Charles's growing unparliamentary convictions, and the dismissal of Secretary Vane, in December 1641, which advertised that Charles no longer wished to be served according to their convictions. After that point, every member of this group except Coventry, who was dead, became either a parliamentarian or a neutral in the Civil War.[61] This highlights the fact that in a monarchy, what drives a man into an 'opposition' stance is not his convictions, but the king's attitude to those convictions. A man is pushed into opposition not because the king disagrees with him, but because the king no longer wishes to hear him or be served by him. It was not until the very end of 1641 that it was clear to Charles's inner circle of advisers that a strong and principled attachment to parliaments was incompatible with Charles's service. Their judgement should be taken seriously, for they had more opportunities to form it than a lifetime's research can ever give us.[62]

In the country at large, it was ship money and the Bishops' Wars which seem to have turned attachment to parliaments into a controversial conviction. In Kent, Sir Roger Twysden recorded some of the conversation of the county gentry about ship money, and the issue appeared to be producing something of a polarisation. Some said that 'if a kingdom were in jeopardy, it ought not to be lost for want of money if it were within it', but others argued that 'in so high a point every man ought to be heard and the reasons of every one weighed, which could not be but in parliament'. This group turned to Chapter 35 of Fortescue, which is Fortescue's most pointed contrast between the lawful government of England and the arbitrary government of France.[63] This line of reasoning was much accentuated in 1639, when the king committed himself to a war without attempting to secure the co-operation of a

61. On Leicester's flirtation with royalism, see n.31 above. For Saville see *CSPD 1641–3*, vol. CCCCXCII no. 107 and vol. CCCCXCVII no. 32.

62. Dr Hutton is undoubtedly right that the royalist party of 1642 were not 'long-established servants of the crown'. Hutton, 'The Structure of the Royalist Party', *HJ*, 24, no. 3 (September 1981), p. 554. When Charles, in 1642, set out to portray himself as the champion of the rule of law, he did so with new servants: among those old Councillors to whom this cause should have most appealed, only Lord Keeper Littleton came to join him at York.

63. Kent AO Twysden MSS U 47/47/22, fragmentary commonplace book of Sir Roger Twysden. I am grateful to Mr Kenneth Fincham for this reference. See Kenneth Fincham, 'The Judges' Decision on Ship Money in 1637: the Reaction of Kent', *BIHR*, forthcoming.

parliament. It was probably the first time this had been done since 1323. It was when this reaction was reaching its height that Charles I was roundly defeated by the Scots, and his authority collapsed.

Among those unsettled times which made people reach for a parliament to put things together again, disputed successions and royal minorities were closely followed by the collapse of effective royal authority. Someone had to keep things going, and a parliament, by sharing the responsibility, seemed the best way of doing it. It is hard not to agree with Professor Hirst that in 1640, things had changed so much since the 1620s that we are in 'a new world'.[64] This fact was immediately symbolised by two highly significant novelties in the business the king laid before the long parliament. There are few more important royal powers than control of foreign policy and control of the spending of money. In 1640, Charles handed over the task of negotiating a treaty with the Scots to the Lords, and the task of paying the English and Scottish armies to the Commons, in both cases because he was unable to do the job himself. The negotiation had to be handed over, partly because, like Charles V at the Peace of Augsburg, Charles I had a repugnance for doing what he knew had to be done. It also had to be handed over because the Scots, with the power of a conquering army, insisted that they would not agree to any treaty unless it were confirmed by an English parliament.[65] The paying of the armies had to be handed over because Charles simply had no money to do it. It was thus by the king's own act that the two houses began to exercise powers that no parliament had exercised for a very long time. Yet even so, it remained the assumption of all seasoned politicians that what was going on was not a long-term shift to 'parliamentary government', but a set of emergency measures designed to put the kingdom together again. The House of Lords, in March 1641, had no idea of what it was implying when it suspended several lawsuits (which infringed the parliamentary privilege of the Prince of Wales) 'during the continuance of the present parliament'.[66] Even Pym was looking forward to a longer tenure of power, not as a member of parliament, but as Chancellor of the Exchequer. The story of the causes of the Civil War is the story of why this rescue operation was unsuccessful, and that story, mercifully, does not have to be

64. Hirst, *The Representative of the People?*, p. 147.
65. PRO SP 16/467/5 and 471/22.
66. *LJ*, IV p. 187.

told here.

For the purposes of this chapter, it is possible to end remarks on the changes in the nature of a parliament brought about during the first two years of the long parliament by looking at two Acts, the Triennial Act and the Act Against Dissolution. These were both made necessary by the immediate exigencies of defeat by the Scots, the Triennial Act because the Scots insisted on it as a security for the peace treaty,[67] and the Act Against Dissolution because those who were lending money to pay the armies on the credit of future subsidies insisted on security for their loans. Yet, however immediate the circumstances that gave rise to them, these two Acts are an intellectual watershed in the history of parliaments in England. They gave the parliament a permanent, institutional existence, and, for the first time, make it accurate to speak of 'parliament' and not of 'parliaments'.

These two Acts, passed within eight weeks of each other, gave Parliament the secure status it had never had before. It is permissible to leave the last word with the Earl of Leicester, writing in his commonplace book in or after 1641, and probably referring to the Act against dissolving the parliament without its own consent:

> The parliaments of England heretofore were like tenants at will, depending upon the will of the lord, that is, of the king, and as the death of the lord was a determination of his will, and a cessation or determination of the parliament [cf. tenants at will, see Coke, 1 Institut. lib. 1 cap. 8]. But since the Act of parliament made in this king's time, the parliament is no more tenant at will, nor hath only *possessionem nudam et precariam*, but is as tenants for years or for life not determinable at the will of the king, and corporations never dying (as it is in the law) the parliament which is a corporation never dies, nor ceaseth at the death of the king, that is, the death of the king is no determination of it, and it is not likely that they will be weary of their immortality.[68]

67. PRO SP 16/471/22: the Scots' formulation, at this stage, was 'once every two years or three years at farthest', and they hoped to refer all disputes between the kingdoms to the two parliaments.

68. Kent AO De L'Isle and Dudley MSS Z 47.

2

Parliamentary History in Perspective, 1604-1629

A historian is like a man who sits down to read a detective story after beginning with the last chapter. The clues pointing to the ultimate dénouement then appear to him in such embarrassing abundance that he wonders how anyone can ever have been in doubt about the ultimate outcome. Much of a historian's working life, then, is spent in drawing attention to those clues which point towards the solution which he knows ultimately emerged. Usually, this is a useful process, but there is one important difference between life and detective fiction: life is not a story written by an author who had decided on the ultimate solution before the story began. A historian must always run the risk of letting hindsight lead him to see the evidence out of perspective. Those who write the story remembering the ultimate conclusion may miss many of the twists and turns which gave it suspense along the way. They may even forget that the result ever was in suspense.

This risk is particularly tempting for historians who describe the years before revolutions. In particular, the study of English Parliamentary history of the years 1604–29 has been so dominated by the knowledge that it preceded a Civil War that it is dangerously easy to treat it as a mere preface, and not as a story in its own right. It is dangerously easy to believe, because the story ended with Parliament in a position to challenge the King for supremacy, that it was bound to end in this way, and that it was the direction in which most of the evidence points. In particular, the use of the word 'opposition' to describe the type of criticism the Crown faced during these Parliaments can easily suggest that the criticisms uttered during these years were such as to lead on logically to Civil War against the Crown. This tendency to see the Parliamentary history of the period as a sort of historical escalator appears in such remarks as Professor Moir's comment on the exclusion of Sir Thomas Parry from the Commons in 1614, that 'the development had begun which led ultimately to parliamentary control of the executive'. It appears in Professor Zaller's claim that 'there was no logical end to this cycle but a total assumption of sovereignty, and this was exactly the position to which Parliament was led in the 1640s'.[1] By themselves, such striking juxtapositions are not necessarily wrong, though they may be seriously misleading. We enter on rather more questionable territory with the statement of Professor Zagorin that in the Civil War the sons of Sir Robert Phelips and Sir Edwin Sandys, two prominent members of the Commons 'broke with family tradition to become royalists' in the Civil

[1] T. L. Moir, *The Addled Parliament of 1614* (Oxford, 1958), p. 104: Robert Zaller, *The Parliament of 1621* (1971), p. 4. I would like to thank Dr. D. M. Hirst, Professor H. G. Koenigsberger, Dr. Ian Roy and Dr. N. R. N. Tyacke for reading and commenting on drafts of this article.

War.[2] They did nothing of the sort: their fathers had left them no tradition of fighting against the Crown. The assumption that armed revolution against the Crown was the logical conclusion of their fathers' speeches in the 1620s is one which is too big to be sustained by hindsight alone: it would have to be sustained by evidence, and there is a good deal of evidence which conflicts with it.[3]

This tendency to see the Parliamentary history of the years 1604–29 as a 'high road to Civil War' is sufficiently deeply entrenched to have survived a somewhat erratic preliminary bombardment from Professor Elton.[4] The traditional view now faces a flank attack from European historians. Professor Myers disputes the common assumption that European Parliaments and estates were institutionally less well developed than the English.[5] Professor Koenigsberger, in a far-reaching study of '*Dominium Regale* or *Dominium Politicum et Regale:* Monarchies and Parliaments in Early Modern Europe', has now attempted a general examination of the reasons why Parliaments and Estates survived in some kingdoms and not in others. He does not find the answer in the institutional and procedural development which has been the dominant theme in most studies of the English Parliament. If this were the main determining factor, it would be hard to account for the survival of the Scottish Parliament, whose procedure left it as susceptible to manipulation by the King as any Parliament in Europe. To Professor Koenigsberger, many of the forces which determined the survival or extinction of Parliaments and Estates appear unpredictable. Among unpredictable influences which helped to determine the outcome of events, he lays particular stress on two: the relations between the different states of multiple kingdoms, and the effects of outside intervention: 'such intervention', he says, 'would alter the relative strength of the internal forces to an extent which is, I believe, unpredictable, even if we were to use game theory or a computer'. To him, the causes of the survival of the English Parliament appear, not in its procedural advances in the early seventeenth century but in the effects of Scottish intervention in 1640 and Dutch intervention in 1688. 'Clearly', he concludes, 'at its most critical and dramatic moments, English history cannot be understood in terms of a closed political system'.[6]

[2] Perez Zagorin, *The Court and the Country* (1969), p. 335.

[3] T. G. Barnes, 'County Politics and a Puritan Cause Célèbre: Somerset Churchales 1633', *T.R.H.S.*, 5th Series, 9 (1959), pp. 103–23. Professor Barnes concludes: 'implicit in the churchales controversy is a warning to those who would search in the counties during the personal rule for the developments leading to civil war'. The years 1640 and 1641 clearly need separate discussion, yet even as late as this, we should remember, when reading the debates, that Civil War was a defeat, not a victory, for those who took part in them. See Russell (Ed.) *The Origins of the English Civil War* (1973), pp. 27–31.

[4] G. R. Elton, 'A High Road to Civil War?', in *Essays in Honour of Garrett Mattingly*, Ed. Charles H. Carter (1966), pp. 315 ff. It is unfortunate that Professor Elton concentrated so much of his argument on the *Apology of the Commons* of 1604. Whoever its authors may have been, the *Apology*, if read with care and without hindsight, can shed valuable light on the Parliamentary session of 1604. Professor Elton's error in this article is in too easily reading the *Apology* in the light of the interpretation Gardiner placed upon it.

[5] A. R. Myers, 'The Parliaments of Europe and the Age of the Estates', *History*, vol. 60, no. 198 (February 1975), pp. 18–20.

[6] H. G. Koenigsberger, '*Dominium Regale* and *Dominium Politicum et Regale:* Monarchies and Parliaments in Early Modern Europe' (Inaugural Lecture delivered at King's College, London, on 25 February, 1975), pp. 25, 23. This lecture is to be reprinted in 'Der Moderne Parlamentarismus und Seine Grundlagen in der Ständischen Repräsentation', published by the Bayerische Akademie der Wissenschaft and by the International Commission for the

In stating these arguments, Professor Koenigsberger has issued a challenge to historians of the English Parliament which we cannot afford to ignore. This belief that the ultimate survival of the English Parliament was not inevitable, and that its survival was due to events occurring in and after 1640, and even more the belief that outside intervention could reverse a trend already in progress, entirely contradicts the ingrained assumption of English Parliamentary historians that Parliament, well before the Civil War, was already set on a course which led to serious challenges to the Crown and ultimately to political supremacy. Faced with so deep-seated a difference, we must go back to the evidence and ask who is right.

The conventional belief that the Parliaments of 1604–29 were a 'high road to Civil War' logically implies two further beliefs. One is the belief that Parliament was a powerful institution; it is only if Parliament is thought of as a great power in the State that it can be made to fill the role for which it is cast, of a potential challenger to the king for supreme power. The other logical necessity to the belief that this period was a high road to Civil War is the belief that the Parliaments of these years witnessed a constitutional struggle between two 'sides', government and opposition, or, in modern language, court and country.[7] Two sides are an essential condition of a Civil War, and where there are not two sides, there cannot be a high road to Civil War.

These two beliefs are logically implied in statements made by well-known historians, and these implications have gained the status of received opinions. 'Every schoolboy knows' that Parliament was growing more powerful in the early Stuart period, and that it was divided into supporters of 'government' and 'opposition'. It is the contention of this article that these two beliefs are false. Before 1640, Parliament was not powerful, and it did not contain an 'opposition'.

Since these two beliefs have become so firmly rooted in our collective historical consciousness, it is interesting to see how tentative our leading Parliamentary historians have been in stating them. The greater reservations concern the belief that Parliament, and particularly the House of Commons, possessed political power. In his Raleigh Lecture on *The Winning of the Initiative by the House of Commons* Wallace Notestein, the greatest Parliamentary historian in this field, conveyed this belief in three phrases only. One was the statement that 'Tudor despotism contained within itself the seeds of its own decay; it was leading on to a more active House of Commons, certain *in time* to demand power'. The second was his conclusion that these years 'gave us . . . a new kind of Commons, that was *by and by* to make inevitable a new constitution'. Both these phrases contain a crucial chronological reservation. The third phrase in which Notestein conveyed a belief in the power of the House of Commons was the crucial ambiguity of his title '*The Winning of the Initiative by the House*

History of Representative Institutions. I am very grateful to Professor Koenigsberger for allowing me to read a typescript of this lecture before publication.

[7] This article is not intended to dispute Professor Zagorin's contention that there was conflict between 'court' and 'country'. It is intended to dispute his contention that this was a conflict in which members of Parliament were able or willing to choose sides, and especially his readiness to classify members of Parliament as 'oppositionists'. See his list of 'oppositionists' on pp. 79–80. For a more detailed discussion of the weaknesses of Zagorin's argument, see G. R. Elton, 'The Unexplained Revolution', in *Studies in Tudor and Stuart Politics and Government* (Cambridge, 1974), II, pp. 183–9.

of Commons'. Notestein himself said that he was describing how the Commons 'gained the real initiative *in legislation*'.[8] That independent members gained the initiative in the legislative process in the House of Commons is undeniable, but the small proportion of their bills which passed into law may leave us wondering whether the initiative in the legislative process in the House of Commons deserves to be described without qualification as 'the initiative'.[9]

Notestein showed an almost equal caution in stating the other belief here discussed, that Parliament was divided into 'government' and 'opposition'. It is true that he used these terms throughout, but, in two little noticed passages of reservation, he denied that the leaders he described were a deliberate opposition with constitutional aims. He said that they proceeded 'without purpose or intent but to do the next thing that came to hand'. Similarly, in saying that the leaders he described ceased to take their cue from Privy Councillors, he said 'Not that they were definitely out to change the constitution. Rather, as leaders of opposition, they were full of devices to overcome particular difficulties, and when these devices led on to new custom, they saw in it nothing out of the way'.[10] Others, unmindful of this qualification, have noticed numerous occasions on which members of both Houses of Parliament failed to function in a coherent 'government' and 'opposition' pattern, but they have developed a tendency to treat such examples which fail to fit their picture as illustrations of the moral obliquity of the characters they are discussing. T. L. Moir complained that the officials and courtiers in the Addled Parliament 'should have formed a cohesive group in the House', though he was well aware that they did not do so.[11] The note of moral condemnation is strongest in Professor Zagorin's discussion of Sir Thomas Wentworth: 'if he held any principles, his conduct was no less marked by mercenary self-interest and lack of scruple. These traits appeared fully in his political *volte-face*'. This moral condemnation was missing from the comments of Wentworth's contemporaries. Bedford, who by 1640 did deserve the title of 'leader of the opposition', wrote to Wentworth after his elevation to the Presidency of the Council of the North, not with a complaint that he had 'changed sides', but with an offer to help to get his nephew a barony. It is then possible to wonder whether Wentworth's offence was against the moral standards of his contemporaries, or against the tidiness of Professor Zagorin's argument.[12]

At the least, the hesitancy shown by historians of the calibre of Notestein in asserting these two propositions, that Parliament was a power in the State, and that it was divided into government and opposition supporters should lead us to wonder whether the assumptions are not open to serious

[8] Wallace Notestein, *The Winning of the Initiative by the House of Commons* (1924), pp. 47–8, 54, 4. [my italics]

[9] Notestein's picture of the winning of the legislative initiative provides a contrast, though not a conflict, with Pym's picture of the last Parliaments of the 1620s as being 'like dying men, *intestabiles,* incapable of making their wills, the good Acts that they were about'. J. Rushworth, *Historical Collections,* III i 21.

[10] Notestein, *op. cit.* pp. 4, 51.

[11] Moir, *op. cit.* p. 167.

[12] Zagorin, pp. 57–8: *The Wentworth Papers,* Ed. J. P. Cooper, Camden Soc. 4th Series 12 (1973), pp. 309–10. I am grateful to my pupil Mr. Richard Cust for an illuminating discussion of Wentworth's early career.

doubt. In any discussion of power, it is essential to remember that Parliament had two Houses. Both in legislation and in judicature, the efforts of the Commons stood no chance whatever of persuading the King without the support of the Lords. Without backing from among the Lords, even the most aggressive verbal noises in the Commons amounted to no more than political tantrums. So shrewd a manager of men as Buckingham was more concerned about his critics among the Lords than among the Commons. We remember that during the Parliament of 1621 Sir Edwin Sandys and John Selden were imprisoned but tend to forget the Earl of Southampton. It should give us pause to find the Venetian Ambassador describing the imprisonment of the Earl of Southampton and 'three or four others of no consideration'.[13]

The ability to obstruct Conciliar legislation conferred much less power on either House of Parliament in this period than it would have done in, for example, the 1530s. From the late Elizabethan period onwards, the desire of Crown and Council to legislate appears to have declined sharply, and the political importance of control of the legislative process declined with it. Opening speeches by the Lord Keeper often warned Parliaments that they were not called for the making of new laws, for there were more than enough already. On those occasions when James told a Parliament that one of the reasons for which it was called was the making of laws, he normally intended the statement as a concession.[14] He was not announcing a 'government' legislative programme, since he had no desire for one. He was saying members could spend their time on issues of their own choice. The legislative initiative, then, was of little importance if the Crown had no great wish to legislate. There was only one piece of legislation particularly dear to the heart of James I which was obstructed by the House of Commons, and that was the Union with Scotland. The Great Contract also failed to pass through the legislative process in 1610, but to describe the Great Contract as an example of an 'opposition' frustrating 'government' legislation would be misleading. Many of the strongest opponents of the Great Contract were inside the government, and their criticisms may have had as much to do with its failure as any Parliamentary 'opposition'. There can only be an 'opposition' where there is a clear 'government' line, and the Great Contract was not such an issue. It is, then, misleading to use the failure of the Great Contract to illustrate the power of a Parliamentary 'opposition'.

There was only one thing which could give Parliament power in a situation in which the King did not wish to be persuaded, and that was control of supply. A monopoly of the power of extraordinary taxation was the only means by which Parliament could, in a situation of conflict, hope to force its will on a reluctant Crown. What use did Parliament make of its power to give or withhold supply, and what were the effects of its use? Professor Koenigsberger, at the end of an exhaustive study of European Parliaments and estates, concluded that 'it seems to be a fairly general rule that a Parliament which failed to insist on the redress of grievances before supply

[13] *C.S.P.Ven. 1621–3*, p 80.

[14] G. R. Elton, 'Tudor Government: Points of Contact: Parliament', *T.R.H.S.* 5th Series 24 (1974), p. 188: *Wentworth Papers*, pp. 63–4.

had no chance of winning its struggle with the monarchy; i.e. a parliament must not agree to grant taxes before the King has met its demands'.[15] By this test, the English Parliament before 1629 was heading for extinction. In 1606, they voted three subsidies and three fifteenths, recognizing the principle that Parliamentary supply should be used to meet defects in the King's ordinary revenue. They did not use the supply as a lever to secure redress of their grievances, since they only presented the grievances the day before the subsidy, and accepted from James what, in his predecessor, would have been called an 'answer answerless'. A few of the grievances, such as the patent for logwood, were briefly redressed before springing up again, but most of them continued unchecked until the Long Parliament.[16] In 1610, a vote of one subsidy and one fifteenth was accompanied by a Petition of Grievances. It was proposed that the subsidy be presented before the grievances on the ground that 'there was no reason to defer our gift till he had answered our grievances for the word of a prince was not a small matter, and he had promised us a good and a gracious answer to our grievances'. The Commons decided to defer the subsidy till the grievances had been presented, but James's reply of July 10, saying the grievances could not be suddenly answered, cannot be described as 'redress'. Once again, the subsidy was voted, and the grievances remained unredressed. When Sir Henry Neville told James 'that in this one Parliament they had already given four subsidies and seven fifteenths, which is more than ever was given by any Parliament at any time, upon any occasion; and yet withal that they had no relief of their grievances',[17] he spoke no more than the plain truth. In the first Parliament of King James, the ability to link subsidies with redress of grievances did not confer any significant bargaining power on Parliament, because the attempt to use it for this purpose was not made. The attempt was contemplated, both then and later. The significant fact is that members who contemplated using this weapon so frequently decided not to do so.

In 1621, when Parliament met after a seven-year interval,[18] members of the Commons were even farther from attempting to use supply as a means of extorting the redress of grievances. The drama of the attack on the patentees in 1621 has distracted attention from the ease with which the subsidies went through. The subject was introduced on 15 February, just over a fortnight after the opening of the Parliament, and an important shift at once appeared in the nature of the bargain involved in a grant of subsidy. In the words of Pym's diary, 'this meeting was to be employed uppon the twoe poynts of suply and grievances, but the former consumed most part of tyme, for the subiect being gracious and acceptable many were desireous to have their part in it'. Instead of redress of grievances, the motive of giving

[15] Koenigsberger, *art. cit.* p. 25.

[16] *The Parliamentary Diary of Robert Bowyer,* Ed. D. H. Willson (Minneapolis) 1941, pp. 164–7. S. R. Gardiner, *History of England* (1893) I. 299. For the text of the grievances, see *Bowyer,* pp. 153–6. One, the cost of passing sheriffs' accounts, was redressed by statute in 1624. On the principle of supply to meet ordinary expenditure, see the preamble of the Subsidy Act, *1 Jac. 1 c. 26.*

[17] Elizabeth Read Foster, *Proceedings in Parliament 1610* (New Haven 1966) II 145–8, 286, 338n. James's answer (*ibid.* 273) can hardly be called satisfactory. For Sir Edwin Sandys' proposal to present the same list of grievances again in 1614, see. *C.J.* I, 465.

[18] It is interesting that these years have never come to be known as the 'seven years of unparliamentary government'.

was now alleged to be 'to procure from his Majestie the love and frequency of Parliaments, to take from the world the opinion of ielousye betwixt the King and his Comons, from our enemyes the hope of our devision, from our selves those mischefes and grievances which the discontinuance of Parliaments hath caused. As we expect ease from his Majesties grace, to doe that which may procure his grace'.[19] The bargain had indeed shifted: it was no longer redress of grievances in return for subsidies, but subsidies in return for the summons of future Parliaments. So eager were the Commons to please in this matter that they did not even accept the very mild suggestion of Pym: 'not to hinder the subsidy; but yet to prepare some bills to go up with it'.[20] This is why the Parliament of 1621 presented the extraordinary spectacle of a session in which the subsidy bill was the only legislation passed. Sir Robert Phelips, at least, appreciated the significance of what had happened: he later complained that 'we have broken all former precedents, in giving two subsidies at the beginning of a Parliament'.[21] It seems that the dramas of the revived Parliamentary judicature, and of the foreign policy debate of the second session, have blinded us to a sharp fall, in 1621, in the bargaining power control of the subsidy conferred on the House of Commons. Even the revived judicature, as the cases of Floyd and Yelverton show, was a procedure which could only be made effective with the King's consent. At no time before 1640 did impeachment deprive the King of a minister whom he was determined to retain.

In 1624, once again, the subsidy was voted before grievances were discussed. The Petition of Grievances of 1624 was presented so late in the Parliament and it received so little attention that the Commons were constrained to present the identical petition of grievances again in the next Parliament. In 1625, it can at least be said that the Commons went through the motions of requesting redress of grievances before supply, but it cannot be said that they had much success in doing so. They did not even purport to regard the answers as satisfactory, and resolved, on the motion of Sir Edward Coke, to petition the King for a 'more full' answer.[22] Some of the 1625 grievances, such as the new imposition on the Turkey merchants and the new imposition on wines, provided staple issues of complaint in the Parliament of 1628. Others, such as the imposition on Newcastle coals and the restraint of building, were echoes of the old petition of grievances of 1610. Nevertheless, the Commons duly voted two subsidies without waiting for their 'more full' answer.

It is necessary here to correct two widely held misapprehensions. The first is that the decision in 1624 to appropriate Parliamentary supply to the forthcoming war with Spain, and to allow it to be paid to Treasurers nominated by the House of Commons, represented an exercise of the power of the purse by the Commons. Appropriation of supply had occasionally been discussed in 1610 and 1614 as a way of increasing the Parliamentary power of the purse, but in 1624 the initiative for the appropriation did not come

[19] Wallace Notestein, F. H. Relf and Hartley Simpson (Eds.) *Commons' Debates in 1621* (New Haven 1935) IV 56, II 84–91. (Hereafter cited as 'Notestein, Relf and Simpson'.)

[20] *C.J.* I 550.

[21] *C.J.* I 658.

[22] Queen's College, Oxford, Ms. 449, f. 243a. I am grateful to Mr. Allen Croessmann for drawing my attention to this MS.; *C.J.* I 802; *Commons' Debates in 1625*, Ed. S. R. Gardiner, Camden Society (1873), pp. 37–41.

from the House of Commons. Both the proposal for appropriation and the proposal for the subsidy to be voted to treasurers nominated by the House of Commons were first stated in public by King James I himself, in his speech to both Houses of 8 March, 1624. The proposal was next repeated by Lord Treasurer Middlesex in the House of Lords, and it was only after this firm official encouragement that it was introduced into the House of Commons by Sir Benjamin Rudyerd on 11 March. Dr. J. N. Ball was undoubtedly correct in saying that 'Rudyerd's detailed propositions came directly from the King', and even in describing Rudyerd as acting, in this speech, as a 'government spokesman'.[23] This appropriation, great though its long-term constitutional significance may have been, was not the result of any pressure by the House of Commons, but an offshoot of the complex balance of forces at court between those in favour of the war with Spain and those against it. Subsequent attempts to make these treasurers account to the House of Commons, as the wording of the Act demanded, were a total failure.

The other misapprehension is that the failure to grant an additional supply in the Oxford session of 1625 represented an important use of the power of the purse for purposes of political coercion. The 1625 Parliament had already voted two subsidies, and Charles was attempting to induce it to vote a second grant of subsidies in one year. The voting of two grants of subsidy in one session and in one year was something likely to provoke popular discontent, especially during a serious attack of the plague, and there was reason in Sir Thomas Wentworth's statement that 'wee feare the granting therof wilbe esteemed by his subiects noe faire acquittal of our duties towards them, or returne of ther trusts reposed in us'.[24] The surprising thing about the request for an additional subsidy in 1625 was not that it was refused, but that it was ever seriously entertained. A similar request in 1610 had been turned down out of hand. There was only one recent precedent for the making of two grants of subsidy in one year. That was the grant of an additional subsidy in the second session of 1621, which James had thrown away by a premature dissolution.

By themselves, these occasions on which supply was voted without redress of grievances need not prove a lack of Parliamentary power: they might only prove a desire to be conciliatory. Such a desire was certainly present in 1621. It is only possible to test the extent of the power conferred on Parliament by the right to withhold supply by looking at the rare occasions on which Parliaments did attempt to use the withholding or delaying of supply as a bargaining counter to extort political concessions. In the

[23] J. N. Ball, 'The Parliamentary Career of Sir John Eliot 1624–1629', Cambridge Ph.D. Thesis, 1953, pp. 40–1. I am grateful to Dr. Ball for lending me a copy of this thesis, which is, as he says, 'the first attempt except for studies of the Petition of Right and of Eliot's leadership in the Parliament of 1626, to rewrite any of the political history of the period 1624–9 both in the light of new materials and from a point of view outside the 'Whig' tradition of English historiography'. *Thesis cit.* p.i. *L.J.* iii 250, *Lords' Debates in 1624 and 1626,* Ed. S. R. Gardiner, Camden Society N.S. xxiv (1879), p. 22, B.M. Add. Ms. 18, 597, ff. 70–2. *H.M.C. Mar and Kellie (Suppl.),* p. 195. It is recorded in an endorsement on the Act itself that 'the grounds of this Act proceeded originallie from the gratious proposition of his Matie. himself'. Judges' resolutions of 26 May 1624, *L.J.* iii 408, and House of Lords Record Office, original Acts, 21 Jac. I c. 33).

[24] *Wentworth Papers,* p. 238. Wentworth said they should refuse a second grant, 'having regard unto our creditts and reputations'.

reign of James I, there was only one such occasion: the Addled Parliament of 1614. The issue here involved was the issue of impositions, in which the House of Commons stood alone. They lacked majority backing from the House of Lords in attempting to force the Crown to abandon its right to impose duties on merchandise without the consent of Parliament. The issue was one of the utmost importance, involving the right of the Crown to place additional customs duties on merchandise at its pleasure. The subsequent history of impositions shows that members of the Commons were not mistaken in the importance they attached to them. The issue was, moreover, being discussed in a second consecutive Parliament. In 1610, the Commons had mustered all their debating talent on this issue. Thomas Wentworth, son of Peter Wentworth, quoted Fortescue, expressing the fear that this meant the end of England's status as *dominium politicum et regale,* a Parliamentary monarchy. Yet, though all the legal resources of the Commons were involved in the assembly of a formidable collection of precedents, John Chamberlain proved justified in his forecast that those involved in impositions 'no doubt will maintain their doings, knowing that though men storm never so much yet *vanae sine viribus irae*'.[25] It is remarkable that the 1610 Parliament, when they were so rightly, and deeply, concerned about impositions, did not attempt to make supply conditional on their abandonment. Even in 1614, when the King threatened immediate dissolution if supply was not granted, a surprising number of members were prepared to vote supply without first insisting on the abandonment of impositions. By my count, the speakers in the final debate on whether to grant the king an immediate supply were 14 on each side. The King, then, lost his supply, not through a collective resolution of the Commons to deny it, but through the success of the opponents of supply in preventing the putting of the question. This issue, then, came to a showdown in spite of the reluctance of a number of distinguished House of Commons men, including Thomas Wentworth (son of Peter Wentworth), Nicholas Fuller, James Whitelocke and Sir Maurice Berkeley, to make an issue of it.[26] When the issue did come to a showdown, there was never a moment's doubt what the result would be. The Parliament was dissolved, leaving so sober a member as Sir Thomas Roe claiming that it was 'a dissolution, not of this, but of all Parliaments'.[27] Impositions continued to be levied without Parliamentary consent until the Civil War, and increased from the £70,000 a year of 1614 to £218,000 a year in the 1630s. In this, the only profound constitutional conflict of the reign of James I, the result had been such an overwhelming victory for the King that there can hardly be said to have been a contest.

It was another round of the same issue which produced the second attempt of the period to use the withholding of supply as a weapon of political persuasion, the withholding of Tonnage and Poundage in 1625. On 14 April, 1624, the luckless Solicitor General Heath had cited the Jacobean Tonnage and Poundage Act of 1604 as a justification of the levying of impositions.[28] This necessarily produced a determination in the

[25] Foster, *op. cit.* II 108 and n.
[26] This calculation counts the six members who moved for a committee as neutrals.
[27] *C.J.* I 506.
[28] Diary of Sir William Spring, Harvard MS Eng. 980, f. 229. I would like to thank Dr. Colin G. C. Tite for lending me a transcript of this MS.

Parliamentary leaders to word the new Tonnage and Poundage Act which had to be passed in the first year of Charles I's reign in such a way that it could not be so cited. In the words of the anonymous diarist:

> 'The reasons that moved the house not to grant it for life, as it was in King James his tyme, was for that the kinges Councell in the Parliament of 18 Jacobi [*recte* 1624] did picke out reasons out of that Act for the ptermitted customs and other impositions wch lay and were imposed on the subts. very grievous unto them, and they had not tyme to examine and redress them'.[29]

Since the Tonnage and Poundage bill was being prepared during a hasty session designed to reach a speedy end to avoid the plague, there was no time for a carefully worded new grant which would have either excluded impositions, or based them, as the Long Parliament ultimately did, on Parliamentary authority. A temporary bill, granting Tonnage and Poundage for one year, therefore appeared the obvious way round the difficulty. There was no intention to deny Tonnage and Poundage, merely to word the Act in such a way that it should not appear to sanction impositions. This plan foundered on the refusal of the Lords to pass the bill for one year only. The Lords' rejection of the bill left Charles without legal authority for Tonnage and Poundage, even for the proposed interim period of a year. Once again, he continued to collect it regardless of any legal authority. Once again, law proved to be no substitute for power, and the Parliamentary right to deny supply proved to be nothing but a boomerang against those who used it.

In spite of this failure, the next Parliament again attempted to use the right to withhold supply as a political weapon. The issue this time was the second of the two serious constitutional crises of the period, the impeachment of the Duke of Buckingham, to which the Forced Loan and the Petition of Right were sequels. On this issue, the balance of forces was as favourable to Parliament as it was ever likely to be. It is probable that Buckingham's overt opponents enjoyed a majority in both Houses, and not just in the Commons. They enjoyed widespread popular support in the country at large, and very powerful leadership within the Privy Council. The Commons had also, rather late in the day, developed an effective procedural device for linking supply with redress. The subsidies were voted in principle early in the Parliament, and the subsidy bill was then delayed in committee while members waited to see what the King would do to meet their demands. In addition, denial of supply was now being used in wartime, when the King was desperately and urgently short of money. If the denial of supply was ever going to be a successful means of extorting concessions, this seemed the most promising occasion possible. Yet even in 1626, there seems to have been no possibility that Charles would allow the combined forces of Parliament and Privy Councillors to coerce him into parting with Buckingham. It appears that Charles's delay in deciding to dissolve the Parliament was more likely to have been due to hope that the Lords would acquit Buckingham, leaving the Commons isolated, than to any hesitation in his ultimate commitment to Buckingham.[30] It is noteworthy that the Privy Seals under which Charles ultimately raised the Forced

[29] Queen's College MS 449, f. 259.

[30] Jess Stodart Flemion, 'The Dissolution of Parliament in 1626: A Revaluation', *E.H.R.*, vol. LXXXVII (1972), pp. 784–90. P.R.O. 31/3/63, pp. 57, 61, 63, 73, 79, 89, 99.

Loan he used instead of the lost subsidies were dated several weeks before the Parliament was dissolved.[31] The decision to raise a Forced Loan if the impeachment seemed likely to succeed had been taken, as a contingency plan, before it was clear to Charles that Buckingham could not count on an acquittal. And the Forced Loan, for all the protests it created, must be counted a success. The money came in, and the final yield was little less than the five subsidies Charles lost by dissolving Parliament. The difference was scarcely worth the holding of a Parliament. It is even possible to exaggerate the universality of the protests the Forced Loan created. In Hampshire, the collectors had to ask for instructions on how to handle money from those who offered contributions before they had been assessed.[32] Once again, the denial of supply had proved a political boomerang, leading only to the injury of those who used it.

The fourth and last occasion on which the threat to withhold supply was used was the Petition of Right, of 1628. On this occasion also, five subsidies were voted in principle, early in the Parliament, and the subsidy bill was delayed in committee while members waited to see whether the King would give his assent to the Petition of Right. As in 1626, the demand came from both Houses, and not just from the Commons. This time, it appeared in the short term that the threat had been successful, since Charles acceded to the Petition of Right. However, it is probable that he only did so because he was confident of being able to evade its intention. When he had it printed, shortly after the session was over, he had it printed with his first answer attached. This first answer, in the opinion of most of the Commons, was unsatisfactory because it did not effectively prohibit forced loans or arbitrary imprisonment: it left Charles under no more legal restriction than he had been under before. The evasion was of course noticed in the Parliamentary session of 1629, but members could do no more than threaten to punish the King's printer.[33]

In the Petition of Right, members of Parliament were faced with the inadequacy of an attempt to bind the Crown by law, without having the power to execute that law. When the Petition of Right was cited in the courts, judges tended to interpret it along the restrictive line of the King's first answer, and Attorney General Heath in 1629 claimed that 'a petition in Parliament is not a law'.[34] Sir Thomas Wentworth had already pointed out during the debates of 1628 that a legal restriction demanding that the Crown should show cause for an imprisonment did not prevent the Crown from citing a false cause, and searching the accused's papers before he

[31] P.R.O. E.401/2442. The Privy Seals there mentioned are dated 1 May (Rutland), 12 May (Devon), 16 May (Herefordshire) and 19 May (Brecon). I am grateful to Mr. D. L. Thomas for this reference. The Bishop of Mende reported Charles's intention to raise money by 'extraordinary ways' on 23 May/2 June. P.R.O. 31/3/63. p. 79.

[32] Robert Ashton, *The Crown and the Money Market* (Oxford, 1960), pp. 39, 41. The comparative figures were £264,000 for the Forced Loan, against £275,000 for the five subsidies of 1628. Hants. R. O. Jervoise MSS DD44/M 69/012 (Deputy Lieutenants to Conway) 8 December and 13 December, 1626.

[33] Elizabeth Read Foster, 'Printing the Petition of Right', *Huntington Library Quarterly*, vol. xxxviii no. 1 (November 1974), pp. 81–3. *Commons' Debates in 1629*, Ed. Wallace Notestein and F. H. Relf (Minneapolis), 1921, pp. 54–6.

[34] *State Trials*, Ed. Cobbett, III 285, 1109, 1125: J. Rushworth, *Historical Collections* II ii 191 and 237–8. For a conspicuous exception, see Hutton's Ship Money judgement, *ibid.* 164–5. The Act of Parliament abolishing Ship Money enacted that the Petition of Right should be put in execution. *Statutes of the Realm 16 Car. I c. 14.*

could get his *Habeas Corpus*. The rule of law was not a useful ideal unless backed by the power to enforce that law.[35]

The conclusion appears irresistible that the withholding of supply was not a powerful bargaining counter. At the end of the Parliament of 1628, the King still had impositions, Tonnage and Poundage, Buckingham, and, as the event was to show, the powers of arbitrary taxation and arbitrary imprisonment. Parliament's inability to sustain a constitutional struggle with the Crown appeared to have been clearly proved. The one challenge of James's reign had achieved nothing, and three in four years at the beginning of Charles's reign had merely called Parliament's survival into question. Hakewill could remark in passing that confirmation of statutes against arbitrary imprisonment would be a useful restraint on the judges, 'especially if there be continuance of Parliaments'. The fact that the question was open now appeared too obvious to call for comment. Perhaps the most perceptive comment was the advice of Rudyerd 'to use such a carriage as may uphold parliaments for though the power of them sinke not at once yet itt may moulder away'.[36] It seemed in 1628 that if Parliament was to continue at all, it would be on the King's terms. It seems an irresistible conclusion that Chamberlain was right that Parliament was '*sine viribus*'—without power.[37]

At first sight it does not appear to make sense that the denial of supply should achieve so little impact at a time when the King was so desperately short of money. Why, when the King was trying to scrape together every penny he could collect, should the threat to deny him supply have so little coercive force? One very obvious reason is that the sums of supply being offered were too small: they fell so far short of the King's needs that they were simply not worth bargaining for. The financial and administrative paralysis which had overtaken other sources of royal revenue had overtaken the Parliamentary subsidy as well, and the Parliamentary subsidy had suffered much more severely than most other forms of revenue. While other forms of revenue were losing value in real terms in face of inflation, the value of the Parliamentary subsidy fell, not only in real terms, but even in money terms. The same overgrowth of patronage and favour which was choking other sources of revenue was working even more acutely on the Parliamentary subsidy. As Delbridge remarked in 1625, 'commissioners tax men higher and lower, at their pleasure, not respecting taxations brought in by the taxation'. Assessment for the subsidy had become yet another way in which a man showed favour or disfavour to his neighbours. The yield of one subsidy, which had been £130,000 in the middle of Elizabeth's reign, fell by 1621 to £70,000 and by 1628 to £55,000. The depression of the 1620s, as well as administrative weakness, probably contributed to this decline. As early as 1604, Parliament had included in a statute the blunt admission that they were unable to grant the King enough money. They granted James Tonnage and Poundage 'although the same

[35] *Wentworth Papers*, p. 293. See also the illuminating comments of Clare, *ibid.* pp. 287–8.

[36] B. M. Stowe MS 366, ff. 124a, 115a.

[37] Above, n. 25, and *Letters of John Chamberlain*, Ed. N. E. McClure (Philadelphia, 1939), II 421 (19 January, 1622). Chamberlain's comment on the Protestation of December 1621 was '*vanae sine viribus irae*, and that there is noe disputing nor contesting with supreme authoritie'.

doe or hereafter shall nothinge in effect countervaile the same your great charges, nor yet wee your saide poor Comons able fullie to gratifie your highness by any means'.[38] Yet it was the very same men whose collective power as members of Parliament was being diminished by under-assessment of the subsidy who, in their local capacities, allowed it to continue.

One of the big mistakes we have made in the past is to suppose that granting too little supply was part of the same process as the withholding of supply. The supposition may be true for 1625, but it is not true for other Parliaments. In 1624, when the supply granted was less than half of what was needed, there was no possible further concession for which members could have been holding out. Grants remained excessively small even at times when members were leaning over backwards to demonstrate their eagerness to vote supply.[39] It is perhaps possible to take members of the Commons at their word when they said that they could not vote more for fear of the reactions of their constituents. 15 February, 1621, the day when Pym recorded that members talked about supply and not grievances because it was more pleasing to the King, was also the day when they decided to abandon fifteenths, 'because they come for the most part out of poor men's purses, whome it is unfit to chardge before we have given them ease'. In November 1621, in debating the proposal for a second grant of subsidy in one Parliament, Crew said 'if there be two taxes in one year . . . there must be two harvests, two springs and two autumns'. He then went on to support the motion for an extra subsidy.[40] It was not only their poorer constituents members wished to conciliate, but also their fellow-gentlemen. It was again on the same day as this extra subsidy was voted that Sir Edward Coke opposed a proposal for a property qualification of £100 a year for knights of the shire, on the ground that this would be a way to have them assessed at so much in the subsidy.[41] It is in debates such as these that it is important to remember that members were not permanent Westminster politicians, but men who lived most of their lives among the people whose money they were being asked to grant. The need to conciliate the King and the need to conciliate the county community could compete in an uncomfortably uneven balance. Sir Robert Phelips, speaking on the subsidy in 1628, denied that he would 'wishe at this time a shewe or face of contradicion', but also said that 'I apprehend it necessary to look back from whence I come'.[42] Our knowledge of Phelips' career in Somerset makes it possible to take Phelips at his word on both points. A similar conflict is implied in Delbridge's apparently self-contradictory statement in the same debate that 'I speake not to lessen the guift but by comand from

[38] *C.J.* I 803; A. Hassell Smith, *County and Court: Government and Politics in Norfolk 1558–1603* (1974), p. 115: *Statutes of the Realm 1 Jac. 1 c. 33.*

[39] The argument in Russell (Ed.), *The Origins of the English Civil War* (1973), p. 103, that members of the Commons did not realize the true cost of government, is true. On the other hand, the work of Dr. D. M. Hirst (*The Representative of the People?*, Cambridge, 1975) makes it impossible to regard it as the whole truth, or even the most important part of the truth. I am very grateful to Dr. Hirst for allowing me to read this book before publication.

[40] Notestein, Relf and Simpson, IV 58, II 466. Alford thought that three subsidies in one year called for three harvests, but also gave his voice in favour of an additional grant. *Ibid.* VI 208.

[41] *C.J.* I 649.

[42] B. M. Stowe MS 366, f. 48 a–b.

my countrey'.[43] It has long been known that members made these protestations about the reactions of their local communities to grants of supply, but in the past it has been suspected that such speeches were no more than polite excuses to cover up a reluctance to subsidize royal extravagance. Some speeches, such as that of Samuel Lewkenor in 1610, clearly fit this interpretation, but it is not sufficient by itself. Two points weigh heavily against placing too much weight on this interpretation. One is members' continued insistence on the poverty of the country on occasions, such as the first subsidy debate of 1621, when they were not attempting to link their own grievances to the subsidy. The other is the discovery of Dr. D. M. Hirst, in his new work *The Representative of the People?* that, with increasingly frequent contested elections, local communities were in a strong position to exert pressure on their members of Parliament, and often carefully followed their actions at Westminster. Members were often alarmed about the effects of such constituency reactions to their Parliamentary activities. For example, Sir Richard Grosvenor, in the recess debate in 1621, complained that 'we that goe home may be made subjects of the peoples fury, if not of disgrace'.[44] Parliament's increasingly close links with feeling in the country at large were doubtless a strength to it in 1642, when its popularity helped to enable it to raise an adequate army. But what was a source of strength in 1642 was only a source of weakness in the 1620s, since it helped to prevent Parliament from voting the supply essential to its own continuance.

Another reason why the threat of withholding Parliamentary supply may have had so little effect on a poverty-stricken king is that the concessions Parliament hoped to obtain may sometimes have done more to diminish the royal revenue than its supply did to increase it. The clearest example of this point is impositions. At £70,000 a year, they were worth the equivalent of a Parliamentary subsidy every year. James was entitled to the complaint he made in 1610: 'is it a fit matter to dispute of taking away 70,000 li. a year from me when you are called to consider of supply and support for me? I have expounded my necessities myself and my Treasurer at large to you, and the first device and dispute is what to take from me'. His warning that if he continued to meet such behaviour 'I shall be the more unwilling to call you to Parliament' made sound financial sense, and all the more financial sense because of James's shortage of money.[45] In 1614, James was asked to choose between impositions, at £70,000 a year, and a sum unlikely to exceed two subsidies, of £70,000 each, with no certainty that they would be followed by more. In terms of financial arithmetic, this choice was simple, and it is hard to see how an impoverished king could have made it otherwise than he did.

Many more minor grievances concerned the collection of royal revenue. Many of the patents attacked in 1606 and 1621 had been granted because existing methods of local government were entirely inadequate to collect the King's revenue. The highly unpopular alehouse patent, for example, was granted to meet a situation in which many people admitted that the traditional machinery of law enforcement, and therefore of revenue collec-

[43] *Ibid.* f. 44a.
[44] Notestein, Relf and Simpson, III 347.
[45] Elizabeth Read Foster, *Proceedings in Parliament 1610,* II 105. See *ibid.* II 273 for James's promise on impositions.

tion, had proved inadequate.[46] The greenwax patent, which was included in the 1606 petition of grievances, was granted because local officials, by returning false names and addresses to the Exchequer, had been making it almost impossible to collect fines imposed in courts.[47] Cranfield, opposing the monopolies bill in the House of Lords in 1621, said it would take from the King £30,000 a year. Gardiner noted that 'either this must be a great exaggeration, or Cranfield must have taken into calculation means of revenue not usually classed among monopolies'. When it is remembered that to Coke, who was largely responsible for the monopolies bill, a monopoly was first and foremost a method of law.enforcement by a private individual, rather than a restraint of trade, it seems that Gardiner's second hypothesis is the more probable. If Cranfield exaggerated, he still calculated the cost of abandoning patents at a lower figure than Lord Keeper Williams, who said that the King had abandoned 37 grievances, each equivalent to a subsidy. If, in 1621, concessions to Parliament were being costed against supply in this way, it would be possible to read an ominous note into Cranfield's warning that he 'wished the Commons to handle the business so as they might make the King in love with the Parliament'.[48]

The cost of using Parliament as a source of supply would appear even higher if the cost of revoking unpopular grants to the King's servants were taken into account. The King's servants, however unpopular they might be, needed to be paid, and if they were not to be paid at the expense of the Exchequer, they had to be paid at the expense of the public. The overwhelming majority of complaints raised by the Jacobean House of Commons concerned methods of rewarding royal servants, and therefore, if met, threatened to create a new drain on the Exchequer. Professor Aylmer's picture of fees to officials as a form of indirect taxation can perhaps be extended to other grants as well.[49] If such grievances as the Duke of Lennox's patent for sealing stockings are seen as forms of indirect taxation, their survival in the face of Parliamentary criticism becomes more intelligible. There are some signs that people in court circles were thinking in these terms. In 1624, James bluntly vetoed a bill which would have forbidden him to grant recusants' forfeited estates to private individuals, on the ground that it would prevent him from rewarding his servants. This, even if not the true reason, was one which could appear convincing to so well-informed a Crown servant as Edward Nicholas.[50] In 1606, in attacking Brouncker's patent for issues of jurors, the Commons were concerning themselves with something which was both a necessary method of law enforcement and a way of rewarding a Crown servant. The Crown was receiving £1,000 a year from fines on defaulting jurors, a source of revenue

[46] Notestein, Relf and Simpson, IV 326–31, VII 312–22.

[47] *Parliamentary Diary of Robert Bowyer*, pp. 126–7; Notestein, Relf and Simpson, VII 372–6, IV 31; *Wentworth Papers*, pp. 232–3; A. Hamilton Bryson (Ed.), 'A Book of the Several Officers of the Exchequer', *Camden Miscellany*, 4th Series 14 (1975), p. 112.

[48] *Debates in the House of Lords 1621*, Ed. S. R. Gardiner, Camden Soc. 1st Series no. 103 (1870), p. 104 and n.: Notestein, Relf and Simpson, III 416: *L.J.* iii 168. Such redress of grievances as happened in 1621 was a consequence, not a cause of the voting of subsidies.

[49] G. E. Aylmer, *The King's Servants* (1961), pp. 246–8.

[50] *C.S.P.D. 1623–5*, vol. clxiv, no. 61. The real reason for the veto appears to have been French diplomatic pressure (P.R.O. 31/3/58, ff. 67a, 70b, 74a, 119, 122). The excuse was presumably chosen because contemporaries would find it convincing.

which had previously been negligible, while Brouncker, the patentee, was receiving relief from a private debt without any cost to the Exchequer. Fanshawe, who was both an Exchequer official and a good House of Commons man, pleaded with the Commons to leave this grant alone, for 'this patent', said he, 'is assigned to a gentleman for satisfaction of a great debt, who is undone if this grant be revoked'. By revoking this patent, the King would have lost his power to reward Brouncker unless out of the Exchequer, as well as his £1,000 a year, and it is not surprising that in 1621, when this patent was the subject of further complaint, the Council decided that 'we conceave this to be absolutely in the kings owne powre as part of his casuall revenue'.[51] As early as 1601, at the conclusion of the monopolies debate, Sir Robert Cecil had bitterly listed all the faithful servants of the Queen who must go without reward if the Commons' complaints were met.[52]

It was, then, possible to ask whether, in financial terms, Parliaments were worth their cost. The mere prospect that they might assemble kept down the yield of some sources of revenue, such as the sale of baronetcies, which was once noted as something which could be worth—'if they knew there would be no Parliament'—£20,000.[53] It was more important that the prospect of future Parliaments hindered the chances of expanding revenue from impositions. It also prevented the King from developing the precedent set in the imposition on Newcastle and Sunderland coals, and in the imposition (or composition, as the King's lawyers preferred to call it) of 4d. a quarter on malt. These were precedents which opened the door to an excise, as the House of Commons were very well aware.[54] Why, then, did James remain so faithful to his promise to the Parliament of 1610 that he would not further expand impositions without consulting Parliament?[55]

It is necessary to ask whether the reasons for continuing Parliaments were as much political as financial. Did James continue to summon Parliaments, not so much for a relief for his financial necessities, which they were unable to give, as for what Professor Elton calls 'a point of contact'? Was James sincere, for example, in telling the Parliament of 1621 that he wished it to search out the causes of the scarcity of money, 'which neither himself nor his Council could find out'?[56] James's treatment of the patentees in 1621 suggests that his desire to be informed of the griefs of his subjects was sincere.[57] It was also convenient to have a body whose deci-

[51] Notestein, Relf and Simpson, VII 387–90: *Parliamentary Diary of Robert Bowyer,* p. 127.

[52] Sir Symonds D'Ewes, *The Journals of All the Parliaments* (1682), p. 653.

[53] Katherine Van Eerde, 'The Jacobean Baronets', *Journal of Modern History,* vol. XXXIII (1961), p. 140, See also *Ibid.* p. 138.

[54] Foster, *op. cit.* II pp. 267–70. The anonymous diarist of 1625 remarked on this clause of the Petition of Grievances 'but note there is no answer to the laying an imposition on a native commodity'. Queen's College MS 449, f. 240b. For the debate on whether this was an imposition or a composition, and for Phelips' fear that it might lead to an excise, see Notestein, Relf and Simpson, II 476 and n. 480–1. The value of this imposition to the King was estimated at £3,500 p.a. Diary of John Hawarde (Wilts. R. O. Ailesbury MSS), unfoliated *sub* 30 November, 1621.

[55] Foster, *op. cit.* II 273. James's fidelity to this promise was not total.

[56] G. R. Elton, 'Tudor Government: Points of Contact; Parliament', *T.R.H.S.* 5th Series, 24 (1974), pp. 183–200; Notestein, Relf and Simpson, V 429.

[57] It is worth recalling James's statement, in his proclamation dissolving the Parliament of

sions had the unquestionable force of law. James did not have a big legislative programme, but, for example, if so important a Crown creditor as Philip Burlamachi wished for the legal benefits of naturalization, it was, other things being equal, preferable to have the means available to satisfy him. The importance of statute as the ultimate source of law was not seriously threatened, but the urgent questions of James's reign were not so much about what the law should say, as about how it could be effectively executed.

It was also considered essential to be able to call a Parliament at the beginning of a war. Again, the reasons for this were not only financial. It appears to have been widely believed that the symbolic gesture of unity involved in a successful Parliament would do much to make foreign ambassadors believe the country was united in a war effort. In 1628, Sir Humphrey May was quite blunt on this point. He said: 'you cannot resolve too soone for ye kinge neyther can you indeede give enough. But lett our harts joyne. Let forrane states knowe wee are united. Wee have here in towne six embassadors and they every day aske after us'.[58] The point of contact provided by a Parliament was probably also essential to the domestic organization of a successful war effort. Men who were to be asked to do their utmost for the prosecution of a war needed to be able to feel that their local grouses about the organization of the military effort could be heard in higher quarters. The history of the years 1625–28 proved that the King was no more able to fight a war with a Parliament than without a Parliament, but this was something which only the event could show. Up to 1625, the possibility of a future war could have appeared a strong argument against allowing Parliament to drift into extinction. What the catastrophic failure of the war effort showed was that Parliament, as well as the King, was too handicapped by the creeping paralysis which had afflicted English administration since the late Elizabethan period to make a substantial contribution to a war effort. To call for war while under-assessing the subsidy, and while attacking military rates and the Deputy Lieutenants, was a contradiction in terms. The war years at the beginning of Charles I's reign did not show a relationship between an advancing institution and a declining institution: they showed a relationship between two declining institutions, both overtaken by the functional breakdown of English administration, and the only question was which would reach the bottom first. Until the intervention of the Scots, in 1639–40, it appeared overwhelmingly probable that the answer would be Parliament.

If Parliament had so little coercive power, its members were dependent, not on coercion, but on persuasion. If Parliament could not, by withholding supply, force the King to do what it wished, its members all had to engage in a process of lobbying designed to persuade the King, of his own free will, to do what they wished. Persuasion, moreover, had to be addressed to the King. As Pym said in November 1621, 'herein lyes the principall part of

1621, that it had 'proceeded some months with such harmony between us and our people as cannot be paralleled by any former time'. J. R. Tanner, *Constitutional Documents of the Reign of James I 1603–1625* (reprinted Cambridge 1960), p. 290

[58] B. M. Stowe MS 366, f. 15a. For Sir Henry Neville's concern with the effect of Parliaments on England's reputation abroad, see Moir, pp. 13–14. On the whole, the comments of foreign ambassadors do not bear out the widespread English belief that they were much concerned with events in Parliament.

our labour to winne the Kinge for hee is the first mover, from whence all prosperitye of this and other affayres of Parliament must be derived'.[59] There was no point in persuading the public at large, except in a situation in which riot or revolution might be contemplated.

If Parliamentary critics of the Crown were entirely dependent on persuasion, it must give us pause before describing them as an 'oppostion'. An opposition, as we know the term now, can hope to force changes of policy, either by changing the government, or by appealing so eloquently to the public that the government is forced to change its ground. In this sense, opposition as we know the term now was impossible. It is also a characteristic of an 'opposition' that it is united by some common body of beliefs, which it does not share with members of the government. This ideological gulf between 'government' and 'opposition' is impossible to find in Parliament before 1640. There were many disagreements on policy, often profound ones, but these were divisions which split the Council itself. On none of the great questions of the day did Parliamentary leaders hold any opinions not shared by members of the Council. Men who depend on persuasion to get their way, and who hold no beliefs incompatible with office, cannot be described as an 'opposition' without grossly misleading modern readers. Their relations with Councillors were more like the relations of modern back-bench M.P.s with the leaders of their own parties than the relations of government and opposition. This is why attempts to divide Parliament into two 'sides' have proved so grossly misleading. Even the impeachment of Buckingham was not a confrontation between 'government' and 'opposition': it was a confrontation between two groups within the Council, in which both sides enjoyed support within the Lords and the Commons, but the less influential group in the Council enjoyed majority support in the Commons. Buckingham himself, whose judgement of men was better than his judgement of measures, regarded his most dangerous opponents as being Pembroke, the Lord Chamberlain, Abbot, the Archbishop of Canterbury, Arundel, the Earl Marshal, and Williams, who had just been sacked from the Lord Keepership of the Great Seal.[60] To describe these men as 'leaders of the opposition' would be an absurdity. After the impeachment had failed, it was Pembroke, and not the leaders of the Commons, whom Buckingham felt the need to conciliate. The contract for a marriage between Buckingham's daughter and Pembroke's nephew and heir is dated 3 August, 1626, only a few weeks after the end of the Parliament, and it reads comically like a marriage alliance ending a war between two great powers.[61] It was probably the withdrawal of Pembroke's support, rather than a hypothetical meeting of leaders of the Commons at Sir Robert Cotton's house,[62] which did most to prevent the renewal of the

[59] Notestein, Relf and Simpson, IV 448.

[60] W. Knowler, *Strafforde Letters* (1739) I, 28 (Ingram to Wentworth). The Bishop of Mende, the Queen's Almoner, regarded Arundel as the prime mover in the impeachment of Buckingham, and tried to lead him to believe he enjoyed the Queen's support. P.R.O. 31/3/63, p. 73 (Mende to Richelieu).

[61] Sheffield City Library, Elmhirst MSS 1351/4. Salvetti noted this contract on 21/31 July 1626, only just over a month after the dissolution of the Parliament. *H.M.C. 11th Report I,* p. 82.

[62] J. N. Ball, *thesis cit.* pp. 222–3. Dr. Ball has found no record of this meeting at Sir Robert Cotton's house, but believes the outlines of the story to be correct. On the importance of Pembroke's attitude to Buckingham in 1628, see also *Cal.S.P. Dom. 1627–8,* vol. xcii, no. 12

impeachment in the Parliament of 1628. It is noteworthy that when Eliot's study was searched, during the impeachment of Buckingham, the only document known to have been taken away was a petition to Pembroke for the office of Deputy Lieutenant in Cornwall.[63] As Buckingham saw it, Eliot had not gone over from the government to the opposition, but had changed his court patron, from Buckingham to Pembroke. Even with the support of such powerful members of the government, the impeachment of Buckingham remained an attempt at persuasion, rather than at coercion. As Dr. Ball remarked, in adopting their 1626 Remonstrance, the Commons 'were implicity admitting that without the willing support of the Crown, the impeachment of a powerful minister could not hope to succeed'.[64]

If persuasion was the object of the exercise, it was essential for Parliamentary critics of current policies to act in alliance with friends in the Lords and in the Council, whose efforts could be used to make their attempts at persuasion more effective. There were always members of the Council who were willing to join in such exercises in persuasion, both behind the scenes and publicly, in Parliament. That they did so does not mean that they had 'gone over to the opposition': it means they were discharging the duty of a Councillor to give good counsel. In the days before the collective responsibility of the Cabinet, the duty of a Councillor was not to toe some mythical 'government' line. It was, in Queen Elizabeth's words to William Cecil, 'that without respect of my private will you will give me that counsel which you think best'. Like his Stuart successors, William Cecil interpreted these words as applying to counsel given in Parliament, as well as outside it, and like his Stuart successors, he accepted that it remained his duty to give good counsel even if he therefore got into trouble with his sovereign.[65]

It was, then, no breach with tradition that in the Addled Parliament, it was Secretary Winwood who moved the motion for stricter enforcement of the recusancy laws. When he was seconded in this motion by the reputedly 'opposition' member Sir Dudley Digges, no unholy alliance between government and opposition had taken place. All that had happened was that two personal friends were speaking together for a cause in which they both believed.[66] In 1621, when Lionel Cranfield encouraged the attack on the referees who had granted the obnoxious patents, he may have been pursuing his own advantage.[67] He was, however, also doing his duty as a servant of the Crown. His chief principle as a Crown servant was that the King's money ought not to be wasted, and in attacking those who wasted it, he was not being false to the principles on which he acted as a member of the government.

Though Solicitor General Heath was not a member of the Privy Council,

(Hippisley to Buckingham, 2 February, 1628). I am grateful to Mr. Paul Fowle for this reference.

[63] *C.S.P.D. 1625–6*, vol. xviii, no. 68. [64] J. N. Ball, *thesis cit.* p. 211.

[65] Conyers Read, *Mr. Secretary Cecil* (1955), I 119. For an example of how Burghley interpreted this injunction, see the story of his Interregnum Bill in J. E. Neale, *Queen Elizabeth I and Her Parliaments,* II (1957), pp. 45–8. Neale's comment that 'Stuart days were not far distant' can be read two ways. See also G. R. Elton, *Studies in Tudor and Stuart Politics and Government* (Cambridge, 1974), vol. II p. 159.

[66] *C.J.* I 475.

[67] Notestein, Relf and Simpson, V 261, III 227. Cranfield succeeded Mandeville, the referee he attacked with most vigour, as Lord Treasurer.

the King had few more loyal servants, and few more dependable Parliamentary spokesmen. Yet there were numerous occasions on which Heath gave Parliamentary counsel which ran counter to the King's immediate wishes. In the first session of 1621, he initiated the attacks on a number of the patents which were questioned. As a law officer of the Crown, he was under no obligation to support methods of law enforcement he believed to be illegal or against the King's profit. In the foreign policy debates of the winter of 1621, Heath was one of the first members of the Commons to press for war with Spain to be prosecuted in the West Indies, and was the man who finally reassured the Commons that it was within the limits of propriety to petition the King on a matter of state. For this, Heath, like some Elizabethan Councillors before him appears to have got into trouble, but he was doing no more than giving the King the advice which he, and a number of the King's other Councillors and servants, believed was the best. In 1625, Heath explicitly supported both the attacks on the Arminian Richard Montagu, and the Commons' right to take cognizance of matters of religion. In all these causes, Heath probably enjoyed the backing of the powerful Pembroke-Abbot group within the Privy Council.[68]

There appear to have been no important issues of principle which divided members of the so-called opposition from their friends in the Council. Those who wanted war with Spain enjoyed the backing of Pembroke, Carlisle and Holland. Those who wanted to see the end of Arminianism were led by George Abbot, Archbishop of Canterbury. Those who wished to restrict the activities of informers enjoyed the public encouragement of the Earl of Salisbury. The English gentry in the 1620s were not a divided society: all the important political disagreements were such that those on both sides could work together within the same Council. Where there is not a divided society, there is not the fuel to sustain a division into two parties. All the leading members of Parliament of the 1620s were legitimately entitled to hope for office. Since they could accept office without abandoning any of the principles for which they pressed while in Parliament, those, like Wentworth and Digges, who accepted office, do not deserve any strictures for 'changing sides'. They saw no sides to change.[69] Cases like these should be regarded, not as the exception, but as the rule.

Sir Dudley Digges makes an excellent case-study for this point, since we possess a document of his which amounts to something approaching a political creed.[70] Every point in this document is consistent, both with his Parliamentary record, and with the royal service into which he ultimately entered. The document is an undelivered letter to King Charles, written in

[68] Notestein, Relf and Simpson, IV 150, II 155, VI 21, V 16, II 123: *C.J.* I 648, 657; *C.J.* I 806. Heath's connections appear to have been with Buckingham, rather than with Pembroke, but this only illustrates the fact that Buckingham's clients were rarely expected to function as a monolithic 'party'.

[69] The only prominent members of Parliament who could conceivably be regarded as excluded from office by their beliefs are Nicholas Fuller, Thomas Wentworth son of Peter, and possibly John Pym after the York House Conference. In all three cases, the obstacle was religious. Sir Roger Owen and Edward Alford were temperamentally unsuited to office, but they held no beliefs incompatible with it. On the range of opinions compatible with office, see G. E. Aylmer, *The King's Servants* (1961), pp. 351–6.

[70] S.P. 16/19/107. This document is hard to reconcile with Zagorin's description of Digges as an 'oppositionist'. *op. cit.* p. 79.

the early months of 1625. One might suspect that such a document, clearly compiled in the hope of office, might not be entirely honest, but it covers almost all the beliefs he expressed in Parliament, including his hostility to Buckingham. He expressed a desire to combat the growing greatness of the House of Austria, to increase the prosperity of England by expanding overseas trade, to reduce the Commissions of the Peace to manageable size, to ensure the efficient management of the King's revenue, the disparking of remote royal forests, the granting to the outports of the right to farm their own customs, and the employment of 'grave counsellors'. Buckingham might perhaps have taken alarm at Digges' determination to 'owne that obligacon only to yor owne royall chaire wthout other dependance', but there was nothing in it to prevent Charles from regarding him as what he later became, a faithful servant of the Crown. The really conspicuous omission from this document is the lack of any suggestion for an increased place for the House of Commons. Digges said he regarded it as a body which had grown too large and contained some factious spirits. In spite of this, he continued to regard it as the proper source of extraordinary supply (warning Charles in the process of the trouble he could expect over impositions and the Tonnage and Poundage bill of 1625), but he seems to have seen no other place for it. This was the man who was a manager of the impeachment of Buckingham and took a leading part in the passage of the Petition of Right. He took a leading part in the attack on the patents and the foreign policy debate in 1621, and did so while hoping for office. He was thought by Chamberlain to have much increased his chances of office by his conduct in the first session of that Parliament.[71] He was a pupil and a friend of Archbishop Abbot,[72] and could have been a welcome recruit to the Abbot-Pembroke group on the Council. It seems clear that he regarded Parliament, not as something to be magnified in its own right, but as one possible place in which to pursue causes which were better pursued in office. To men such as Digges, a division between government and opposition was meaningless.[73] A division between 'ins' and 'outs' had meaning, but this affected, not his beliefs, but only the forum in which he pursued them.

Another issue conspicuously missing from the Digges memorandum is that of religion, and in this Digges may not have been entirely typical of his fellow-members. His persistent opposition to bills for scandalous ministers suggests that he was a long way from being a Puritan by any definition. Other members, such as Rudyerd, felt a much deeper concern about the issue of Arminianism than Digges did. Digges was merely against Arminianism: Rudyerd detested it. However, in the opening years of Charles I's reign, even the strongest feelings about Arminianism were not enough to produce a Court-Country or government-opposition polarization. So long as many of Arminianism's most effective opponents were still

[71] *The Letters of John Chamberlain*, Ed. N. E. McClure (Philadelphia, 1939) II 385–6, 389, 392.

[72] Digges was not merely a fair-weather friend to Abbot. After Abbot's hunting accident, when other ambitious people were avoiding him, Digges rode post to pay him an immediate visit. *Letters of John Chamberlain*, II 394–5.

[73] It is typical of the early Stuart structure of politics that in 1614 Digges, a supposedly 'opposition' member, was in charge of a 'government' bill for the creation of County Record Offices. Moir, pp. 19, 203: *C.J.* I 487.

in the Council, and had access to the King's ear, it was not yet necessary for opponents of Arminianism to sever their court connections in order to pursue their principles. So long as Abbot, Pembroke, Manchester and Sir John Coke were about the Court, there was no reason why their fellow-critics of Arminianism should not be there too.[74] It was not until 1626 that John Preston wrote to 'a gentleman in Northamptonshire and a noble Lord' (possibly Knightley and Saye) to tell them that Buckingham could be no further use to them.[75] To others with closer connections with Buckingham, such as Harley and Fleetwood, opposition to Arminianism and support for Buckingham appeared compatible for a good deal longer. Harley's hatred of Arminianism was never in doubt, but in the Parliament of 1626, he still found it compatible with a defence of Buckingham.[76] Arminianism was an issue capable of producing a polarization into two sides, pro- and anti-government, but it would be using hindsight to claim that before the death of Buckingham it had already done so. Buckingham was a man whose intentions were often surrounded by confusion, and even after the York House Conference, his anti-Arminian dependents, such as Harley and Fleetwood, could have believed that his support for Arminianism no more represented his last word than his support for Spain had done in 1621.[77] It was of the essence of the attacks made on Arminianism by Pym that he thought his views, and not those of the Arminians, were the orthodox doctrines of the church of England, and the idea that belief in the orthodox doctrines of the Church of England turned a man into a member of 'the opposition' was one which many people took a number of years to absorb.

What has already been said should suggest that many members of Parliament were concerned to adopt a conciliatory approach to the Crown, but this belief is difficult to sustain from the record of Parliamentary proceedings. The reason for this difficulty is that the evidence for conciliation consists, not of what is in the record, but of what is not in the record: on many issues, conciliation was best expressed by silence, and we have all been too preoccupied with collecting the speeches of conflict to notice the silences of conciliation. Yet, like Sherlock Holmes's dog in the night time, they are significant when they are noticed. Fortunately, in some cases, Sir Robert Phelips' irresistible urge to draw attention to his own virtue enables us to say that the silences were deliberate, and not the result of loss of interest.

The most deafening of these silences was on the issue of impositions, in the Parliaments of 1621 and 1624. Impositions were an issue on which, as James Whitelocke had pointed out in 1610, silence could well be taken for consent, 'and therefore if we let this pass *sub silentio* all posterity is bound by it and this will be as great a record as can be against them'.[78] Yet in

[74] N. R. N. Tyacke, 'Arminianism in England in Religion and Politics 1604 to 1640' (Oxford D.Phil. Thesis, 1969), pp. 134, 194.

[75] I. Morgan, *Prince Charles's Puritan Chaplain* (1957), pp. 164–5.

[76] Diary of Sir Nathaniel Rich, House of Lords Record Office, f. 37v: Diary of Bulstrode Whitelocke, CUL MS Dd 12–20, ff. 59b, 58b, 40a.

[77] G. E. Aylmer, *The King's Servants* (1961), pp. 353–4, 374–9.

[78] Foster, *op. cit.* II 109.

1621, despite Chamberlain's fears,[79] the issue of impositions remained unmentioned until the arrival of the King's angry letter of 5 December, almost at the end of the Parliament. Phelips then lamented '[we] have never meddled with impositions (though highly concerning the subjects' interest) to make this a Parliament only of union . . . What then the cause of this soul-killing letter from his Majesty'?[80] In 1624, one of the articles in the impeachment of Cranfield was the laying of additional impositions without the King's consent. Phelips and Sandys warned the Commons not to raise the general issue of impositions, 'lest we rush upon a rock which will endanger our hopes'.[81] If there are any two members of the Commons from whom silence on impositions is exceptionally significant, they are Phelips and Sandys, who were probably the two members most profoundly concerned about this issue. Until the Parliament of 1629, there was a similarly deafening silence about the unparliamentary collection of Tonnage and Poundage. No member seems to have expected the King to stop collecting Tonnage and Poundage, and the subject was mentioned only in occasional discussion of bills to make the King's collection of it legal. The depth to which this acceptance of a *fait accompli* had gone is best shown by a revealing verbal gaffe by Sir Edward Coke in 1628. In the course of a debate on pirates, he complained bitterly that the King was not spending Tonnage and Poundage for the purposes for which it had been *given* (my italics).[82] Similarly, for most of the Parliament of 1628, there was a deafening silence on the great issue of the previous Parliament, the Duke of Buckingham. This time it was Rich who drew attention to the silence. After discussing the precedent of 1297, he asked 'Do we desire anything so high, have we called in question any ministers, do we demand any punishment on ill officers? Those are the men indeed that go about to trench upon power'. There is some point in the conclusion of Sir Robert Phelips, in a public act of contrition for his previous silences over impositions, that 'moderation is of great use, the times considered, but a silent moderation is the destruction of great councells'.[83]

Similarly, we have probably overrated the willingness of the Commons to take up privilege issues, since the speeches of those who wished to take them up are recorded, and the silences of those who did not wish to take them up are rarely so explicitly recorded. We know about the attempts of Mallory to raise a privilege dispute about the imprisonment of Sir Edwin Sandys after the first session of 1621, but it is only from Pym's private diary

[79] Chamberlain's fear that the Parliament of 1621 would be of little use because 'the prerogative is grown a *noli me tangere*' was a fear that the Parliament would break over the issue of impositions. The allusion is presumably to Bishop Neile's '*noli me tangere*' speech about impositions, which had done so much to wreck the previous Parliament. Chamberlain thought impositions, as well as patents, had become so grievous 'that of necessity they must be spoken of'. *Letters of John Chamberlain* II 313: Moir, p. 117.

[80] *C.J.* I 658. The picture of Phelips as being, not an opposition member, but a mediator between Somerset and the Court is supported by the fact that one of his earliest political actions was to lend the Crown £1,000 in 1613. His fellow-lenders, Burlamachi, Vanlore, Courteen and Sir Baptist Hickes, will hardly serve for a roll-call of leaders of the opposition. B. M. Cotton MS Titus B iv, f. 101b.

[81] Diary of Sir William Spring, Harvard MS Eng. 980, ff. 209, 221–2.

[82] B. M. Stowe MS 366, f. 145b.

[83] B. M. Stowe MS 366, ff. 185b, 173b. Phelips' attempt to reopen old arguments over impositions was brusquely silenced by Rich's advice that they should pass it over, 'ascribing all that is past to councells of necessity'.

that we can discover his conviction that that motion was at first 'well past over' by the House. Similarly, it is only from the surprised note '*quaere quaere*' in Sir Thomas Barrington's diary that we can tell that he shared Pym's misgivings about the introduction of this dispute.[84] In 1629, Barrington's views on the big privilege dispute about Tonnage and Poundage do not emerge from the public debates, and it is only from a private letter to his mother that we can tell that he thought the whole introduction of the topic to be distinctly ill-advised.[85] Pym and Barrington were both good House of Commons men and they may have been very far from alone among good House of Commons men in their belief that many privilege disputes were started which would have been better left alone.[86] It would be possible to multiply the list of silences by running through long lists of unredressed grievances passed over in silence by subsequent Parliaments, but it is doubtful whether the process is necessary. The silences on the two big issues of Buckingham and impositions are enough to show that in the two big constitutional conflicts of the period, Parliament accepted defeat.

We can, then, conclude that Professor Koenigsberger is right in ascribing the ultimate success of the English Parliament to the effects of Scottish and Dutch intervention. This ultimate result was so far beyond Parliament's reach in 1604 to 1629 that they were not even trying for it. In both of the two big constitutional conflicts members of the House of Commons were not the initiators. In the first, over impositions, the issue appears to have blown up to the equal surprise of all the participants, James, Salisbury and the Commons. There is no reason to believe that there was any thought in Salisbury's head over impositions except the need to fill the Exchequer. In the second, over the impeachment of Buckingham, we should follow Buckingham himself in seeing the initiative as coming, not from members of the House of Commons, but from within the Privy Council. Dr. Ball is undoubtedly correct in seeing the concern of those who managed the impeachment of Buckingham as being, not with long-term constitutional objectives about the power of Parliament, but simply with the immediate political issue of getting rid of Buckingham.[87]

If Parliament was not engaged in the pursuit of supreme power, and if its leading members were not divided from their friends among the Council by any issue of principle which turned them into an opposition, then much of the history of Parliament in this period needs to be re-written. If we abandon the two main analytical tools which have been used to tell the story, we must put something in their place. For even if we abandon the picture of a government and an opposition struggling for power, which was always an anachronistically Gladstonian picture of the Parliaments of this period, the fact remains that they were not very happy Parliaments. How unhappy they were is a question which will doubtless need re-examination. In particular, we will have to reassess how much these Parliaments were occupied with conflicts, and how much with relatively uncontentious legislative busi-

[84] Notestein, Relf and Simpson, IV 441, III 410.

[85] *H.M.C. 7th Report, App.* p. 544.

[86] See Phelips' remarks on the deliberate passing over of the 1614 imprisonments in 1621. *C.J.* I 658. For a valuable attempt to place privilege issues in perspective, see the forthcoming article by D. M. Hirst in the *Historical Journal.*

[87] J. N. Ball, *thesis cit.* pp. 143, 181. See also pp. 8, 18.

ness, but it would be straining the evidence beyond belief to picture them as models of harmony. What, then, was the trouble about?

Some of it must undoubtedly be laid at the door of King James I. James may not have been an anti-Parliamentary ruler, as he appears in traditional accounts, but neither was he a particularly competent Parliamentary manager. The misunderstandings of 1604, and of the second session of 1621, arose mainly from the perennial uncertainty about James's intentions.[88] To say that James was a much better king than Charles, and enjoyed much better relations with his Parliaments, is not to say that he was a good king, or enjoyed good relations with his Parliaments.

However, it is impossible to follow Professor Elton in laying all the blame on incompetent kingship.[89] The faults in English administration were more fundamental than can be blamed on any one man, and they were too apparent during the Elizabethan war with Spain to make it a tenable thesis that they were entirely caused by an incompetent king who had not yet come to the throne. Of all the general theses which have been propounded about the early seventeenth century, the one which most closely fits the Parliamentary evidence is Professor Everitt's picture of a permanent tension between the centre and the localities.[90] This tension was apparent even before 1588. It was no fault of Jacobean kingship, but a standing institutional weakness, which made Lord Keeper Nicholas Bacon warn the Parliament of 1576 that if the J.P.s did not execute the laws more effectively, the Queen would be 'driven cleane contrarie to her most gratious nature and inclination to appoint and assign private men for profitt and gaines sake, to see her penal laws to bee executed'.[91] This speech summarizes most of the issues that disturbed Parliaments for the next half-century. To accept this is not to turn members of the Commons back into representatives of an embattled 'country'. It has become a truism that a successful career in local government, which was what many leading members wanted, required backing both at court and in the country.[92] The idea that it was necessary to dispense with either was a profound threat to the careers of such men as Wentworth or Phelips.

In this context, it is interesting to see what meaning members of the Commons attached to the word 'country'. In the debate on the summer recess of 1621, nine members of the Commons expressed agitation about the reactions of 'the country' if they came home without passing any bills. By 'the country', they did not mean themselves. They meant the people they would have to meet when they went home, who appeared to them to need to be conciliated every bit as much as the King did. This need appeared to cause them irritation, as well as alarm. Coke complained that

[88] I hope to discuss the second session of 1621 elsewhere. On 1604, see the important article by N. R. N. Tyacke, 'Sir Robert Wroth and the Parliament of 1604', *Bulletin of the Institute of Historical Research* (forthcoming), and *H.M.C. Salis* xvi, pp. 141–4.

[89] G. R. Elton, *Studies in Tudor and Stuart Politics and Government* (Cambridge, 1974) II pp. 161, 166.

[90] Alan Everitt, *The Local Community and the Great Rebellion* (Historical Association, 1969), pp. 5–10. During such a conflict, the distinction of being the local community's representative at the centre was likely to be an uncomfortable one.

[91] A. Hassell Smith, *County and Court: Government and Politics in Norfolk, 1558–1603* (Oxford, 1974), p. 124.

[92] T. G. Barnes, *Somerset 1625–1640* (1961), pp. 289–90; Hassell Smith, pp. 42–3; J. P. Cooper, *The Wentworth Papers*, pp. 5, 7.

'if we shall goe into the country and tell them the difference twixt a prorogation and adiournment, theay will not understand us. *Non est discrimen intelligendum inter illiteratos*'. Delbridge, member for Barnstaple, protested that 'I had rather never have gone home then goe home in this manner. I doe dislike it, I protest I thinke it will doe that hurt that I wish I were in Heaven'. Edward Alford expressed alarm at the prospect of going home without passing the Bill of Informers, because 'the King hath commanded us to tell the country this bill should pass'. Sir Thomas Wentworth, who had promised the passage of this bill while speaking as a subsidy commissioner during the Easter recess, was probably quietly asking himself the same question.[93] It is interesting to note the unanimous belief of these speakers that what 'the country' wanted was not assertions of Parliamentary privilege or discussions of foreign policy, but the passage of bills.

The issue of informers is a typical example of the tension which faced members of Parliament as representatives of the centre in the localities, and representatives of the localities in the centre. In their local capacities, they were sensitive to their neighbours' hostility to informers, and wished them abolished. In their capacity as Westminster legislators, they knew that without the aid of informers, much of their legislation would be unenforceable. In 1604, 11 out of 17 penal statutes passed called on the services of informers. Even in 1624, Pym pointed out that while they were in the middle of passing a Statute to exclude informers from the Westminster courts, they were simultaneously passing another to call on the further services of informers for the enforcement of the laws against recusants.[94] The need to reconcile their central and their local capacities constantly put members of Parliament into this state of helpless conflict with themselves. They needed to conciliate the King, and they needed to conciliate their neighbours, and it was becoming increasingly impossible to do both. Sir John Eliot, in 1628, expressed their desire to conciliate both court and country in a characteristically vivid image:

> There are two townes in Kent that serve for sea markes, when you see them both beeing at sea, it is a signe you are safe, but if you see but one of them the mariners know they are in no good rode and are out of hart and fearing shipwrack untill both bee discovered.[95]

Parliament was, in Professor Elton's phrase, the 'point of contact' between the centre and the localities. But in a situation of permanent tension between the centre and the localities, the point of contact becomes the point of friction. In this conflict, Parliament was not the champion of one side: it was a collection of those whose interests did not permit them to let two sides develop. The conflict between the central government and the county communities was one in which almost every member of Parliament had divided loyalties. The conflict between these divided loyalties was one of

[93] Notestein, Relf and Simpson, III 325–406: *The Wentworth Papers*, pp. 152–5. The nine members concerned were Sir Edwin Sandys, Sir Robert Phelips, Sir Samuel Sandys, Sir Edward Coke, Sir Dudley Digges, Neale, Alford, Sir Edward Montagu and Delbridge. They provide a representative cross-section of the speakers of the House. For an authoritative discussion of the relationship of M.P.s with their electorates, see D. M. Hirst, *The Representative of the People?* (Cambridge, 1975), *passim*.

[94] Bodl. MS Tanner 392, ff. 1b, 34b. Hassell Smith, pp. 120–1.

[95] B. M. Stowe MS 366, f. 74b.

the most important reasons for their powerlessness. The conflict between 'court' and 'country' was not fought out between members of Parliament and the King: it was fought out within the members' own minds.

3

The Foreign Policy Debate in the House of Commons in 1621

On 3 December 1621 the House of Commons resolved to submit a petition to King James I, asking him for stricter enforcement of the laws against Catholic recusants, asking 'that your Majesty would propose to yourself to manage this war with the best advantage, by a diversion or otherwise, as in your deep judgement shall be found fittest, and not to rest upon a war in these parts only, which will consume your treasure and discourage your people', and that 'our most noble prince may be timely and happily married to one of our own religion'.

King James, who was away at Newmarket, lost his temper with hearsay reports of this petition, and his response created a political crisis which led to the dissolution of the parliament. Subsequent accounts of this dispute have been derived, in their main outlines, from the utterances of King James. The petition is still seen, in James's words, as an attempt by 'some fiery and popular spirits of some of the House of Commons to argue and debate publicly of matters far above their reach and capacity, tending to our high dishonour and breach of prerogative royal'.[1] Faced with such a challenge as James offered, no Stuart House of Commons, even if it regretted having initiated such a debate, could refrain from defending its right to conduct it. The defence was regarded by King James as a challenge to his royal authority, and led him to ask: 'what have you left unattempted in that petition of yours except the striking of coin?'[2]

In these passages, James laid down what have since become the two main points of orthodoxy on this subject: that the debate was started on the independent initiative of the House of Commons, and that by starting it, the Commons had attempted a constitutional encroachment on his royal authority. J. R. Tanner was following James when he said that 'the Commons were provoked to the annexation of a new province. They drew up a petition to the king on matters of foreign policy.' He follows James's other point in claiming that 'the Commons, here the real revolutionaries, had now thrown over all the Tudor limitations which warned them off matters of state'. I have in the past followed James in

[1] For the text of the Commons' petition of 3 December and of James's letter of the same date, see J. Rushworth, *Historical collections*, I, 40–4 and J. R. Tanner, *Constitutional documents of the reign of James I, 1603–1625* (reprinted Cambridge, 1960), pp. 276–80. I would like to thank Professor Elizabeth Read Foster for reading and commenting on a draft of this article.

[2] Tanner, op. cit. p. 286 (James's answer of 11 December)

ascribing the debate to the independent initiative of members of the Commons: I said parliament was making an attempt 'to fill an obvious void by debating foreign policy and forming a policy of their own'. Professor Ruigh is equally convinced of these two points: in 1971, he said that 'when the Commons demanded that "the voice of Bellona" replace "the voice of the turtle", it was apparent to all that their action was unprecedented'. He falsely accuses Coke of misquoting the writ of summons in support of the Commons' petition, and follows James in the somewhat curious claim that 'if mere discussion was presumptuous, the remonstrance passed on 3 December was tantamount to high treason'.[3]

Professor Robert Zaller, in his book on *The parliament of 1621*, has printed a large amount of evidence which is entirely incompatible with this interpretation. In particular he has discovered that the first formal motion that the Commons should petition the king for war with Spain was moved by Sir George Goring on the instruction of the duke of Buckingham. He has shown that, before offering their petition, the Commons had 'concluded that Goring's motion had the King's blessing'. He has pointed out that the silence of the Councillors in the face of this motion could well be taken for consent, and, indeed, that the Councillors themselves so took it. He quotes Secretary Calvert, that they had freely taken part in the debate of war with Spain and the prince's marriage, 'as being not all that while controlled from Newmarket, we thought we had done well'.[4] This evidence is hardly compatible with James's belief that the debate was initiated by 'fiery and popular spirits', nor with his belief that it constituted an attempt to snatch control of policy out of the hands of the Council. Professor Zaller's evidence makes it impossible to regard this debate as having anything to do with 'the winning of the initiative by the House of Commons'. However, Professor Zaller, whose book is subtitled *A study in constitutional conflict* is apparently too certain that the main outlines of the parliamentary story are unquestionably known to have attempted the reassessment demanded by his own evidence. He still believes that the Commons wished to 'wrest control of the war' from the king, and that the result of the debate 'virtually usurped the monarchy'.[5] These are James I's two original assumptions, still standing in the face of Professor Zaller's own evidence. It is therefore still necessary to reassess the significance of this debate in the parliamentary history of the period. James I was away at Newmarket throughout the debate, and is therefore not necessarily a particularly well informed source on its motives and progress.

Even if the facts of the story had been as James I believed, it would not follow that they bore the constitutional significance he ascribed to them.

[3] Tanner, pp. 274, 276; Russell, *The crisis of parliaments* (Oxford, 1971), p. 296; Robert E. Ruigh, *The parliament of 1624* (Cambridge, Mass., 1971), pp. 9–10, 12. For the text of the writ of summons, which Coke quoted correctly, see P.R.O. C. 218/1.

[4] Robert Zaller, *The parliament of 1621* (Berkeley, 1971), pp. 151–4.

[5] Zaller, op. cit. pp. 150, 182.

The belief that the Commons were committing a constitutional impropriety is based, in Tanner, and in much discussion since, on the belief that the Commons should not have been debating foreign policy at all. In this, we have been influenced by the belief that Queen Elizabeth's list of 'matters of state' which she believed the Commons should not discuss, represented a long-standing restriction on their freedom of debate. It therefore used to be possible to regard every debate on one of these 'matters of state' as an encroachment by the Commons on the royal prerogative. In fact, as S. R. Gardiner pointed out long ago, 'it was by Elizabeth that the first serious attempt was made to restrain liberty to debate upon principle'. The work of Professor J. S. Roskell has since reminded us that on this point Gardiner was right.[6] The limitation which debarred the Commons from debating foreign policy was a new one. It then becomes one of the striking features of the 1621 debate that the Crown had so nearly succeeded in inducing parliament to accept a novel restriction on its freedom of speech.

Professor Elizabeth Read Foster has also recently called attention to the significance of the fact that the Petition of 3 December was a petition of grace, and not a petition of right. A petition of grace was not an instruction or direction: it was a request, submitted in all humility to a superior for his consideration. Professor Foster quotes Sir Edward Coke, that if it had been a petition of right 'that required an answer, I would never prefer it or give my consent to the preferring of it, but it's only a petition of grace'.[7] It was difficult to construe a petition of grace as an attempt to dictate to the king in the conduct of policy. Members regularly compared such petitions of grace to prayers to God, who remained free to answer the prayers or ignore them as he saw fit. As Crew put it, using divine right imagery entirely acceptable to James, 'we do petition to the lieutenant of God; he may do as he pleaseth'.[8] On another occasion, apparently in a private conversation about monopolies, Coke told James 'I hope every one that saith, Our Father, which art in Heaven, does not prescribe God Almighty what he shall do so do we speak of these things as petitioners to his Majesty, and not as prescribers etc.'[9]

Professor Foster quotes numerous Tudor precedents, some of which were also quoted in 1621, for petitions to the Crown on matters of state, not all of which were given unfavourable responses. In 1586 both Houses petitioned for the execution of Mary, Queen of Scots, and received no rebuke for doing so. Sir Robert Phelips quoted the occasion in 1553 when

[6] S. R. Gardiner, *History of England* (1893), IV, 256–7, J. S. Roskell, *The Commons and their Speakers 1376–1523* (Manchester, 1965), pp. 50–1.

[7] Elizabeth Read Foster, 'Petitions and the Petition of Right', *Journal of British Studies*, XIV, I (Nov. 1974), 33.

[8] Wallace Notestein, F. H. Relf and Hartley Simpson, *Commons' debates in 1621* (New Haven, 1935), II, 495. Further references are to this edition unless otherwise stated. Only volume and page numbers will be cited.

[9] B. M. Harl. MS 389, f. 30a (Meade to Stuteville, 3 March 1621).

the Commons had petitioned Mary to marry within the realm, and the occasion in 1599 when the Commons had petitioned Queen Elizabeth to marry. The complete failure of both these petitions should serve to establish that a petition of grace did not direct royal policy.[10]

It was a different matter if attempts were made to tie grants of supply to royal responses to petitions. Such attempts had been made in the past. Crew quoted the case of 1563, in which the Speaker petitioned the queen to marry when presenting the subsidy bill.[11] In 1587, a precedent correctly quoted by Sir George More, the Commons had debated asking the queen to accept the sovereignty of the Low Countries, and had intended to petition her to do so until the queen, who was not at Newmarket, persuaded them that such a petition would not be welcome. On this occasion, unlike 1621, the Commons were prepared to use supply as a means of securing a favourable response. In the draft speech in which the Speaker had planned to present the 1587 petition to the queen, he had intended to say that 'the affairs of your royal estate are not to be directed by us, but only to be managed by yourself'. Sir John Neale comments that this was 'a dutiful, tactful statement, but its lack of sincerity and the desire of the Commons to direct their sovereign were revealed in the conditional character of their financial offer'.[12] Conversely, in 1621, the unconditional character of the Commons' financial offer could be held to show their sincerity in similar dutiful, tactful statements that they did not want to direct the king's prerogative. The Commons of 1621 had already voted an additional subsidy before they even began to consider their petition, and showed no sign of regarding it as anything but a free gift. Thus, even if the facts of the case had been entirely as James supposed, the Commons would not have committed the constitutional impropriety with which he credited them. Even if the petition had been entirely the work of fiery, popular spirits, it would not have represented, either any breach with Tudor practice, or any threat to James's authority. If he did not welcome its contents, he needed to do nothing but ignore it. James's response to this petition is a particularly clear example of his tendency to make constitutional issues where he had no need to do so.

But were the facts of the case precisely as James alleged? Where was the initiative in the preparation of this petition? James himself, in his blanket prohibition of debate on foreign affairs and royal marriages, allowed one crucial exception: 'these are unfit things to be handled in Parliament *except your King should require it of you*' (my italics).[13] If the king did require such a debate of members, then loyalty demanded that they should join into it with enthusiasm. And this debate took place precisely because members believed the king had required it of them. Sir Edward Coke, in

[10] Foster, ubi supra, pp. 27–32; II, 492–3.

[11] Parliamentary diary of John Hawarde (Wilts. R.O., Ailesbury MSS): unfoliated, *sub* Dec. 3: J. E. Neale, *Queen Elizabeth I and her parliaments*, I (1953), 123–8.

[12] J. E. Neale, op. cit. II (1957), p. 180.

[13] Tanner, p. 286.

the final debate on the petition, said that 'we advise nothing but what his Majesty liketh'. Phelips, whose desire for favour makes him a more convincing witness than Coke, said that 'if I thought this petition would be offensive to the king I would not have it spoken of'. Recorder Finch said that the petition contained no presumption, 'for originally it comes from the king who tells us there is no hope of peace'.[14]

In a discussion of the initiative for this debate, it is necessary to distinguish three different issues on which the Commons have been held to be guilty of constitutional encroachment. The simplest view is that of Tanner, that they were guilty of encroachment in discussing war and foreign policy at all. The second issue, that on which Professor Zaller concentrates, is about the type of war which was being contemplated. To Zaller, the Commons appear to have been attempting to press their view about how to conduct the war, and 'about the nature and purpose of the war itself'. He believes that the Commons, on their own initiative, were attempting to transform a local war for the recovery of the Palatinate into a general war against Spain, and thereby to deprive the king of control of foreign policy.[15] The third issue, and the one which James most strongly held against the Commons, was the introduction of the prince's marriage into the debate. These three charges are separate, and need separate answers.

These three charges, moreover, need to be considered in relation to three separate periods of time. They need to be considered in relation to the first session (ending on 4 June) in relation to the first nine days of the second session (opening on 20 November), and in relation to the time between Goring's motion for war with Spain, on 29 November, and the completion of the petition on 3 December. The mood and actions of the Commons changed very much from one of these periods to another, and it is only by distinguishing the three that it is possible to apportion responsibility for the development of the petition.

James's picture of 'fiery and popular spirits', itching to meddle with matters of state, is very hard to reconcile and the deafening silence of the Commons on matters of foreign affairs and the prince's marriage during the first session. These were already burning issues before the first session, a fact which makes the Commons' silence on them the more significant. When the king charged the Commons with unauthorized meddling in these matters, three members, Digges, Phelips and Crew, immediately drew attention to their self-restraint in refraining from any such debate during the first session. Crew said that though they might

[14] II, 496, 492, 493. On Phelips' desire for court favour, see notes 16, 34, 54 below. For his apparent hopes for office in 1624, see Somerset R.O., Phelips MSS 216/32b (Harley to Phelips, 23 March 1623/4). 'Sr. I am glad I have an opportunity to do you service and I pray you take this in pawne of yr. further power in England. yr. affectionate frend and servant, Ro. Harley.' The probability is that Harley was acting on behalf of Buckingham. Unfortunately, the letter leaves no clue to the nature of the enclosed 'this'.

[15] Zaller, pp. 145–51.

meddle with such subjects, 'all the last sessions we did not, which is remarkable'. Phelips, though also claiming the right to debate these subjects, had no wish to debate them against the king's will. He said that 'we spake not of the match with Spain in the first sessions, but the way was traced out to us by the Lords, and not to excuse it, for I do not acknowledge it yet an error...'. Calvert proposed 'to lett the kinge know upon what grounds wee proceeded, and that if wee were mistaken, wee are sorry'.[16]

The Commons were not merely using hindsight in claiming credit for their self-restraint during the first session. On the last day of the first session Digges drew attention to the fact that the House was 'unwilling to pry into anie matters of State, which they had forborne all this while'. This restraint was in spite of the fact that they had expected these topics to be raised. Phelips said, at the end of the first session, that 'the children of the king are in a miserable estate, relieved by other charyty; and I came with a resolution to have had somewhat donn for ther reestablishment and that we might not spend sommer upon sommer in speculation of ther miseries without redress'.[17] On 18 December 1620 the Venetian ambassador had expected parliament to try to induce James to break off the Spanish treaty and marriage negotiations 'which is the special object of the generality', but noted with surprise on 2 April that parliament was refraining from debating foreign affairs: 'the Parliament is working harmoniously with the King, and each strives which can please the other most. Thus the former proceeds cautiously.'[18]

This silence did not come easily to some of the Commons. One reason for the intensity of their intervention in the case of Floyd, who had rejoiced over the defeat of the Elector Palatine in Bohemia, was that it enabled them to express their feelings about foreign affairs without formally appearing to debate them. Part of the shock they felt on hearing of the imminence of the summer recess was that, as Edward Alford pointed out, it meant 'we shall have no wars'.[19] The Commons left behind them a declaration, at the end of the first session, that whenever the king were willing to enter a war, they would be willing to assist him. It is interesting to note that James so welcomed this declaration that it was translated into foreign languages, and circulated abroad.[20] The final gesture of the supporters of war in the Commons during the first session was kept for the closing minutes of the session, and was made, in typically

[16] II, 503; II, 504; V, 233–4; V, 233 and below, note 62.

[17] IV, 415–16; III, 348.

[18] *C.S.P. Ven. 1619–21*, p. 500: ibid. 1621–3, p. 2. See also B. M. Harl. MS 389, f. 37b. 'The Parliament meddles not at all with the match, nor will not (as is sayd) unlesse the king himself motion it to them, and then they have their answer ready.' Meade to Stuteville, 10 Mar. 1620/1.

[19] II, 403.

[20] B.M. Harl. MS 389, f. 92a. The French ambassador reported that some people even credited James with helping to draft this declaration. P.R.O. 31/3/55 (unfoliated): Tillières to Puisieux, 7/17 June 1621.

theatrical style, by Sir Edward Coke. As the House was about to rise, he burst out, 'out of his zeal', into the prayer from the Liturgy for the king's children, at which 'all the house cried out, Amen, Amen'.[21] Nobody could accuse Coke of seditious conduct for praying in the words of the Book of Common Prayer. He had allowed his feelings to be crystal clear, while scrupulously refraining from offering any advice on a decision which he recognized to be the king's alone.

Any explanation of the treatment of foreign policy in the parliament of 1621 must fail unless it can explain, not only the Commons' debating of matters of state in the second session, but also their studied refusal to debate them in the first session. Why did the line of the Commons change so radically? Sheer impatience would have been a possible explanation, since they had been waiting patiently from February to November for a royal decision which did not come. According to Meade, the decision had been widely expected to follow the return of Digby from his continental embassy, and it was the return of Digby which abruptly precipitated the decision to bring forward the beginning of the second session from February 1622 to November 1621. Chamberlain reported on this decision that 'though yt be verie short warning, yet yt seems the urgent necessitie will admit no longer delaie', and he is unlikely to have been alone in wondering what this haste was likely to bring forth.[22]

It is in this context that we must judge the Commons' own justification of their action. In their explanatory petition of 9 December, they said they had been invited to discuss war by the speeches of Lord Keeper Williams, Digby, and Lord Treasurer Cranfield, at the conference between the Houses of 21 November. The use of the Lord Keeper's speech to set out an official agenda for a parliamentary session was so well recognized a practice that it is hard to see how any House of Commons discussing the matters presented to them by the Lord Keeper could possibly be held to be meddling in matters which were none of their business. This is the Commons' summary of what they were told at the conference:

When your Majesty had reassembled us in Parliament by your royal commandment sooner than we expected, and did vouchsafe by the mouths of three honourable Lords to impart unto us the weighty occasions moving your Majesty thereunto; and from them we did understand these particulars;

That notwithstanding your princely and pious endeavours to procure peace, the time is now come that Janus' temple must be opened. That the voice of Bellona must be heard, and not the voice of the Turtle.

That there was no hope of peace, nor any truce to be obtained, no, not for a few days.

That your Majesty must either abandon your own children or engage yourself in a war, wherein consideration is to be had, what foot, what horse, what money will be sufficient.

[21] IV, 417; II, 430; V, 398.

[22] B.M. Harl. MS 389, f. 37b: *Letters of John Chamberlain*, ed. N. E. McClure (Philadelphia, 1939), II, 405–6.

That the Lower Palatinate was seized upon by the army of the King of Spain... That the King of Spain at his own charge had now at least five armies on foot.

...We therefore, out of our zeal to your Majesty and your posterity, with more alacrity and celerity than ever was precedented in Parliament, did address ourselves to the service commended unto us.

...And although before this time we were in some of these points silent, yet now being invited thereunto and led on by so just an occasion, we thought it our duties to provide for the present supply thereof, and not only to turn our eyes on a war abroad, but to take care for the securing of our peace at home.[23]

This is an entirely correct report of the conference of 21 November and it would appear to be a sufficient defence for the Commons against Tanner's charge that they ought not to have been debating foreign affairs at all. Indeed, they did not report everything they could have said in their own defence. They perhaps prudently did not report Lord Keeper Williams's claim that his speech was 'warranted to a syllable by his Majesty's directions, as (I hope) my Lords of the Council will bear me witness'.[24] They did not report his command that they should defer domestic business till after Christmas, bestowing upon it only 'such howers as may be well spared from this forreigne occasion'.[25] It was not in the time they spent on foreign affairs in the second session, but in the large amount of time they spent on domestic affairs that they risked ignoring the Lord Keeper's instructions about the nature of their business. Nor did they report the words Barrington ascribes to the Lord Keeper, that the king trusted them to be ready with the sword in their hand, and 'the manner he leaves to your resolution'.[26]

This conference, then, should serve for proof that the Commons were invited, in the king's name, to discuss a war. The claim of James, and of Professor Zaller after him, is that the Commons then offended by discussing the wrong sort of war. James said that at the conference they had been invited only to discuss a local war for the relief of the Palatinate, and not to discuss a general war against the king of Spain. Which type of war the Lords had in fact invited the Commons to discuss could be a matter of some doubt. Digby's speech, on which the Commons had to rely for detailed directions on matters of foreign affairs, did, it is true, concentrate on the relief of the Palatinate. However, he also stressed strongly that what threatened the Palatinate was 'the current of the Spanish army', and when he said that 'the state of religion be in great hazard, for the King of Spaine hath nowe six armies in the field',[27] it was at least possible for an honest man to believe that he thought a local war with Spain in the Palatinate might grow into a general war with Spain in other

[23] Tanner, pp. 280–1.

[24] *L.J.* iii, 167.

[25] IV, 425.

[26] III, 418. These words would have authorized the most general of foreign policy debates. It is curious that they were reported only by Barrington, but he is not usually a misleading reporter.

[27] IV, 426, 428.

places. As Sir Edward Coke said, 'the King of Spain maintains 6 armies, his forces have gotten the Palatinate, so then we must fight against the Spaniards. But we desire that we might fight against Spain.'[28] Coke might be forgiven for thinking that the two propositions had a certain broad similarity. The note on Digby's speech in Hawarde's diary, that 'in this I did not well conceive his meaninge', appears to have been made without benefit of hindsight, and so deserves to be given the more weight.[29] It is the more possible that confusion could have arisen about Digby's meaning, since in private he was attacking the Spaniards 'non seulement en termes plains de chaleur, mais entièrement accompagné de violence, ce qui fait estonner tout le monde'.[30]

It is not then surprising that some members of the Commons wanted clarification about the proposals they were being asked to support. Such clarification was not an unreasonable thing for them to want: if they were to finance a war, they needed to have some idea of the type of war they were being asked to finance, since it would make a considerable difference to the cost. As Perrott had asked prophetically on 5 February: 'howe shall we treate of provision for the Pallatinate and not meddle with matters of State?' It is natural, then, that the Commons should have been slow to start the foreign affairs debate to which Lord Keeper Williams had invited them. On the motion of Sir Robert Phelips, they deferred the debate until the following Monday, 26 November. Digges, who opened the debate, said he had used this interval to clear himself at court, and he is unlikely to have been the only member who did so. He also, in spite of the instructions of the Lord Keeper, took the precaution of asking the privy councillors for leave to be heard in matters of State.[31]

The debate of 26–28 November was a confused one, because none of the speakers who took part in it was entirely certain what was being asked of him. The debate did not show any division between 'court' and 'country' speakers. Indeed, the first three speakers were living illustrations of the difficulties in the way of making any such distinction. Digges was hoping for office at the time he spoke, was a personal friend of Archbishop Abbott, and was bound to judge the foreign policy situation in the light of his experience in a recently concluded diplomatic mission to the Netherlands. Rudyerd owed his office as Surveyor of the Court of Wards to the influence of the earl of Pembroke, was feoffee to uses for Pembroke in 1618, and in 1620 was answering Pembroke's letters for him.[32] These two could well be regarded as spokesman for the war party

[28] II, 496.

[29] Hawarde's diary, *sub.* 21 Nov.

[30] P.R.O. 31/3/55, ff. 216–17. Tillières commented that though James had agreed to reassemble parliament in order to satisfy Digby, 'pour moy, ie croy que s'il peut honnestement, qu'il rompera le dit Parlement'. Tillières to Puisieux, 8/18 Nov. 1621.

[31] IV, 15; III, 445.

[32] Sheffield City Library, Elmhirst MSS 1358/1; S.P. 81/8/155, quoted Zaller, p. 17 (Rudyerd to Nethersole).

on the Council. Sir Miles Fleetwood, who spoke third, could reassure anyone who feared to be involved in a Conciliar split, since, in addition to being a downright Protestant, he was also well known to be a dependent of Buckingham.

Digges, who was the first to discuss a diversionary war against Spain, did so in the belief that it was necessarily entailed in a war for the recovery of the Palatinate. His argument, a very reasonable one from a recent envoy to the Netherlands, was that an open war could more easily permit the collection of allies than an underhand one. In short, Digges thought the king was going to have to choose between an open war and defeat, and he was therefore recommending 'the safest way'. Of the next four speakers, Rudyerd and Sackville, simply contented themselves with expressing support for war and willingness to vote supply, and Fleetwood and Perrot tentatively supported Digges's proposal for a war of diversion.[33] The first speaker to draw back was Sir Robert Phelips, who made the distinction later regarded as crucial by James, between a local war in the Palatinate, and a general war against Spain. He did not know which type of war the king favoured, and moved to defer supply until the king had declared himself.[34] This was a reasonable proposal because until it was known what type of war was wanted, it was impossible to know how much supply was needed. In this, he was followed by Sir Edward Giles, who thought they were being asked to support a local war: 'we must fight with the Spaniards in the Pallatinate and be friends with them every where elce'. This also was not an attempt to direct the war, but only a proposal to defer supply until the nature of the war was clear. Giles made his own preference for a naval war perfectly clear, but had no intention of trying to direct the decision.[35] It was only at this stage of the debate that the first councillor, Secretary Calvert, took part in it, and he attacked Phelips and Giles, not for directing the king in matters of state, but for trying to avoid a subsidy though he also, significantly, in the light of later events, commended Phelip's motion to take measures against the papists at home.[36]

The next speaker, Sir George Hastings, did attempt to make detailed proposals about how the war should be fought. He also thought that war against Spain in the Palatinate implied war against Spain elsewhere, and wanted an army sent to the Netherlands and Spanish shipping interrupted. This speech did not catch the mood of the House, and was dismissed in Pym's diary in the words 'here were interposed some unseasonable motions'.[37] It was only at this stage that the first attempt was made to cast doubt on the propriety of the debate, not by a councillor, but

[33] For Fleetwood and Perrott's support for a war of diversion, see Edward Nicholas, *Proceedings and debates* (1766), II, 209–10. It is perhaps not coincidental that of these two speakers, one was connected with Buckingham, and the other with Pembroke.

[34] IV, 437–8; VI, 197; V, 404.

[35] IV, 438; III, 453. He said that if they gave supply, they should 'lett the King dispose it as he pleases'.

[36] *C.J.* I, 646.

[37] IV, 439.

by the veteran Sir George More, who reassured himself with the precedent of 1587, and confined his proposals to support for a subsidy.

After More's speech, opposition to the holding of a foreign policy debate began to find voice, and it did not come from councillors: it came from private members who were anxious to get back to the business of passing bills into law. Glanville, always an enthusiast for the passage of legislation, said that he 'will not play the statesman',[38] and, while supporting a subsidy, argued that parliament would be better occupied, not in debating foreign affairs, but in passing the bills for monopolies, free trade, informers and continuance of statutes. He was supported by Sir Thomas Wentworth, who wanted to defer the subsidy, as well as going back to bills. He was particularly concerned with the bill for continuance of statutes, and feared, justifiably, as the event proved, that the debate would mean they would 'loose the fruite of a Parliament'.[39] Crew, who spoke between Glanville and Wentworth, also wanted to get back to bills. He wanted, in particular, to deal with old crown debts and the reform of licences to alienate. On supply, he wanted to defer the grant, and wait to know 'against whome we are to fight'. Crew admitted to a preference for war in the West Indies, but, at this stage, was making no proposal to offer the king any formal parliamentary advice. According to Nicholas's report, he moved 'that when [we know our enemy] we may give with alacrity'. His proposal to continue with bills until the king's wishes were clear might be regarded as hyper-cautious, but it was hardly an act of overt opposition. It is important that it is in the context of this sincere desire for instruction about the king's wishes that Crew first introduced the only explosive topic to be introduced by an independent Commons' initiative: the prince's marriage. He expressed a hope that 'wee might see him timely married to one of our owne religion', but hastily dropped the subject with the words: 'but this is nott fitt for mee to enter into'.[40] At this stage, he still had no thought of formally petitioning the king about the prince's marriage. The day's debate was closed by Digges, who strongly expressed the hope that the desire to know the enemy would not be used as an excuse to defer supply. He admitted he would like to see a general war against Spain, but again underlined the point that the Commons were not formally offering advice: 'we declare nothing yet, though we all see which way we incline'.[41]

This had been a thoroughly confused day's debate, in which, as there was no clear 'government' line discernible, so there was no clear 'opposition' line either. Each man spoke according to his own conviction, combining uncertainty and desire to please in almost equal proportions.

[38] *C.J.* I, 646.

[39] III, 457–8. For his concern with the bill for continuance of statutes, see W. Knowler (ed.), *Straforde letters* (1739), I, 15.

[40] IV, 440; V, 213. Nicholas (II, 215–16) does not mention his introduction of the prince's marriage.

[41] III, 458. Nicholas (II, 216) quotes him as saying: 'we desire to know of the king our enemy, and we must take time to be satisfied by the king of that'.

The second day's debate, of 27 November, fits even less well with conventional patterns of parliamentary history than the first day. It did however, produce one single 'fiery and popular spirit', who made the attempt with which James credited the whole House, to take control of foreign policy out of the king's hands: this was Wilde, who moved 'that if the King will not declare the enemie he would give us leave to declare him'. How far this was from the general mood of the House is best shown by its reaction to the speech: in the words of Pym's diary, Mr Wilde 'began to speak too liberally of the House of Austria, but was quickly stopt by the dislike of the House'.[42] The Commons' silencing of Wilde should be a warning to anyone who believed they intended to dictate policy to the king. It also provides a very sharp contrast to the ample tolerance the Commons had extended to similarly exuberant speeches in Elizabethan days.

Wilde was followed by Sir Thomas Edmondes, the only councillor to oppose the whole debate. He claimed, with more confidence than his fellow-councillors appear to have felt, that the king did not now hold it fit to open an offensive war against Spain, though he added that 'twill come in its due time'.[43] He urged the Commons to confine themselves to voting supply. Neale, who spoke next, had to point out to him that this was an impossible injunction: the supply must be 'answerable to the occasion', and they could not assess and levy it without knowing against whom it was to be employed.[44] Pending the resolution of this doubt, he too wanted to pass bills for the benefit of his constituents. Pym, the fourth speaker of the day, shared the doubt of many members about whether it was possible to fight the king of Spain in the Palatinate 'and yet to keepe peace in other places'. Like Neale, he would have preferred a general war, but made clear that he was not trying to force the king's hand, and moved for a grant of suppy 'without anie mencion of the warr',[45] leaving the king more time either 'to accomplish his desired peace' or to declare war. Meanwhile, like many other members he wanted to get back to the passage of bills.[45] Sir Thomas Wentworth was equally unhappy with the uncertainty about what type of war was being proposed, and also wanted to vote a small sum while waiting to discover the king's wishes, warning the House to leave war and peace to the king.[46]

Ironically, in the light of later events, it was a privy councillor, Sir Richard Weston, who reassured Wentworth that all these were topics fit for a parliament. Faced with all this caution, he felt the need to add 'commendation of the gravity, warines and good affection of the Howse'. He then seems to have given tentative encouragement to the demand for a war of diversion,[47] and certainly left some confusion among the diarists.

[42] V, 214; IV, 441.

[43] III, 459.

[44] III, 460; IV, 441; VI, 200.

[45] IV, 443.

[46] *C.J.* I, 648.

[47] *C.J.* I, 648; IV, 444; II, 455; III, 464; V, 217. On Weston's attitude to a war of diversion, the accounts of *C.J.* IX and Barrington appear to contradict those of Pym and Bel. Weston's

The most probable resolution of this confusion seems to be that Weston was in favour of a war of diversion, but not yet. When he was followed by Solicitor General Heath, with an entirely unambiguous proposal that they should send ships abroad to take away the king of Spain's West India treasure, it looked as if at last the Commons had got a clear lead.[48] Apart from Wilde, the first member to make a firm proposal that the House should support a general war against Spain was the solicitor general.

Yet, even with this degree of official encouragement, the reluctance to enter into an overt discussion of what the king's foreign policy should be persisted. Sir Edward Coke, who followed Weston, said that 'I would that I had now no vote', though honesty forced him to add that he 'would not wish no voice'. He did what he usually did when nervous: he rambled. The fact that his rambles were made up of a long list of all the iniquities committed by Spain since his childhood has distracted attention from the anti-climax of his conclusion, which was a proposal to go on with bills.[49] Sir Robert Phelips was equally cautious, and appeared to be censuring the rashness of Weston and Heath when he said that "they which speak of a war with Spain speak not seasonably'. He still wished to defer to a grant of supply 'till the King be assured of the fine of this business and how he must draw his sword'.[50] There may well have been a suspicion, possibly even a justified suspicion, that councillors were giving spurious support to a proposal for war with Spain in order to get a larger supply, which could then be spent for other purposes. Such a suspicion certainly appeared to underlie the remarkable proposal of Sir Nathaniel Rich, that they should ask the king's leave to confirm any league he might make by act of parliament. This was indeed an attempt to give parliament a share in the direction of foreign policy, and may explain why Rich was sent to Ireland after the conclusion of the parliament. Like Wilde's speech, however, Rich's did not meet the mood of the House. Of the remaining speakers on that day, Finch, Digges, Towerson, Caesar and Sir William Strode confined themselves to supporting a grant of supply, and Mallory, Seymour and Sir Guy Palmes joined the crescendo of proposals to go back to the passage of bills.

At this stage of the debate, Goring's report to Buckingham was a fair summary of the mood of the House: 'I doubt not but having disported themselves they will every day more and more let his Majesty see that it was nothing but theyr zeale that first transported them and a desire that

speech is a possible subject for the Venetian ambassador's reports of 29 Nov./10 Dec. and 12/23 Dec., that 'some of the Councillors who have hitherto belonged to the Spanish faction' were arguing in parliament for war, and that 'those considered most Spanish in sympathy seem to have made more clamour than others, for the purpose of offending his Majesty, and lighting a conflagration'. *C.S.P. Ven. 1621–3*, pp. 175, 184. Pym (IV, 444) makes Weston against a war of diversion but his account does not conflict with the resolution offered here. See also III, 464; V, 217; VI, 323. The diaries seem to establish, by their variation, that Weston did not give a clear and unambiguous lead on the issue of a war of diversion.

[48] II, 455; *C.J.* I, 648.

[49] III, 465, 468; *C.J.* I, 648.

[50] *C.J.* I, 649; III, 469.

his Majesty might know the stream of theyre affections which is as greate as ever was to any King, and no way to crosse upon his prerogative or direct him in his councells.'[51] Goring was on surer ground in saying the House had shown no desire to cross the king's prerogative than in saying they had shown a zeal to his service. Except for Wilde and Rich, the members had entered no further into foreign policy than was necessary to deciding how much supply to vote. In voting one subsidy on 28 November they showed both their willingness to assist the king and a desire to avoid being entangled in the making of his foreign policy decisions. What was much clearer than any intention to trespass on the king's prerogative was a strong disposition, in which both Phelips and Wentworth had been prominent, to avoid being led into a foreign policy debate at all. The Commons were not rushing eagerly into a foreign policy debate: they were being dragged into it by the councillors. When they had done their duty by voting supply, they returned, on the morning of 29 November, to a list prepared by Sir Edward Coke of patents which had not yet been condemned. The sum was no doubt inadequate, but this was the only time an early Stuart parliament voted a king two grants of supply in one session. It was this, rather than the foreign policy debate, which probably represented the spontaneous inclination of a majority of members. Alford's slogan, 'that we may not forget England while we provide for the Palatinate',[52] was nearer the mood of the House than it has been taken to be.

It was into this atmosphere that Goring dropped his officially inspired motion of 29 November that the House should petition the king for open war with Spain. The Commons did not have the certain knowledge we now have that Goring was moving this motion on Buckingham's command, but, as Professor Zaller observes, 'Goring's connection was notorious'.[53] In a time when Buckingham's favour was so high, and Buckingham himself was away at Newmarket, Goring was likely to be a better guide to official thinking than any of the sworn councillors. Goring's motion, moreover, answered precisely the point of doubt which had been vexing the Commons ever since the conference of 21 November: what exactly was the proposal for which the king wished them to demonstrate their support? Their ready compliance with official wishes was shown in the Commons' swift reaction. There was only one speaker after Goring, who moved his motion near the end of the day's debate. This was Sir Robert Phelips, who two days earlier had been protesting that proposals for war with Spain were not seasonable. He clearly thought Goring's motion indicated that they now were seasonable, and hastened to

[51] Zaller, p. 150.

[52] VI, 202. On 28 November the only member to speak of war with Spain was the courtier Sir Thomas Jermyn, and he drew no response from the House (VI, 208). See also the reaction to Calvert's speech, VI, 205.

[53] Zaller, p. 152.

do his duty to the Court. He now 'confidently affirms that as the state of things are, our saftie and happines can not be secured but by a difference with Spaine'. Phelips himself, in a series of draft petitions written during his imprisonment in the Tower, confirmed that he spoke for a breach with Spain because he believed that he was conforming to the king's wishes. In a draft petition to an unnamed Lord, he said:

I spake not positively but with qualification and comparison, not after but before [sic] his Matie had signified his pleasure to have that subject dealt with. Not upon a design or premeditation, but suddenly and upon the occasion of a proposition from Sir G. Gor. at the rising of the House, wch induced me to think that something sayed to that purpose might conduce to his Mats. ends. I had no purpose to derogate from the dignity and greatness of these princes with whom his Maty. is now in treaty much lesse was it my intention undutifully hereby to search into the king's proceedings, as having care how unfitt it is for private men to speak and how impossible for them rightly to iudge of the high causes and secrett counsells of princes. I could amplifye and enforce this point with sundry and evident arguments of my innocency herein; but not knowing whether you will have opportunity to make use of them or no, I will stay....

It is not surprising that Phelips felt somewhat disillusioned with Buckingham and Goring: 'I have bin so unfortunate in all my addresses to my Ld. Marq. (uppon whom as you know I principally relye) that I am utterly discouraged from presuming any further to trouble his Lp.' He was finally reduced to drafting a letter to Goring, calling himself Goring's 'unprofitable servant', and asking to be brought to a legal trial, 'that so I may stand or fall by the sence and censure of the laws of the kingdome the proper birthright and the best protection of the subiects thereof'. This incident must have made an important contribution to the distrust which disrupted Phelips' attempted alliance with Buckingham between 1624 and 1625.[54] The conversion of Phelips, the chief opponent of proposals for a general war, was taken to indicate the mood of the house, and Goring's proposal passed on to a committee to draft the petition without further debate. Thus, on two out of the three subjects on which they were accused of encroaching on the royal prerogative, the Commons were proceeding on request, and doing what they believed they had been invited to do.

The third subject on which the Commons were accused of encroachment on the prerogative was the mention, in their petition, of the prince's marriage. This subject was not included in Goring's motion, and there is some difficulty in finding out what was the source of the initiative for the proposal to petition the king that the prince should be married to a Protestant. The first mention of this proposal in the diaries is not a proposal that it should be included in the petition, but a proposal that it should be excluded from the text of a petition already drafted. On the afternoon of Saturday, 1 December when a text for the petition was being

[54] v, 225; vi, 213. Somerset R. O. Phelips MSS 224/82, 224/90 and intervening numbers, esp. 224/88. There is no proof that any of these draft petitions were ever sent.

considered in committee, Sir Robert Bevill moved the exclusion of this clause, and Sir Humphrey May, Chancellor of the Duchy of Lancaster, expressed unease about its inclusion.[55] It seems an inescapable deduction that the proposal first appeared in a text which was laid before this Committee.

The procedure for drafting the petition for which Goring had asked was that a text was prepared by a sub-sub-committee of six, whose members remain unnamed in the *Commons' Journals*.[56] It was their text which was laid before a committee on the afternoon of Saturday, 1 December and reported to the House on Monday, 3 December. The initiative must have come from one of these six unidentified members, at a drafting meeting unrecorded in the diaries between it was not a public proceeding. It is possible to make reasonable conjectures about the identity of three of the six members involved. Sir Edward Coke, who reported the petition to the House, is likely to have been involved in its drafting. John Pym is likely to have been a member, since two clauses of the petition are taken from his speech of 28 November. One was his proposal that the enforcement of the recusancy laws should be transferred to 'choice commissioners to be thereunto especially appointed', though the petition prudently omitted Pym's further proposal that some of these commissioners should be drawn from the two houses of parliament. The other clause which can be traced to Pym's speech of 28 November is one of his arguments against the toleration of Popery: 'it hath a restless spirit, and will strive by these gradations: if it once get but a connivancy, it will press for a toleration; if that should be obtained, they must have an equality; from thence they will aspire to superiority, and will never rest till they get a subversion of the true religion'. Coke and Pym, however, had both been too cautious in their desire to avoid intrusion on matters of state to be likely sources of the proposal on the prince's marriage.

The third person who can be identified as a likely member of the drafting committee is Crew. The final clause of the petition, dealing with the general pardon which was expected at the end of the session, asked for the pardon to cover reform of the procedure on licences to alienate and *ouster le mains*, and for an end to the 'new invencion' whereby a licence to alienate in order to create a use was expected to describe the use in the licence. This clause is clearly modelled on the concluding section of Crew's speech of 26 November, and while it is possible that Pym's speech made such an impression that parts of it were copied into the petition by other members, Crew's concern with *ouster le mains* created so little response that no one except Crew is likely to have put it into the

[55] v, 228. Alford defended its inclusion.

[56] *C.J.* I, 655. This silence may explain Pym's otherwise mysterious remark in 1624 that 'sum had receaved benefitt by the clerk's book'. B.M. Add. MS 46, 191, f.88a. See my note on 'The Examination of Mr Mallory After the Parliament of 1621', *Bulletin of the Institute of Historical Research* (1977); below, pp. 81-8.

petition.[57] It was Crew who was the only member who had mentioned the prince's marriage on the floor of the House. The words of the petition, that the prince should be 'timely and happily married to one of our own religion', bear a close resemblance to the words of Crew's speech of 26 November, that the prince should be 'tymely marryed to one of our owne religion'. It is then a reasonable conjecture that it was Crew who first wrote the proposal on the prince's marriage into the text of the petition. This would then explain the decision to send him to Ireland after the end of the session.

If Crew was responsible, something had happened since 26 November to change the belief he had then held that 'this is nott fitt for mee to enter into'.[58] When the propriety of the petition was debated by the House, on 3 December Crew now believed that the general invitation to discuss matters of state warranted a discussion of the prince's marriage. He said that 'Queen Hester in the case of religion durst do that which, if the clemancy of the king had not been, might have cost her her life. It was told us that the temple of Bellona was open whereupon we were invited to the discourse of this war. Doth not this invite us? May not the king say, if the match with Spain proceed, that we never spake against it?' These words would seem to show Crew believing, though with considerable hesitation, that leave to debate matters of state probably covered the prince's marriage as well as war. Sir Edward Coke similarly believed that there was at least covert official encouragement for such a motion: he said that 'the prince his marriage must move either directly or indirectly from the King', and then quoted in his defence the same passage from Lord Keeper Williams' speech of 21 November which had been quoted by Crew. Recorder Finch shared the same belief that he was proceeding with official encouragement: 'we are not now to point out when and where his Majesty should marry his son; we only do humbly present it, for originally it comes from the King who tells us there is no hope of peace'.[59] Those who believed the petition on the prince's match enjoyed official encouragement must have been strengthened by the intervention of Solicitor General Heath. Answering Noy, who was now left as a solitary opponent of war with Spain, Heath explicitly defended petitioning the king on the marriage as well as the war. He said: 'we have warrent for the matter in our petition. Matter of warr and the marriage of the prince are *arcana imperii* yet we may petition the King humbly on them both'.[60] In stressing

[57] Rushworth, I, 43; IV, 440; III, 457. On uses and licences to alienate, see Conrad Russell, 'Land sales 1540–1640: a comment on the evidence', *Economic History Review*, 2nd series, XXV, I (1972), 117–21, and the reply of Professor Stone, ibid. p. 123.

[58] V, 213.

[59] II, 494, 496, 493.

[60] VI, 223; II, 498; *C.J.* I, 657. There is no truth in Zaller's contention (p. 154) that on 3 December 'the government suddenly presented a united front against the petition'. Sackville, the chief opponent of the petition, has no more claim to be considered a member of the 'government' than Perrott, who was one of its chief supporters. Weston's speech, though dubious, amounted to a request for precedents rather than outright opposition (II,

the submissive character of a petition of grace which did not demand an answer, Heath was trying to soothe the fears of those who still thought the petition might be taken to be an attempt to direct the king in matters of state. In saying that 'if we may present our petitions to God, who is the king of kings, no doubt we may much more do it to the King',[60] he gave explicit sanction to the use of the same argument in favour of the petition by Coke and Crew. He also said he was 'satisfied with the matter of the petition, drawn to the general by direction from the king: the particulars follow as consequents'. It was Heath's intervention which ended the debate, and finally secured the House's approval of the petition which later caused so much offence to James.

What was the source of this belief that there was official encouragement to petition the king on the prince's marriage? There is no encouragement to be detected in any public proceedings of the House for a petition to the king on this subject. Heath's support came after the petition had been drafted. It is of course possible that members' belief that they were being encouraged to petition the king on the marriage, as well as war, was simply wishful thinking. There are many Elizabethan precedents for such wishful thinking, and it is possible that Goring's motion simply led the Commons, or rather the drafting committee, to take the bit between their teeth. Once the clause was in the petition, it was a much harder task to get it out than it would have been to get it in. Many members, of whom Phelips was the most influential, had no wish to exercise freedom of speech in any way displeasing to the king, and yet at the same time were committed to maintaining a theoretical right to free speech on any subject. Once the clause was in the petition, its exclusion would have involved an implicit admission that the subject was one on which the Commons had no right to offer advice. People who would willingly have passed the subject over in silence could yet feel bound to resist any suggestion that the Commons had no right to discuss it. It was possible to believe that the inclusion of this clause was a gross imprudence, but that its deliberate and overt exclusion on grounds of principle would have been an intolerable sacrifice of dignity. It is then possible that the insertion of this clause was simply a successful piece of opportunism by Crew.

There is, however, another possible explanation. By its very nature, this explanation cannot be tested, and therefore can be offered only as a conjecture. This is that Goring, or some other member with court connexions, had encouraged the raising of the prince's marriage by remarks made in private conversation. It derives its force from the fact that on every other issue under debate, most speakers had refrained from plunging into debate until after they were certain of official encouragement. On the morning of 3 December Goring reported to Buckingham

489; Hawarde *sub* 3 Dec. v, 221–1; v, 229). Chamberlain on 4 January recorded that the king's servants, and especially Heath, had been in trouble for not opposing the petition 'more earnestly'. *Letters of John Chamberlain*, II, 418.

with apparent unconcern that the petition was about to be reported to the House, and described the clause on the Prince's marriage as 'yt third pointe which was from my motion'. He said nothing of note had happened since 29 November except the sending for Sir Edwin Sandys, and told Buckingham that 'if ought of consequence happen yor. Lop. shalbe sure to have it with all possible speed'. If there was any 'united front' against the petition, Goring clearly had yet to learn of its existence.[61] Wishful thinking is hardly a sufficient explanation for Crew's change of attitude between 26 November and 3 December. Nor is it a sufficient explanation for the change of front of Sir Robert Phelips, who, throughout these debates, was peculiarly careful to avoid any speeches on matters of state which he believed would be offensive to the Court. If Goring and Buckingham were capable, for motives which were probably mischievous, of drumming up a petition for war with Spain, which they clearly did, they were equally capable of using private lobbying to procure a petition against the Spanish match. Since the match was extremely unpopular with a number of vocal members whose previous silence was due to an earnest effort to be conciliatory, it is unlikely that the amount of lobbying necessary to initiate a debate on the match would have been very considerable. Even a slight hint that a petition against the Spanish match would be helpful would have been likely to be enough to initiate a debate. If such hints had been intended constructively, it is likely that some friend among the councillors and those with court connexions would have tried to change the wording of the petition, from a petition against any Catholic marriage to one simply against the Spanish marriage. If Buckingham and Goring encouraged the motion to go through in the form in which it did, they did it, not to break off the Spanish marriage, but to break off the parliament.[62] The timing of Goring's motion for war with Spain would support a hypothesis that it was designed to break off the parliament: it was timed to interrupt a debate on the explosive case of Lepton and Goldsmith, on which a thorough investigation could have proved extremely damaging to Buckingham.

It must be stressed that such an explanation of the petition on the prince's match is pure conjecture. All that can be said in its favour is that it is no more improbable than the alternative conjecture, that the subject was introduced simply by an opportunist action by one member. In either case, it seems clear that the members involved in the preparation of the petition believed that they were proceeding, if not according to the letter, at least according to the spirit, of the conference with the Lords of 21 November and of Goring's motion of 29 November. Digges and Crew,

[61] See also note 18 above. B.M. Harleian MS 1580, f. 430a.

[62] James's letter of 3 December and his answer of 11 December show that it was, as Sackville foresaw, the introduction of the Spanish match into the Petition which offended him more than any other issue. See Tanner, pp. 279, 284–5, and II, 487–8. Sackville said the mention of the prince's match 'would be like the drug colloquintida which being taken by the king with the rest will make him cast out all the rest.'

who initiated the debate, and did some damage to their own careers in the process, should perhaps be allowed the final words. On 5 December they replied to the king's indignant letter with injured innocence: Digges said:

Wee search no further than the revealed will of the Kinge. Wee knew as much before touching the match with Spaine etc, yet no man spoke of them till occasioned by those pointes which were commended to us by the kinge from the Lordes. Soe it cannot be interpreted in us as an itching desire.

Crew concluded:

We dispute it [the prerogative] not here, but were petitioners invited'.[63]

It is not surprising that the king's outraged response to this debate cast members' minds back to the *Apology of the Commons* of 1604. On that occasion, as on this, members' shock was caused by royal censure for debating matters they believed they were officially invited to debate. Commons' protests that they had been 'misunderstood' when they offended the king are such debased currency that they are rarely given much attention, but on these two occasions, the excuse was the plain truth: the Commons had been misunderstood.

This material raises questions about the intentions of James and his councillors and questions about their relations with each other, to which the parliamentary evidence cannot provide an answer. It entirely confirms the criticisms which have been made of James as a parliamentary manager, and shows one of the major parliamentary storms of his reign as being caused by simple uncertainty about his wishes, uncertainty in which the councillors all shared.

On the other hand, though this debate shows a familiar picture of James, it shows a rather more unfamiliar picture of the House of Commons. It shows a House of Commons in which Court–Country and Government–Opposition divisions, in terms of which debates have normally been analysed, were entirely inoperative. A high proportion of the members who spoke in these debates had some court connexions, though, in a situation of so much uncertainty, this does not permit them to be classified as speaking for 'the government'. Few, if any, members, consciously and deliberately spoke against the Crown's wishes, and the whole debate shows a desire to follow an official line, if once it could be made apparent, which is entirely incompatible with the notion of a parliamentary 'opposition'. Above all, the debate shows a willingness to accept, in practice if not in theory, royal limits on freedom of speech. This willingness suggests a change in the Commons since Elizabethan days. The silencing of Wilde on 27 November contrasts sharply with the hearing which appears to have been given to Throckmorton's much wilder speech in 1587. Indeed, this debate goes a long way to suggest that familiarity was slowly bringing the Commons to work within the new limits on their freedom of speech, and that if James had not demanded so

[63] v, 233. For damage to Digges' career, see *Letters of John Chamberlain*, II, 416.

humiliating a submission, he would have had a chance, which Elizabeth had never had, of getting his ideas about freedom of speech accepted as a matter of common practice. In a story of Jacobean foreign policy, of the Jacobean council, or of the incompetence of parliamentary management, this debate deserves an important place, but in 'a study in constitutional conflict' in the early seventeenth century it has no claim to inclusion.

However, though the initiation of the foreign policy debate deserves no place in 'a study in constitutional conflict', the debates on free speech, beginning from the receipt of the king's first letter on 5 December, do deserve a place in a study in constitutional conflict. The Commons' obstinate rearguard defence of the principle that they were allowed to debate foreign affairs was a constitutional issue, and the Protestation asserting their right to freedom of speech is a constitutional document. However, in the immediate political context of 1621, the sentiments expressed in the Protestation remained in the realm of pious aspiration. There was no chance whatever that parliament would succeed in manoeuvring James into a war, and every chance that their persistence in an argument they had had no wish to begin would end only in their own dissolution and the discrediting of the case for war. John Chamberlain, who viewed the 1621 Protestation without benefit of hindsight, commented: '*vanae sine viribus irae*, and...there is noe disputing nor contesting with supreme authoritie'. The dispute between king and Commons provided a talking point sufficiently exciting to divert all attention from the demand for war. An attempt to pressurize the king into war, organized by a number of councillors, had looked like becoming irresistible in October 1621, and had petered out by January 1622. James had exchanged a demand for war for a dispute with his parliament. With hindsight we may say that James was the loser by this bargain. In the short term, however, since parliament was certain not to meet the full cost of a war, James could well have believed that he had had the better of the bargain. A row with his parliament may have seemed preferable to a war the country could not afford to fight. Since the motives of so many of the leading actors in the 1621 dissolution still remain obscure, it is perhaps best to leave the last word with Sir Thomas Wentworth: 'as for the disaster fallen upon this so hopeful a Parliament...when I cannot think a thought of it but with grief, will it well become me to be silent'. On the greatest mystery in this story, the motives and aims of King James, it is still impossible to add to the words of Goring in his letter to Buckingham of 29 November: 'His Matyes ende is not knowen to any.'[64]

[64] *Letters of John Chamberlain*, ed. N. E. Mc.Clure (Philadelphia, 1939), II, 421; W. Knowler (ed.), *Straforde letters* (1739), I, 15. See also note 30 above. Zaller (p. 154) draws attention to the fact that there is no sign that James held Buckingham and Goring to blame for their share in initiating the foreign policy debate (VII, 621 n; B.M. Harleian MS 1580, f. 401 a). Goring originally wrote 'his matyes ende is not knowen to any fleshe', but crossed out the last word. The note is not a postscript, but a marginal note opposite the report of his motion for a breach with Spain. I am grateful to Mr David Hebb for drawing my attention to the potential significance of this note.

4

The Examination of Mr. Mallory after the Parliament of 1621

AFTER THE dissolution of the parliament of 1621, Coke, Hakewill, Phelips, Mallory and Pym were imprisoned, and Crew, Perrot, Rich and Digges were sent to Ireland. In a group of cases which should be seen together with these, Sir Peter Hayman was sent to the Palatinate, and Viscount Saye and Sele and Sir Jerome Horsey were imprisoned, for their resistance to the benevolence for the relief of the Palatinate.[3] Sir Francis Seymour was questioned by the privy council for his resistance to the benevolence, but, to Buckingham's indignation, appears to have escaped punishment through the intervention of the duke of Lennox. Buckingham's letter to Cranfield makes an explicit connection between the imprisonments over the benevolence and his offence at members' behaviour in parliament. Writing

[1] I am grateful to the Trustees of the British Library Board for permission to publish this document. In my transcription I have standardized the use of capitals, expanded the contractions and modernized the punctuation; spelling is as in the original. An abbreviated version of this letter was printed over 70 years ago by W. C. Waller, who did not however anticipate my argument. 'An extinct county family: Wroth of Loughton Hall. I' (*Trans. Essex Archaeol. Soc.*, new ser., viii (1903), 155–6).

[2] Wroth had been appointed to a walkership in Waltham Forest in May 1603. *Calendar of State Papers, Domestic, 1603–10*, p. 10.

[3] R. Zaller, *The Parliament of 1621* (Berkeley and Los Angeles, 1971), p. 188; Chamberlain to Carleton, 4 Jan. 1622, *Calendar of State Papers, Domestic, 1619–23*, p. 333.

from Newmarket on 3 February 1622, he quoted to Cranfield instructions from the king about those who refused the benevolence: 'first, that they would spare no man, and secondly that they would principally deal with those that were of the Parliamt. especiallie those wch. were most refractarie, amongst whome Sir Francis Seymour was one of the chiefe'. Refusal of the benevolence outside parliament was to be used as an excuse to punish Seymour for his conduct inside parliament. Rather than escape, said Buckingham, Seymour should be sent to the Palatinate in person, 'that others may be scared by the example'. Cranfield annotated this passage with a marginal 'x', but Seymour's subsequent immunity suggests that Buckingham's fear that he might try to get favour by the lord steward was justified.[1]

Yet, when we have established that these two groups of imprisonments should be seen together, we have established neither their real causes nor their ostensible grounds, which at the time remained a closely-guarded secret. Even John Chamberlain was only able to deduce from the names of the prisoners that it was thought they were attacked on parliament business. On 19 January 1622, he noted that the council were examining Phelips twice a week, but appears to have gained no clue to the contents of the examinations.[2] Phelips himself said on 5 August 1625, that he was 'delivered without injuringe the libertye of the House in wordes or writinge, and taxt with nothinge but only with speakinge against the Spanish matche'.[3]

The examination of one of the imprisoned members, preserved among Sir Robert Phelips's parliamentary papers in Somerset Record Office, sheds much light on the first half of Phelips's statement. As the only known examination of any of these imprisoned members of the Commons, it is worth some study. The questions make it clear that it is not Phelips's own examination, and it is endorsed, in what is probably his hand, 'Mallery; Coke and Lepton'. The document contains no material on Coke and Lepton, and if Phelips preserved any material on that subject, it unfortunately does not appear to have survived. On the other hand, an analysis of the questions in the examination gives every reason to suppose that it is in fact the examination of Mallory. As fellow-sufferers, the two members could well have exchanged information, possibly in order to concert their defence. Moreover, the 1621 debates contain some evidence to suggest a personal friendship between Mallory and Phelips. On 25 April, it was Mallory who moved that Phelips be allowed his privilege in a lawsuit in the exchequer. On 2 May, it was Phelips who seconded Mallory's highly

[1] National Register of Archives, Sackville MSS., ON 2421. Seymour's 'refractoriness' probably concerned his leading part in the attack on the referees. On the interaction between the benevolence and the general issue of parliamentary control of taxation, see Marc L. Schwarz, 'Lord Saye and Sele's objections to the Palatinate benevolence of 1622: some new evidence and its significance', *Albion*, iv (1972), 12–22.

[2] Chamberlain to Carleton, *Cal. S.P. Dom. 1619–23*, pp. 333, 337.

[3] *Debates in the House of Commons in 1625*, ed. S. R. Gardiner (Camden new ser., vi, 1873), p. 81.

important motion that Sir Edward Villiers should be suspended from the House, and Phelips who seconded Mallory's motion to prevent the Speaker from shielding the referees by his untimely rising.[1] There is, then, no inherent improbability about supposing that Mallory and Phelips may have continued as defendants the concerted action they had carried on in parliament. Mallory, who was said to be 'much dejected' at his arrest, could also have felt in need of moral support.[2] The presence of this document in Sir Robert Phelips's papers is then at least no argument against the supposition that it is the examination of Mallory. Since Mallory was not a particularly prominent member, information about the ostensible grounds for his arrest could be of particular interest. Gardiner described him as a member 'of whose special offence we are ignorant'. Zaller's suggestion that his imprisonment was 'presumably connected with his part in the plot against Buckingham', for which Sir Edward Villiers had been used as a stalking-horse, is highly probable.[3] However, as Buckingham's letter about Sir Francis Seymour shows, the real reasons for an imprisonment need not be the same as its ostensible grounds, and an examination can give interesting information about ostensible grounds.

Since the identification of Mallory as the subject of this examination depends on a comparison between the questions asked and Mallory's known speeches and actions, it seems best to print the document first, and then compare it, question by question, with Mallory's known record in the House. For convenience in this process, I have given numbers to the questions, which are added in square brackets.

Somerset Record Office, DD/PH/216/11[4]

Endorsement[5]*:* Mallery; Coke and Lepton
25th of January 1622

[1] The examination of [*blank*] before the Lords Mandevil, Treasurer, Arundell, Sir Thomas Calventry, Sir Randall Crew. First whether I was not the first mover that Sir Edwin Sandis should be sent for, and whether I did not say that he was committed for Parliament business?

[2] Whether I did not hould that the Parliament was not to medle with his majesties hye prerogative as the marriag of his sonne, war peace & religion and coyne?

[3] Whether I lyked or mislyked the protastation or whether I gave my voyce with or noe?

[1] *Commons' Debates 1621*, ed. W. Notestein, F. H. Relf and H. Simpson (7 vols., New Haven, 1935) (hereafter cited as *N.R.S.*), vi. 98, 97; v. 131, 283.

[2] Zaller, p. 188.

[3] S. R. Gardiner, *History of England from the Accession of James I to the Outbreak of the Civil War*, iv (1896), p. 267; Zaller, p. 230n.

[4] The original spelling of the document has been retained, except that all abbreviations have been extended. A minimum of punctuation and capitalization has been introduced where necessary to make the meaning clear.

[5] Probably in the hand of Sir Robert Phelips. I am grateful to Mr. D. M. M. Shorrocks for his help in identifying this. I have not been able to identify the handwriting of the document.

[4] What did I speake at the committy?
[5] After Sir Richard Weston had tould the house upon the king second letter that nowe all doubts weare cleard and they might well procede with there business, did not you answer that you weare worse satisfyed than before?
[6] Why did you move to have the prerogative disputed in the house whether maye not the king committ anie Parliament man for offencas [*sic*] during the Parliament?
[7] Sir Randall Crewe did question me for matters donne in the former Parliament and did urge yt with muche btternes.[1]

1 Februarii Keeper, Treasurer, Mandevil, Arundell
[8] By what authority and whoe went with you to Sir Edwin Sandis? What conferenc [*sic*] had you there by the fyre syde at ten of clocke at night the servants being put out and none but you there? What conferenc had you upon the way?
[9] Why did you move to have an accounmpt [?*sic*] taken of the messag knowing the kings commaund to the contrary?
[10] Why did you move to have his majesties letters examined say . . .[2] they have trenched into yor pryvileges?
[11] Who was that, that stood at your elbowe and moved against the reading of the kings letter?
[12] I was tould by one of the Lords that I had spoken 38 tymes & all seditiously that I had carried an hygher hand against his majestie than ever anie subiect did in that place and that my offence was an hygher trason than Empson & Dudlys and deserved to have my head taken of my shold[3]
[13] Did not you say yf the house had called you to accoumpt you would have mayd sport?
[14][4] I was tould by one of the Lords that yf I had bene as carefull to look to the Clark as I was to the Speaker manie things had not bene knowen that nowe comes to light.

This document presents an immediate difficulty, in the date 1622 at the head of it. January and February 1622 are highly probable dates for Mallory's examinations, which would then have coincided with those of Sir Robert Phelips. However, in old style dating, these dates should have been recorded as 25 January and 1 February 1621. It is highly improbable that the examinations really took place in 1623, since Mallory and Phelips were released on 9 August 1622.[5] The two likeliest possibilities are then, either that the author was using new style dating, or that he made an error in writing the year. There is little doubt that the correct dates should be 25 January and 1 February 1621/2. 1 February is recorded as the date of a council meeting, but though 24 and 26 January are so recorded, 25 January is not. It is possible that there is an error of one day in the first date, but slightly more probable that the body concerned was a committee of the council, rather than the full council.

Question 1, concerning the motion to send for Sir Edwin Sandys, was one

[1] There is no punctuation between one page and another but it seems grammatically possible and logically probable that questions 7 and 8 represent two separate sentences.

[2] Blot in MS., obliterating about 3 letters, probably *-ing*.

[3] Margin: *-ers*. [4] Margin: *T*. [5] Zaller, p. 189.

of the most serious issues. Sandys, who was in fact being kept away from the House for his activities during the first session, had been induced to agree to the council's polite fiction that he was not attending the second session because of illness. So long as this polite fiction was unquestioned, parliamentary business could continue, but if it were once established officially that Sandys had been restrained for parliamentary business, the rest of the session could be lost in a privilege dispute. It was on the first day of the second session, 20 November, that Mallory demanded to investigate the issue, moving, 'that Sir Edwin Saniss may be called for, being now not in the House'. This was a disruptive motion, and the disconcerted note in Barrington's diary, '*quaere quare*' was entirely to the point. Mallory was then definitely 'the first mover that Sir Edwin Sandis should be sent for'. Three days later, it was again Mallory who 'renewed the motion towching Sir Edwin Sandes, to examine the cause of his committment'. Hawarde reports him as seconding Spencer's motion on this subject. Pym's diary does not record a direct statement that Sandys was committed for parliament business, but this is clearly the innuendo of the words he records. The Commons's final decision to send to Sandys, on 1 December, was taken on Mallory's third moving of his motion, and on this occasion, as well as dwelling on the theme of parliamentary privilege, he added the potentially dangerous motion that Sandys 'be required to set down under his hand, as he is a gentleman, for what he was questioned'.[1]

Questions 2 and 3 appear to be simply leading questions, of the sort which could have been asked of any active member, and seem to be designed to produce an incriminating answer. They do, however, shed some light on Phelips's subsequent relief that he was 'delivered without injuringe the libertye of the House in wordes or writinge'. It seems possible that one of the objects of the questions was to obtain submissions which could be quoted against parliamentary claims to privilege.

Question 4 probably relates to the Grand Committee to draft the final Protestation. It was Mallory, on Monday 17 December, who reminded the House of their agreement the previous Saturday to go into Committee. We have two recorded speeches by Mallory at the Committee. The first, at its setting up, was a motion that 'the key . . . be brought up and that none goe oute', presumably to prevent the carrying of reports to the king. The second was a motion: 'the Committee to take it into consideracion, if a member of the house be Committed after the Parliament, if this bee not a breache of the privileges, and to see if there have bin any such'.[2] This, an apparent revival of the case of Sandys, could have been a ground of complaint.

[1] *N.R.S.*, iii. 410; iv. 434; ii. 484 & n. The diary of John Hawarde (Wiltshire Record Office, Ailesbury MSS.) reports a sharply hostile reaction by Lord Clifford and Sir Thomas Wentworth to the attempt to open the case of Sandys, and support from Sir Peter Hayman.

[2] *N.R.S.*, vi. 242, 339, 342. May protested at Mallory's motion to lock the doors that 'tis a fundamentall liberty of the house that att a Committee every man may goe out of the house that will'.

Neither of these speeches adds any proof to the identification of Mallory, but it may safely be said that they do not conflict with it.

Question 5 deals with the second letter from King James, delivered to the Commons on 14 December, with an injunction from Weston, in the king's name, that they should then proceed to other business. Mallory's immediate riposte was to move that every member should have a copy of the letter, and the next morning he moved 'that we may consider of our liberties. The King hath sent a gracious answer but we are worse than afore, for he saith our privileges are not by inheritance and that we must not trench into his prerogative'. The similarity of these words to those alleged in question 5 is striking. With Mallory's opening of this dispute, the last chance of an amicable conclusion of the parliament had probably disappeared.[1]

Question 6 is another general question, which could be asked of almost any member. Two possible subjects for this question are his joining in the attack on Lepton and Goldsmith on 13 December, and his reply, on 24 April, to the king's speech saying that the referees should not be questioned unless for corruption 'because it was *Humanum errare*'. Mallory, who had throughout been forward in the attack on the referees, replied 'that it is fitt an inquisition should be made who it is should doe so ill offices for the house'.[2] Such passages again contribute nothing to an identification, but do not conflict with it.

Question 7 contains no precise matter admitting identification, but again asks for self-incrimination.

Question 8 returns to the main cause of complaint, the Sandys case. The Commons ordered on 1 December 'that Sir Peter Heyman and Mr. Mallory should go to Sir Edwin Sandys on Monday, to bring him to the House if he were able, if not to require him to send a declaration in writing whether he were examined and committed for any Parliament business or no'. It was probably on this occasion that the conference with the servants put out took place, and Mallory and Hayman appear to have obtained their declaration in writing. On 18 December, immediately before the dissolution, it was 'ordered that Sir Peter Hamond shall burne the paper he hath of Sir Edwin Sandes contayninge a declaration of his commitment'.[3] If even the Commons wished to burn this paper, it must indeed have been dangerous, and it is noteworthy that it was Mallory's fellow-actor in this business, Sir Peter Hayman, who was sent to the Palatinate.

[1] *N.R.S.*, vi. 336, 237, ii. 521–2; *Commons Journals*, i. 663, 664.

[2] *N.R.S.*, ii. 517, vi. 95.

[3] *N.R.S.*, ii. 484, vi. 245; *Commons Journals*, i. 669. Hawarde records that this paper was burnt on Hayman's own motion (Diary, 19 Dec.). The paper would have been likely to confirm that Sandys was committed for 'parliament business'. These words may have been carefully chosen, since the surviving examinations of Sandys concentrate, with a consistency unlikely to have been accidental, on matters which were parliament business, but not actually done in parliament (Inner Temple, Petyt MS. 538/19 fo. 3). Mallory's claim to privilege would then involve the nove' extension of privilege to private conversation outside the house of commons.

Question 9 again seems to refer to Mallory's interventions on 14 and 15 December, and shows a tendency in the second examination to go again over the ground covered in the first examination.

Question 10 again paraphrases Mallory's speech of 15 December, about the king's second letter.

Question 11, alas, we are in no position to answer: the man who stood at Mallory's elbow appears to have escaped the scrutiny of posterity.

Question 12 alone would serve for the elimination of Coke, Phelips and Hakewill as possible subjects of this examination. No councillor in his senses could have accused them of speaking so few as thirty-eight times. Pym spoke thirty-eight times, but he is eliminated on the fact that none of the questions bears any relationship to any of his known speeches. Mallory in fact spoke sixty-two times during the parliament, but there is nothing improbable about the hypothesis that the record available to the councillors was not as good as that collected by Notestein, Relf and Simpson. The comparison with Empson and Dudley, echoing Coke's attack on Mompesson, is an interesting one, and an early example of the fact that the idea that treason could be committed by making a division between the king and people was one which both parliament and council could use.

Question 13 appears to refer to a remark made in private conversation, and cannot be identified with any material in the recorded debates.

Question 14, on the clerk and the Speaker, is an interesting one. Mallory had been a vigorous critic of the Speaker, and the particular reference here is probably to his motion at the beginning of the debate of 15 December, that the House should go into Committee, 'that we be not troubled this day with the Speaker'.[1] The clear innuendo of the question is that the clerk thereafter reported Mallory's speeches to the council. Mallory himself clearly read it this way, since he moved, at the beginning of the parliament of 1624 'that the clerke may enter no mans name, and only the determinacions of the House'. In this, he was surprisingly opposed by Pym, who claimed that many men had been helped by the clerk's book.[2] The big sign 'T' in the margin of this passage, which is not in the same hand as the rest of the document, could possibly be a note by Phelips to recommend action on the point, though a handwriting identification on one letter is clearly impossible.

It can then be said with confidence that this examination fits Mallory, and that it does not fit any other imprisoned member of 1621. It provides a rarely vivid councillor's eye view of debates, and shows how explosive the issue of parliamentary privilege might appear to a council committed to

[1] Zaller, p. 168; Hakewill, in 1628, recalled that 'I was chargd with wordes out of the clerkes book' (British Library, Stowe MS. 366 fo. 87v); E. Nicholas, *Proceedings and Debates of the House of Commons in 1620 and 1621* (2 vols., Oxford, 1766), ii. 330.

[2] Brit. Libr., Harley MS. 6383 fo. 88. It is interesting that Mallory's motion against the clerk was seconded by his fellow-sufferer Sir Peter Hayman. It is tempting to imagine that the clerk had been irritated by the amount of work involved in Mallory's demand that he produce a copy of the king's letter for every member.

maintaining quiet and order. It also shows very clearly the council's concern over the restraint of Sir Edwin Sandys. Whether it takes us much further in explaining the 1621 imprisonments as a whole is a more difficult question. There is also one interesting omission. The Palatine benevolence, used by Buckingham to excuse his attacks on so many other members, was questioned as illegal by Mallory on 27 April, and the questioning forms no part of these examinations. In the light of this fact, and in the light of Buckingham's letter about Seymour, it appears unsafe to eliminate any theme as not being a ground of Mallory's imprisonment simply because it is not included in this examination.[1] It is then possible that Mallory's highly provocative speeches of the first session, on Sir Edward Villiers and on the referees, had as much to do with Buckingham's support for his imprisonment as the matters recorded here. However, the Seymour letter shows that Buckingham and James did not always speak with one voice, and there is no reason to believe that James was prepared to punish members of parliament in order to protect Sir Edward Villiers. It is then possible that the highly 'constitutional' tone of this examination reflects the reactions of James, but not the political malice which first led Buckingham to attempt to provoke James to these reactions. Dr. Zaller's conclusion that 'Mallory's seizure was presumably connected with his part in the plot against Buckingham' could then stand as a picture of Buckingham's motives, while leaving this examination as providing the better picture of the minds of James and the rest of the council. The unanswered question then becomes whether Buckingham or James is seen as the prime mover in the imprisonments of 1621. That is a question to which this examination does not provide the answer.

[1] *N.R.S.*, iii. 97. There is no reason to believe that these were Mallory's only examinations.

5

The Theory of Treason in the Trial of Strafford

'We are of opinion, that upon all that your Lordships have voted to be proved: that the Earl of Strafford doth deserve to undergo the pains and forfeitures of high treason by law.'[1] This answer was returned to the house of lords by eight of Charles I's judges, led by Chief Justice Bramston. Like the judges, I am not in this article concerned with the question of fact: I am concerned with what Miss Wedgwood has called 'Pym's manufactured theory of treason'[2]: I am concerned to suggest that the judges may have had legal reasons for their answer. I do not for a moment deny that they were under very considerable pressure: the influence of the mob on the attainder of Strafford is well known, and the anonymous diary of the Lords' proceedings, Harleian Manuscript 6424, gives a most unsavoury picture of concerted party manoeuvring by the opposition peers.[3] But Bramston, at least, had already shown that he was not susceptible to intimidation,[4] and I believe that the judges' answer may have been inspired, not only by fear, but also by generally accepted doctrines of law and political theory. The theory of treason may have been extended during the trial of Strafford, but many elements of it already had a long, and sometimes even respectable, history. Most of the new elements in it, moreover, had been

1. House of Lords, Braye MS. 2, fo. 142b; *L.J.* iv. 239; Brit[ish] Mus[eum] Harleian MS. 6424, fo. 64b. For the text of the questions to the judges, see Lords' MSS., Apr. 1641. I would like to thank Mr. Cobb, of the House of Lords Record Office, for his help in finding manuscripts, and in deciphering some particularly awkward pieces of pencil scribble among them.

2. C. V. Wedgwood, *Thomas Wentworth: A Revaluation* (London, 1961), p. 359. Even if this theory was constructed by the Long Parliament, it does not follow that it can therefore be called Pym's. It is dangerously easy to slip into a shorthand in which Pym is used as a figure for the whole of the Long Parliament. The attainder of Strafford was supported by D'Ewes, Glyn, Maynard, Palmer, Marten, Haselrigg, Culpeper, Falkland, and, I firmly believe, by Hyde. These were all able men, and none of them renowned for their political docility. And even if the 'conspiracy' theory of the Long Parliament be accepted, there is more evidence to support this theory in the proceedings of the Lords than in those of the Commons. Saye and Sele, Warwick, Bedford and Mandeville were all influential people, and there is no more evidence to suppose that Pym controlled them than to suppose that they controlled Pym.

3. See fos. 39a, 60a, 64b, and the earl of Warwick's timing of the introduction of the Bill, fo. 58b.

4. See below, 'The Ship Money Judgments of Bramston and Davenport', ch. 8, pp. 81-88, and *Journal of Sir Symonds D'Ewes*, i (ed. Notestein), 121-3 for evidence that the judges had been solicited. It is true that Bramston was among those who denied being solicited, but Falkland, who interviewed him, may be supposed to have had some reason for his very forcible claim that the judges had been under pressure. Rushworth, *Historical Collections*, iii. 140.

first worked out, not by Pym, but by Charles I and his immediate supporters.[1]

The 1352 treason statute had been the basis of the law ever since it was passed. Taken in the literal sense, this statute restricts the idea of treason to personal offences against the king. But running beside this tradition, and sometimes confused with it, is another, possibly owing something to Roman law,[2] but probably more to recurrent panic, of treason against the state, or against the stability of the kingdom. The essence of this doctrine of treason is the idea of making a division between the king and the people. This doctrine was sometimes applied by act of attainder, as in the case of Elizabeth Barton, sometimes by common law constructions upon the clauses of levying war or of compassing the king's death, as in the case of the Oxfordshire rebels in 1597, sometimes, as in the case of Empson and Dudley, by both. The case of Empson and Dudley is perhaps the most important for this purpose, since it had been well known to Pym for twenty years, and had come to him stamped with the oracular authority of Sir Edward Coke. In the course of the proceedings against Mompesson in 1621, Coke had produced the indictment of Empson and Dudley, and Pym, as a young member, had taken it all down carefully in his notes.[3] It has a remarkably close resemblance to some of the charges used against Strafford.[4]

It should be easy to understand that it might be held to be treason to make a division between the king and his people: it was Strafford who said: 'under a heavier censure than this, I am persuaded no gentleman can suffer'.[5] Unity was the great obsession of

1. See Charles I'squestions to the judges about Sir John Eliot's offence in 1629, which appear to be destined to elicit the answer that Eliot had committed treason: 'whether, if the Parliament men conspired to defame the king's government, and deter his subjects from obeying and assisting him, of what nature would be their offence?' *Cal. S.P. Dom. 1629*, cxli. 44. There is a much fuller account of these questions in *Autobiography of Sir John Bramston*, Camden Society, 1st ser., xxxii (1845), 49–53. This account specifically mentions treason, and since Sir John Bramston's father had been counsel for Eliot, the account may perhaps be more accurate than its late date would suggest. See also the remarks of Finch and Berkeley, below p. 92, n. 3, p. 97, n. 1.

2. See Holdsworth, *History of English Law*, v. 208–11 for the influence of Roman law on the growth of the parallel doctrine of sedition. See also M. V. Clarke, 'Forfeitures and Treason in 1388', in *Fourteenth Century Studies*, pp. 134–5.

3. *Commons' Debates in 1621*, ed. Notestein, Relf and Simpson, iv. 92: 'as much as in them lies by their oppressions they withdraw the hearts of the subjects from the king.' (Per Sir Ed. Coke, upon this ground Empson was indicted of treason.) See also *ibid.* iv. 110, and 136 ('Empson and Dudley's offences, which were nothing to this man's, were reputed high treason because they subverted the laws and withdrew the hearts of the people from the king'). The doctrine that treason can be committed by a minister who serves the king in such a way as to make him odious seems clearly stated here.

4. The indictment of Empson is printed in Coke's *Fourth Institute*, p. 198. In addition to the above point of resemblance, it accuses Empson of acting for his own advancement (Coke has a marginal note: '*ambitio*'), and of trying to govern the kingdom according to his will.

5. In his last letter to the king. Rushworth, *Trial of Strafford*, p. 743.

seventeenth-century politicians, of Pym as much as of Laud. As usual, they were obsessed by that of which they felt the lack: 'men and brethren, what shall we do? Is there no balm in Gilead? If the King draw one way, and the parliament another, we shall all sink.' Rudyerd was quite right: a deep division of conscience between the king and his parliament was something the seventeenth-century constitution could not accommodate.[1] Moreover, in a period when kings normally lacked the power to preserve their authority by force, all political theorists with the possible exception of Machiavelli were unanimous in feeling that allegiance must be based on love and not on fear. It was felt that subjects could only be expected to give loyal obedience to a policy of whose main outlines they approved: as soon as they were subject to the mere will of another man, they could be expected to rebel. For example, this was the ground of Norton's original draft of the recusancy Bill of 1581. It was generally felt, except by *politiques* such as Bodin, Elizabeth or Oldenbarnevelt, that religious division from the government was itself seditious: that a man could not be expected to be loyal to a policy which he thought was leading the country straight to Hell. This was the doctrine applied by the Commons against Montague,[2] or by the Star Chamber against Prynne[3] and Traske.[4] A secular version of this doctrine, a charge of making the king's authority odious to the people, was used against Mompesson. But Mompesson was not accused of high treason: he was accused of high crimes and misdemeanours, even though Lord Spencer saw fit to ask 'whether he be not guilty of praemunire, treason, etc.?'[5]

Why is it that making a division between the king and the people is sometimes treason, sometimes sedition, high crimes and misdemeanours, or, in the case of Buckingham, 'sundry misprisions'? Obviously, this distinction is a barometer of political panic: the vast majority of accusations of treason for making a division were made in the years of the Wars of the Roses, the Reformation and the

1. In 1628. Rushworth, *Historical Collections*, i. 501. It is in the same speech that Rudyerd said: 'this is the crisis of parliaments; we shall know by this if parliaments live or die.'

2. *Common's Debates in 1625*, Camden Society, 2nd ser., vol. vi (1873), ed. Gardiner. Montague was accused of making a division, and of sedition. See pp. 47, 49, 52, 69, 179. Pym was in charge of this case also, and again the doctrine was supported by the authority of Sir Edward Coke (p. 69).

3. Prynne was accused of being 'a mover of the people to discontent and sedition', and of having 'endeavoured to infuse an opinion into the people that it is lawful to lay violent hands upon princes that are either actors, favourers or spectators of stage plays': *Proceedings against William Prynne*, Camden Society, new ser. xviii (1877), ed. Gardiner, 1–2. For this, Finch held him 'reus laesae majestatis' (*ibid.* p. 10). Many of the Star Chamber, including Heath explicitly and Richardson by implication, held that this was high treason (*ibid.* pp. 17, 20). See also Rushworth, *Historical Collections*, II. i. 220–39.

4. Holdsworth, *op. cit.* viii. 407.

5. *Debates in the House of Lords, 1621*, Camden Society, 1st ser., ciii (1870), ed. Gardiner, 134.

Civil War. But in legal terms, what has to be present in an indictment to make it treason? If it is to be based upon the statute, it must allege a compassing of the king's death: it must allege that the division made it so serious that the people are liable to rise against the king and threaten his life. This doctrine of constructive compassing of the king's death was used against Strafford, but it was not invented in this case: it had of course been the basis of the treason legislation against papists, it appears in such fifteenth-century cases as that of Sparhauk,[1] and it runs all through the attainder of Elizabeth Barton.[2] It is not used against Wolsey or Buckingham, Bacon or Mompesson, Montague or Manwaring, who were not accused of treason. It was, however, used by those of the Star Chamber judges who believed that Prynne had committed high treason by writing *Histriomastix*. This seems to be one touchstone. Another possible, though less reliable, touchstone is that those who are accused, as Strafford was, of accroaching royal power, may be accused of treason. This treason was not in the statute, but it appeared in article 16 of the impeachment, and it was argued by D'Ewes and Perd, among other members, that it was treason at the common law.[3] This argument has recently been accepted by Professor Chrimes, who believes as firmly as the Long Parliament that common law treasons survived, and that accroaching royal power was among them.[4]

A theme which is new in Strafford's case is the accusation, not merely of making a division, but of making a perpetual division. This idea of perpetual division was stated by most of the managers, but it is perhaps best stated by Pym:

It doth exceed all other treasons in this, that in the design and endeavour of the author, it was to be a constant and permanent treason; other treasons are transient, as being confined within those particular actions and proportions, wherein they did consist, and those being past, the treason ceaseth. The powder treason was full of horror and malignity, yet it is past many years since: the murder of that magnanimous and glorious king, Henry the Fourth of France, was a great and horrid treason; and so were the manifold attempts against Queen Elizabeth

1. Quoted by St. John. Rushworth, *Trial of Strafford,* p. 686.

2. 25 Hen. viii, c.12. The idea of constructive compassing of the king's death comes out very clearly in this Act. She was accused of saying that Henry was no longer king in the reputation of God, and of claiming false revelations, 'intending thereby to make such a division and rebelling in this realm among the king's subjects whereby the king's highness should not only have been put to peril of his life, but also in jeopardy to be deprived from his Crown and dignity royal'. Strafford, in one of his petitions to the Lords, admitted that this was 'a treason within the statute 25 E.3, by compassing the king's death' (Braye MS. 2. 141b).

3. *Journal of Sir Symonds D'Ewes* (ed. Notestein), i. 64.

4. S. B. Chrimes, 'Richard II's Questions to the Judges', *Law Quarterly Review,* 72 (1956), 366-84. This charge had been made against Latimer after the passing of the 1352 statute. See Plucknett, 'The Impeachments of 1376', *Trans. R. Hist. Soc.,* 5th ser., i. 160.

of blessed memory; but they are long since past; the detestation of them only remains in histories and in the minds of men, and will ever remain: but, this treason, if it had taken effect, was to be a standing perpetual treason, which would have been in continual act, not determined within one time or age, but transmitted to posterity, even from one generation to another.[1]

The idea behind passages such as these is that expressed in the phrases, 'subverting the fundamental laws' and 'erecting arbitrary and tyrannical government'. It is an idea of permanent alteration of the type of constitution existing in England. It is in his next sentence that Pym says 'to alter the settled frame and constitution of government is treason in any state'. The suggestion here is that Strafford is proposing to alter the constitution to one in which the king's authority rests on will, and is unfettered by any restraints. This authority, an authority of force, will be odious to the people, who will be likely to rise against it. Therefore, it was argued, to introduce an arbitrary government was to risk a civil war, and so to compass the king's death.[2] The idea that the king's death can be compassed by making his authority so obtrusive that it becomes odious is not a new one, but the idea of alteration of government is new. Even if Pym is right in saying that it was part of the case put up in 1388, it is certain that nobody had been accused of it since. It is of the essence of this accusation that it can only be made against a powerful minister. Manwaring had been accused of arguing for a different form of government, but he had not been accused of altering the government: even Pym does not seem to have feared that he had the power to do it. Strafford, on the other hand, if he had the intention, had also the power.

Mr. Cooper has recently recalled attention to the importance of this fear of alteration of government as a contributory cause of the Civil War: 'consciousness of what had happened abroad, of what absolutism meant in practice, was one factor which made some Englishmen think it necessary to fight a civil war.'[3] It is worth pointing out what a very different idea this is from the precedents on which its legal use was based. Empson and Dudley, it is true, had been accused of subverting the laws, and Wolsey had been accused of subverting 'the due course and order of your Grace's laws',[4] but this means something rather different from the charge which is made against Strafford. Empson and Dudley may have been thought to be behaving tyrannically, but I know of no evidence to suggest that

1. Rushworth, *Trial of Strafford*, p. 669.
2. This case is well argued by St. John, *ibid.* pp. 685–9.
3. J. P. Cooper, 'Differences between English and Continental Governments in the Early Seventeenth Century', in *Britain and the Netherlands*, ed. Bromley and Kossmann (Oxford, 1960), p. 73.
4. The articles against Wolsey were printed in Coke, *Fourth Institute*, pp. 89–95.

they were suspected of setting up a tyrannical government as a separate type of constitution. Wolsey is said to have reduced the commonwealth to the state of being 'greatly decayed and impoverished', but again the idea seems to be a matter of personalities and practical issues, rather than of general theory. A charge of this sort has far less theory and drama about it than the charge against Strafford: it is simply a matter of getting rid of a particular nuisance. With Strafford, on the other hand, the accusers, in a mark-of-the-beast mood, have identified him with what they regard as a general and overspreading evil theory. It is an example of how the seventeenth-century tendency to take everything back to first principles increased the bitterness of each particular conflict to which they were applied.

In considering this notion of alteration of government, it is necessary to answer the recent arguments of Dr. Hinton, for if he is correct, the government of England was already an absolute monarchy.[1] If so, how could it be further altered? If we must assume, as Dr. Hinton assumes, that the English government was either a mixed monarchy or an absolute monarchy, the better case is for mixed monarchy. I accept the dictum of J. W. Allen that 'there is hardly anywhere to be found any suggestion that the king can make law'.[2] It is true that there are many fears that *other people* may think the king can make law, but this is an entirely different point.

I believe the antithesis between mixed monarchy and absolute monarchy is an artificial one: the terms are too imprecise. Pym's 'arbitrary government', in which the king does whatever he pleases and everyone else has to endure it, is easy enough to understand. But it is not at all the same thing as the doctrine of 'absolute monarchy' with which Dr. Hinton credits Sir Edward Coke: 'the king is God's lieutenant, and therefore must do no wrong.'[3] If this is absolute monarchy, then it may be that a number of people believed England was an absolute monarchy. But this form of absolute monarchy, if it was believed in, is very different from arbitrary government, and an endeavour to introduce arbitrary government could still be regarded as an endeavour to alter the constitution. And I am by no means certain that I know what absolute monarchy is. From what is it absolved? From parliament? From liability to take counsel? From duty to heed counsel? From the common

1. 'English Constitutional Theories from Sir John Fortescue to Sir John Eliot', *EHR* lxxv (1960), 410–25; 'The Decline of Parliamentary Government under Elizabeth I and the Early Stuarts', *Camb. Hist. J.*, xiii, 2 (1957), 116–32; 'Government and Liberty under James I', *ibid.* xi (1953), 48 ff., especially p. 48, on James I: 'partly by the circumstances of his succession but in greater measure by the tradition of English public law, he exercised his rule as the absolute king of a free monarchy.' See also p. 53, where Dr. Hinton categorically asserts that the king by himself made law.

2. *English Political Thought 1603 to 1660*, p. 11.

3. *Commons' Debates in 1621*, ed. Notestein, Relf and Simpson, ii. 253. This quotation is not used by Dr. Hinton, but I hope it is a fair summary of the doctrine he is describing.

law? From fundamental or divine law? From other people's interpretation of these laws? These, and each possible combination and permutation of them, are all different ideas, and if we are to discuss absolute monarchy, it must be clear which of them are classified under that heading, and which are not.

Mixed monarchy seems easier to define, and I think a number of Long Parliament members may be said to have believed in it. For example, it appears from his speech on article 19 that the younger Whitelocke, who chaired the committee against Strafford, held very much the same doctrine as his father.[1] But any attempt to say who held this doctrine and who did not falls on the subtleties of the idea of counsel. The king had always had to take counsel. But did he have to take it from particular people? And how much heed did he have to give to it when he had taken it? It is one of the peculiarities of seventeenth-century parliamentarians that they think of themselves as the king's council to such an extent that if one only read their speeches, one might forget that there was ever such a body as the privy council at all. (This, incidentally, is one reason why it is impossible to measure the importance of parliament simply by the number of Acts it passed.) Between the saying the king must hear their counsel and ought to act on it, and claiming a share in the sovereign power, so that the king cannot act without them, is a psychological razor-edge so fine that I think most members did not know on which side they stood.

It is also difficult to disentangle the Whitelocke doctrine of mixed monarchy and shared sovereignty from the lawyers' idea, expressed by St. John in his Ship Money speech,[2] and which I think was also the basis of D'Ewes's political thought, at least until the summer of 1641. In this view, the king is the fountainhead and solely supreme, but he is supreme only within the framework of a given order, and his power is only valid if it flows down through its proper channels. Parliament has no sovereignty, and is not equal with the king, but it is the only channel through which the king can tax or legislate. This is a different doctrine from that of mixed monarchy, but it shades imperceptibly into it, and any attempt to draw a dividing line between them I regard as unprofitable. The MacIlwainian view of declaratory legislation within a framework of fundamental law is also hard to classify. As Dr. Hinton argues, it gives more importance to the courts, but as Mr. Cooper has pointed out in a recent criticism of Dr. Hinton's thesis, 'an essential feature of parliament was that it was a court'.[3]

1. Rushworth, *Trial of Strafford*, pp. 509–12.

2. *State Trials*, iii. 859–64. See especially p. 861, 'His Majesty is the fountain of justice; and though all justice which is done within the realm flows from this fountain, yet it must run in certain and known channels'.

3. J. P. Cooper, *ubi supra*, p. 65.

The argument about mixed monarchy and absolute monarchy thus becomes a case of undistributed middle. To credit Hooker, for example, with a belief in either would be absurd. In 1628, when Pym says 'I know how to add sovereign to his person, but not to his power',[1] he is not claiming mixed monarchy: he recognizes the sole supremacy of the king. But to say that Pym therefore believed in absolute monarchy would be misleading.

It is of course impossible to do justice to this problem in an article to which it is merely necessary background, but it seems clear that whatever the constitution of England was believed to be, and whatever names historians give to different conceptions of it, they will all be found to preclude the development of arbitrary government. This fear of alteration of government at least existed. The earliest example of it I know is from the reign of Elizabeth: from Peter Wentworth's queries on freedom of speech in 1587. He asked: 'whether the prince and state can be maintained without this council of parliament, not altering the government of the state?[2] Very clear in this remark is the idea which gives a different flavour to the doctrine of treason in the trial of Strafford – the idea of the state, a permanent and public entity, in whose fate the safety of the king is perhaps involved, but which exists on its own and can in itself be offended against. The idea of an offence against the state appears, for example, in Coke's report of the case *De Libellis Famosis*: 'greinder imputation a le state ne poit estre qu'a y mitter tels corrupt hommes a seer en le sacred seate de Justice, ou davoir ascun medling en, ou concernant ladministrat' de justice.' Public libels, he says, are worse offences than private ones, because in this case 'le libeller traduce et slaunder le state et gouvernement que ne mourust pas'.[3] In this, or in the fears expressed by the 1610 parliament of alteration of government through growth of impositions or proclamations, there is very clearly the idea of a constitution. There are not merely good and bad kings: there are good and bad forms of government. This idea seems, as far as I can gather, to be somewhat less prominent during the period of frequent parliaments in the sixteen-twenties[4]: there is no fear of alteration of government expressed in the impeachments of the sixteen-twenties, unless possibly in Pym's speeches against Buckingham and Manwaring. But after the dissolution of parliament in 1629, the atmosphere is rather

1. Rushworth, *Historical Collections*, i. 562. There is also some indication in the speech that at this time Pym was dabbling in the contract theory. See below, p. 98, n. 4.

2. J. E. Neale, *Elizabeth and Her Parliaments*, ii. 155.

3. *Fifth Report*, 125a. See also *Journal of Sir Symonds D'Ewes*, i. (ed. Notestein), 83, where Serjeant Hyde is accused of saying that those who spoke against monopolies 'spoke against the State'.

4. It was at the end of this period, in 1628, that the judges had before them a collection of precedents of treason by making a division, and rejected them. R. v. *Pine, State Trials*, iii. 359–68.

different: the return made to Strode's Habeas Corpus accused him of sedition. Littleton, appearing for Selden, argues that sedition is a civil law offence, 'but it was resolved 11 R. 2 n. 14, we are not governed by the civil law'. The offence of sedition is essentially an offence against the state, as appears from the argument of Sir Robert Berkeley in this case: 'so it is concerning the incendiaries of state, they ought to be restrained and suppressed, lest others should be stirred up by them to the same combustion.' Berkeley goes on: 'seditio est quasi seorsum itio, when the people are severed from the king. And in this sense sedition is no stranger in our law; and such sedition, which severs the people from the king, is treason.'[1] Sedition, it is argued in R. v. *Strode* (the case in which it became known to the common law courts) is an offence *laesae majestatis*. Pym appears to be adding nothing to Berkeley when he says in the trial of Strafford: 'that law term, laesa majestas, whereby they express that which we call treason, was never more thoroughly fulfilled than now; there cannot be a greater lesion or diminution of majesty than to bereave a king of the glory of his goodness.'[2] It is the same idea, more crudely expressed or more crudely reported, which is produced by Nathaniel Fiennes in the debates on the attainder Bill: 'if it be treason to kill the governor, then sure 'tis treason to kill the government.'[3]

How was Strafford supposed to have attempted to kill the government? This is almost the same question as to ask what the government was. What did parliament most fear to lose? I think it would be generally agreed that one of the things they most feared to lose was the right of being the sole channel of legislation. From 1610 onwards, the Commons had been expressing fears about the growth of proclamations. One of the rights which distinguished most continental kings from English ones was the right to make law without consulting their estates, and I think it would be generally agreed that the English parliament was afraid of losing control of legislation. And they accused Strafford of attempting to deprive them of it. In article 4, they accused him of saying that an act of state should be as good as an Act of Parliament. This could have been, of course, no more than Strafford said it was, a defence of the position of proclamations as *leges temporis*.[4] But it is interesting, as a guide to what the article was taken to mean, to study the ways in which it was misreported. The author of Harleian MS. 6424, which

1. *State Trials*, iii. 257–8 and 246–9.

2. *Two Speeches by John Pym,* printed for John Bartlett, 1641, p. 3.

3. *Verney's Notes of the Long Parliament,* Camden Society, 1st ser., xxi (1845), ed. Bruce, 54.

4. The Commons would have been much more alarmed if they had known of the letter Strafford wrote to Coke after his first Irish parliament, threatening to pass by proclamation all the Acts parliament had refused, 'it being necessary this people should see his Majesty will without more ado be obeyed'. Wedgwood, *op. cit.* pp. 162–3.

is a more pro-Straffordian account than any other except perhaps the *Brief Relation,* reports him as saying that *any* act of state should be as good as *any* Act of Parliament.[1] By itself, this might mean nothing. The greater vividness with which it suggests the idea of a changed constitution might be accidental. But it is interesting to set it beside Sir Framlingham Gawdy's misreport of the same article: 'that an act of state should be as good as a law.'[2] A similar misreport, though not on the same article, was made by the usually accurate D'Ewes. Article 3 had accused Strafford of saying that the Irish were a conquered nation, and 'the king might do with them what he pleased'. These words are capable of being used to present a very large vision of tyranny, but D'Ewes, who was distinctly hostile to Strafford at this stage of the trial, narrows them down to one specific point: 'that the king might put upon them what laws he pleased.'[3]

It is very hard to say how much the members were aware of continental parallels: they quote Sejanus and Nero more often than Richelieu or Philip II, and it would sometimes be possible to think that Israel was nearer at hand than France. But though I doubt whether many members knew very much about the continent, it is clear that Pym, at least, was aware that continental governments were different from the English one. In his speech against Manwaring, in which the idea of alteration of government appears very clearly, Pym rejects Manwaring's quotations from continental political theorists: 'most of his places are such as were intended by the authors concerning absolute monarchies, not regulated by laws or contracts between the king and his people.'[4] This, incidentally, is almost the only place in which I have found the phrase 'absolute monarchy' used as a definition.

However vague and generalized the members' interest in the continent is likely to have been, they may well, in considering article 4, have thought of the Edict of Restitution. 'L'Empereur', says Pagès, 'qui pendant si longtemps n'avait pas osé réunir une Diète d'Empire dans les formes traditionelles, semblait résolu à se passer de la Diète, comme aussi de l'union electorale, qui perdait en fait l'autorité qui lui avait été jusqu'alors reconnu. Toute la constitution du Saint-Empire s'en trouvait faussée, au profit d'un pouvoir monarchique absolu.'[5] Not only did the form of the Edict of Restitution appear similar, but it was even dealing with the same matter – the attempt to recover church property. If members thought of this parallel, it is easy to understand their alarm.

1. fo. 28a.
2. Diary of Sir Framlingham Gawdy, Brit. Mus., Add. MS. 14828, fo. 36a.
3. Brit. Mus., Harleian MS. 162, fo. 358a.
4. *State Trials,* iii. 348. See also n. 1, p. 96.
5. G. Pagès, *La Guerre de Trente Ans* (Paris, 1952), p. 113.

In article 19, Strafford was accused of framing a new oath, and punishing people for not taking it, without any authority by Act of Parliament. Whitelocke argues that this is an illustration of his words, that he would make an act of state as good as an Act of Parliament. The argument of article 19 is that Strafford is assuming the legislative power himself: 'it is well known, that a new oath cannot be imposed without assent in parliament. It is *legislativa potestas*.' Whitelocke accuses him of acting 'to make his authority equal to an Act of Parliament'.[1] Of course it is very doubtful how much substance there was in this claim that the power to impose an oath was a legislative power: Prynne supports it with eighty-seven statutes, *not one* of which proves his point.[2] I think, though, that this article may make sense if it is assumed that it was not the mere imposing the oath which was thought a legislative power, but the power to punish for refusing it. If this is assumed, the doctrine about oaths takes its place as just another embellishment on Magna Carta 39 – that no one shall be punished except *per legem terrae*.

If it be asked what else, beyond the legislative power, parliament thought should appertain solely to it, the answer must be the power to tax. And this also they accused Strafford of taking away from them. It is true that they took some account of Strafford's doctrine of emergency, but Strafford's certainty of emergency was turned against him, as showing that he was reducing parliament's consent to taxation to a mere formality. Article 21 admits that he 'counselled his Majesty to call a parliament in England', but goes on to say: 'yet the said Earl intended, that if the proceedings of that parliament should not be such as would stand with the said Earl's mischievous designs, he would then procure his Majesty to break the same, and by ways of force and power to raise monies upon the subjects of this kingdom.' Roughly the same charge appears in the words of article 23, that the king was 'loose and absolved from all rules of government' – a remark which is likely to have had a sinister ring for anyone whose mind was running on the civil law. This part of the charge, the power to tax under emergency powers, was one of the few parts which survived all stages of the proceedings in both Houses, and found its place in the Lords' final votes on the attainder Bill.[3]

There was one other constitutional security which was specially valued by members of the Long Parliament: the security of living under settled and known rules of common law. This is a security about which they grow more strident as they come to feel less secure in the enjoyment of it. The claim made by the opponents of the

1. Rushworth, *Trial of Strafford*, pp. 509–12.
2. Prynne, *Breviate of the Prelates' Intolerable Usurpations, etc.* (1637), p. 219.
3. House of Lords, Braye MS. 2, fos. 142a–b. See Appendix below for these votes.

High Commission, that common and statute law were the only forms of *lex terrae,* was a very dubious one. It is a claim, I think, which grows stronger in proportion to the fear of alteration of government. When there is division between the king and the people (by the people I mean what I think members meant, what Mr. Cooper describes as 'the political nation'), then there is more need to distrust the prerogative, more need to keep things secure from its effects. This has grown, by the time of the Long Parliament, into a doctrine shared by most members, that the lives, liberties and estates of subjects are only to be touched by common or statute law: that they belong to a sphere of government in which the prerogative has no place. Because the members feared the destruction of common law, they thought that lives, liberties and estates came within the sphere of common law; because Strafford had proceeded by prerogative against men's lives, liberties and estates, they accused him of intending to destroy the law. Hyde, in the debates on the Council of the North, was as extreme as any of them: he said the Council of the North proceeded 'in an arbitrary way, like a court of Chancery. That no Habeas Corpus, injunction, prohibition or writ of error should lie against it, that by this means no man's estate or liberty was safe.'[1] What is new here is the idea that if this can happen in some cases, no man is safe. What is new is the distrust: in other words, division. Articles 4 to 9 of the impeachment all show Strafford exercising power over lives, liberties and estates, and are gathered together into one general formula in the attainder Bill. The managers' panic interpretation of this is perhaps best expressed by Maynard: 'if any one such design as this should take effect, that the law and justice should be taken from the throne, and will placed there, we are without hope of ever seeing remedy.'[2]

If this charge could be supported, then it appeared that Strafford had attacked all the most important elements of constitutional security. It remained to show, if this case of alteration of government was to be brought within the scope of the old treason law, that Strafford had made the king's authority odious to the people, and so threatened his life. This was very cleverly done by an appeal to the Bible. In article 2, Strafford was accused of saying 'that the king's little finger should be thicker than the loins of the law'. Maynard, in opening the case, says of this: 'your Lordships may consider what a transcendent speech this was, out of whose mouth it came, what sad accidents happened upon it; nothing could move this Lord to utter: but his will and his violence must out, though he

1. Journal of Sir Symonds D'Ewes, Brit. Mus., Harleian MS. 163, fo. 488a. On the same page D'Ewes records a speech of his own, saying that 'by the course here taken all law must needs in the issue be destroyed'. Fears such as these were constantly expressed in the course of the Long Parliament.

2. Rushworth, *Trial of Strafford,* p. 129.

burst a kingdom in pieces for it.'[1] No sad accidents had happened upon Strafford's speaking these words. But very sad accidents had happened upon the speaking of these words in 1 Kings 12, by the young counsellors to Reheboam: 'thus shalt thou speak unto this people: – my little finger shall be thicker than my father's loins. And now whereas my father did lade you with a heavy yoke, I will add to your yoke: my father hath chastised you with whips, but I will chastise you with scorpions.' When Reheboam repeated these words to the people, they replied: 'what portion have we in David? neither have we inheritance in the son of Jesse: to your tents, O Israel: now see to thine own house, David.' The words did not merely make a division between the king and the people: they caused a civil war. The application to the case of Strafford is obvious.

This idea that Strafford's attempt to take away the law destroyed allegiance appears elsewhere in the trial. Maynard, opening the case, argues that 'it is the law that gives that sovereign tie, which with all obedience and cheerfulness, the subject renders to the sovereign'.[2] Pym handles this point very cannily: he confines himself to saying that 'the vigour and cheerfulness of allegiance will be taken away, *though the obligation remain*'. But the impression had been conveyed: one of the pirate pamphlets of his closing speech quotes him as saying simply that allegiance will be taken away.[3] This idea of destroying allegiance by making the king's authority odious is not new: it had appeared against both Elizabeth Barton and Empson and Dudley. There is also a parallel to it in an interesting piece in the *Somers Tracts,* which concludes a highly royalist discussion of the suppression of the liberties of Aragon: 'all this notwithstanding, such is their memory of their ancient liberties and privileges fixed in the hearts of the people; and so many are the discontents – as if ever there came apt occasion, by any public commotion within those kingdoms, it is to be doubted, that they will once again, to the danger of the king's estates, make proof of their fortunes.'[4] The suppression of the liberties of Aragon, dwelt upon by D'Ewes during the debates on the attainder Bill, is the only specific continental parallel mentioned during the trial.

1. *Ibid.* p. 131. Though Strafford seems to have proved that he spoke the words the other way round, this still remains an example of the audacity of his choice of allusions.

2. Rushworth, *Trial of Strafford,* p. 129.

3. *Ibid.* p. 662; *Mr. Pym's Speech in Answer to Thomas Lord Strafford's Defence* (John Aston, 1641), p. 2. In the same part of his speech, Pym argues that if the king rules as a conqueror, then the people are restored to the right of the conquered, to recover their liberty if they can.

4. *A Discourse of the State of Spain* (1607), by Sir Charles Cornwallis. *Somers Tracts* (1810), iii. 312. Journal of Sir Symonds D'Ewes, Brit. Mus., Harleian MS. 163, fo. 457a. D'Ewes says 'there are two ways to subvert the laws of a realm, the one by circuity and length of time, the other speedy and violent by an army'. Whether it is accurate to speak of Philip II 'subverting the laws' of Aragon, or whether it is not, both these very different authors seem to believe he had done so.

Where there is no legal machinery of unity between king and people, authority must rest, not on consent, but on force: there will be a Hobbist state of war between the king and the people. And in article 15, Strafford is accused of levying war against the king and his people, by using soldiers to enforce his decisions on paper petitions. This, it is argued, being a levying of war for public ends and against the king's law, must be a levying of war against the king. St. John's elaboration of this point is taken almost verbatim from the discussion of the 1597 Oxfordshire case in Coke's *Institutes*.[1] He says, too, that 'against the law or kingdom is against the king, it cannot be severed'. It would seem that the obvious line of defence against this article would have been to deny that the war was levied against the king. But Strafford believed in unity as profoundly as Pym and St. John, and he never denied, in the whole of his defence, that if he had levied war, it was against the king. His defence was that he had not levied war: 'these be wonderful wars, if we have no more wars, than such as three or four men are able to raise, by the grace of God we shall not sleep very unquietly.'[2] It was Glyn who was left to wrestle with this defence on behalf of the Commons. His argument is that the number of soldiers is insignificant: if they are enough to overpower a man, it does not matter whether they are four or four thousand.[3] Glyn's argument, in fact, relies on a Hobbist

1. Rushworth, *Trial,* pp. 680–1, Coke, *Third Institute,* p. 9. The Commons had finally succeeded in obtaining the MS. of Coke's *Institutes* on 13 Feb. *D'Ewes* (ed. Notestein), i. 358.

2. Rushworth, *Trial of Strafford,* p. 639. These words are spoken in the course of Strafford's defence to the parallel case of article 27. On pp. 636–7, his words read as if he were granting that a levying of war against the people was against the king: he certainly makes no attempt to make any distinction between them. It is worth quoting, on this article, an observation of Mr. Cooper's: 'the French monarchy in the 1630's and 1640's collected its taxes by military force. The intendants and tax farmers had permanent bodies of fusiliers at their disposal; where these did not suffice, they used military force. . . . It is difficult to think of English parallels to this, save perhaps in the conduct of the royalists in the west in the last phase of the civil war, or in the treatment of the Irish.' It is in precisely this point that article 26 accuses Strafford of recommending the practice of the French monarchy. (J. P. Cooper, *ubi supra,* p. 73). This fear of 'French government' is a long-continued fear, and can be found for many years before and after the Long Parliament. See, for example, a passage with a very close resemblance to article 15 in *A Discourse of the Common Weal* (ed. Lamond), p. 94. See also a parallel to article 21 in a speech by Montagu in 1681: 'This is not to be used as an English Parliament, but French, to be told in the king's speech what we are to do, and what not' (Cobbett, *Parliamentary History,* iv. 1318). I would like to thank Miss G. Hampson for this reference. There is another parallel to article 15 in the 1628 debates (Gardiner, *History of England,* vi. 235): 'they have rent from us the light of our eyes, inforced a company of guests worse than the ordinances of France.' This speech was by Sir Thomas Wentworth. In May 1641 Francis Gamull member for Chester wrote to his father in law that 'Richelieu the Cardinal . . . hath as Strafford endeavoured nay brought them to the most servile state that ever subjects were. So that we see all or most neighbour nations are infected with this malady'. M. F. Keeler, *The Long Parliament,* Philadelphia 1954, p. 183; Harleian MS. 2081, fo. 93b.

3. ' 'Tis as ill to be forced by 4 as by 4,000, and the force makes it levying war.' Verney, *Notes of the Long Parliament,* p. 44.

concept of war: a situation in which the will to contend by force is sufficiently known, and there is no other way of settling disputes.

The Commons thought this article particularly important, since they regarded it as treason in itself, within the 1352 statute. There is even a story told that the Commons tried to force a vote on this article on the spot. I am strongly inclined to disbelieve this story,[1] but it is none the less significant, as showing what sort of impression article 15 had created. And the Commons did succeed in getting article 15 across: the author of Harleian Manuscript 6424 reports the supporters of the Bill in the Lords as still arguing that it was plain treason by the 1352 statute.[2] It held its place in the attainder Bill when many articles had fallen by the wayside, and in the final votes of the Lords, when some parts of the attainder Bill (such, for example, as Strafford slandering the house of commons to his Majesty) have also fallen by the wayside, article 15 still survives, and is the subject of four separate votes. In fact, it appears from the Lords' votes that it was almost entirely upon articles 15 and 23 that the Commons won their case in the Lords.[3] Both of these were outside the main stream of the treason argument. They were both treasons by levying war, and so reducible to the terms of the statute. They both involved the assumption that levying war against the people was levying war against the king, but they did not involve the main body of argument which had been put up by the Commons. They did not involve, either, the vexed legal questions which Strafford surprisingly conceded to the Commons at this late stage, the question whether the salvo to the 1352 statute, allowing parliament to declare further treason was still in force, and the question whether there were treasons at the common law.[4]

1. Wedgwood, *op. cit.* part iii, chap. 4, n. 19; Brit. Mus., Add. MS. 47145. I am deeply suspicious of this manuscript, a fragmentary account containing such strange items as a circumstantial account of proceedings on article 28, which all other accounts, and Strafford himself in the course of his defence, are quite explicit in stating to have been dropped. Its authority in this point, however, is confirmed by another anonymous account (Brit. Mus., Lansdowne MS. 209, fo. 97b). These manuscripts are in apparently different hands, and though they have a resemblance to each other in formulae and phraseology which is closer than their resemblance to any other account, their resemblance is not close enough to justify the assertion that they come from a common source. However, even if these are two completely separate accounts, I am inclined to reject them. I find it hard to see why such an important event should have been omitted by Rushworth, D'Ewes, the *Lords' Journals* (which are normally most punctilious in recording the Lords' adjournments to debate points of procedure), and by the author of the *Brief Relation,* whom I would have expected to seize on this point as an illustration of the Commons' sharp practice. I would like to thank Mr. J. P. Hudson, of the British Museum Manuscript room, for his help in comparing these two manuscripts.

2. fo. 62a.

3. See Appendix below.

4. House of Lords, Braye, MS. 2, fos. 140b–141b. This is a surprising petition, since it is inscribed: 'tra. 5 May 1641', and so would appear to have been written on the same day as his famous letter to the king. The argument is very different from that of the letter: he asks for more time, and argues that though treason may have been declared in the past, it had only been declared for offences which were already felonies and capital. However, though it is not mentioned in the marginal rubrics of the *Lords'*

continued

Nor did the Lords' votes involve anything of the doctrine of constructive compassing of the king's death, to which Oliver St. John had devoted such labour. This doctrine played a curious part in the trial of Strafford. Pym admitted that a large amount of his argument had no precedent since 1388, because 'all that time, hath not bred a man, bold enough to commit such crimes as these'.[1] The doctrine of constructive compassing of the king's death had been the bridge by which this new idea of alteration of government was linked to the old doctrine of treason against the king's person: it was the doctrine whereby an offence against the state was punished under a law which was designed to protect the king's person. It had plenty of valid historical precedent, but it did not survive the course of the trial. Neither the attainder Bill nor the Lords' votes contain any mention of a possible danger to the king's person: Oliver St. John's labour was spent in vain.

This doctrine of constructive compassing of the king's death was a dangerous one to play with. In the first place, it was not what the members were really worried about. They were worried, no doubt, by the fear of civil war, but I do not think that even at this early stage they were very worried by the fear of the king's death in that war. Even St. John, who refused to take part in the trial of Charles I, is unlikely to have been moved by a passionate fear of Charles's death at the hands of some stray Felton. He was much more moved by the normal parliamentary concern for his own liberty and property, which he thought Strafford was threatening. And this is another reason why the doctrine of constructive compassing of the king's death was a dangerous one. It was a charge which had been levelled against the king's servants before, but when it was used against them, it was not so much a charge of treason, as of making traitors. And as such, it was nothing to throw against Strafford unless Pym

continued

Journals, its authenticity is confirmed by the anonymous diary Harleian MS. 6424, fo. 61a. If it was written on the same day as the last letter to the king, I think it shows Strafford's desire to avoid division between king and Lords. On the points in question, whether the salvo was still in force, and whether there were common law treasons, this petition is perhaps as good evidence as we have. The question of the salvo is probably unanswerable, since the treason statutes of 1399 and 1553 are insolubly ambiguous on the point. Vaughan (*Verney's Notes*, p. 53) argues that 1 Mary cap. 1 allows parliament to declare treasons, but not to punish for them unless they are committed after the declaration. The best discussion of the question by a legal historian that I know is by J. F. Stephen, *History of the Common Law*, ii. 250–3. After a great deal of hesitation, he decides that the Commons' abandonment of the impeachment should be taken as a tacit admission that the salvo was no longer in force. Strafford's petition seems to destroy the force of this point. The question of common law treasons is even thornier: the authority of Coke is against it, and yet, to take an extreme example, the 1352 statute had not made it treason to violate the queen regnant, and yet, if such an event had happened, I believe it would have been punished as treason. On the salvo, see also Elton, *The Tudor Constitution* (Cambridge, 1960), p. 86, for the duke of Norfolk's admission that the salvo was in force, and also Rezneck, 'The Parliamentary Declaration of Treason', *Law Quart. Rev.* xlvi (1930), 80.

1. Rushworth, *Trial of Strafford*, p. 669.

and St. John themselves were prepared to play their part, and threaten the king's life by rising up against Strafford's arbitrary government. This made it a dangerously double-edged doctrine. It was quite true that the constitution in which they all believed (there are fewer differences between Pym and Strafford than is commonly supposed) could not function if there was division between the king and the parliament. Serious division meant danger of civil war, and in a civil war the king's life was endangered. But it takes two to make a division, and it was quite open to somebody who thought Strafford was right and Pym was wrong to maintain that Pym was making a division, making a civil war likely, and thereby compassing the king's death. It is, in fact, in the course of the debates on article 2 that the author of the *Brief Relation* quotes Strafford as saying that Pym 'might one day perhaps be attacked for persuading the House of Commons to commit the same crime that was laid upon him as a charge of treason'.[1] It was in fact one of the charges against the Five Members that 'they have traitorously endeavoured, by many foul aspersions upon his Majesty and his government, to alienate the affections of his people, and to make his Majesty odious unto them'.[2]

Perhaps this is why, after the trial of Strafford, which was the first of the Long Parliament's treason cases, this doctrine of constructive compassing of the king's death falls into the background. In the trial of Laud the Commons argued that 'treason may be against the realm as well as against the king'.[3] This is a straightforward offence against the State. In the trial of Charles I himself the change in the doctrine of treason is unconcealed by any legal fiction. It would of course have been ludicrous to execute Charles for constructively compassing his own death, and he had to be tried only for offences against the State. The new idea in the trial of Charles I is that 'the State' and 'the people' are terms which can be used interchangeably. But the State, and any alteration in its government, were always the concern of the Long Parliament, and the trial of Strafford is in many ways a bridge used to close the gap between these new accusations and the old ones.

The gap had been closed before the trial of Strafford was over. The indictment, and St. John's argument of law, are still concerned with the king's person. But the questions put to the judges referred to them as matter of fact only the alteration of government. The 'facts' they were given were: 'that the Earl of Strafford by words, counsels, actions, hath endeavoured to subvert the fundamental laws of the kingdom by introducing an arbitrary government. That the earl of Strafford hath exercised a tyrannical power against

1. *A Brief and Perfect Relation* (1647), p. 12.
2. Rushworth, *Historical Collections*, III. i. 474.
3. *L.J.* vii. 125.

the laws of England over the lives, liberties and estates of his Majesty's subjects.'[1] It was upon these facts that the judges found Strafford guilty of treason. Alteration of government is treason in itself. This perhaps is a manufactured theory of treason, but it is not simply Pym's theory of treason. It is the theory which was foreshadowed in Coke's prosecution of the Oxfordshire rebels, and in Berkeley's prosecution of Strode.

But even this was a double-edged doctrine. English government could be altered in two ways. If parliament might be deprived of its just rights, so might the king. It was another article against the Five Members that 'they have traitorously endeavoured to subvert the fundamental laws and government of the kingdom of England, to deprive the king of his royal power, and to place in subjects an arbitrary and tyrannical power over the lives, liberties and estates of his Majesty's liege people'. If the king and his parliament could not agree, government had to be altered somehow. If government were altered, everyone, Pym and Strafford equally, feared that something like Hobbes's state of nature would follow.

This fear of disorder and chaos was strengthened by the intensity of the idea of order in seventeenth-century political thought. All political thought before the civil war, from Pym's to Filmer's, rested upon the doctrine of the Great Chain of Being.[2] The idea of order in this doctrine was very precise: each part of the Great Chain which made up the universe corresponded both to the macrocosm of which it was a part, and to the microcosm which was part of it. And all this order was only held together because there was unity: 'God is one', said Laud, 'and loves nothing but as it tends to one.'[3] The whole was united in God, and the political microcosm was to be united under the king. So long as there was unity and harmony between the king and the subjects, or between fire and water, there was harmony. As the unity of the cosmos was secured by natural law, so the unity of the body politic was secured by fundamental law. This was a very comforting doctrine while things went well, but as soon as disorder began, the comfort ceased. For the only alternative to this one God-given harmony was thought to be chaos.[4] This is what the Long Parliament feared was coming back. It was St. John, not the most poetical of men, who said: 'take the polity and

1. House of Lords MSS. Apr. 1641.

2. On the doctrine of the Great Chain of Being and its influence in the seventeenth century, see A. O. Lovejoy, *The Great Chain of Being*, E. W. M. Tillyard, *The Elizabethan World Picture*, W. H. Greenleaf, 'James I and the Divine Right of Kings', *Journal of Political Studies*, v (1957), 36–48 and J. W. Gough, 'Flowers of the Crown', *ante*, lxvii. 86–93.

3. In his opening sermon in 1628: *Works* (ed. Scott, 1847), i. 163 and 155–81 *passim*.

4. Denzil Holles, in his speech on the Protestation, expressed fear of a state of 'general dissolution, and all things return, as in the beginning, in antiquum chaos' (Rushworth, *Historical Collections*, III. i. 243). See also Greenleaf, *ubi supra*, p. 41.

government away, and England's but a piece of earth, wherein so many men have their commorancy and abode, without ranks or distinction of men, without security in anything further than possession, without any law to punish the murthering or robbing one another.'[1] Hobbes himself never put it as well as this. The nightmare which helps to increase fear is of Hobbes's Leviathan on one side, and of Hobbes's state of nature on the other. There is little in Hobbes which is not found in the Long Parliament, save the crazy courage with which Hobbes accepted that this choice had become unavoidable, since the king and his parliament would never be able to agree. It is these same fears which gave the bite to Pym's fear of arbitrary government, as they did to Strafford's fear of insubordination and anarchy. And one or other of these, it appeared, was the inevitable consequence of a division between the king and the people, in which neither side would make concessions, and there was no authority to settle the dispute short of force. And once it is granted that such a division can be made by one person (a premise which neither side denied) it is easy to understand Strafford's conviction that 'under a heavier censure than this, I am persuaded no gentleman can suffer'.

APPENDIX

The Lords' Votes on the Attainder Bill

At the Restoration, the proceedings on the attainder of Strafford were erased from the *Lords' Journals*, but the marginal rubrics were not. The marginal rubrics for 5, 6 and 7 May record four separate sets of votes on the Bill, but the votes themselves have hitherto been unknown (*L.J.* iv. 236–7). In the Braye MSS. in the House of Lords Record Office (vol. 2, fos. 142a–b) there are recorded a series of thirteen votes which I believe are those taken by the Lords on these days. They are headed *Die Mercurii 5 Maii 1641*. The first five votes appear under this heading, the next five under the heading *Die Jovis 6 Maii,* and the last three under the heading *7 Maii.* The votes under *6 Maii* concern the two parts of article 23 the charge of saying that the king was absolved from rules of government, and the Irish army charge. On this day the *Lords' Journals* record two sets of votes. Under 5 May, on which day the *Journals* record one set of votes, are the votes on article 15, and under 7 May, on which day one set of votes is recorded in the *Journals*, are the final votes of alteration of government, and the vote to refer the question of law to the judges. Fortunately, it is possible to check the accuracy of this record against Harleian MS. 6424 (fos. 62b–64a). It is, however, impossible to check the dates in this manuscript, since the diarist has put all the attainder bill proceedings together under the heading of 4 May. It is, however,

1. Rushworth, *Trial of Strafford*, p. 699.

possible to check the matter. There are some differences in the wording, of which the most significant is that the Lords' diarist records (fo. 63b) a vote on article 15 to the effect that the soldiers had acted in obedience to Strafford's orders. The votes on article 23 are not recorded in full in the diary, but in the main the matter is the same. The last three votes are almost identical, except that the words: 'above and contrary to the laws' appear in the first vote where they do not in the Braye MS. They are perhaps an echo of the words of the second vote of 7 May: 'above and against the laws.' The number of votes on article 15 is the same, and the contents almost identical. I therefore feel justified in printing the text of the Braye MS. as an authentic record of the Lords' proceedings.

They are as follows:

Die Mercurii 5 Maii 1641

1/ Resolved upon the question: that going by way of Bill in the discussing of the matter of fact in this whole cause the rule shall only be the persuasion of every man's conscience.[1]

2/ Resolved etc. that the Earl of Strafford gave warrant for the sessing of soldiers upon men's lands in Ireland, and the same was executed accordingly.

3/ Resolved etc. that the sessing of soldiers was done for the disobeying of the Earl of Strafford's orders made upon paper petitions between party and party against their consents.

4/ Resolved etc. that the sessing of soldiers was with armies and officers in warlike manner.

5/ Resolved etc. that the sessing of soldiers was with armies and an officer conducting them.

Die Jovis 6 Maii 1641

6/ Resolved etc. that the Earl of Strafford did counsel and advise his Majesty that he was absolved from rules of government.

7/ Resolved etc. that the Earl of Strafford said unto his Majesty that in cases of necessity, and for the defence and safety of the kingdom if the people did refuse to supply the king, the king is absolved from rules of government. And that everything is to be done for the preservation of the king and his people. And that his Majesty was acquitted before God and man.

8/ Resolved etc. that the Earl of Strafford used these words to his Majesty, that his Majesty having tried all ways, and refused in cases of this extreme necessity, and for the safety of the kingdom, you are absolved from all rules of government, and are acquitted before God and man, or words to that effect.

9/ Resolved etc. that the Earl of Strafford said to the king these words: you have an army in Ireland, which your Majesty may employ to reduce this kingdom, or words to that effect.

10/ Resolved etc. that these words (to reduce this kingdom) were spoken of the kingdom of England.

1. It would seem from Harleian MS. 6424 (fo. 63a) that this vote was proposed by Manchester.

7 Maii 1641

11/ Resolved etc. that the Earl of Strafford hath by his words counsels and actions endeavoured to subvert the fundamental laws of the kingdoms of England and Ireland, and to introduce an arbitrary power.
12/ Resolved etc. that the Earl of Strafford hath exercised a tyrannous and exorbitant government above and against the laws, over the lives, liberties and estates of the subjects.
13/ Resolved by vote that this question be put to the judges; that upon all the Lords have voted to be proved, that the Earl of Strafford doth deserve to undergo the pains and forfeitures of high treason by law.

'We are of opinion upon all that your lordships have voted to be proved: that the Earl of Strafford doth deserve to undergo the pains and forfeitures of high treason by law.'

These several votes cover the whole of the attainder Bill, with two exceptions. I have found no record of any vote on the clause of the attainder Bill in which Strafford was accused of slandering the house of commons to his Majesty, nor upon the clause accusing him of being an incendiary of the wars between England and Scotland.

6

The Authorship of the Bishop's Diary of the House of Lords in 1641

THE ANONYMOUS DIARY, British Museum Harley MS. 6424, is the only record we have of the debates of the house of lords during the Long Parliament, and this fact alone gives it considerable value as a source. Our picture of the comparative importance of the Lords and Commons in the seventeenth century can be distorted by the great disproportion between the numbers of Lords' and Commons' diaries that have survived. The keeping of diaries is doubtful evidence on comparative political importance: there are no diaries of the privy council. It may be that the importance of the Parliamentarian Lords in the origins of the Civil War has been underestimated.[1] This manuscript, moreover, was written by a keen observer of Parliamentarian party management. It is true that much of the information it contains, such as the articles against Strafford or the texts of the king's speeches, can be found in other sources. But it also contains much otherwise unrecorded evidence about the political alliances of 1641. It is valuable, for example, to know that the petition on behalf of Osbaldeston, Williams's accomplice in the subornation of perjury case, was presented by the earl of Bedford, and that in return, Bishop Williams moved the motion to give thanks to the twelve peers who had petitioned for a parliament.[2] The clauses of the Triennial Act whereby power to summon a parliament was given to the lord keeper and to a committee of peers were inserted as Lords' amendments. It appears that in the original Commons' draft the power to summon a parliament devolved directly from the king to the sheriffs.[3] It is interesting

[1] Professor Lawrence Stone (*The Crisis of the Aristocracy* (Oxford, 1965), p. 7) attempts to explain 'weaknesses which seriously reduced their influence over the events of 1640–2'. Before explaining the reduction of the aristocracy's influence, one should be certain that it was in fact reduced.

[2] British Museum, Harley MS. 6424 fo. 8r: fo. 52r.

[3] *Ibid.* fo. 12r.

that Savill asked for a night's time 'wherein to recollect his notes' before voting on the attainder of Strafford, and that Essex, Mandeville and Say moved that those Lords who would not take the Protestation should have no votes on the Attainder Bill.[1]

The authorship of this diary has been discussed by Professor Coates, who made a very tentative suggestion that the diary might be by Juxon. He based this suggestion on the argument that the diarist was likely to have been neither one of the twelve bishops impeached in December 1641, nor one of the thirteen bishops impeached for making the canons.[2] The Protestation and impeachment of the twelve bishops is, as Dr. Coates says, recorded 'quite imperturbably', and with the bare minimum of detail.[3] It is, moreover, improbable that a man who distrusted Bishop Williams as much as this diarist appears to have done would have signed a petition which was largely of his devising.[4] But even if it seems likely that he was not one of the twelve bishops, the evidence is too tentative for the Protestation of the twelve bishops to be a reliable test for elimination.

Dr. Coates's evidence for the suggestion that he may not have been one of the thirteen bishops is worth quoting in full, since the passages in question are the only ones which prove the author to have been a bishop. The diarist almost invariably uses the third person, but in his entry for 16 August 1641 he says:

> the bishops that are impeached for making the canons desired till Michaelmas or Michaelmas term to make their answer, which by Essex, Say, Mandeville, Wharton, Paget, was vehemently opposed, neither would they have us be in the House while this question of time was debated, although the bishops themselves consented that when the merit of the cause was judged, they would withdraw.[5]

The second passage is for 28 October: 'although the night before it was assented that this day the general bill for sequestering us might be debated, yet now they would and did debate the request of the Commons to sequester the thirteen, which after a long time was ordered that both this request and the bill should be respited till November 10'.[6] In both of these passages, the first person is used for the whole bench of bishops, but not clearly for the thirteen. The first passage, however, ends with a reference to the whole bench of bishops as 'they'. This is not the only occasion on which the author refers to the whole bench of bishops as 'they': on 24 February, he records Mandeville's motion that the bishops should withdraw from the trial of Strafford, and adds, 'the Lord Marshal, Lord Privy Seal,

[1]Harley MS. 6424 fo. 63v: fo. 60r.

[2]*The Journal of Sir Simonds D'Ewes*, ed. W. H. Coates (New Haven, 1942), pp. xvi, 3, 410–11.

[3]Brit. Mus., Harl. MS. 6424 fo. 99r.

[4]See his report (*ibid.* fo. 44r) of Williams's attack on Laud ('His Grace (saith he) abounds in passion and rashness'), and fos. 54r, 65r, 88r.

[5]*Ibid.* fo. 92r. In his account of this debate, he drops his impersonal manner enough to call the supporters of the 13 bishops 'the good lords'.

[6]*Ibid.* fo. 98v.

Lord Say, Paget, Brooke and divers others being earnest upon the same point, the bishops desired only to make answer for themselves, which the violence of the opposers would not suffer, and therefore when the Lord Strafford came in again to the bar, the bishops of their own accord walked forth'.[1] The fact that he referred to the thirteen bishops in the third person cannot therefore be a sufficient ground for arguing that he was not one of them. It could be argued with equal force that these passages suggest that he was one of the thirteen, since the only occasions on which he lapses into the first person are in discussions of the thirteen, and moreover on discussions of the one specific point of the amount of time they should be allowed to put in their answer. However, no certain deductions can be drawn from this evidence.

Nor can any deductions be drawn from the hand, which appears to be that of a secretary. All deductions about the authorship must be tentative, since it can be proved that the diarist at least once reported a day on which he did not attend. He reports the impeachment of the twelve bishops on 30 December 1641, and then gives an equally brief report of the charge against the Five Members on 4 January. All bishops present on 30 December were in prison on 4 January, so one of these reports must be of a proceeding in his absence.[2] He also wrote up proceedings afterwards: under 3 July, he records that the king 'this afternoon' passed the bill for poll money, but refused the bills for star chamber and high commission 'till he were better satisfied in them yet on Monday next he passed them'.[3]

However, it may be assumed that during the period covered by the diary, from 14 January 1641 to 4 January 1642, the diarist attended with at least reasonable frequency. This suggests that Juxon is an improbable author, since Fuller says that because of his other occasions he was 'seldom seen' in the parliament.[4] The diary ends with eight folios of notes, possibly for a speech, on bishops' baronies, their right to make canons, their relations with the secular authority, and the greed of the laity for church property.[5] Fuller also says that the best defenders of the bishops' baronies were the bishops of Rochester and Bristol.

Fortunately, one of the days the diarist reports in most detail is 4 May, the day on which the Protestation was taken. It is also one of the rare days on which he refers to the house of lords as 'we', and it seems highly probable that was a day on which he attended the House. If so, the diary must be by one of the bishops who took the Protestation on 4 May. The diary gives the text of the Protestation in full, together with the attempts to get ministers to notify the crowd that it had been taken, so that they should go away. If the diarist took the Protestation on 4 May, he was one of the following bishops: Lincoln, Gloucester, Carlisle, Bath and Wells, Hereford, Bristol, Rochester or Llandaff.[6]

[1] *Ibid.* fo. 39r. [2] *Ibid.* fos. 99–100. [3] *Ibid.* fo. 80r.
[4] T. Fuller, *Church History*, ed. J. S. Brewer (Oxford, 1845), vi. 237.
[5] Brit. Mus., Harl. MS. 6424 fos. 100–8.
[6] *Ibid.* fos. 58v–60v. *Journals of the House of Lords* (hereafter cited as *L.J.*), iv. 234.

A clearer elimination is possible for 4 August. On that day the diarist records that 'the Bishop of Lincoln in the Parliament House (*hora 5a pomeridiana*) tells the Bishops of Gloucester and Bangor, which I overheard and Bangor repeated to me presently that the King told him: Canterbury had drawn him to the canons' making against his judgement'.[1] The bishops of Lincoln, Gloucester and Bangor can then be eliminated on internal evidence. This passage proves that the diarist was in the House on the afternoon of 4 August, when the House was called. The bishops of Carlisle, Bristol, London and Coventry and Lichfield were absent, and can therefore be eliminated.[2] It is also possible to eliminate the bishop of Peterborough on internal evidence, as well as on the strength of his absence from the taking of the Protestation.[3]

This leaves a list of five possible authors, the bishops of Durham, Bath and Wells, Hereford, Rochester and Llandaff. There is tentative evidence against four of these. The bishop of Durham was absent at the calling of the House on 2 November. The diarist records the proceedings of that day against Father Phillips the queen's confessor, but misdates them to 3 November.[4] The bishops of Hereford and Bath and Wells were given leave to visit their dioceses on 21 August, and are unlikely to have been present on 25 and 26 August. These days are both reported in the diary.[5] On 26 August the diarist also records that Bishop Manwaring of St. David's was sent for 'and upon the Bishop of Llandaff's certificate, if he could not be found in his diocese. The bishop of Lincoln affirmed that he roved from alehouse to alehouse in disguise, and the Bishop of Lincoln moved his bishopric might be sequestered to the King'.[6] Everything that can be learnt of the diarist's biases suggests that his sympathies are likely to have been against both Lincoln and Llandaff in this question, and therefore that he is unlikely to have been Llandaff. If this passage is regarded as evidence for eliminating Llandaff, then only John Warner of Rochester would remain as a possible author.

There is one other test on which elimination might be possible. There is only one committee whose proceedings the diarist reports, the Committee for Innovations in Religion, set up on 1 March. He records an order for regulating its proceedings, and an exchange on 6 March between the earl of Bristol and Bishop Williams about its scope and the witnesses it should send for. On 12 March, he records what he says is its first meeting,

[1] Brit. Mus., Harl. MS. 6424 fo. 88r.

[2] *L.J.*, iv. 340.

[3] He says Sir John Clotworthy told Lord Lanerick, who told the queen, that Newport, Mandevill and others at Mandevill's table 'on Sunday last' were in earnest conversation how to take and keep the queen and the prince. 'This Mr. William Lake told the Bishop of Peterborough, Dr. Wemyss and myself at Dr. Wemyss' house after dinner August 18, 1641'. Brit. Mus., Harl. MS. 6424 fo. 94r.

[4] *L.J.*, iv. 418: Brit. Mus., Harl. MS. 6424 fo. 98r. The report, being brief, might be based on hearsay.

[5] *L.J.*, iv. 374; Brit. Mus., Harl. MS. 6424 fo. 94r.

[6] Brit. Mus., Harl. MS. 6424 fo. 94r.

and adds a note of the date of the next meeting. He records, though he does not report, a meeting of a sub-committee and assistants at Bishop Williams's house, which he says is to report to the full committee.[1] It appears possible, though not certain, that the diarist was a member of this committee. Its episcopal members were Winchester, Chester, Lincoln, Salisbury, Exeter, Carlisle, Ely, Bristol, Rochester and Chichester.[2] On this test, John Warner of Rochester would remain a possible author, and a second test would eliminate the bishops of Durham, Hereford, Bath and Wells and Llandaff. It can only be argued that the author was one of these four if both these eliminations are rejected.

It remains to consider how probable a candidate John Warner may be. Except for the Protestation of the twelve bishops on 30 December, there is no event recorded in the diary on a day on which Warner can be proved to have been absent. His first recorded absence was from the calling of the House on the afternoon of 6 November. On that day, the diarist records the morning's proceedings, but remains silent from dinner-time on that day until 25 November.[3] It is also possible to test Warner's known biases and preoccupations against those of the diarist. The diarist shows an intense interest in the proceedings of the Scots, which are recorded on 33 of the 100 folios of the diary. In March 1640 Warner had got into trouble for a sermon against the Scots on the text, 'O Lord, forget not the voice of thine enemies'.[4] The diarist's interest in the trial of Strafford was probably shared by almost every member of the House, and offers no clue to his identity. It is perhaps more significant that he gives a great deal of space to Bishops' Exclusion, and to the defence of the thirteen bishops accused for making the canons, while remaining comparatively silent on demands for the abolition of episcopacy. He shows a particular interest in the time allowed to the thirteen to put in their answer.[5] Warner in 1660, listing his activities in parliament, said: 'how I carried myself in the Parliament of 1640, in maintenance of the King's right, keeping of the praemunire for making the canons, and in defence of the bishops' sitting in Parliament, I appeal to the Lords if living'. Warner was also largely responsible for organizing the defence of the thirteen bishops.[6] He was one of the thirteen, but not one of the twelve.

[1] *Ibid.* fos. 43v, 45r, 49r, 54r.

[2] *L.J.*, iv. 174.

[3] *L.J.*, iv. 426: Brit. Mus., Harl. MS. 6424 fo. 99r. There are two references to Warner in the third person. The first (fo. 57v) is a statement that the marriage of Princess Mary to the prince of Orange was celebrated 'verbatim according to the English form' by the bishop of Ely, and that the bishop of Rochester preached on Psalm 45.7. The second (fo. 58v) is that on the news of the first Army Plot 'the Earl of Stamford wished the Bishops of Carlisle, Bristol and Rochester to give thanks for our great deliverance, which is greater than that from the Gunpowder Treason'. There is no remotely possible author who is not mentioned in the third person.

[4] *D.N.B.*, *s.v.* Warner, John (1581–1666).

[5] Brit. Mus., Harl. MS. 6424 fos. 92r–93r, 96r, 97r, 98v. He also shows a considerable interest in procedural questions concerning the 13 bishops.

[6] Bodl. Libr., MS. Tanner 49 fo. 23r; MS. Eng. Hist. b. 205 fo. 26r: *L.J.*, iv. 401.

The diarist records some other more unexpected points in detail. He shows a close interest in the bill for transferring Durham House to the earl of Pembroke,[1] and in the bill for the clerk of the market.[2] Warner was on the committees for both these bills.[3] The diarist gives a remarkably thorough report, including large numbers of precedents, on the arguments about setting up a Custos Regni during the king's absence in Scotland. Warner was on the committee for this bill.[4] He was also on the committee for the depredations of the French, in which the diarist is clearly interested.[5] This material, while not conclusive, is suggestive, and there is no material to suggest that Warner was not the author. It then seems reasonable to suppose that the diary is that of John Warner.

What manner of man was Warner, and what sort of biases can be expected of him? He is not mentioned by Gardiner or Clarendon, or even by Sir Philip Warwick, who was one of his executors.[6] It may then be worth recording some information about him. The main biographical details are recorded in *The Life of John Warner* by Edward Lee-Warner,[7] but something may be added about his political and religious outlook. He appears not to have been an Arminian in pure theology. His will might suggest an imputation doctrine of Justification, though it does not prove it.[8] His letter to Jeremy Taylor, about Taylor's *Unum Necessarium*, is more specific. He quotes Augustine, that all men are 'damnationi obnoxios', and that 'sola gratia redemptos discernit a perditis, in unam perditionis massam concreverat ab origine ducta communis contagio'. He claims that the Fathers had discussed these questions less 'till Pelagius had pudled the stream'.[9] Clearly, Montague, for example, would not have found his theology pleasing.

Even if he was not an Arminian, he must be classified in the political terms of 1640 as a Laudian. The petition of the parishioners of St. Dionis Backchurch, one of his livings, shows that he held the full Laudian position on the altar. He also shared Laud's dislike of lecturers, 'and in his pulpit has compared lecturers to ballad-singers and hobby-horse sellers, for that they in the fair or market have the most crowd, while mercers or goldsmiths who sell rich commodities have nothing to do'. He also had a strong concern with economic problems of the church. His parishioners charged him with raising burial dues at pleasure, and with raising tithes 'against Christian charity and humanity'.[10] He spent large sums of money for the

[1] Brit. Mus., Harl. MS. 6424 fos. 88r–v, 89v, 90v.
[2] *Ibid.* fos. 80v, 90r–v.
[3] *L.J.*, iv. 343, 313.
[4] Brit. Mus., Harl. MS. 6424 fos. 85r, 86r–v, 87r–v, 88v, 98v, 90r–v: *L.J.*, iv. 341.
[5] Brit. Mus., Harl. MS. 6424 fos. 7v, 56r, 66r: *L.J.*, iv. 302.
[6] Brit. Mus., Lansd. MS. 989 fo. 14v.
[7] E. Lee-Warner, *The Life of John Warner* (1901).
[8] Brit. Mus., Lansd. MS. 989 fo. 13r.
[9] *A Letter Written by the Lord Bishop of Rochester* (London, 1656), pp. 65, 70.
[10] *Cal. State Papers Dom. 1641–3*, vol. ccccxciii no. 28; Public Record Office, S.P. 16/493/28. The full report contains a large amount of material on economic problems of the church which is not printed in the *Calendar*.

repair of church fabric at St. Paul's and Rochester, and on the buying in of impropriations.[1] The notes at the end of the diary contain a considerable amount of material on impropriations, and also a complaint, which sounds typical of Warner, that the clergy were rated for subsidies at a far higher rate than the laity.[2] In his treatise *Church-Lands not to be Sold*, Warner subscribed to the full Laudian position, that 'lands so given for the service and to the servants of God, change their common quality or nature; and are by dedication and God's acceptation become God's, and therefore holy', and that 'King Henry the Eighth, so decryed for a notorious sacrilegist, yet never did he take away the lands of bishops, nor cathedrals'.[3] The second statement does no credit to Warner's history. He was appointed to the high commission while still dean of Lichfield, and appears, from the scanty surviving records, to have undertaken the unpopular task of arbitration in alimony cases.[4]

He had a sensitive eye for opposition to the Crown, perhaps sometimes before it existed. In 1626, he preached a sermon before the king on the text: 'they said among themselves, this is the heir; come let us kill him'. It is not surprising that 'this sermon so startled the Lords and Commons that they earnestly moved the King that I might be hanged at Whitehall Gate'. Warner subsequently regarded this sermon as 'a full and clear prophecy' of Charles's subsequent fate.[5] The prophecy was perhaps partly self-fulfilling. His sermon of February 1649 on *The Devilish Conspiracy* of the Jews against Christ their king returned to the same theme with rather more justification. In that sermon, he expressed the view which the diarist clearly shared, that the Lords had a large part in beginning the war.

> If those Rulers or Princes of the People were as our Lords; then they must know that these men were deep in the first plotting and carrying on this Treason; and were as chief instrumentall means in bringing Ch. the King [*sic*] to his end; though towards the end, or last act of the Tragedy (his condemnation and execution) for feare or policy they appeared not, or drew their necks (as we say) out of the coller.[6]

He remained concerned about the loyalty of the Scots, and in his will he left £80 per annum to support four Scottish scholars at Balliol until they were fit to take orders in the Church of England. They were to be selected by the archbishop of Canterbury and the bishop of Rochester.[7]

[1] Brit. Mus., Lansd. MS. 989 fos. 13–14. Bodl. Libr., MS. Tanner 49 fo. 23r; MS. Top. gen. c. 75(1); MS. Eng. Hist. b. 205 fo. 9. I would like to thank Mr. N. J. Tyacke for these references.

[2] Brit. Mus., Harl. MS. 6424 fos. 100–8.

[3] *Church-Lands not to be Sold* (1648), pp. 4, 18.

[4] *Cal. State Papers Dom. 1633–4*, vol. cclii no. 57; *Cal. State Papers Dom. 1639–40*, vol. ccccxxxiv no. 37; *Cal. State Papers Dom. 1640*, vol. ccccxxxiv no. 27.

[5] Bodl. Libr., MS. Tanner 49 fo. 23r.

[6] *The Devilish Conspiracy* (London, 1648), p. 9.

[7] Brit. Mus., Lansd. MS. 989 fo. 13v.

There is also a surviving catalogue of his library.[1] He possessed a number of books which are quoted in the notes at the end of the diary, but since these are largely such common works as Matthew Paris, Speed's *Genealogies*, Linwood and Camden, they cannot be used to support the case for Warner's authorship. His library does show, however, that we must add one more to the list of those who were interested in science without having any sympathy with Puritans. He possessed Tycho Brahe's *Historia Caelestis*, Agricola's *De Re Metallica*, Robert Recorde's *Castle of Knowledge*, and numerous other scientific works. He also had, for his lighter moments, a copy of *Don Quixote*. His total collection amounted to 1,742 volumes.

None of this personal information adds anything towards a proof that Warner was the author of the diary, but it is all readily compatible with his authorship, and, like the internal evidence of the diary, it contains no evidence against his authorship.

[1] *Bibliotheca Warneriana* (London, 1686).

II

MONEY

7

Monarchies, Wars and Estates in England, France and Spain, c.*1580*-c.*1640*

In matters of parliamentary history, the English (and Anglophones) have for many years enjoyed a tendency to thank God that they are not as other men are. S.R. Gardiner claimed that "the Parliament of England is the noblest monument ever reared by mortal man".[1] It is very easy for those who can base their history on the comfortable confirmation of hindsight to indulge the pleasing fantasy that there is something specially English about parliaments. Yet such a claim must be subjected to critical scrutiny, and it is perhaps fitting that this scrutiny should, in the first instance, come from an Englishman.

It is not the object of this article to attempt comparisons for the whole of Europe: such a task, though clearly important, is beyond my present limits. Moreover, comparisons between estates which had to deal with major monarchies and estates whose dealings are with local princes and dukes are not always comparisons of like with like. Since ignorance restrains me from serious discussion of the institutions of Sweden and Denmark, and since the constitution of the Dutch republic in the seventeenth century was *sui generis*, this article will concentrate on comparisons between the three great monarchies of Europe: England, France, and Spain. It is the central theme of this article that the relations between these three monarchies and their various parliaments and estates show more in common than we have sometimes been led to suppose. It is not the purpose of this article to explain why parliaments ultimately showed more power of survival in England than they did in France or Spain. That is a question which must be tackled by a detailed discussion of the events of James II's reign. Parliament was not sitting during 1688, and James's attempts to control membership of Parliaments through controlling municipal corporations had made so much progress that it was James II's critics, not James, who were determined to prevent the assembly of the Parliament due to meet in November 1688. The key to England's later development was the successful Dutch invasion of 1688,

[1] S.R. Gardiner, *History of England* (1893) I 2.

and that subject is beyond the chronological scope of this article.[2] My present objective is the much more limited one of examining similarities and differences among the three countries, not as clues to a distant and uncertain future, but as subjects worth investigation in their own right.

Recent work in this field has begun to escape from the baleful influence of Montesquieu, whose insistence on the separation of powers, and on the notion that it is their proper function to provide checks and balances to each other, is alien to seventeenth-century thought in any country, and to English thought in any century. As Professor Major has said, "We must therefore abandon the liberal assumption that the kings and the estates were natural adversaries." As he rightly stresses, most men "saw the strength of the state as dependent on cooperation between the King and the people".[3] With this assumption firmly in mind, it is possible to see strong estates without being forced to look for a weak monarchy, and conversely, in England, it is possible to see a weak monarchy without being forced to look for a strong Parliament. The French Estates examined by Professor Major certainly do not appear, around 1600, to be in any danger of withering away. They met frequently, and defended their interests vigorously. Some of their members even produced what sounds remarkably like a doctrine of the Ancient Constitution.[4] The Cortes of Catalonia, as described by Professor Elliott, seems to be quite as firmly entrenched in Catalan law and sentiment as the English Parliament ever was in English sentiment. Professor Jago has now now discovered clear evidence of vitality in so unexpected a place as the Cortes of Castile.[5] Conversely, while new importance has been discovered in French and Spanish representative assemblies, the tendency of recent work on England has been to play down both the importance and the constitutional aggressiveness of English parliaments.

In particular, the belief that the English Parliament enjoyed particular strengths in procedure has come under review. Dr. Lambert has recently called in question the procedural advances formerly supposed to have taken place in English Parliaments, while Professor Major has stressed that "in terms of administration and privileges, the English Parliament lagged far behind the national diets of most continental countries and the provincial estates of France".[6] This claim is undoubtedly justified, and

[2] See J.R. Western, *Monarchy and Revolution: The English State in the 1680s* (1972), J.R. Jones, *The Revolution of 1688 in England* (1972) and H.G. Koenigsberger, *Dominium Regale or Dominium Politicum et Regale: Monarchies and Parliaments in Early Modern Europe*, King's College, London (1975).

[3] J. Russell Major, *Representative Government in Early Modern France*, New Haven (1980), pp. 179, 177.

[4] Major, *op. cit.*, p. 186.

[5] Charles Jago, 'Habsburg Absolutism and the Cortes of Castile', *American Historical Review*, vol. 86 (1981), pp. 307-26.

[6] Sheila Lambert, 'Procedure in the House of Commons in the Early Stuart period', *E.H.R.* vol. 95 (1980), p. 735-81: Major, *op. cit.*, p. 198.

there are three main respects in which it is justified. One is the appointment of officials: French or Catalonian estates were able to appoint their own officials and their own presiding offices, while in England the king (or the Council) had gained control over the nomination of the Speaker, and had always had control of the nomination of the Lord Chancellor in the House of Lords. The clerks and all the permanent officers were royal appointments, and answerable to the man who appointed them. English Parliaments had no legal being between sessions, unlike some French estates, which had become recognized as corporations.[7] Men like the syndic of Agen or the *diputats* of Catalonia enjoyed a right to speak for estates in between sessions, and, which is perhaps more important, held a tenured office, which gave them a legal standing in between sessions. The contrast with members of the English House of Commons, whose privileged status expired 16 days after the day of dissolution, is painful. It underlines the point that the purpose of the 16 days was to allow members time to go home. Most continental estates had committees which remained in being during a recess, and many had control of collection of the taxes they voted, and access to their own independent funds: two vital resources the English Parliament conspicuously lacked.

It is interesting to look, with these limitations in mind, at the English crisis of 1640-2. Two of these limitations Pym succeeded in remedying. He succeeded in getting a committee to remain in session during the summer recess, and in his capacity as its chairman he issued orders which, according to one of his critics, lacked only the letter "R". He proposed, in the Ten Propositions, to appoint a committee charged with the enforcement of the Propositions between Parliaments.[8] In a little noticed procedural innovation, the first subsidy act of 1641 transferred control of collection of the subsidy from commissioners named under the Great Seal to commissioners named by Act of Parliament.[9] These innovations might have looked much less revolutionary on the continent than they did to some in England. On the other hand, he did not succeed in creating any person or body authorized to speak to the king on behalf of the House of Commons. Individual lords might visit the king with authority from the House, but there was no procedure for commoners to do so. The Speaker, whose job it had once been to speak to the king on behalf of the Commons, could not do the job effectively, because he was a royal nominee. When Pym went to see the king, he went as a private member, bearing no

[7] Major, *op. cit.*, p. 166.

[8] *C.S.P.D. 1641-3*, vol. ccccIxxxiv, no. 63: *L.J.* iv 287. Pym had made a similar proposal before, though the earlier one had not been for a specifically Parliamentary commission. *Commons' Debates in 1621*, ed. Wallace Notestein, F.H. Relf and Hartley Simpson, New Haven (1935) ii 464.

[9] *16 Car. I c. l.*

authority from the Commons. When the Commons as a whole wanted to negotiate with the king, they had to do so by means of written and published declarations. In the summer of 1642, the attempt to restore amity between king and Parliament by these public written declarations looks a bit like trying to mend a marriage by means of lawyers' letters. The influence which might have been exerted by officers like the Catalonian *diputats*, with power to speak to the king privately in the name of the assembly, could have been immense.

Money, the Root of All Evil?

If, then, we approach the evidence without any a priori assumptions about the specially "parliamentary" character of the English, we may look for common themes, and stand some chance of finding them. The most obvious common theme is the strain put on working partnerships between monarchies and estates by the continuous, growing, and apparently insatiable need of the monarchies for money.

As Sully put it, "My master placed me in office to increase his revenue, and not to deliver justice".[10] The note was one which any early seventeenth-century minister of finance would have recognized, though not all of them could afford to be so frank about it. Robert Cecil was making more or less the same point when he said in 1610: "I speak not by way of menace; for when it comes to that I shall be miserable. I do not say the King shall send you an Empson and a Dudley, but this I say, the King must not want".[11] In 1615, the president of the Spanish Council of Finance complained that "the spending of eight million ducats in a year is unheard of," only to find, at the end of the year, that expenses would clear nine million, "a figure of which there is neither record nor tradition." In 1618, the Spanish Council of Finance told Lerma that the sums of money he was trying to send to Germany and Italy simply did not exist, only to get a reply from the king in person: "These provisions are so vital that the Council of Finance must find them. Germany cannot possibly be abandoned".[12] However much monarchies might believe in ruling justly or legally, a need for money this intense was liable to take priority over all other needs, and therefore to be pursued in a potentially arbitrary spirit.

These royal needs for money are so constant across Europe that it is hard to blame them on the extravagance of any particular king. Moreover, the chronology of royal needs for money shows enough similarities to raise the question how far these extraordinary needs had common causes. It seems that in all three kingdoms, the kings who inherited the throne after the wars and the rapid inflation of the 1590s were faced with urgent

[10] Major, *op. cit.*, p. 380.
[11] Elizabeth Read Foster, *Proceedings in Parliament 1610*, New Haven (1966) ii 310.
[12] J.H. Elliot, *The Revolt of the Catalans*, Cambridge (1963), pp. 187-90.

pressure to consolidate their finances and increase their sources of income. Sully and Robert Cecil were, at least in part, working on the same treadmill. In 1618, when the monarchies were just beginning to get their heads above water again, the outbreak of the Thirty Years' War produced soaring demands for money. These created strains across Europe in the middle 1620s. The difficulties in the English Parliament of 1626, the Catalan Cortes of 1626, and the Sardinian Parliament of 1624-5 came so close together in date that it is reasonable to ascribe at least some of their difficulties to the wars which all of these assemblies were being asked to finance. In all three countries, these financial troubles appear to have risen to a peak around 1640. The revolts of Scotland, Ireland, Catalonia, and Portugal, all happening within a period of little over two years, raise the question how far the difficulties of the monarchies had pushed them into putting excessive pressure on their outlying kingdoms.

Moreover, these peaks in royal financial needs came at the same time as two periods of particular economic hardship. The exceptional inflation of the 1590s coincided with a long period of bad weather, in which it was almost literally true that "the rain it raineth every day". 1597, in particular, was a year of record grain prices and of numerous local outbreaks of famine. It was the wrong time to demand exceptionally large war taxes, and it is not surprising to find occasional complaints that the poor were selling their pots and pans to pay subsidies. In the 1620s, the connection between war and bad economic conditions is not coincidental. The depression of the 1620s was largely caused by currency manipulations which themselves were the result of the Thirty Years' War. In the 1620s, taxes were going up in a time of unemployment, unpaid rents, and general economic hardship. In Castile, Olivares was painfully aware that the burden on taxpayers was near the limit of what they could bear. In England, both Sir Edwin Sandys and John Winthrop were worrying about the prospect of a peasants' revolt on the level of the famous one in Germany.[13] It was a situation in which parliaments and estates were bound to think twice about sanctioning exceptional rates of taxation. Moreover, it was a period of physical shortage of coin. Not all excuses by taxpayers claiming they lacked the coin to pay taxes are necessarily credible. Yet when some taxpayers in Devon in 1627 offered to pay the Forced Loan in goods because they could not pay it in coin, it seems at least a reasonable hypothesis that they were facing a genuine difficulty.[14] England, France, and Spain all seem to have reached the top of the demographic curve between 1625 and 1640, and in all three countries the top of the curve was marked by epidemics and serious concern over the

[13] *1621 Debates*, iv 304: *Winthrop Papers*, Massachusetts Historical Society, Boston (1929) I 124.

[14] *Proceedings in Parliament 1628*, ed. Mary Frear Keeler, Maija Jannson Cole and William B. Bidwell, New Haven (1977-83) II 304, 310, 314.

food supply. It was the wrong time to have to feed armies.

Why were the monarchies' needs for money so large? Inflation is an obvious and correct answer, yet it does not appear to be sufficient. What appears to produce the greatest need for money is a rapid increase in the costs of war, and in the interest-paying debts wars left behind them. Since the Hundred Years' War, gunpowder and fortifications had changed the character of war considerably. In particular, the development of the bastion had led to long sieges and consequently to much longer campaigns. Yet in most countries, subjects' legal obligation had not changed to keep up with changing military necessities. In most countries, the obligation to feudal military service lasted for only forty days, a uselessly short time for a seventeenth-century campaign. Richelieu's attempts to raise an army by feudal tenures in 1635 and Charles I's in 1640 were failures[15] and in Catalonia it was doubtful whether even this military obligation existed unless the prince was present in person.[16] Moreover, firearms created a pressure for uniformity of equipment, lest, as the Duke of Somerset told Lord Russell, troops be supplied with "shot as fit as a shoe for a man's hand".[17] The proportion of costs of war which fell on the Crown for providing standard equipment, and not on the individual knight or soldier providing his own, rose considerably. The whole range of responsibilities covered by the Ordnance Office marks a trend which could be accurately described as "the socialization of war". In Spain, where this trend went farthest, it seems to have outstripped the state's administrative resources, and gone into reverse. The Spanish experience with *asiento* provides an interesting framework for the study of those in England who have been classified as "the concessionary interest".[18] In the period between 1588 and the 1620s, this trend was spreading from land warfare to naval warfare. The last war fought effectively with privately-owned ships, privately financed and making their profit from plunder, was the Armada campaign of 1588. From then on, steady increases in tonnage (whether militarily justified or not) led to increasing pressure for large fleets of permanent royal ships.[19]

Royal ships had to be financed out of taxation: they could not be financed out of a royal right to conscript privately-owned merchantmen. This was the dilemma which led Charles into such legal confusion in the Ship Money case. He was still entitled to conscript ships, which he did not

[15] G. Pagès, *La Guerre de Trente Ans*, Paris (1949) p. 207: *C.S.P.D. 1640* vol. cccclxiv, no. 9; S.P. 16/487/35.

[16] Elliot, *op. cit.*, pp. 206-7.

[17] Julian Cornwall, *The Revolt of the Peasantry 1549* (1977), p. 134.

[18] I.A. Thompson, *War and Government in Habsburg Spain, 1560-1620* (1976), pp. 256-287.

[19] On matters of piracy, I am indebted to the advice of Dr. David Hebb, whose work on Piracy and English Politics should soon be in print.

need to do, but not to tax to build a navy, which he did need to do. The Ship Money case nearly went wrong in court through the confusion created by Charles's pretence that all he was doing was conscripting privately-owned ships for a period of six months. This pretence was forced on him by the failure of his legal rights to keep pace with his naval needs.[20]

Perhaps the best symbolic example of the effect of changing military needs on law and property is the crying need of monarchies for saltpetre. Since saltpetre is normally found where there is human habitation, shortage of gunpowder put the saltpetre men under constant pressure to override property rights. In 1628, the English saltpetre men calmly justified digging under churches on the grounds that "the women piss in their seats, which causes excellent saltpetre".[21] It is not surprising that the House of Commons, hearing this story, was not impressed: they gave a much higher priority to property rights, and a much lower one to military necessity. They recognized the gunpowder shortage as real, and were quite capable of complaining about it, but they simply did not regard it as worth this sort of disruption. It was a straightforward clash of priorities.

It seems to be this clash of priorities which dominates the relations of monarchies and estates throughout this period. Monarchies were occupationally inclined to give priority to issues of defence and national security: those, after all, were the issues administrators found on their desks day after day. Under pressure, monarchies and their servants were liable to argue, like the Spanish Junta on Fortifications, that "no law can stand in the way of natural defence". They had no great objection to law, and strongly preferred to do things legally if possible. Yet when a legal right came into conflict with an urgent necessity of defence, they gave priority to the urgent necessity. When Olivares found that he could not get corn to an army defending Catalonia unless he paid for it on the spot, he exclaimed, "If the constitutions do not allow this, then the devil take the constitutions". The conditional clause is an essential part of this sentence. It is the same voice as Strafford's in 1640, threatening to hang some of the London aldermen who would not contribute to a war against the Scots. As Professor Elliott has said, "In both countries, the restrictions on royal authority which had been received from an earlier age prevented the Crown in a very different age from doing certain things that it considered administratively essential".[22]

Parliaments and estates, facing such vast administrative necessities, almost inevitably developed an occupational deafness to such arguments.

[20] See 'The Ship Money Judgements of Bramston and Davenport', above, pp. 137-44.

[21] *1628 Debates* I v 350. For another example of the constancy of military needs, see the complaints made by the Cortes of Castile in 1593, Thompson *op.cit.*, pp.211-2. If the references in this document to 'mules' and 'Moors' were altered to 'horses' and 'Scots', it would be easy to pass it off as an English document.

[22] Elliot, *op. cit.*, pp. 356, 118-9, 375.

If they once allowed that the king had to have money, on grounds of necessity, then the very principle of consent to taxation was put under threat; as Sir Francis Seymour put it, "If his Majesty be persuaded by any to take from his subjects what he will, and when it pleaseth him, I would gladly know what we have to give." Even where they recognized the royal needs, they tended to think that these needs did not override the liberties and privileges of their own communities. As Sir Robert Pheips said in 1628: "We have provoked two potent kings, the one too near . . . The dangers are not chimerical, but real. I acknowledge it, but it must be done in a true proportion of our dangers at home. I more fear the violation of public rights at home than a foreign enemy".[23] In bringing the king face to face with a more local scale of priorities than was to be found at court, representative assemblies were only doing their job. The king could be presumed to know about military necessities: what he did not know, unless someone told him, was the effect the satisfaction of these necessities might have on many of his subjects. The Sieur de Selves, syndic of Agen, is a man who seems to have in many ways resembled Sir Robert Phelps: they were not concerned with the pursuit of major consitutional objectives, but with the liberties, traditions, and privileges of their own communities.[24] When these were threatened by the pressure of war finance (or the payment of post-war debts), their reactions were essentially defensive.

The problem seems usually to have been not desire to withhold supply in order to secure redress of any particular grievance but sheer incomprehension of the sums needed. In the English Parliament of 1626, Secretary Coke made a long financial statement in the hope of explaining how much was needed, but the diarists who reported it filled in the noughts at random. In 1625, he told the Commons that the navy for that year had cost £200,000 and the figure was reported as "20,000".[25] Not all estates were as optimistic as those of Languedoc and Brittany, who asked in the 1590s for taxes to be reduced to the level of the reign of Louis XII.[26] Yet plenty of assemblies, like the English Parliament of 1624 or the Scottish Parliament of 1633, could pride themselves on voting more than had ever been voted before, while they were still not voting enough. Perhaps the most eloquent statement of incomprehension of royal financial demands comes from a deputy in the Catalan Cortes of 1626, reporting to his town council. He said the king was demanding:

> the horrific sum of £3,700,000 ducats – which, at 11 reals to a Castilian ducat, works out at 4,125,000 Barcelona lliures, which, as I understand and as can well be believed, would mean the total ruin and destruction of this kingdom

[23] *1628 Debates*, ii 56, 61.
[24] Major, *op. cit.*, pp. 282-8.
[25] Russell, *P.E.P.*, pp. 270, 236. the diarists' error is repeated in my book, and I am grateful to Professor Michael Young for drawing my attention to it.
[26] Major, *op. cit.*, pp. 214, 217.

> . . . They say that to raise this money, a tax of one thirtieth would be levied on all grains, vines, oils and other fruits for a period of fifteen years, so that all Catalonia would be desolated . . . So be brave and constant, for if we allow ourselves to be oppressed in this way, not only we but all our descendants in perpetuity will be slaves and captives. We want to please our king, as is only right and proper, but in such a way that we all stay alive, not being – as we are not – a conquered, but a free people, as we have made clear in all the offers we have made, and as can be found in the volumes of all the constitutions.

This, like the complaints of English members who feared the prospect of annual subsidies, is not the voice of men pursuing power, but of men trying to avoid power and the responsibilities that come with it. Professor Elliott is surely right that in these circumstances kings and estates were speaking two different languages.[27] They were not so much in opposition to each other, as like the proverbial parallel lines, which could never meet.[28]

A Clash of Priorities

Like other dialogues across a language barrier, the dialogues of kings and estates in the early seventeenth century tended to lead to misunderstandings. One of the reasons this happened was that royal need for money interfered with the process of bargaining and mutual concession which usually went with a grant of supply. This was not usually anything so crude as insistence on redress of grievance before supply. It was more a matter of cooperation and mutual willingness to oblige, the *servicio* and *merced* of Spanish thought, or the contribution and retribution of Robert Cecil's speeches. The monarchies could not take part in this sort of bargaining, for they needed every penny of the supply they were offered, and usually more as well. Moreover, supplies granted by estates often did not raise enough to make it worth royal concessions to get them. In the Irish Parliament of 1634, Wentworth was said to have met a petition for confirmation of the Graces by telling them that "they had more already than their six little subsidies were worth". In 1595, Henri IV told Matignon, "The time is not right to hold such assemblies, which ordinarily do more to free my subjects from expenses than to assist and aid me in my affairs, because no one now looks further than his individual welfare".[29]

Also, as grants of supply got bigger, many estates, especially in the Crown of Aragon, spaced them out over more years: the subsidy voted by the Cortes of Valencia in 1604 was still being collected 21 years later. In

[27] Elliot, *op. cit.*, pp. 237, 236, 119-20.

[28] Andrew Marvell's image of the lines which, though truly parallel, could never meet, was anticipated by Sir Richard Weston in the Parliament of 1625. Russell, *P.E.P.*, p. 244.

[29] Aidan Clarke, *The Old English in Ireland* (1966), p. 88: Major, *op. cit.*, p. 267.

England, the long-running grant of four subsidies in 1601 prevented any further grant of supply in 1604.[30] By making their grants so long, many estates ensured that their meetings would be less frequent, and so underlined the point that in times of great financial necessity, it was likely to be the Crown, and not the estates, which was the champion of frequent meetings. Members were often aware of the risk of pressing the people beyond their ability, and when Sir Edward Coke, in 1625, objected to a poll tax on the ground that the last had caused a peasants' revolt, it is unlikely that he was just indulging in antiquarianism.[31] Members had duties to those they represented, and the idea that their duty and their loyalty might come into conflict was one they found uncongenial.

To kings, it all seemed rather different. It became an increasingly urgent question whether this much time, and this much fuss, were worth spending in order to get so little money. In particular, the pressure caused by estates on royal and conciliar time caused more and more irritation in official circles. The classic case is Philip IV's disruption of the Catalan Cortes of 1626, by setting an arbitrary date for his departure. In 1621, announcing the summer recess, James I made a more reasonable case: he pointed out that the two terms, the judges and the Privy Council had been in constant attendance on Parliament, and therefore unable to give time to other business. Moreover, the presence of so many justices of the peace and deputy lieutenants at Westminster had led to "the interruption of government in the country".[32] In 1626 and 1628, the haste arose from the progress of the campaigning season, in the end becoming so undignified that Hakewill was provoked to ask whether the King would prefer five subsidies on Monday or four on Friday.[33] Yet, when delay could mean the loss of a whole campaigning season, such haste was intelligible. It did not make serious give and take in parliaments very easy. To kings in a hurry, concern with issues of law and privileges when the safety of the kingdom was at stake could look like pettifogging. As Olivares complained, "We always have to look and see if a constitution says this or that. We have to discover what the customary usage is, even when it is a question of the supreme law, the actual defence and preservation of the province – really, Sir, the Catalans ought to see more of the world than Catalonia".[34]

Facing this sort of royal impatience, it seemed that estates could not win. If they were, as kings saw it, "responsible", they reduced consent to a

[30] *Letters of Sir Francis Hastings*, ed. M. Claire Cross, Somerset Record Society, vol. 69, Frome (1969), pp. 85-6. It is interesting that Hastings, having given this very discouraging reply to the suggestion that he should speak in favour of a subsidy, nevertheless did so. *C.J.* i 242a, 995.

[31] Russell, *P.E.P.*, p. 245.

[32] *1621 Debates*, iv 383, ii 3.

[33] Russell, *P.E.P.*, p. 245.

[34] Elliot, *op. cit.*, pp. 400-1.

rubber stamp and weakened their relations with those they represented. If they were not "responsible", the king simply lost any incentive to call them. The Cortes of the Crown of Aragon, in particular, seemed to illustrate that the more independent estates were, the less the king called them. In Naples in 1643, after two parliaments had objected to the size of the taxes demanded, the viceroy reported that the assembly damaged the public peace and the king's service. It was not called again.[35] This was all too common a story.

It would be a mistake to think that kings did this sort of thing out of attachment to a theory called "absoloutism". No king wanted it said that he had no respect for the law or that his people did not love him. With the ghosts of Mariana and Ravaillac in the background, no king wanted to be typecast as a tyrant. Even in 1641, Olivares did not want to abolish the constitutions of Catalonia, but only those which impeded good government and the billeting of an army. Apart from the fact that tyranny implied a failure in kingcraft, it seems doubtful, looking at the variety of meanings of the word "absolute" in the seventeenth century, whether kings could believe in "absolute monarchy" before historians had invented it.[36] Professor Major, commenting on Henri IV's dealings with the estates of Brittany in 1593, says, "Clearly, Henri's goal was to obtain money to carry on the war, not to establish an absolutist regime".[37] The same would be said of Charles I's levying of the Forced Loan in 1627. Charles had an attachment to the rule of law, yet he believed that the law must be compatible with his obligation to defend his kingdom. In fact it was not, but it should cause little surprise that both kings and estates avoided so stark a choice whenever they possibly could. Kings who dispensed with estates did not do so because estates were bad; they did so because being able to defend their kingdoms was good. It was the usual argument which gives priority to national security over laws and liberties. Those who use this argument are not against laws and liberties; they just think national security comes first.

These royal difficulties seem to have come to a head all over Europe in the years 1625-1640. Yet their origins lie many years further back. The escalating cost of warfare, because of firearms, the development of the bastion, and other things, was a sixteenth-century problem. If it is a correct explanation of royal difficulties, why should its effects have caught up with monarchies about a hundred years later? It seems that, faced with exceptional demands, monarchies could, for a while, increase revenue, borrow money, sell lands, or otherwise live off their fat. In France

[35] H.G. Koenigsberger, 'The Italian Parliaments from their Origins to the End of the Eighteenth Century', *Journal of Italian History*, vol.1 (1978), pp. 18-49.

[36] J.W. Daly, 'The Idea of Absolute Monarchy in Seventeenth Century England', *H.J.* vol. 21 (1978), pp. 227-50.

[37] Major, *op. cit.*, p. 224.

increased taxes, in Spain silver from the Indies, and in England the dissolution of the monasteries put off by at least a couple of generations the evil day when the monarchy would have to come to terms with the limitations of its resources. Moreover, rising costs of war were cumulative: new weapons were invented, so that by 1621, obligations to produce weapons specified in the English statute of 1557 were already obsolete. A bill for provision of arms "according to the modern form" ran into trouble in the House of Commons, largely because of the expense it entailed. The growth of navies also meant that expenses continued to grow. All three monarchies borrowed heavily for the wars of 1585-1604. All three placed severe pressure on taxpayers in the course of trying to clear these debts. All three therefore faced the beginning of the Thirty Years' War having already strained their financial systems a good deal more than was wise. It is during the Thirty Years' War that their relations with their estates seem to have approached the point of collapse. A war of this duration was likely to underline the central weakness: the use of occasional assemblies to supply taxes that were now needed regularly was no longer a satisfactory system. Estates had developed to finance short campaigns. If they were to finance long ones, they would have to become semipermanent. There were social, as well as intellectual, obstacles in the way of such a development.[38]

The period 1620-40 was also one of trouble in the relations between different parts of multiple monarchies in all three countries. Here the flashpoints were war and religion, yet in the period before the Peace of Westphalia it is impossible to separate the two entirely. Religious dissidents were dangerous partly because they provided the enemy with an opportunity for indirect aggression, and thus defence, as well as piety, provided a motive for imposing religious uniformity on outlying kingdoms.

One does not normally think of France as a multiple monarchy, yet there is one small case in which it faced the problems of one. In this case it is instructive to find that Louis XIII behaved exactly like Charles I in Scotland. This is the case of Béarn, which was part of the kingdom of Navarre, and in which Protestantism had been legally established. Louis decided that it was intolerable to rule over one Protestant and one Catholic kingdom, and marched south to conquer Béarn, at a cost the Estates of Languedoc estimated at nine million livres.[39]

The English and the Spaniards were not so lucky; their outlying kingdoms were a great deal bigger, and a great deal harder to suppress. The locus classicus of this story is the Spanish monarchy. Here, the trouble seems to arise from the cost of war. It was the strain of war on the

[38] Cecil's Great Contract of 1610 is the only attempt to bridge this gap of which I am aware, and it was too novel to be successful.

[39] Major, *op. cit.*, pp. 449, 474.

taxpayers of Castile which drove Olivares, through the Union of Arms and the ideas connected with it, to put more and more pressure on the outlying kingdoms. The story ended, at the crisis of the Thirty Years' War, with the revolts of Catalonia, Portugal, Naples, and Sicily.

What is not so widely appreciated is that the same problems, caused by the same wars, created similar problems in the British Isles. In 1627, Secretary Coke proposed that the English should copy the Union of Arms.[40] Nothing so definite happened, but Anglo-Irish relations during the years 1626-8 illustrate the process which led Coke to think of a Union of Arms. Charles's decision to make war on Spain, in 1625, raised the problem of the defence of Ireland. There were two rival approaches to this problem, that of the Irish and English Privy Councils. The Irish Privy Council assumed that the army was there to defend them against Catholics, and therefore that arming large numbers of Catholics was contrary to the object of the exercise. The English Privy Council, on the other hand, favoured a scheme to win the loyalty of the Catholic Old English by concessions. In return, they were to pay for and organize an army capable of defending Ireland against foreign invasion. These negotiations concluded in the grant of a substantial set of concessions called the Graces, in return for a payment of £40,000 a year for three years and more "from time to time". By the time this agreement with the Old English was concluded, the war was ending, so the Graces were never confirmed.[41] Having raised the expectations of the Old English, the government reverted to the policy of the Irish Protestants, of treating them as people of doubtful loyalty. The whole thrust of English policy in Ireland under Wentworth was towards the tightening of English control. This story ended when the Old English joined with the native Irish in the rebellion of 1641. Ireland is another case where centralizing pressure, begun in response to the needs of a war, ended in the rebellion of an outlying kingdom.

Points of Difference

So far, this discussion has concentrated on the similarities among England, France, and Spain. An article which left the matter there, though true, could be seriously misleading. It is necessary to touch, however cursorily, on some of the differences. The English Parliament was highly unusual among European estates in that it was a national assembly and consequently enjoyed a hold on public and patriotic sentiment that many European estates would not enjoy. In France, most estates were provincial – not estates general, but estates particular. As the monarchy grew more self-assertive, it grew easier to hold their

[40] S.P. 16/527/44.
[41] Aidan Clarke, *op. cit.*, pp. 28-43.

particularity against them. In the Spanish monarchy, what constituted a nation was an uncomfortably moot point. I know no European equivalent of Sir Edwin Sandy's speech of 1607, in which he discussed what constituted *unus grex*, one people, and said, "It is not *unus grex* until the whole do join in making laws to govern the whole; for it is fit and just, that every man do join in making that which shall bind and govern him, and because every man cannot be personally present, therefore a representative body is made to perform that service".[42] A nation is a body which has one parliament. Yet though this sentiment might strengthen parliaments within England, it only made the British problem, on which Sandys happened to be speaking, even more acute.

Sandy's speech also illustrates the strength the English Parliament had as the source of a uniform national system of law. The firmness of its hold on the legislative function seems, in Europe, to be paralleled only in Catalonia. Under James I and Charles I, this hold on legislative power was not of urgent importance, since there was very little desire for new laws. Yet it gave parliaments a fixed place in English legal thought, which would have taken a long time to eradicate.

It seems clear that the differences between the English polity and the polities of France and Spain, which became increasingly obvious after 1689, cannot be said to be caused by the procedural strength of English parliaments. The complete absence of a parliament during the key year of 1688 will serve to underline the point. Yet, for those who are unhappy at ascribing the differences between eighteenth-century England and eighteenth-century France or Spain to the success of William III's military gamble in 1688, it is possible to find institutional peculiarities which explain the extent to which eighteenth-century England was a self-governing country. These peculiarities should be sought, not in English parliamentary history, but in English local government.[43] One is the question, to which Professor Major has drawn our attention, of control over the collection of taxation. This appears to have been as vital as consent to its levying. In France, the choice is between tax-collection machinery controlled by the provincial estates and *élus* appointed by the king and answerable to him. In France, central and local control of collection can be seen as alternatives. In England, everything seems to be undistributed, and probably undistributable, middle. With the exception of the customs (which accounted for most of the Stuarts' successes in unparliamentary taxation), English tax collection was more or less immutably under the control of the justices of the peace in one capacity or another. Dispensing with parliaments did not very much increase the king

[42] *The Parliamentary Diary of Robert Bowyer 1606-1607*, ed. D.H. Wilson, Minneapolis (1931), pp. 258-9, 265n.

[43] J.S. Brewer and John Styles, *An Ungovernable People: The English and their Law in the Seventeenth and Eighteenth Centuries* (1980), pp. 11-21.

of England's freedom of manoeuvre, since his dependence on the justices of the peace was unalterable.

The relations of the king with the justices of the peace seem to have involved an interdependence so total that it amounted to a mutual stranglehold. They held office by royal appointment and could be dismissed at the king's pleasure. Yet the king's business would not be done unless he appointed men whose standing in their local communities was sufficient to ensure obedience. JPs who served the king too zealously lost their local standing and therefore their power to compel obedience. JPs who did not serve him zealously enough were dismissed. Until the creation of Pym's excise, England conspicuously lacked a sales tax of the sort which was the mainstay of many continental finances. Without such a tax, the English depended on taxes on land, which had to be levied by those who knew where the land was, and what it was worth. It is in this area, from the justice of the peace down to the parish constable, that English self-government was peculiarly strong. The paradox is that this level, the one on which French representative institutions were peculiarly strong, was one on which the English had no representative institutions at all, unless we count those parishes which genuinely elected their constable. The strength of English self-government depended on justices of the peace, who were appointed by the Crown. Quarter Sessions might on occasion set itself up as the representative body of its county, but it enjoyed no elective claim to do so. Self-government and representative instititions are not necessarily synonymous.

The other peculiarity of England, which in a period of frequent wars was peculiarly important, was its literal and metaphorical insularity. This is why the English were able to enjoy an undercurrent of resistance to war and to the militarization of the country, which other countries may have coveted but could not share. It is interesting to wonder how many English taxpayers felt as little involvement in their government's wars as the Kentish yeoman in the 1590s who complained that "the Spaniards be long a-coming, and I would they were come". In France or Spain, a man who talked that way would have run much more risk of being taken at his word. When they lost wars, the enemy did come into the kingdom, and the military effort had to continue. When the English lost a war, they could in Sir Robert Phelips' phrase, "like the tortoise, withdraw themselves into their own shell".[44] There was only one enemy from whom the English could not retreat in this fashion. That enemy was Scotland. One defeat by Scotland started a train of events which forced the English to prepare an effective war. Like the Dutch, they learnt to fight an effective war by doing it against their own king.

[44] Peter Clark, *English Provincial Society from the Reformation to the Revolution: Politics, Religion and Society in Kent 1500-1640*, Hassocks (1977), p. 277: Russell, *P.E.P.*, p. 84.

The difficulties caused by the rising costs of warfare seem to have been common to most of the countries of Europe. Yet in most countries, the upheavals caused when they came to a head proved manageable. There were only two countries where these financial and administrative problems came to a head at the same time as the other main difficulty of the period, the collapse of royal attempts to impose uniformity of religion. In those two countries, the resulting dislocation was considerable. Those countries were England and the Netherlands.

8

The Ship Money Judgements of Bramston and Davenport

MUCH has been written on the Ship Money trial, but very little on the judgments of Bramston and Davenport.[1] The extremist utterances of Sir Robert Berkeley and Sir George Croke have been thoroughly discussed, but the cool and dispassionate judgments of the chief justice of the King's Bench and the chief baron of the Exchequer have been almost ignored. In Gardiner's *History* they have half a sentence between them : the bare statement that they 'placed themselves for technical reasons' on Hampden's side'.[2] In Sir David Lindsay Keir's article in the *Law Quarterly Review* for 1936, they receive a little more attention, but they still appear to him to have shirked the main issue : the chief justice appears under the title of 'the temporizing Bramston'. He asserts, indeed, that 'nine of the twelve judges had no doubt that Ship Money was a legitimate charge on the subject'. Whether we accept this as true must depend on our view of what 'Ship Money' was, and this was one of the main points of difference in the trial. 'And now', wrote Henry Parker in 1640, 'all our controversy ends in this, whether the Ship Money be a pecuniary or a personal charge. For though the intent of the writ, and the office of the sheriff, be to raise moneys only, yet the words of the writ, and the pretence of state, is to build and prepare ships of war. The kingdom generally takes this to be a mere delusion and imposture, and doubtless it is but a picklock trick, to overthrow all liberty and propriety of goods, and it is a great shame that so many judges should be abettors to

1 I would like to express my gratitude to Mr. J. L. Barton for the benefit of his legal knowledge.

2 *History of England*, viii. 279.

such fraudulent practice contrived against the state.'[3] From this stricture Bramston and Davenport should be exempted.

The king's ostensible case rested heavily upon the claim that he was raising, not money, but a ship. The power of defence was in the king, and it was commonly recognized that he had the power to command services for this purpose. The case advanced for the Crown in court had nothing to do with taxation : it simply involved the claim that for urgent cases of defence, the king might claim naval service, and levy money towards it from those who were unable to serve in person. The words of the second extrajudicial opinion were that in time of danger 'your Majesty may, by writ under the Great Seal of England, command all the subjects of your kingdom, at their charge, to provide and furnish *ships*'. And the words of the first writ, the 4 Augusti, were : 'we command you, firmly enjoining you, in the faith and allegiance wherein you are bound to us, and as you do love and honour us, that you cause to be prepared and brought to the port of Portsmouth before the first day of March now next ensuing, *one ship of war*'. There is nothing in the record of any levy of funds for the general upkeep of the navy ; if the terms of the writ were to be executed, there would have to be an actual Buckinghamshire ship, built (or hired, as Finch suggested[4]), and taken to Portsmouth for actual service, with the implication that it would be employed on an actual campaign. This ostensible case for the Crown was very hard to answer, for the precedents proved beyond all doubt that in time of danger the king might command service for the defence of the realm : Elizabeth, impounding the merchant fleet in 1588, had done no less. To object statutes against unparliamentary taxation in reply to this case

[3] *The Case of Shipmoney Briefly Discoursed* (1640), p. 40. This pamphlet is an interesting contrast to that of Prynne, who begged the whole question by entitling his pamphlet *A Humble Remonstrance Against the Tax of Ship Money*.

[4] Cobbett's *State Trials*, iii. 1224. This in reply to the maxim quoted by Croke : 'lex non cogit ad impossibilia.' Finch states the issue as clearly as anyone : 'my brother Hutton and my brother Croke would have it to be raising of money by reason of the clause in the writ for the distribution of the surplusage, but the record is "ad assidend" omnes homines et ad contribuendum navem vel partem navis non habentes, etc.', which shows it cannot be for money. Neither is there any colour for money, for it is to find a ship.' In Finch's judgment there is also some indication of how the Crown attempted to square this claim with its actual practice : 'the words are but "parare" ; not for the building, but preparing a ship : and it was not meant they should build it there, but that they should contribute to the building of a ship in the most fit and convenient place.'

was nothing to the point.

On this fact the king's counsel and the judges who judged for him leant very heavily during the trial. All of them (except perhaps Trevor and Vernon, whose opinions are too brief for proper analysis) argued for the Crown on the assumption that Ship Money was a service and not a tax.[5] The most explicit statements to this effect are from Weston and Berkeley. Weston, answering St. John's objection that if the case were decided for the king, all property would be in his mercy, declared ; 'there is no such fear, for the writ is expressly to raise a ship. There appears no money in this case to be coming into his Majesty's hands '.[6] It was Sir Robert Berkeley, the extremist, who said : 'it is to be observed that the principal command in the shipping writ is not to levy money, it is to provide a ship. It is not a debt, vi termini, but rather a duty to be performed, as a means conducing to the principal end.'[7]

Neither St. John nor Holborne, neither Hutton nor Croke, ever properly answered this case. The case they answered was a case for unparliamentary taxation, and they relied upon the great statutes against unparliamentary taxation : 'but there is a law saith, he shall not tax his subjects without consent in Parliament '.[8] None of them, except Hutton,[9] spent any energy trying to *prove* that Ship Money was a tax ; they simply assumed it. And it was the great objection to the Crown's arguments, not precisely that they were bad law, but that they rested on a false statement of the case, and so were irrelevant. The money, it is true, was used for naval purposes, but this was not the test which seemed important to the judges at the time. The test was whether it were paid into the central funds, whether it went into the king's coffers. It is one of the interesting points in the financial attitudes of the period that any money paid

[5] See, for example, Littleton, *State Trials*, iii. 951, and Bankes, *ibid.* 1015 and 1029–32. Of those who argued at any length for the king, the only exception appears to be Crawley, who actually listed among the royal prerogatives : 'to impose taxes without common consent in Parliament.' Admittedly this is only a doctrine of emergency (justified out of Bodin), but even so Crawley here accepted something to which neither Finch nor Berkeley ever committed himself. *State Trials*, iii. 1083–4.

[6] *Ibid.* iii. 1075.

[7] *Ibid.* iii. 1095. For Jones on this point see *infra*.

[8] Holborne, *State Trials*, iii. 1013.

[9] Rushworth, *Historical Collections*. II, pt. ii, Appendix p. 171. Davenport's central point is also touched very briefly in Sir George Croke's concluding paragraph.

into central funds, for whatever purpose, was regarded as being for the king's own use.[10] And the money was paid into central funds: it was paid to the treasurer of the Navy. It was spent on the navy, but it was spent as a general levy for naval upkeep, and not for the discharging of a specific service in a specific emergency. This, in the first place, was contrary to the terms of the writ; there had been no command to pay money to London for the maintenance of the Navy; there had been a command to bring one ship of war to Portsmouth. No attempt to execute the terms of the Ship Money writ was ever made, save in the single case of the City of London.[11] If the money was paid into central funds, it was a tax, and the fact that it was a tax was the fact which had to be established before judgment could be given to Hampden.

It is to this point that Bramston and Davenport, and only Bramston and Davenport, addressed themselves. They had, it is true, the last sentence of the judgment of Jones as a starting point: 'that Mr. Hampden shall be charged with the 20s. with this limitation and condition, that none of it comes to the King's purse, for if it do, my opinion is against it.' Davenport followed immediately after this argument, and followed it up in point of logic. First he commented upon the failure to observe the terms of the writ: 'the next thing upon the Sci' Fac'; the question upon this record is, whether this doth appertain to the king. My reason is this, because in the very writ 4 Augusti it is expressly provided that it shall be employed to no other use, but the preparation of the ship therein mentioned, and by no means to any other purpose. It doth not now appear, who were the collectors therein appointed to receive the money, whereby to become chargeable over to the king. It doth not appear upon this record, that any ship was provided, or that any fault was in them that were employed, or surplusage in the collectors' hands: though it was a worthy and gracious act

[10] For extreme example of this view, see *Parliamentary Debates in 1610*, Camden Society, first series, no. lxxi(1862), p. 9. For the use of the phrase 'the king's coffers' to cover all government financial departments, *ibid.* pp. 57, 175, 177. For a contrary use by Finch, see Rushworth, *Historical Collections*, iii, 1138.

[11] Miss M. D. Gordon, 'The Collection of Ship Money in the Reign of Charles I', *Transactions of the Royal Historical Society*, 3rd. series, iv (1910). Except in 1635, London built its own ships, which was done far more cheaply than the king could do it. It seems clear that the City of London ships were *not* permanently added to the royal navy, but used for a temporary period of service, see *Cal. S.P. Dom. 1639*, p. 417/110.

in his Majesty, yet this is not so legally executed, as the king may have a writ of Sci' Fa'.'[12] The best answer Finch could make to this objection was the claim that though a ship had been prepared, if it had not been prepared, it would have been because contributions had not been paid. In fact, out of £199,700 to be raised by the 1635 writs, £194,864 had been levied and paid to the treasurer of the Navy, and, despite a clause in the 4 Augusti that any money not spent on the ship was to be returned to the contributors, £23,323 was paid over to the exchequer.[13] From Davenport's objection about the lack of a collector who should be responsible for providing 'the ship', arose a further question: if judgment were given in the king's favour, how should it be executed? 'Nothing is put into the record to bring this to the king', said Davenport (indeed, it was the heart of the king's ostensible case that it was *not* to be brought to him). 'If judgment be for the king, it must be with this limitation and condition, that it shall not go into the proper coffer of the king, as my brother Jones observed. And in my conscience, if it were paid to him, he would be a loser by it.'

Here the king was caught in a procedural tangle made inevitable by his own dishonesty. He wanted the money for himself, and so was obliged to use a form of procedure which would bring it to himself. The writ of Scire Facias, which the king used, could be used for levying debts, but it could not be used for levying debts due to someone else; if judgment on this writ were given for the king, the money could not be paid to anyone but the king. But the king had left out of his case any statement, or even any other implication, that the money was to come to him. Thus, if judgment were given for the king, it was impossible to see how it should be executed, impossible to see to whom the money should be paid. Davenport, later re-echoed by Bramston, exposed this flaw with an accuracy which was merciless. 'Whom Mr. Hampden should satisfy, or to whom the money should be paid, non constat, as was well opened upon the demurrer; for it is not "si dominus rex valet aut debeat onerare", but that the defendant "oneretur et inde

[12] *State Trials*, iii. 1212–16.

[13] Gordon, *ubi supra*. This was the only year in which money was paid from the Ship Money fund to the exchequer: in other years the fund had to be supplemented out of the exchequer.

satisfac' ". Nothing is put into the record to bring this to the king, therefore " quod oneretur " cannot be executed at all ; and according to the books of 39 Edw. 3 and 49 Edw. 3, if judgment is to be given, and it cannot be executed, there it shall not be given at all. . . . Therefore to give judgment " quod oneretur ", and not to know to whom (for to the king it cannot) would be wrong ; therefore I cannot see how judgment can be given, " quod oneretur ".' 'Truly,' said Sir John Bramston in the last minutes of the trial, 'of all the exceptions I have heard, none sticketh with me but this exception.'[14] It destroyed the whole of the king's case : it established that there was nobody to whom the money could be paid but the king. And if it were paid to the king, it was a tax. If it was a tax, from this there followed the whole of Hampden's case, all the statutes against unparliamentary taxation, culminating in Hutton's thunderous conclusion : 'the people of England are subjects, not slaves ; freemen not villeins ; and are not to be taxed de alto et basso and at will, but according to the laws of this kingdom.'[15] That Bramston and Davenport did not say these words is not important. They, and they alone, had established the essential premise from which these words followed as night follows day ; they alone had shown that they were relevant to the case. That they accepted the king's ostensible case merely shows that they kept a cooler head than Hutton or Croke ; it takes nothing away from the force of their judgment for Hampden.

Their coolness also saved them from some of the legal extravagances of Holborne : the case put to the court, said Bramston, 'is not against the great laws on the subjects' liberties, because it is not a tallage, but a service'.[16] Sir Robert Berkeley was right when he said that if this ostensible case were settled against the king, 'salus populi will be clean out of the law' : the prerogative would practically abolished. But so was St. John right, when he said that if the actual case were settled for the king, 'if the subject hath anything left to him, he is not beholding to the law for it, but it is left entirely to the goodness and mercy of the king' : the

[14] *State Trials*, iii. 1250.

[15] Rushworth, *Historical Collections*, II, pt. ii. Appendix p. 176. The most interesting fact about these words is that they had been used on the other side by Sir Robert Berkeley (*State Trials*, iii. 1090), as part of his contention that Ship Money was not a tax, and Hutton is here using them as a quotation.

[16] *State Trials*, iii. 1249.

force of statute law would be practically abolished. This fear that a judgment either way would wreck the balance of the constitution was one which was painfully present to the judges during the trial ; most of them lamented that it was the hardest case that had ever come before them. And from these extravagances on one side or the other, Bramston and Davenport, by the accuracy of mind they succeeded in bringing to the case, were able to escape. Berkeley's law, if accepted, would split the kingdom down the middle ; so, if accepted, would St. John's claims to the unalterable supremacy of statute : but Bramston's and Davenport's law would not. Bramston, apart from the distinction of being twice a reader in the Middle Temple before he was a serjeant, had been defending counsel for Bristol on impeachment, for Darnel in 1627, and for Sir John Eliot in 1629, and it is interesting that the Parliament in the Treaty of Uxbridge, and later Oliver Cromwell, wanted to restore him to his post of chief justice (a preferment he was not willing to accept). There is no need to doubt his son's statement that the ground of his judgment and Davenport's was 'that the king might command the service, but he could not receive the money' :[17] and there is no need to doubt that it was good law.

There are many other good things in these judgments, which I shall not treat at length. Unlike Sir George Croke, they refrained from kicking against the prick of the fact that the assertions of the king's writ were not traversable, but they succeeded in exposing the dishonesty of the king's claim to emergency simply by demonstrating that he had not stated the actual existence of an emergency in his writ.[18] But this is an argument they shared with many others, and there is no need to elaborate upon it. Davenport also had

[17] *Autobiography of Sir John Bramston*, Camden Society, first series, no. xxxii (1845), p. 80. This is not an altogether reliable account, being written by Bramston's son in his extreme Royalist old age under the Restoration : for example, in a long eulogy of his father's legal career, he never once mentions that he was counsel for Darnel. But for this very reason, his statements on the extent of his father's opposition to the king over Ship Money are unlikely to be exaggerated.

[18] These arguments shed some interesting light on an exchange between St. John and Littleton. St. John had claimed that the king already had provision by tenures, by tonnage and poundage, and from the Cinque Ports, which were adequate for the defence of the sea. Littleton replied that all these were for the preservation of merchants, and that the king might levy more for an emergency. But, as Bramston and Davenport pointed out, the preservation of merchants was the one and only specific aim mentioned in the writ.

many other points, of great interest in themselves, but not of such far-reaching implications as the two above. The assessment at the sheriff's will and pleasure, he said, was arbitrary and illegal. The first writ, the 4 Augusti, was not returnable, and had not been revived by the mittimus, which followed a year and a half later. Instead of sending the record itself, the king had only sent the tenor of the record. Now the king had chosen to proceed by Scire Facias, 'and so it is, Dyer 4 and 5, and 22, clearly held by the court, that upon the tenor of a record, no Sci' Fa' could lie'. If it could, there could be two executions on one judgment. The main general conclusion from these points is that the king had much cause to regret the death of Attorney General Noy.

One thing more must be said. Jones had declared that if the money went into the king's coffers, his opinion was against it, and if he had examined the record as carefully as Bramston and Davenport had done, he should have judged as they did. If he had done so, the court would have been divided 6–6. There was no procedure for a casting vote, and the normal procedure in such cases was to go on adjourning the case until the parties settled out of court. In the Hampden case, this is a prospect on which there is no need to elaborate.

9

The Wardship of John Pym

'As Athene from the brain of Zeus, so Pym might seem to spring full panoplied at 37 years into the Parliament of 1621'. Other historians have used less eloquent language than C. E. Wade, but there has been general agreement in lamenting our lack of non-political information about John Pym. The only attempt to investigate his private life, by S. Reed Brett, produced very little information, and some of that is inaccurate.[1]

Fortunately for historians, the Pym family was unlucky in the matter of wardship, and the wardship of John Pym, in 1585, was the third in the family during the century. It is thus possible to compare the information on the Pym estates, and on the Crown's dealings with them, which arises from the wardship of John Pym, with that which arises from earlier Pym wardships. It appears that from 1505 to 1579, when John Pym's grandfather Erasmus died, the list of the family's properties was reasonably constant. The manor of Exton and Haukrege was sold but there are no other significant changes. One manor, that of Stone in the parishes of Sidbury and Sidmouth, was in Devon. It was successfully suppressed at the 1505 *Inquisition Post Mortem,* but was the subject of a separate Inquisition in 1530, when it was valued at £18. In 1574, Erasmus Pym sold it to his eldest son Alexander 'of the Middle Temple' for £400, 'provided that the said Erasmus shall not without

1 C. E. Wade, *John Pym* (1912), p. 16. J. H. Hexter lamented our lack of any data on the personal life of Pym (*The Reign of King Pym,* Cambridge, Mass., 1941, p. 193). A. P. Newton said that 'Of those who have exercised a commanding influence on English history, there is perhaps no one whose career had been less studied than Pym's' (*The Colonizing Activities of the English Puritans,* New Haven, 1914, p. 71). S. Reed Brett, *John Pym* (1940). I would like to thank Mr. Andreas Mayor for drawing my attention to the documents which led me to start this investigation, and Professor J. Hurstfield for the benefit of his knowledge of the records and procedure of the Elizabethan Court of Wards.

his free consent be compelled to travel out of the county of Somerset'.[2] At some time after this date it was sold, and in 1627 it was in the hands of the Colleses of Pitminster.[3] There is no evidence that John Pym ever owned it.

The remaining properties were all in Somerset, and there are four *Inquisitions Post Mortem* on them during the sixteenth century.[4] Inaccurate though Inquisition valuations may be, they do not support S. Reed Brett's claim that 'the Pyms were among the great landowners of the west country'.[5] The lands were valued at £26 3s. in 1505 and at £22 1s. 8d. in 1529. In 1579, on the death of John's grandfather Erasmus, the total was increased by the inclusion of the manor of Langham and Poole, successfully suppressed at the two previous inquisitions,[6] and valued at £11 1s. With this inclusion, the total valuation amounts to £48 3s. 6d. *per annum.* This total included former chantry lands in Cutcombe valued at £4 15s. 8d. but the general impression is of a family whom the Dissolution had passed by. They had acquired no former monastic estates, and had no impropriations, advowsons, leases or other ecclesiastical perquisites. They had, moreover, seen the Rogerses and the Colleses, two families who did benefit from the Dissolution, advanced above them in their own parish of Cannington. Their manor of Cannington, being no longer the chief manor in the parish, had its name changed to the manor of Brymore. Erasmus Pym appears not to have been a J.P., and though he was on the commission of sewers, he was not a member of the quorum.[7] So far from being among the great landowners of the west country, the Tudor Pyms can only be classified as minor gentry.

2 S[omerset] R[ecord] O[ffice], DD/BW, Pym MSS. no. 95. These MSS., recently deposited in the Somerset Record Office, represent the surviving nucleus of the collection formerly in the possession of Mr. Philip Pleydell Bouverie, part of which was calendared by the Historical Manuscripts Commission. *Tenth Report* 6, pp. 82–89. I would like to thank Mr. D. Shorrocks, of the Somerset Record Office, for drawing my attention to these MSS.

3 M. J. Hawkins, *Sales of Wards in Somerset,* Somerset Record Society, vol. 67 (1967), p. 96. P[ublic] R[ecord] O[ffice], C.142/48/46.

4 *Calendar of Inquisitions Post Mortem* 13–20 Henry VII, no. 930 (on the death of Alexander Pym I, 1505): P.R.O., C. 12/46/115 (Reginald Pym d. 1529). P.R.O., C. 142/187/61 (Erasmus Pym, d. 1579). P.R.O., C. 142/206/20 (Alexander Pym II, d. 1585).

5 S. Reed Brett, *op. cit.* p. xxvi.

6 J. Collinson, *History of Somerset* (Taunton, 1791), ii. 25.

7 Erasmus Pym is not listed in Brit. Mus., Lansdowne MS. 1218 (*Liber Pacis I* Eliz.), nor in Brit. Mus. Egerton MS. 2345 (*Liber Pacis 16* Eliz). For the commission of sewers, *Calendar of Patent Rolls, Elizabeth,* vol. v, nos. 1849 and 1853.

The recurrence of wardships may be one reason for their failure to advance beyond this status. The fact that Erasmus Pym was a minor almost throughout the 1530s may help to explain the Pyms' failure to benefit from the dissolution of the monasteries,[8] and the wardship which arose on the death of Alexander Pym, in 1505, was exploited with enough efficiency to have put a considerable strain on the estate. Alexander Pym had been out with Perkin Warbeck, and could not expect favourable treatment for his heir.[7] He did not get it: Henry VII, faced with a four-years' wardship, decided to keep the wardship in his own hand, and got approximately £50 a year out of the estate.[9] The widow, moreover, was still enjoying her dower in 1530.[10] Compared with this wardship, that of Henry VIII's reign was undisturbing. It was before the statute of wills made it necessary to leave a third of an estate in wardship, and only £8 13s. 4d. out of £41 9s. 8d. descended to the heir, Erasmus Pym. The land and the wardship of the body were obtained by Sir Thomas Elyot, author of *The Governour,* for £80.[11]

This information gives some comparative basis for assessing the much better documented events which followed the death of John Pym's father Alexander, in January 1585. Alexander, who was a successful lawyer and a careful estate manager,[12] had considerably improved the family's status, becoming a J.P. and even an M.P.,[13]

8 Erasmus Pym was granted his livery on 11 Feb. 1539. *Letters and Papers of Henry VIII,* xiv, i. no. 403 (38).

7. E. Chisholm Batten, 'Henry VII in Somerset', *Somerset Archaeological Society* xxv. 72. I would like to thank Dr. Phyllis Hembry for this reference.

9 P.R.O., E.36/212, fos. 68, 72: E.36/248, fos. 39, 65, 93, 135, 218, 219.

10 P.R.O., C. 142/48/46.

11 *Letters and Papers of Henry VIII,* iv, pt. iii, 5508, no. 1, 24313, no. 13.

12 He was able to pay £400 for a manor at a time when he had no income from land, and helped to provide the Middle Temple Reader's Feast in 1578: S.R.O., DD/BW, Pym MSS., no. 95: *Middle Temple Records, Minutes of Parliament,* vol. i, ed. Charles Henry Hopwood (1904), p. 224. As a landlord, he introduced two major changes: he reduced almost all leases to one life, instead of two or three, and gave himself the right to immediate eviction for arrears of rent, instead of distraining. Both these changes were subsequently reversed by Sir Anthony Rous and John Pym. P.R.O., Wards 5.36; S.R.O., Pym MSS., nos. 80, 90. His second marriage to the sister of John Colles of Pitminster, probably also increased his standing in the county. Pym MSS., nos. 82, 85.

13 Brit. Mus. Royal MS. 18, D. III, fo. 25. Burghley's political atlas (fo. 26) marks the Pyms at Wollavington, among a fairly small number of landed gentry. *Official Returns,* i. 415: Alexander Pym was elected for Taunton in 1584, but it is doubtful whether he lived long enough to take his seat.

but it is still doubtful whether the wardship was big enough to tempt any of the leading speculators in wardships. The three people most likely to be interested in it were John Pym's mother Philippa, and his two uncles, William Pym and John Colles. Of these three, the best placed was John Colles, who, in addition to being trusted with a large number of administrative commissions, was also county feodary.[14] He used his position to obtain wardships for himself on other occasions, but this time he appears to have confined himself strictly to acting in the interests of his sister. He was therefore faced with a problem in discharging his duty of valuing the estate. If his sister were to get the wardship, Colles would want the estate to be valued as low as possible in order to enable her to buy the wardship at a favourable price. On the other hand, if he returned a low valuation before the wardship was granted, he might make it look a good bargain to other Somerset country gentlemen. It was therefore in Colles' interest to postpone his valuation as long as possible.

It is worth recording some further information about John Colles, since he is the key figure in the story of the wardship, and his influence during John Pym's childhood may have been an important counterbalance to that of his stepfather, Sir Anthony Rous. He appears to have been a trusted county administrator: he was a commissioner for the militia before the Armada, a Deputy Lieutenant, and was one of six Somerset gentlemen who acted in 1586 as commissioners for the plantation of Munster.[15] Like other Elizabethan county administrators, he was not above suppressing information for a friend, and at least once attracted the attention of an informer.[16] He appears to have been prosperous, and in his will his greatest enthusiasm appears to be about his coach and its furnishings.[17] Dr. Phyllis Hembry has shown that he was a successful

14 H. E. Bell, *The Court of Wards and Liveries* (1953), p. 43. *Acts of the Privy Council, 1587–1588*, p. 96; *Cal. S.P. Dom.*, Add. 1547–80, vol. cxxi, no. 83; P.R.O.E., 178/1967. E. Green, *Preparations in Somerset against the Armada* (1881), p. 47. P.R.O., Wards 9.400, fo. 258v and E. Green *op. cit.* p. 51 for wardships Colles obtained for himself.

15 E. Green, *op. cit.* p. 31, *Acts of the Privy Council, 1585–1586*, p. 9. P.R.O., S.P. 14/33, fol. 3v. He may also have been identical with the John Colles who had an interest in the Duchy of Lancaster manor of Buckby. P.R.O., DL 28/10/23. I would like to thank my wife for this reference.

16 P.R.O., Wards 9.527, 25 Aug. 43 Eliz.

17 P.C.C. 63 Windebank.

speculator in episcopal lands.[18] He signed the Bond of Association, and chose Bedford as his correspondent when he detected a sect of the Family of Love,[19] but he cannot be classified as a puritan. His profits in episcopal lands were largely organized through his family's friendship with the family of the Marian bishop Bourne, and in his will he said nothing about Justification, Election, or other puritan shibboleths, and confined himself to expressing belief in the resurrection of the flesh, life everlasting, 'and all other articles of my faithe whiche a Christyane man oughte to beleeve'. For Colles, these articles would be likely to coincide with those which enabled him to keep his coach, his geldings, and his wethers.

It is remarkable how little evidence there is of any puritanism in John Pym's family background before his mother's marriage to Sir Anthony Rous. The nearest thing there is to evidence of puritanism is the religious clause of the will of his other uncle, William Pym: 'and first I bequeathe my soule to Almightye God applying and apprehending by a livelye true faithe his loving mercyes freelye given me in Christ Jesus oure Savyour and onlye hoping through his grace to sleepe with him and with a resurrection to rise to the enjoyinge of the glorious fellowshippe and blisse of the sons of God and my body to the earth.' As evidence for puritanism, this is very slender, and it is immediately followed by a bequest of 12d. for works at Wells cathedral. The detail in which his will lists his cushions and silk carpets suggests a desire for soft living which was probably beyond his income.[20] The wardship would have been a valuable addition to his resources, and he might be expected to press to get it. On the other hand, he had suffered a series of matrimonial misadventures, which, if discreetly exaggerated in the right quarters in London, might handicap his chances of getting the wardship of the body, if not of the lands.[21]

18 Phyllis Hembry, *The Bishops of Bath and Wells* (1967), pp. 134, 149 and other refs.

19 P.R.O., S.P. 12/174/9; *Acts of the Privy Council 1578–1580*, p. 445. The executors of his will were Sir Edward Phelips and Henry Walrond.

20 P.C.C. 81 Wingfield. This will, which contained some passages which might have made probate doubtful, was proved before Sir John Bennett, who was subsequently vigorously attacked by John Pym for taking bribes for probate of wills. *C.J.* i. 583. See below, p. 158, n. 51.

21 Agnes Billey appears to have remained in doubt from 1579 to William Pym's death in 1610 whether she was married to William Pym or to one Toby Andrewes, and to have lived in marriage alternately with both gentlemen. When she died, in the 1630s, she was Mrs Andrewes. S.R.O., D/D/Ca, Act Book 62, 23 July 1579; P.C.C. 81 Wingfield; S.R.O., DD/BW, Pym MSS. no. 224.

The evidence we have about John Pym's mother Philippa is very slender, but what there is suggests that she was addicted to worrying. She had the expensive habit of getting unnecessary entries made on the patent rolls, and her funeral sermon suggests that she was one of those pathetic predestinarians who believed they were predestined to damnation.[22] The great decline in the quality of her signature might suggest ill-health, though there is no direct evidence for it.

These three appear to have been the main interested parties when the procedure for a wardship was set in motion. Alexander Pym died on 5 January 1585, almost immediately after his election to parliament, and by a curious irony his successor in the Taunton seat was Francis Bacon.[23] On 11 February, the clerk of the Court of Wards recorded the issue of a writ of *diem clausit extremum*, the normal writ for an *Inquisition Post Mortem*, which was to be taken by a commission of four among whom John Colles, as feodary, was of course included. The writ which arrived at Taunton, however, though it was issued on 11 February, was not a *diem clausit extremum*, but the much more peremptory *mandamus*.[24] It may have been partly the *mandamus* which produced an increase in the valuation of the lands from £48 to £52.[25] Part of the increase was accounted for by the fact that Alexander Pym had recently purchased the manor of Hawkwell, valued at 30s. 3d., from Francis, earl of Bedford. It is unfortunately impossible to say how close a connection this may indicate between Bedford and Pym's father. The inquisition also recorded two uses of the property created by Alexander Pym. In both of them, his feoffees to uses included John Colles. The first use, dated 1581, was to protect his wife's jointure from wardship, and his feoffees to uses included Edward Hext of Ham, with whom

22 P.R.O., C. 66/1267 (one of two entries): C. Fitz-Geffrey, *Deathes Sermon Unto the Living* (London, 1622), p. 29, 'These her teares, I doubt not, but God treasured up in his bottle: sure I am, they have been many times my comfort; for they assured me that she had in some good measure those graces for whose want she wept, seeing it is grace that makes us complain of the want of grace.' The theology of this passage sounds rather forced in a preacher who elsewhere quoted Cartwright with approval. *The Curse of Corn-hoarders* (Exeter, 1631), p. 25.

23 Brit. Mus., Lansd. MS. 1218, fo. 51 (Burghley's Parliament-Book).

24 P.R.O., Wards 9,171 (docket book of writs); C. 142/206/20. I can offer no explanation for this discrepancy. Since Alexander Pym had only been dead five weeks, there is unlikely to have been a question of concealment.

6. The valuation of those lands which Alexander Pym had inherited from his father v25 increased by £2 10s. above the valuation on the death of Erasmus Pym, in 1579.

he had shared a chamber in the Middle Temple.[26] The second use was dated a week before his death, and left the remainder of his property to be held to the use of his wife. This second use could have no legal validity, since under the statute of wills a third of the estate had to descend direct to the heir, and therefore became liable for wardship. The crown appears to have overridden this second use, and there is a note on the particular of the estate: 'a third to discend to the Quene notwithstandinge the conveyance aforesaid'.[27] The only result of this second use appears to have been an abortive threat of proceedings in the Court of Exchequer for alienation without licence.[28] The Inquisition, taken on 3 April 1585, records John Pym's age as ten months and fourteen days. Since the source for this information was probably the boy's uncle, and since there was little advantage to be gained from his returning the age as ten months rather than twelve or six, this may be taken to be an authentic record of the date of John Pym's birth, which would then be 20 May 1584.

However accurate the record of John Pym's age may be, the valuation of the estate was of course inaccurate, and the inaccuracies began to emerge within a few months. The most important was the omission of the manor of Wollavington Throckmorton, purchased by Alexander Pym from Francis Throckmorton (of the Throckmorton plot) in February 1581. Since the manor was valued in the deed of conveyance at £35, it represented a considerable portion of the estate. In reality, the manor was probably worth much more than this, since the purchase price was £1700, 'all which payments to be made in and upon the Fante Stone in the Temple Church in the suburbs of London or in and upon the place where the Fante now standeth'. At this price, Alexander Pym would have bought the manor at the astonishing rate of 48½ years' purchase. The valuation of £35 appears to have been a reasonably accurate assess-

26 *Middle Temple Records, Minutes of Parliament*, vol. i, ed. Charles Henry Hopwood (1904), pp. 177, 179. This is the same Edward Hext whose letter to Burghley on the treatment of vagrants was printed in *Tudor Economic Documents*, ed. R. H Tawney and Eileen Power (1924) ii. 339. Alexander Pym probably shared Hext's harsh views on the poor, but the views of Pym's stepfather Anthony Rous appear to have been the opposite of Hext's. Brit. Mus., Harl. MS. 6995, fo. 127.

27 P.R.O. Wards 9, 681a, 1586, no. 5.

28 S.R.O., DD/BW, Pym MSS. no. 113. The order book of the Court of Exchequer, P.R.O., E. 12/5, has no record of subsequent proceedings.

ment of the rental value (John Pym assessed it in 1614 at £37).[29] The explanation of the high purchase price appears to be that the real value of the manor consisted in the entry fines, rather than the rents. One of the Throckmorton leases preserved among the Pym papers shows an entry fine of £43 13s. 6d. on a rent of 45s. 10d. *per annum* and for a lease of three lives. When John Pym made a lease of the home farm, in 1607, he obtained an entry fine of £545 on a rent of 69s. for a lease of 41 years.[30] It was an important addition to the estate, and its purchase may have been the occasion of the sale of the outlying manor of Stone. The title to it was disputed in a lawsuit, which it is interesting to discover that Alexander Pym, though a common law barrister, brought in the Star Chamber,[31] and all hope of concealing the purchase appears to have disappeared on the attainder of Francis Throckmorton. On 13 August 1585 Philippa Pym received a patent pardoning her for holding it without a licence to alienate.[32] From this patent, it appears that the manor was held in chief of the Crown, paying a rent of 2s. a year, and that it had formerly been the property of the duke of Somerset, The patent is also our only source of information on the contents of Alexander Pym's will.[33] He appears to have left the manor to his wife for twenty-one years, and then to John Pym and the heirs of his body, and failing them to his daughters Katherine and Jane, and failing them to his heirs. The patent also pardoned the failure to declare this manor at the Inquisition.

It is not clear whether this discovery was made before or after the grant of the wardship of the body to Philippa Pym, but it is clear from the particular of the estate which Philippa Pym submitted when she petitioned for the wardship that the valuation on which she purchased it was that of the Inquisition. Two copies of her

29 S.R.O., DD/BW, Pym MSS. nos. 86, 142. This manor was never properly declared. In 1604 a tenement on it was held by Sir Edward Dyer, holder of the patent for concealments and Sir Anthony Rous tried to fine him 6d. for not living on his tenement. Pym MSS. no. 117: J. Hurstfield, *The Queen's Wards* (1958), pp. 40–41.

30 S.R.O., DD/BW, Pym MSS. nos. 77, 122.

31 The suit was introduced as a fraud case, but it soon became clear that since the alleged fraud consisted in pretending to a non-existent title, the case was really about the title to the manor. P.R.O., Sta. Ch 5, P.32/34, P.38/33, P.66/23.

32 P.R.O., C.66/1255.

33 S.R.O., DD/BW. Pym MSS. no. 109, a use of the manor of 'Wollavington' (sc. Wollavington Throckmorton) created by Philippa Pym a fortnight after her husband's death, records that Alexander Pym made a will, but gives almost no details of its contents.

particular survive, one in the Public Record Office, and the other attached to her counterpart of the indenture granting the wardship. The fact that this particular was prepared by John Colles is probably sufficient proof that he acted as his sister's intermediary, since the particular was not an official document, but a private one prepared by the petitioner for the wardship.[34] The price at which Philippa purchased the wardship was £60, paid in three annual instalments. This was a normal price, if anything slightly below the average for the period, and a favourable rate of payment.[35] Her first obligation for payment was dated 16 May 1585, and the date of 16 May 1586 on the indenture is probably a clerical error. The indenture contains one interesting clause, to the effect that once every four years John Pym should be brought before 'the bushoppe of Bathe and Wells to be examyned and talked withall as well for the knowledge of his or their bringing upp in lerninge as in other vertuous and decent qualities as to his or their estate and degrees appertaineth'. This clause, however, needs no special explanation, since the text of the standard lease in the Court of Wards formulary book shows that an examination by the bishop was a normal alternative to examination by the Court of Wards, and the wording in this indenture is identical with that in the formulary book.[36]

All this time, John Colles had not conducted his feodary's survey of the estate. He had thus achieved his object of not committing himself to a low valuation of the estate until his sister was certain of the wardship. Such postponement of the feodary's survey, though unusual, was not unique. The indenture contained the standard clause to the effect that if any lands were discovered which had not been included in the Inquisition, Philippa Pym could

34 P.R.O., Wards 9.681a, 1586, no. 5. Philippa Pym's copy of the particular, and the indenture, to which it is attached, are at present in my possession: *Sotheby's Catalogue,* 21 July 1965, no. 785. A photostat copy of these documents is deposited among the Pym MSS. in the Somerset Record Office. The two copies of the particular are not identical. *Sotheby's Catalogue, loc. cit.* no. 786 (the earl of Bedford's licence to alienate the manor of Hawkwell to Alexander Pym) is or was in the possession of Mr. Alf E. Jacobson, of Colby Junior College, New Hampshire, U.S.A. I regret that I have not been able to see it. The particular and the indenture have since been sold: *Sotheby's Catalogue 29 Oct. 1968,* No. 402.

35 P.R.O., Wards 9.386, fos. 39v, 115v, 202v. J. Hurstfield, *The Queen's Wards,* pp. 86–87.

36 P.R.O., Wards 10. 27.

have them at a rate of three years' purchase. The Court of Wards already knew that the manor of Wollavington Throckmorton had not been included in the Inquisition, and Colles was probably under some pressure to carry out his survey to see what more the Crown could obtain. When he finally carried it out, on 1 September 1587, the result suggests that he may have been under some pressure. He surveyed in Latin, which he did not normally do, and produced a formidable document six folios long, which is more detailed than any other surviving survey of his except that of the very valuable Portman wardship.[37] In his survey, he listed individually each copyhold tenant, his rent, his type of land, and the number of acres he held. At the end of this immense exhibition of willingness, he returned a valuation of the estate a few shillings *lower* than that of the *Inquisition Post Mortem*. The manor of Wollavington Throckmorton remained suppressed by the same method as in the particular. The manor of Wollavington Pym, which had been in the Pyms' hands for a long time, was split into two parts, both confused under the name of the manor of 'Wollavington', and the Court of Wards was left to assume that one of these parts represented the manor of Wollavington Throckmorton. Historians might have made the same assumption, but for the fact that we possess a series of court rolls of the 1590s from Wollavington Throckmorton, and of thirty-three tenants identified on the rolls, not a single one appears in Colles's feodary's survey.[38]

It is fortunately possible, by comparing the feodary's survey with surviving estate documents, to gain some picture both of the inaccuracies of the survey, and of the agriculture of the Pyms' manors. There appear to be some tenants missing from the feodary's survey, and there is one man who is recorded in the survey as holding one tenement at a rent of 6s. 8d. who had in fact been granted the year before two tenements at a rent of 23s. 6d.[39] John Colles could not plead ignorance of this grant, since he himself was a witness to it. On the whole, however, the estate documents suggest that Colles's estimate of the rent rolls was no more than reasonably inaccurate,

3. P.R.O., Wards 5.36. The document is very different from the brief English s37 'eys which Colles normally produced. See P.R.O., Wards 5.36 and 37 *passim*.

38 S.R.O., DD/BW, Pym MSS. no. 117.

39 S.R.O., DD/BW, Pym MSS. no. 112.

and that the real under-valuation was achieved by ignoring the entry fines and heriots. The story shows that one of the best reasons for relying on heavy entry fines rather than high rents might be that it made it easier to obtain favourable valuations for taxation: an accurate list of the rent rolls, while perfectly honest, might be a gross under-valuation of the estate. It is possible that one reason why Inquisition valuations rose so little during the sixteenth century is that they represented only rents, and omitted entry fines. Such omission would depress valuations most in the west, where entry fines were often higher than elsewhere, but it would produce some distortion anywhere where entry fines existed at all. The individual manors listed start with Cutcombe Raleigh, held of East Greenwich, containing, according to Colles, ten tenants and 336 acres, and valued at £4 4s. The adjoining manor of Cutcombe Mohun was listed as containing 18 tenents and 858 acres, and valued at £10 10s. 6d. This manor had been valued at £10 in 1505, and the figure shows signs of being distinctly traditional. Nevertheless, as far as rent is concerned, it may be accurate. There is one case in which two grants of the same tenement in Cutcombe, of 1579 and 1641, are bound together. During that period the rent was actually reduced, from 8s. 6d. to 6s. 8d., but the entry fine was increased from £6 13s. 4d. to £125,[40] on a lease of three lives. Since it appears that Alexander Pym had kept almost all his grants copyholds for one life only, entry fines must have been a fairly frequent occurrence. Both the Cutcombe manors were on the slopes of Exmoor, including part of Dunkery Beacon, and were primarily pastoral: some grants prohibit the conversion of pasture to tillage.[41] Both of them appear to have included considerable amounts of wood. Hawkwell, the manor bought from the earl of Bedford, was also in the parish of Cutcombe, and was listed by Colles as containing two tenants and 220 acres, and as worth 30s. 3d. *per annum*. In 1620, John Pym let it out on a lease for three lives, at a rent of 15s. 1½d., and at an entry fine of £510. He excepted out of this lease woods, mines, quarries, and ground 'where the fullers' racks stand'.[42] Since

40 S.R.O., DD/BW, Pym MSS. no. 239.
41 S.R.O., DD/BW, Pym MSS. no. 135; nos. 190, 239.
42 S.R.O., DD/BW, Pym MSS. no. 155. The mine is likely to have been of either copper or lead.

there is no parallel clause in any of Pym's other leases, it may be presumed that the manor included a mine, and a quarry. How profitable they were, what was mined, and whether they existed when Bedford sold the manor, remain unknown. They were certainly not mentioned by Colles.

The manor of Langham and Poole, also in the far north-west of Somerset, was listed by Colles as worth £8 13s. 9d. There are too few estate documents about this manor to provide any real check on Colles's valuation, but it certainly omitted the fact that the manor included large woods and some marlpits.[43] A ward's woods were supposed to be reserved to the Crown, but it is doubtful whether this reservation was often made effective. The manor of Brymore, where the Pyms lived, was valued at £10 9s. 8d. This again is a traditional valuation, and is probably misleading by the omission of entry fines in much the same way as the Cutcombe valuations. This manor probably contained a higher proportion of arable than the upland manors, and was on the edge of the orchard country outside Taunton. The manor of Wollavington Pym was a low-lying fenland manor on the edge of Sedgemoor and was broken up into a large series of small enclosed plots. There is no evidence that the Pyms ever tried to follow the example of their neighbour Lord Poulett at Cossington, by consolidating these plots into larger enclosures. When John Pym later wanted to lease large areas there, he composed them of a scattered series of small plots. Colles valued it at £6 10s. *per annum*. In 1614, perhaps after some purchases, John Pym valued it at £20.[44] Another check on this valuation is provided by the home farm occupied by William Pym. Colles valued it at £4 (blot) 4d. When William Pym died, in 1610, it remained, according to the custom of the manor, in the occupation of the lady who, after his death, consented to be recognized as his widow, until the 1630s. John Pym then decided to lease it at an economic rent, instead of an economic fine, and let it out to a rich

[43] P.R.O., Sta. Cha. 5 P.42/318; S.R.O., DD/BW, Pym MSS. no. 96.

[44] S.R.O., D/D/Rg. 137 (Cossington Glebe Terrier); S.R.O., DD/BW, Pym MSS. nos. 165, 169, 219; no. 141.

yeoman for £100 a year.[45] The remainder of the estate consisted of various tenements in Huntspill, Puriton, Downend, Edington and Cossington. These were officially classified as mixed farming, and were part of the 'oozy grounds' at the mouth of the river Parrett. Colles valued them at a total of £6 3s. 4d. The only other source of income listed was an annuity out of the manor of Bomson, of £4 12s. 4d. *per annum*.

These details suggest that the lease of the Crown's third of the estate, including as it did the right to receive entry fines and heriots, would be a valuable acquisition, and this acquisition was gained, sometime during 1585–6, by William Pym.[46] The jottings on the particular of the estate in the Public Record Office show that the Court of Wards had some difficulty in making up the Crown's third part of the estate. The lands which were left to descend to the heir, which therefore came into the Crown's hands, were the manor of Cutcombe Mohun, the only one of the officially listed manors which was held by knight-service in chief, the manor of Hawkwell, and the annuity from Bomson. These added up to £16 12s. 3d. The clerk, having incorrectly added them up to £16 7s. 4d., noted that 18s. 3d. was still lacking, and the Court made it up by adding the lands in Edington, which had been supposed to be part of Philippa Pym's jointure. These lands were leased to William Pym at a rent of £17 12s. 6d. William Pym, however, immediately fell into arrears with his rent to the Court of Wards, and these arrears were carefully recorded by John Colles. In a year and three quarters,

45 William Pym claimed in his will that 'I geve to Agnes that I did a long time take for my wife till of late shee hath denied me to be her husband (although wee were married with our friends' consent, her father, mother, and uncle at it, and now shee sweareth shee will never love me, neither wilbe persuaded by no preachers nor any other which hath happened within these five yeares; and Tobye Andrewes the beginner which I did see with myn owne eyes when he did more than was fitting. And this by the meanes of Robert Musgrave and their abetters I have lived a miserable life these sixe or seven yeares, and now I leave revenge to God and Tenne pounds to buy her a greate horse, for I could not these many years please her with one great enough'. P.C.C. 81 Wingfield. Proceedings may have been considered about this clause, since there are copies in *Cal. S.P. Dom.* James I, vol. lvii, no. 61 (endorsed 'libellous scandal'), and in Huntington Library Ellesmere MS. 703 (I would like to thank Professor J. Hurstfield for this reference). In 1614, however, Agnes Pym was enjoying the widow's tenement, and in 1635 the same tenement had recently been occupied by 'Agnes Andrewes widow deceased'. S.R.O., DD/BW, Pym MSS. nos 141, 224.

46 P.R.O., Wards 9.197, fo. 93v (Calendar of Leases). The actual lease has not survived.

he had fallen behind by £18 12s. 6d. out of £30 5s. 10d.[47] Moreover, there is no record either in the Receiver General's account or in the feodary's accounts, of any payment of William Pym's entry fine on this lease, and it must be presumed he did not pay it. Sometime during 1588–9, a new lease was made, for which Philippa Pym paid an entry fine of £13 6s. 8d. in ready money.[48] Later feodaries' accounts show that this was a lease of the same properties at the same rent, which Philippa Pym paid punctually.[49] William Pym's lease must have been cancelled for non-payment, and transferred to Philippa. The fine she paid for the lease was a reasonably favourable one, being slightly below the average for Burghley's Mastership.

While the lease was passing from William Pym to Philippa, the exhibition granted for the maintenance of the ward was going through the opposite process. The exhibition of £6 13s. 4d. was a normal small exhibition, and was paid to Philippa until Michaelmas 1587.[50] The cause of the difficulty was a clause in the will of Erasmus Pym, confirmed by a deed of Alexander Pym's, under which Erasmus' younger son William, and his wife after him, were to be paid an annuity of £20 a year out of the manors of Cutcombe Mohun, Cutcombe Raleigh and Langham and Poole.[51] This deed had not been mentioned at the Inquisition, and Cutcombe Mohun had been leased by the Court of Wards in all innocence of the knowledge that this annuity was chargeable on it. It must remain a matter for speculation whether the fact that he was not getting his annuity was among the reasons for William Pym's failure to pay the entry fine on his lease. Faced with non-payment, William Pym distrained for the annuity, as under the deed which granted it he was entitled to do, whereat Philippa rashly began a lawsuit against him in the Court of Wards.[52] Philippa may have acted in this against the advice

47 P.R.O., Wards 9.681a, 1586, no. 5: Wards 9,444 (feodary's accounts).

48 P.R.O., Wards 9.386, fo. 227v.

49 P.R.O., Wards 9.480, fo. 130; Wards 11/11/5.

50 P.R.O., Wards 9.444.

51 P.C.C., 7 Rowe; P.R.O., Wards 9.85, fo. 460. This annuity presumably remained chargeable on John Pym's estate until the death of William Pym's widow in the 1630s.

52 The pleadings for this lawsuit have not survived, but it is listed in one of Hare's indexes as 'Regina v. Pyme'. This means that the plaintiff's case must have been presented by the Attorney of the Wards, who pleaded on behalf of the ward, and therefore that Philippa, the committee of the ward, must have been the actual plaintiff. P.R.O., Wards 9.296, 29 Eliz. The object of the lawsuit may have been simply to make William Pym incur costs he could not afford.

of John Colles, since Colles, when called as a witness, could only say that the deed granting the annuity was a good one. The court therefore ruled that William was entitled to the annuity and to his arrears. This created a further problem about the Crown's third part of the estate, since out of an estate of £52, £30 was assured as jointure to Philippa, and £20 as annuity to William. The Court therefore ruled that when the annuity had been granted 'the residue of all the said ward's lands as well discended as in joyntor to be leyable to satisfaccon her Mat.s iiide parte'.[53] This ruling, that the Crown was entitled to take part of the jointure to make up its third part, was a new one, and though it was subsequently confirmed in Price's case 9 James I,[54] the Court appears to have been unhappy about it, and to have decided not to act on it. Philippa Pym kept a lease of the same third part as before the decree, and instead the exhibition for the maintenance of the ward was paid to William as part of his annuity. John Colles, when he recorded the payment of the exhibition to William Pym in his accounts, was careful to record also that he was paying it in virtue of '*quoddam decret*' of the Court in Hilary Term 1587.[55] There is no record of how Philippa Pym reached the next stage in this story: it may have been by the influence of her new husband, Anthony Rous. This stage is recorded in an entry on the Patent Roll, dated 20 November 1588, recording the grant of the wardship to Philippa.[56] The entry does not simply record the words of the indenture, but repeats several times that she is entitled to the wardship of the body, and to the exhibition, and to receive the exhibition '*per manus feodarii*' without giving any account of it. The entry also states that Philippa was entitled to the exhibition for all the period since Alexander Pym's death. This entry contradicted the Court's decree, and appears to have been effective: John Colles's next surviving account, dated ten years later, records that the exhibition was paid to Philippa and her husband Anthony Rous, '*sic sibi concess. per litteras Domine dicte Regine patentes*'.[57] How William Pym's annuity was made up after

53 P.R.O., Wards 9.85, fo. 460. Her Majesty was not to be 'prejudicied' of her full third part.

54 H. E. Bell, *Court of Wards and Liveries*, p. 107; Ley, *Reports* (1659), p. 42, Since it anticipated the ruling in Price's case, Pym's case deserves a place in the history of Wards law. The precedent it created is unlikely to have pleased Philippa Pym.

55 P.R.O., Wards 9.444.

56 P.R.O., C.66/1312. The entry is 'per ipsam reginam'.

57 P.R.O., Wards 9.480, fo. 160.

the exhibition was returned to Philippa is not recorded.

This appears to be the end of the complications of the Pym wardship. There is no record of Pym's mother exercising her right to arrange his marriage. His wife is first mentioned in his estate documents in 1607, and it is probable that he had only married her shortly before that date, by which time he had been out of wardship for two years. There is no record of the size of his wife's marriage portion, but his wife's sister received a marriage portion of £600. If John Pym received as much, he can be regarded as having made a reasonably, but not remarkably, good marriage. Whether his mother arranged his marriage or not, she is likely to have regarded it as satisfactory. Pym's father-in-law, John Hooke of Bramshott in Hampshire, had, like his mother, married into the Rous family. His son, Henry Hooke, was admitted in 1607 to the Middle Temple chamber of Francis Nicolls, another member of the Rous circle. John Hooke appears to have been fairly prosperous: although his *Inquisition Post Mortem* only valued his estate at £5 *per annum*, he left in his will annuities of up to £150 a year in addition to the main legacy to his heir, and though he lived at least twenty miles from the sea, he burnt coal as well as wood. He appears to have been a moderate puritan, carefully reciting the doctrine of Justification, and stating his confidence of his Election, and following up this religious clause by bequeathing 40s. to his parish church. He appears to have been on good terms with his 'deare and loving sonne' John Pym, whom he left as an overseer of his will. Although he was only granted arms in 1600, he appears to have been of sufficiently high status to marry a daughter into the Dering family.[58]

John Pym passed very painlessly through the processes of coming of age. His mean rates, the profits of the land between his coming

58 P.C.C., 75 Capell; *Visitation of Hampshire*, ed. W. Harvy Rylands (Harl. Soc., 1913), pp. 83–84. John Hooke had married Barbara, daughter of Richard Rous of Devon. *Middle Temple Records, Minutes of Parliament*, ed. Charles Trice Martin (1904), p. 487. P.R.O., C.142/685/52. In 1625, Henry Hooke, Pym's brother-in-law, was assessed at £10 for the Forced Loan: P.R.O., S.P. 16/177/1. The religious clause of John Hooke's will is as follows: 'I doe first bequeath my soule to Allmightie God by whose mercie and grace thorowe faith in Christ Jesus I doe hope assuredlie to bee saved acknowledginge and confessing my flesh to bee a most vile and wretched synner and that there is no meane or merit in mee to attaine everlasting salvation but only by faith in Christ Jesus whose death hath washed awaye my synnes, which I most assuredly believe. And by whose meditation and intercession unto God the Father for mee I doe verile hope to be partaker of those heavenly joyes promised to his elect, dying in the faith of Jesus Christ'.

of age and suing for livery, were to be paid to John Colles, who was still in office as feodary. His payment of £3 10s. 6d. cannot be supposed to have been exorbitant. The payment was completed on 24 October 1605, immediately before the Gunpowder Plot.[59] For the livery of his lands, he naturally chose to sue for a special, rather than a general, livery, since a general livery demanded a precise description of the estate he claimed to inherit, and would inevitably have raised the old question about the title to Wollavington Throckmorton. For a special livery, the normal rate after wardship was about half the annual value of the lands. The table of liveries lists his payment as £26 12s., which would have been almost exactly half the official value of his estate. This would have been as good a rate as his father's livery payment of £46 4s. 10½d. but it was not in fact what he paid: the Receiver General's accounts show that in fact he only paid £20, and the entry in the table of liveries probably represents the value of his obligations.[60] The actual livery '*fideli subdito nostro* John Pyme' is duly enrolled in a volume whose flyeaf is decorated with persistent attempts to imitate Burghley's signature.[61] In many ways, the Pym wardship was a complicated one, but it is doubtful whether any of the complications, unless perhaps the activities of Sir Edward Dyer at Wollavington Throckmorton, left John Pym with any particular cause of grievance against the Crown. There is some evidence that he felt concern about the subject of wardship in general,[62] but the complications in his own wardship had all been introduced by the complexity of his family's actions. Wherever possible, the Court of Wards tried to treat the Pym wardship as a typical run of the mill transaction. In so far as they failed to do so, the fault is entirely that of Pym's relations. Whether Pym appreciated this point must, for the present, remain an unanswered question.

59 S.R.O., DD/BW, Pym MSS. no. 146. On Sir Edward Dyer, see p.152, n. 29 above. In one of the numerous documents Pym drew up to protect his estate from wardship, he specified that the king was allowed 'all such profett as he may or ought to have'. S.R.O., DD/BW, Pym MSS. no. 199. Also nos. 139–147.

60 P.R.O., Wards 9.400, fo. 502v. Pym's subsequent concern with the Gunpowder Plot may appear the more genuine for the fact that when it was discovered, the motion to give thanks for their deliverance was moved by his neighbour and his father's friend Sir Edward Hext, and the committee to prepare an Act for public thanksgiving included his stepfather Sir Anthony Rous. *C.J.* i. 257, 258.

61 P.R.O., Wards 9.254, fo. 20v; Wards 9.402, fos. 359r, 360v; Wards 9.384, fo. 235v, Wards 9.385, fos. 21v, 169v, 221r.

62 P.R.O., Wards 9.70, fo. 188r.

Appendix I
Robert Cecil and his Father's Wardship Leases

The effects created by the prolonged vacancy in the Mastership of the Court of Wards after Burghley's death have been superbly described, first by one of the wards clerks, and later, with more detachment, by Professor Hurstfield.[1] There is therefore no need to elaborate on the delays suffered by those who were seeking wardships during this period. But an examination of the wardship leases (P.R.O. Wards 12 4-10) shows that these delays were suffered, not only by those seeking for grants, but also by those whose grants had already been signed by the Master, but had not yet passed the Great Seal. There are large numbers of such leases bearing a double date, the first the date on which they had been signed by Burghley, the second the date on which they had been re-signed by Robert Cecil as the new Master.[2] There is often over a year's difference between the two dates.

It is also well known that Robert Cecil raised the rates, both for the wardship of the body and for fines for leases.[3] It appears that this policy did not only apply to new leases: those who had already had their prices fixed by Burghley might find them altered by Robert Cecil. Unfortunately, most of the leases concerned have suffered too badly in the 'hell-like fish-cellar'[4] to be very easily legible, but some cases are clear. The lease to Joan Barton of lands in Shropshire and Flint endorsed by Burghley 29 June 1598, and by Robert Cecil 14 February 1599/1600, appears to have given Robert a free hand, since Burghley had omitted to enter the amount of the fine.[5] But on the lease to Catherine Yonge, widow of Thomas Yonge, of lands in Essex, Burghley had entered the fine.

[1] J. Hurstfield, *The Queen's Wards* (1958), pp. 283-97; P.R.O. Wards 9. 525, 21 May 40 Eliz.

[2] These leases are scattered throughout P.R.O. Wards 12, 4-10, but the majority are in Wards 12 4, 5, and 6. I would like to thank the staff of the Public Record Office for their kindness in allowing these very fragile documents to be exposed to the risks of production in the search-room.

[3] Hurstfield, pp. 298, 312-14: H.E. Bell, *Court of Wards and Liveries* (1953), pp. 58, 60

[4] H.E. Bell, p. 180.

[5] P.R.O. Wards 12. 5.

Robert Cecil crossed it out, entered a new fine of almost exactly three years' value (£21 on £7 12*s*.), and added a note in his own hand: '2 yeares fine increase by me'.[6] Actions such as these may have contributed something to the growing agitation against wardship in the early years of James I's reign.

[6] P.R.O. Wards 12. 6. See also the lease to Simon Musgrave, dated 10 February 1599-1600, which is only partially legible, but which has clearly had the original fine crossed out. P.R.O. Wards 12. 7.

Appendix II
John Pym and the Queen's Receivership[1]

THE EARLY CAREER of John Pym has always been shrouded in mystery. It has been known that he held the office of receiver of Crown lands for Hampshire, Wiltshire and Gloucestershire, which he first exercised during 1607.[2] It was not known that this was not his only office in land administration: he was also appointed, on 24 August 1608, to the office of queen's receiver for the same counties. For this office he received the surprisingly large annual salary of £140 13*s* 4*d*[3] and had extremely light duties. He had to collect the rents from seven manors, for which he was already collecting the rents as king's receiver, and pay the rents to the queen instead of the king. After Anne of Denmark's death, he continued to hold an extra receivership for these manors, first as receiver to Prince Charles, and then as receiver to Queen Henrietta Maria.[4]

Three points of particular interest arise from the grant of this office. The first is the remarkably high salary, not accompanied by any allowance for poundage. A number of other receiverships for the queen are recorded on the same roll, and all of them have the same high salary without poundage. The queen's receiver for Lincolnshire was paid a salary of £500, and the receiver for Kent, Surrey and Sussex £739. The post of queen's receiver was one which had not existed since the death of Katherine Parr, and it

1 The late Miss Evelyn Gore spent a lifetime working on John Pym, and left a very valuable unfinished draft for a projected biography of him. I am grateful to Mr. Paul Gore and to Mr. John Gore for their help in getting me access to this work, for allowing me to use it, and for allowing me to retain a copy of it. The discovery here recorded is Miss Gore's, and the responsibility for any errors in its presentation is mine. *Conrad Russell.*

2 He began to exercise the office of king's receiver between 19 March and 22 Apr. 1607 (Public Record Office, L.R. 7/112; E178/3097).

3 P.R.O., C 54/1967 m. 132.

4 See P.R.O., L.R. 7/55 *passim.*

looks as if the absence of vested interests had created some scope for administrative reform. Lord Carew, president of the queen's council, or whoever else drew up the terms of these appointments, appears to have been interested in moving away from piecework payments towards putting administration on a proper salaried basis.

The second point concerns the comparative size of Pym's income from office and from land. He had a salary of £100 as king's receiver, together with poundage which probably averaged about £40 a year,[5] so his minimum income from office was £280. He occasionally gained extra poundage for paying in sums not part of his normal charge, such as the £133 6*s* 8*d* allowed him for poundage on the sum of £6,601 5*s* 10*d* paid in to the Crown from Sir Giles Mompesson's wood sales.[6] His total income from office almost certainly exceeded £300. The complete income from his Somerset property will probably now never be known, since a complete survey, rental and set of accounts, formerly in the possession of Miss Gore, seems to have disappeared after her death. Using this document, Miss Gore estimated that at the beginning of James I's reign Pym had a median annual income from land of between £400 and £500, inflated by occasional large entry fines such as one of £545.[7] This coincides fairly closely with such estimates as can be made from surviving estate documents, and though the Somerset property yielded more later, it is doubtful whether, at this date, it yielded more than £500 a year at most. At this date, then, something between thirty-five and forty per cent of Pym's annual income probably came from office.

The third point concerns Pym's security when he entered bonds for his good behaviour in office. His security was his brother-in-law William Cholmeley of Highgate, Middlesex. He had been one of Pym's feoffees to uses in 1614, and was the man Pym used as an intermediary when negotiating with Cranfield for his release from imprisonment after the parliament of 1621.[8] He was not an important or influential connection, and Pym's persistent use of him suggests a lack of more influential friends.

5 For Pym's poundage, see P.R.O., L.R. 7/113–20.

6 National Register of Archives, Sackville MS. ON 7847. I would like to thank Professor Roy Schreiber for this reference. The document is undated, though after 1617. Cranfield's reasons for allowing Pym a double rate of poundage can only be a matter for conjecture.

7 C. J. Sawyer and Co., *Catalogue no. 155* (Jan. 1940), no. 159. I would like to thank Messrs. Sawyer for a great deal of help, and for permission to quote from their catalogue. This MS., if rediscovered, would clearly be the most valuable single source on Pym's early adult life. The payment of £545 to which Miss Gore referred is identifiable in Somerset Record Office, Pym MS. no. 122. The value of Pym's property should not be compared with valuation figures for other Somerset properties. The valuation figure for Pym's property which would have been produced at an inquisition *post mortem* was £100 6*s* 8*d* (Pym MSS. nos 139–146 (1614)).

8 Somerset R.O., Pym MS. no. 146; Hist. MSS. Comm., *4th Rept.*, p. 305.

10

Charles I's Financial Estimates for 1642

THE TWO YEARS before the outbreak of the Civil War are generally thought of as a well-documented period. So, in many ways, they are, yet it is not always appreciated that, among the many types of source which are exceptionally rich, royal archives are a significant exception. Of all the people around Charles in these years, only one was the sort of paper-hoarder who inspires the devotion of historians. That one was Edward Nicholas, clerk of the council, and Secretary of State from early December 1641. Perhaps no one else would have done what Nicholas did with Charles's commission to Newcastle and Legge to seize Hull, on 11 January 1642, and kept a record of his authorization not to make a record.[1]

Nicholas accompanied the king on his hurried departure from London on 10 January 1642, and it may safely be supposed that this hasty departure hindered him from keeping his papers with the tidiness that was natural to him. Among the Nicholas papers now in the British Library, Egerton MS. 2541 is catalogued as a volume of Admiralty and Irish papers. The description is correct, for a large majority of the documents in the volume belong to these two categories. However, the volume also contains several stray items on English politics. These items should, in effect, be regarded as strays from *State Papers Domestic*. Since the foliation, and the binding, are not contemporary with the manuscripts, and many of the documents have been folded, it is probable that Nicholas left the material in the form of a pile of loose papers. One of these papers, which has come to rest on what is now fos. 266–71, is headed 'A Briefe View of His Majesties Ordinary Receipts which are likely to continewe for yeare 1642'. In the margin of the first folio, it bears the date '28 Dec. 1641', and it is annotated on the last folio by Nicholas.

The document begins (fo. 266r–v) with a three-column account of the king's sources of revenue, listing under each item the total revenue from that source, the amount committed in the form of assignment and anticipation, and the amount which remains unassigned. Folio 267 is blank. Folio 268r–v, the middle section of the document, lists receipts 'included in the bill of Tonnage and Poundage', and receipts 'which as wee conceive will hereafter totally faile', and amalgamates the two in a grand total. The third section of the document, fo. 270r–v, lists 'payments upon the ordinary for the years ensueing 1642 unprovided for'. This appears to be, not a list of items of expenditure, but a list

[1] Public Record Office, SP 16/488/50, sign manual warrant authorizing Nicholas to make no entry in the Signet Office. I am grateful to Dr. G. E. Aylmer, Professor Linda Colley and Mr. Richard Stewart for their comments on an earlier draft of this article.

of the amounts by which items of expenditure exceed the revenues assigned to meet them. It is exactly what it says: a list of 'payments . . . unprovided for'. Since the document has been folded, probably not as a single item, it appears that the notes on fos. 267v, 269v and 271v were endorsements, but it is hard to be certain exactly to which folios. The accounts are in a consistent hand throughout, possibly of exchequer provenance. The endorsements on fos. 267v, 269v and 271v, and the date at the head of fo. 266, are probably in another hand, and certainly in a different ink. Edward Nicholas has summarized the document on fo. 271.

This document clearly belongs to the family of revenue balances which run from 1635 to 1641, and shows distinct affinities with other members of this family. The balances hitherto known divide into two generations. The first are balances of 1635 (Public Record Office, T 56/2, E 407/78/5; House of Lords Main Papers, 29 December 1640 etc), showing the king's revenue and expenditure in settled times, but before the improvements of the sixteen-thirties had been completed. The second group, mostly bearing the date 16 August 1641, are copies of the balance drawn up by Pye and Wardour to assist the financial planning of the Long Parliament. These give a medium of revenue and expenditure for the five years 1636–41. The beginning of a third stage is suggested by Bodleian MS. Clarendon vol. 20, no. 1539, since this goes on from listing the revenues and expenditures of the last years of the sixteen-thirties to distinguishing between those 'esteemed legall' and those 'held illegall': it begins to move on from assessing what the revenues were to assessing what they might become in future. The balance here printed is an extension of this third stage of balance-making, in that it attempts to calculate the king's likely income in a future situation. Its peculiarity is that it is drawn up to meet a hypothetical situation, in which the king would no longer enjoy any grant of tonnage and poundage. The object of the document is to tell the king (or the Treasury commissioners) what income would be available to meet what expenses if there were no more tonnage and poundage. This conclusion is strengthened by a copy of part of this manuscript, now University of London Goldsmiths' MS. 34.[2] This copy, dated 5 January 1642, repeats fos. 266r–v and 270r–v. That is to say, it lists expected future income and expenditure, but altogether omits tonnage and poundage and the revenues 'likely to faile', most of which can be classified as monopolies.

We have then a revenue balance, dated 28 December 1641, showing how the king may live without tonnage and poundage. We also have an order to appoint a commission, dated 11 December, with instructions to do precisely that, so it appears reasonable to entertain the hypothesis that the two may be connected The 11 December document is an order in council with the king present, for a commission to balance His Majesty's revenue and retrench his household expenses. It recounts that:

This day his Majesty was pleased to declare how necessary he thought it at this time to enter into a serious consideration of his subsistence, and so order his expenses, as not to live longer from hand to mouth, as of late he had done by reason the Bill of Tonnage and Poundage hath not been passed to him for continuance, as usually and time out of mind it

[2] There is no clue to the original provenance of the Goldsmiths' manuscript.

had been to his predecessors, but only for a few months or weeks, and so renewed; which his Majesty further declared to be dishonourable for him to accept any more in that way; but that his resolution was firm no way to infringe the liberty and propriety of his subjects, nor yet to suffer himself to be starved or bought out of any more flowers of his Crown.

The commissioners were accordingly instructed

to frame a balance of his Majesty's said revenues and of all his expenses ordinary and extraordinary, and to make such retrenchment of his Majesty's expenses, as well Household as otherwise, that he may be able to subsist, though below his kingly dignity, upon his own Revenue without burdening his subjects, in case the duties of Tonnage and Poundage shall be refused to be granted him in such sort as they have been granted to his Royal predecessors.[3]

The document in Nicholas's papers would appear to be the balance here requested. There is no further report to indicate how the king could so retrench as to live without tonnage and poundage: indeed, it was probably the conclusion drawn from the balance that he could not do so.

It is a striking feature of the commission that it envisages tonnage and poundage ceasing by Charles's refusal to take it, rather than by a parliamentary refusal to grant it.[4] The story of tonnage and poundage during the Long Parliament is a long one, and this is not the place to tell it, but a brief account of its status in December 1641 is in order. The Long Parliament had granted Charles tonnage and poundage by no less than five successive short-term acts. The one then current, 16 Car. I, c. 29, was due to expire on 1 February 1642. These acts recited that they were passed on this short-term basis because the parliament intended to produce a new book of rates, which was not yet ready. They also condemned impositions, thereby reversing the judgment in Bate's case, while continuing them on a temporary basis (by authority of the acts themselves) until the new book of rates should be completed.[5]

These acts, then, firmly asserted the principle that all customs duties existed by parliamentary authority, while they had not yet used this authority to settle the duties on any workable long-term basis. Moreover, the acts had changed the basis of collection. They swept away the whole of Charles's system of assignment of customs revenue to particular items of expenditure. Instead, the money was administered by the parliament, who doled it out (by their own authority) to the navy and the king's household. Charles, then, was still receiving the money, but

[3] *Calendar of State Papers, Domestic, 1641–3*, pp. 194–5 (the original adds nothing to the Calendar): P.R.O., SP 16/476/106 (misdated), SP 16/138/63 (misdated), PC 2/12 p. 200. 'Tonnage and poundage' in the language of 1641 represents *any* customs duties to be granted by a bill of tonnage and poundage. In practice, all customs except the Ancient Custom had come to be classified either as 'tonnage and poundage', and therefore legal, or as 'impositions' and therefore illegal. Any customs duty, then, could continue legally only if assimilated to the category of tonnage and poundage through inclusion in a tonnage and poundage bill.

[4] For strikingly similar reasoning, see *The Letters of Queen Henrietta Maria*, ed. M. A. E. Green (1856), pp. 53, 69 (17 March and 11 May 1642). For Charles's remarks when he gave the royal assent to yet another temporary tonnage and poundage bill on 31 Jan. 1642, see *Lords Journals*, iv. 554.

[5] 16 Car. I, cc. 8, 12, 22, 25, 29; *Constitutional Documents of the Puritan Revolution*, ed. S. R. Gardiner (Oxford, 1889), pp. 159–62.

had no control over its collection and administration.[6] The loss of this control had thrown a carefully planned system of assignment of particular revenues to particular expenses into total confusion, and one of the immediate objectives of the balance appears to be to gather the information needed for a re-planning of the system of assignments.

It is unfortunate, from the point of view of modern historians, that the balance conceals many things by lumping together assignments and anticipations under one common heading. By doing so, it perhaps offers us a clue to its authorship, for the confusion of assignment and anticipation under a common heading was a practice characteristic of Sir Robert Pye,[7] auditor of the exchequer, who, together with Sir Edward Wardour, clerk of the pells, had been responsible for the balance of August 1641, now in Bodleian MS. Clarendon vol. 20, no. 1539. Pye and Wardour, then, may be the 'we' of this document. They were likely to be well informed, since, in addition to being trusted king's servants, they were also John Hampden's father-in-law and John Pym's feoffee to uses[8] respectively. Moreover, Pye was on the parliamentary committee preparing the new book of rates, which finally finished its work in July 1642.[9] This fact may help to explain why the authors of the balance, though clearly instructed to proceed on the assumption that tonnage and poundage will not continue, never state in their own words that it is unlikely to do so.

The editing of this document has presented problems, since in its present form it is likely to be deceptive to a modern reader. On the revenue side of the balance, the trouble lies in the confusion of assignment with anticipation. Assignment is a regular earmarking of particular revenue to particular expenditure. Though annoying to officers of the Receipt, who did not see the money, it is in no sense deficit finance. Assigned income differs from unassigned income in that there is no element of discretion in the spending of it, but it is emphatically part of total income.

The figure quoted as 'clere' in the revenue side of the balance is a figure of unassigned income only, and no clue to the king's total income. Since many readers may wish to grope both towards the king's total income, and towards the extent of anticipations, I have tried to help with the process. Anticipations, the spending of revenue before it is received, may more resemble deficit finance, and the total sum of anticipations is a figure of debt. It is thus very different indeed

[6] 16 Car. I, c. 22: there is a copy of the parliament's printed tonnage and poundage accounts in the Harley Papers, British Library Loan MS. 29/46. It shows, from 25 May 1641 to 9 June 1642, the payment of £118,292 to the king's 'private use', and of £129,914 to the maintenance of the navy. I am grateful to Miss Norah M. Fuidge for a transcript of this document. For a premature and unsuccessful attempt by Pym to sweep away Charles's system of assignments, see *Journal of Sir Symonds D'Ewes*, ed. W. Notestein (New Haven, Conn., 1923), p. 192 (29 Dec. 1640).

[7] G. E. Aylmer, *The King's Servants: the Civil Service of Charles I, 1625–42* (1961), pp. 195–6, 381. For Pye's views on assignments, see *Notebook of Sir John Northcote*, ed. A. H. A. Hamilton (1877), p. 113. On 7 March 1642, Sir Robert Pye was paid £200, and his clerk another £200, for making a balance of revenue and other services (P.R.O., E 403/2814, p. 38).

[8] Somerset Record Office, DD/BW, Pym MS. no. 146; P.R.O., C 66/2048 m. 29.

[9] *An Ordinance of Parliament Concerning the Subsidie of Tonnage and Poundage* (1642). This information is printed on the flyleaf of the copy in the Guildhall Library, but not of the copy in the Goldsmiths' Library or the copy in Beinecke Library, Yale. I am grateful to Miss Norah M. Fuidge for transcribing this item for me.

from assignments. There is no complete figure for assignments in force in 1641, so the true figure for the division between assignment and anticipation is undiscoverable. However, the main outlines of the system of assignment in use up to this point appear to be those worked out in 1635, and included in the 1635 balance (P.R.O., T 56/2). Editorial practice, then, has been to print with column 2, of 'assignments and anticipations', a figure of the assignment on that source of revenue in 1635. It cannot be assumed that this is identical to the amount of assignment in 1641, but it can perhaps be said that in most cases the figures may have a broad similarity. The account of anticipations in Bodleian MS. Bankes 5/45 shows an increase between 1635 and 1641 from £330,217 to £550,000. At least, it seems that the element of anticipation is unlikely to be greater than the difference between the figure for 1635 assignments (printed in brackets), and the 1641 combined figure for assignments and anticipations. Total revenue, then, is likely to have had some very approximate resemblance to the sum of the figure listed as 'clere' in the 1641 balance plus the assignment figure from 1635. Since adding these two figures together multiplies the king's apparent income sixfold, it clearly makes some difference to any picture of the king's income.

On the expenditure side, the balance here printed again does not give any picture of total budgeted expenditure, but only of expenditure for which no assignment exists. Again, it would give so misleading an impression to confuse this figure with the total cost of government in 1641 that I have supplied, against each item of expenditure, the amount assigned to it in the 1635 balance, P.R.O., T 56/2, and to be met out of continuing sources of income. Items of expenditure to which no assignment was made in 1635 were paid out of the Receipt, and are marked 'receipt' in brackets. The total cost of each item should then be taken to have an approximate resemblance to the sum of the amount here listed as 'unprovided for' plus the part of the 1635 assignment which was on sources of revenue still continuing. By supplying the 1635 figures in brackets, I have hoped to make it possible to gain a picture of the amount of money Charles's advisers thought he needed to pay his ordinary expenses.

Finally, it is worth noting some discrepancies between the document here printed and the balance of August 1641, Bodleian MS. Clarendon vol. 20, no. 1539. The August balance distinguishes between revenues 'esteemed legall' and others 'held illegall'. It is significant that in this respect, the classifications of August and December are by no means identical. The discrepancies may provide some clue to the movement of royal thinking between August and December. The most significant is that of purveyance, which was listed as 'held illegall' in August, and as 'like to continue' in December. Perhaps this should be linked with the sentence in the 11 December commission in which Charles announced his determination not to be starved or bought out of any more flowers of his Crown. It is possible that in August he had been willing to consider a Great Contract-type solution to the problem of purveyance, and that with the general hardening of his line in December, he had firmly set his face against any such thing. Other such discrepancies have been indicated in footnotes.

One other discrepancy is that five items listed under a general 'customs' heading in August are now shifted out of the tonnage and poundage heading, and listed with revenues not likely to continue. These are the pretermitted custom, Alderman Abell's wine project, the imposition on tobacco and two impositions on seacoals. These serve to illustrate the increasing difficulty in distinguishing between custom and imposition, on the one hand, or between imposition and monopoly on the other. They are also, perhaps, one more barometer of increasing royal pessimism about the terms on which any future grant to tonnage and poundage might be made. Charles found, when he reviewed the record of his parliaments on tonnage and poundage, that it made such pessimism seem warranted by experience.

British Library, Egerton MS. 2541 fos. 266–71[10]

[*fo. 266*]]*Marginated*] 28 Dec. 1641

A Briefe View of His Majesties Ordinary Receipts which are likely to continewe for the yeare 1642

	Charge	*Assignacons Anticipacons*	*Remayne*
Allome workes*	12,500	12,160 [1,233]	340
Composicons for the kings house ultra wines*	36,237	36,237 [30,330]	0
Composicon of xii d. per halder [*sic*] upon sea coales	[*blank*] [1,838][11]		
Post fynes	2,275	1,300 [1,382]	975
Wyne licences*	2,700	2,633 [333]	67
Greenwax	3,265	300 [nil]	2,965
Old and new draperies	997	746 [nil]	251
Issues of jurors	1,000[12]	0 [114]	1,000
xl *s.* per cent of gold and silver transported*	5,760	150 [not listed]	5,610
Ballasting of shippes	466	0 [not listed]	466
Chiefe butlerage	500	278 [278]	222
Sundry minute farmes	413	0 [nil]	413

[10] Printed by permission of the Trustees of the British Library board. Standard abbreviations have been extended and capitalization modernized, but spelling is as in the original. Sums of money are given in pounds: 'li.' and 'l.' where occasionally given in the original have been omitted, as has 'O.O.' for shillings and pence throughout. Items marked* are those listed in Bodleian Library, MS. Clarendon 20, no. 1539 (16 Aug. 1641) as 'held illegall'. Figures in square brackets are those of the assignment in 1635, taken from P.R.O., T 562, except those marked †, which are omitted there and the figures quoted are from P.R.O., E 407/78/5. I am grateful to Dr. G. E. Aylmer for drawing my attention to this document.

[11] Bodleian MS. Clar. 20, no. 1539, 16 Aug. 1641.

[12] This patent had been listed as a grievance both in 1606–7 and in 1621: its powers of survival are remarkable (see *Commons Debates in 1621*, ed. W. Notestein, F. H. Relf and H. Simpson (7 vols., New Haven, Conn., 1935), vii. 387–90).

	Charge	*Assignacons Anticipacons*	Remayne
Court of wardes and liveries	75,088	75,088 [61,257][13]	0
Duchie of Cornewall	19,435	16,541 [1,777]	2,894
[*fo. 266v*] Duchie of Lancaster	10,522	10,438 [11,220][13]	84
Receivors generall	83,964	69,940 [65,529]	14,024
Hanaper	7,695	7,005 [3,252]†	690
Alienacons	5,986	3,920 [3,657]†	2,066
First fruites	5,646	593 [93]†	5,053
Annuall tenthess of the clergie	12,598	0 [not listed]	12,598
The mynte	13,270[14]	11,729 [7,177]†	1,541
The antient revenew of the Pipe[15]	9,093	7,325 [8,283]†	1,768
Recusants in the North[16]	14,222	7,158 [1,933]	7,064
Recusants in the South	4,424	184 [195]	4,240
New Yeares guifts	2,178	2,178 [2,284]	0
Clerke of the faculties	339	21 [22]	318
Respite of homage	837	837 [64]	0
Dover Castle rents	100	0 [nil]	100
Reliefes	[*blank*]	[*blank*]	[*blank*]
Stalled debts and seisures	1,593	0 [nil]	1,593
Moyty of uncustomed goods	693	693 [341]	0
Fines and amerciaments	684	0 [nil]	684
Summa Total	334,480	267,454	67,026

[*fo.267v*][17] 28 Dec. 1641

[13] Both the courts of wards and the duchy of Lancaster are noted in P.R.O., T 56/2 as bearing assignments greater than the revenue they yielded.

[14] Bodleian MS. Clar. 20, no. 1539 lists £12,541 13*s* 10¾*d* for the warden of the mint, and £11,886 4*s* 9*d* for the master worker of the mint. It is not clear which is intended here, nor why the other is omitted.

[15] The Pipe is omitted from the revenue side of P.R.O., T 56/2.

[16] The northern recusant revenue had been raised from a figure of £9,835 in P.R.O., T 56/2. In percentage terms, this is perhaps the biggest increase in any single source of revenue.

[17] Fo. 267 is blank.

A Briefe view of the State of his Majesties Ordinary Receipts for the yeare ensueing 1642

[*fo.268*] Titles of the Receaptes in the Ballance included in the Bill of Tonnage and Poundage

vizt.

Greate customes	172,500
Petty farmes	72,500
Newe imposicons	119,583
Impost of iii d. sup. libr.	5,004
Impost upon wines	30,092
Composicons for wynes in the outportes	5,000
Sugars	2,000
Impost upon seacoales	[*blank*][18]
French wynes portu Cestr	346
Cottons and bayes	200
Summa	407,225

Titles of the Receipts in the Ballance which as wee conceive will hereafter totally faile

vizt.

Imposte upon tobacco		11,000
Retayling tobacco		13,052
xl s. per tonne upon wines per Abell		30,000
Soapemakers of London	29,128	30,828
Soapemakers of Bristoll	1,200	
Castile soape	500	
[*fo.268v*] Mr. Sands his graunt of xii d. upon seacoales		10,000
Pretermitted customes		17,863
Copras farme		1,050
Sole makeinge of glasses		1,500
Starrechamber fines		1,912
Corporacon of Westmr.		1,100
Playing cards and dice		741
Bever hatts		500
Clarke of the markett[19]		336
Unwrought clothes		100
Sundry minute farmes		973
Clenseinge[20] and dying of silke		[*blank*]
Corporacon of starchmakers		[*blank*]
Gold and silver threed		[*blank*][21]
Suma totalis		120,955

Some Totall vizt.	Of the titles of the receipts included in the bill of tonnage and poundage 407,225 Of the titles of the receipts that are like hereafter totally to faile 120,955	528,180

[18] £100 in Bodleian MS. Clar. 20, no. 1539.

[19] See 16 Car. I, c. 19.

[20] The paper has been folded at this point, and the transcription is doubtful.

[21] See 16 Car. I, c. 21.

[*fo.269v*][22] Titles of the Receipts included in the Bill of Tonnage and Poundage and other tytles likely hereafter totally to faile[23]

[*fo.270*] Payments upon the ordinary for the yeare ensueing 1642 unprovided for

Privy purse	5,000
[+2284 assigned on continuing sources]	
The queenes Majesty	3,800
]+28,794 assigned on continuing sources]	
The prince and the rest of his Majesties royall children	23,400
[+3,000 assigned on continuing sources; 9,500 assigned on lapsed ones]	
The queene of Bohemia and her children ultra pencons	19,150
[receipt 1635]	
The cofferer for the king and queenes house	51,250
[+60,549 assigned on continuing sources; 27,444 assigned on lapsed ones]	
The kings Majesties roabes	5,000
[5,000 assigned on lapsed sources]	
The greate wardrobe ultra surplusages	13,065
[+2,651 assigned on continuing sources; 13,065 assigned on lapsed ones]	
Tapestriemakers with the painter at Mortlake	2,250
[not in T 56/2]	
Master of the horse for provision of horses	2,114
[receipt 1635]	
Threr of the chamber	16,981
[+13,500 assigned on continuing sources]	
The band of gentlemen penconers	6,000
[receipt 1635]	
Jewelhouse[24]	4,756
[receipt 1635]	
Liveries of the guard[24]	1,306
[receipt 1635]	
Halberts for the guard[24]	240
[receipt 1635]	
Paymaster of the workes[24]	11,654
[not in T 56/2]	
Office of thordnance ultra extraordinaries	6,000
[receipt 1635]	
Provision of gunpowder	[*blank*]
Castles and forts	9,247
[+4,732 assigned on continuing sources]	
Master of the armoury	400
[receipt 1635]	
Secretaries of State for intelligences etc.	1,400
[receipt 1635]	

[22] Fo. 269 is blank.

[23] *862* added in a much later hand.

[24] These four items omitted in Goldsmiths' MS. 34, though included in the grand total.

[*fo. 270v*] Ambrs. and agents with transportacons and the bills of the master of ceremonies 20,200
[receipt 1635]
The posts [4,225 on receipt 1635] [*blank*]
Lord Privy Seales dietts 379
[receipt 1635]
Dietts of justices of assise 2,040
[receipt 1635]
Barons of the exchequer 300
[receipt 1635]
Lieutenant of the Tower for wages and dietts of prisoners 1,515
[receipt 1635]
Dietts of prisoners in the Gatehouse 500
[receipt 1635]
Master of the revells[25] 333
[receipt 1635]
Provision of tents and pavilions[26] 2,358
[receipt 1635]
Keepers of houses parkes lodges gardens with repaires etc. 2,200
[+3,560 assigned on continuing sources]
Repaire of castles[27] 1,656
[+32 assigned on continuing sources]†
Repaire of stables 190
[receipt 1635]
Rents of houses with repaire of the same 612
[+66 assigned on continuing sources]†
Liberatees of the exchequer and receipt 1,865
[receipt 1635]
Rewards upon the generall dormant 975
[+40 assigned on continuing sources]
Messengers for riding charges 890
[receipt 1635]
Creacon money 1,112
[+558 assigned on continuing sources;
867 assigned on lapsed ones]
Perpetuities 633
[+4,530 assigned on continuing sources;
200 assigned on lapsed ones]
Annuities and pencons 87,437
[+27,849 assigned on continuing sources;
20,872 assigned on lapsed ones]
Fees to severall his Majesties officers 21,685
[+16,251 assigned on continuing sources;
8,803 assigned on lapsed ones]

[25] The master of the revels has been cut back from £425 to £333. It is tempting to see political significance in this very rare case of retrenchment.

[26] Tents and pavilions has increased from £1,413 in 1635. It is tempting to see the costs of the Bishops' Wars behind this very large increase.

[27] Except for the £32 assigned in 1635, this seems to be a new heading of expenditure. Again it seems reasonable to connect it with the Bishops' Wars.

Interest money	22,473
Suma Total	352,366
[*fo.271*][28] Total ordinary receipts clere	67,026
Payments for ye ordinary	352,366
Soe there wants to pay ye ordinary payments	285,340

[*fo.271v*] Payments upon the ordinary unprovided for the yeare ensueing 1642.

This document does not show Charles I in quite such as desperate position as it appears to do: it is probable that the £334,480 it shows for Charles's gross revenues is nearer his real income than the £67,026 it shows for his net revenues. Yet, even if this document is given the most optimistic interpretation possible, the picture it gives of Charles's financial situation is gloomy enough. Nicholas's figure that there wanted £285,000 to meet the ordinary payments appears to be correct, and moreover, it was the best information available to the king. The figures should be compared with Charles's ordinary income when the Long Parliament met, which was £899,368 per annum. This figure, moreover, understates Charles's loss, since it excludes ship money, forest fines and knighthood fines, all of which had been classified as extraordinary income.

Moreover, this document sharply underlines the point that there was a high correlation between buoyant sources of revenue and illegal sources of revenue. Items like the greenwax and the hanaper were never likely to grow much. Income from receivers general, the duchy of Lancaster and the duchy of Cornwall had been heavily mortgaged, in effect, by the making of long leases at high entry fines to finance the wars of the sixteen-twenties.[29] It was unlikely that much increase in these items could have been achieved until the leases had run out. Among legal sources of revenue, only the court of wards and the northern recusant revenues showed anything approaching the buoyancy of impositions. In fact, the document goes a long way to highlight the dependence of early Stuart finance on the customs.[30]

In so doing, it also illustrates the fact that Charles simply could not make a settlement with the Long Parliament unless a new revenue settlement, and a proper grant of tonnage and poundage in particular, were part of the bargain. If he gave up sources of revenue the parliament regarded as illegal, he simply could not carry on unless he were given new sources of revenue instead. On 23 January 1641, he had told the house of lords that 'what parts of my revenue that shall be found illegal or grievous to the public, I shall willingly lay down, relying entirely upon the affections of my people'.[31] By 11 December he seemed to have decided that he could not rely upon the affections of his people. His trust had been fading by September, when he replied to information from Nicholas that the parliament were about to tackle his revenue: 'I pray God it be to good purpose, and there be

[28] This folio is written in the hand of Edward Nicholas.

[29] This is based on Birmingham Reference Library, Coventry manuscripts, Grants of Leases.

[30] See also Aylmer, pp. 64–5.

[31] *Lords Journals*, iv. 142.

no knavery in it'.[32] This document, when Charles received it, can have done nothing to convince him that the parliament was tackling his revenue to good purpose. In agreeing to lay down the revenues 'held illegall' without getting any replacement, Charles had emphatically got the worst of both worlds. It is worth noting that he received this information of the extent of the devastation to his revenue five days before the first appearance of the articles against the Five Members. It can have done nothing to diminish his willingness to prosecute them.

Charles's resentment at the failure of the Long Parliament to settle his revenue has an important place in his final declarations before the outbreak of the Civil War, and, perhaps more important, in the private messages sent from York to Westminister.[33] As he complained, 'our owne personall wants were notoriously known, and unkindly unprovided for'. Since they had asked to look into his revenue, 'we might have expected some fruit of that pretended care'.[34] He was, in the end, entitled to his question: 'will there never be a time to offer to, as well as to ask of Us?'.[35] In that question, much of Charles I's *casus belli* is contained. Looking at the figures in this document, it is hard to see, without a revenue settlement, what other option was open to him. On his parliaments' record on financial questions, Charles's gloomy assessment of their intentions was to be expected. Whether it was also correct is a question to be considered elsewhere.

[32] A. Fletcher, *The Outbreak of the English Civil War* (1981), p. 159.

[33] See, for example, Hist. MSS. Comm., *8th Rept.*, i. 211b (Bankes to Northumberland, 16 May 1642). For Charles's attempt to secure a life grant of tonnage and poundage from the Commons, and Pym and St. John's success in frustrating it, see *The Private Journals of the Long Parliament*, ed. W. H. Coates, A. S. Young and V. F. Snow (New Haven, Conn., 1982), pp. 183, 185–6; *Lords Journals*, ii. 396–7.

[34] Brit. Libr., E 241(1), *An Exact Collection of Remonstrances* (1643), p. 520, 12 Aug. 1642.

[35] *Ibid.*, p. 140.

III

RELIGIOUS UNITY

11

Arguments for Religious Unity in England, 1530-1650[1]

Père Lecler, in his survey of *Toleration and the Reformation*, concluded that 'among all the countries that were divided by the Reformation . . . England comes last so far as tolerance is concerned. Even the simple freedom of conscience which was gradually extended to the whole of Europe, was constantly threatened in England by police inquiries'.[2] With the exception of Spain, Italy and possibly Scotland, the English government was more successful and persistent in its attempts to enforce unity of religion than its counterparts. The explanations of this fact are probably largely political: in most European countries, the willingness to listen to tolerationist arguments was in proportion to the practical difficulty of suppressing dissenters. As Professor Owen Chadwick said, 'Catholic France accepted the Edict of Nantes in 1598 . . . not because Catholic France affirmed toleration to be merely right, but because without the Edict France must be destroyed'.[3] The victory of toleration was normally a victory of expediency over principle. Featly, for example, says that 'toleration of different religions falleth in some respects, within the compass of the mysteries of State, which cannot be determined in the Schools, but are fittest to be debated at the Council table'.[4]

In the eyes of contemporaries, the arguments for religious unity were rarely beaten in debate until they had already been defeated by events. There were, it is true, some doubts about the utility of persecution, since it was often recognised that force could not create faith.[5] But there were few

[1] I would like to thank my wife for a great deal of help in the preparation of this article. She has helped to stimulate my interest in the subject, made a considerable contribution to the argument of the article, and placed at my disposal a large amount of material which she had collected.

[2] J. Lecler, *Toleration and the Reformation*, trans. T. L. Westow, London 1960, ii. 493.

[3] *From Uniformity to Unity*, ed. G. F. Nuttall and Owen Chadwick, London 1962, 9. See also Owen Chadwick, *The Reformation*, London 1964, 404 and N. M. Sutherland, *Catherine de Medici*, Historical Association 1966, 11–12.

[4] Prynne, *Canterburies Doome*, London 1646, 342.

[5] The admission that force could not create faith was compatible with a defence of persecution. See P. R. L. Brown, 'St. Augustine's Attitude to Religious Coercion', *Journal of Roman Studies*, liv (1964), 111–12. I would like to thank Mr. Brown for a number of helpful comments on an earlier draft of this article. Bishop Sandys (*Works*, London 1841, 46), faithfully following Augustine, quotes *Ep.* 204: 'he that is constrained is driven whither he would not go willingly: but when he is entered by constraint, then he feedeth

continued

doubts about the persecutors' major premise, the need for religious unity: that both Christian duty and political prudence demanded, wherever possible, that a State should be maintained in the unity of one religion. There were doubts about how far this aim was practicable, but almost none about how far it was desirable. It was very difficult to put up an effective case against persecution while the need for religious unity went unquestioned. The debate on persecution was about means, and it was hard to make much progress with this debate while the ideal of religious unity, the end of persecution, was left unchallenged.

This article is concerned with the arguments used for religious unity (which were far more widely maintained than those for persecution) because they have received disproportionately little attention beside that given to the early arguments for toleration.[1] The case for religious unity took many forms. So did its definition: some people thought it demanded a much more precise identity of belief and practice than others did. But the central points of the case, those which can be handled within the scope of an article, are remarkably similar in all strands of opinion. This body of common assumptions, too automatic to be easily made matter for debate, constituted the real force of the desire for religious unity in Tudor and Stuart England. Most of these assumptions about the nature of the church and of society were part of the common stock of ideas of medieval Christendom and at first were too much taken for granted to be thought in need of much justification. It is from the end of the period, from men like Edwards and Laud, who were aware of writing under challenge, that many of the most explicit statements of these principles come.

One of these assumptions was that unity is part of the purpose of Christianity: that a devotion to Christianity must necessarily involve a devotion to unity. As Laud said: '. . . the spirit of God, which is one, and loves nothing but as it tends to one. Nay, as the spirit of God is one, and cannot dissent from itself, no more ought they whom the Spirit hath joined in one . . . therefore he that divides the unity of the church practises against the unity of the spirit.'[2] Contention was one of the fruits of the flesh, not of the Spirit: 'St. Paul writes, as long as there are contentions among you, are ye not carnal? . . . Nomen ecclesiae nomen unitatis et pacis, saith Augustine . . . although a man hold all the articles of religion, and break the unity of the church, yet is he not of the church. Yea, albeit he have never so great a multitude of hearers at his sermons'.[3] One of the most interesting points about the persistent attacks on Machiavelli is the

continued
with a good will'. But Augustine's struggles with the problem of the freedom of the will were too subtle for most people, and the commoner position is Hooper's, that though force cannot create faith, it can prevent false doctrine from breaking forth in public: John Hooper, *A Godly Confession and Protestation of the Christian Faith, Later Writings of Bishop Hooper*, ed. Parker Society (hereafter referred to as P.S.), Cambridge 1852. 87,

[1] On the arguments for toleration see W. K. Jordan, *History of Religious Toleration*, London 1932–40, and J. Lecler, op. cit. and bibliography.

[2] Sermon 6 (1628), in *Works*, Oxford 1847, i. 163.

[3] Whitgift, Sermon on the Queen's Accession Day, 1583, in *Works*, P.S., iii. 595.

way he is accused of preaching the doctrine: 'divide and rule'.[1] He had in fact maintained nothing of the sort, and the identification in his opponents' minds appears to be that since Machiavelli was wicked, and wicked people caused division, Machiavelli must have preached division. Division, in fact, was regularly thought of as one of the Devil's means of seducing mankind. A popular pamphlet of 1642, purporting to be a letter from the Devil to the English Roman hierarchy, recounted how 'the only means in our princely wisdom conceived to be the breaking the bond of unity and peace, thereby to provoke the great God of Heaven to leave them to themselves, and to our powerful strategems'. The pamphlet then described an agreement between the Devil and his servant, Attorney Contention, to sow discord: 'yea, he shall not omit to set the father against the son, and the son against the father'.[2] On a more serious level, disunity was thought a scandal to Christians and to the Christian Church. As the *Homilies* said: 'O how the church is divided . . . O how the coat of Christ, which was without seam, is all to rent and torn! O body mystical of Christ, where is that holy and happy unity, out of the which whosoever is, he is not in Christ?'[3] John Dod said: 'it is for dogs and swine to be barking and biting at one another: but to see sheep and lambs tearing one another, all the world would wonder at it'. How, he asks, can Christ's sheep be so divided? His answer is a common one: it is because of the sin of pride.[4] But whose pride? If, as Dod tried to persuade his hearers, the pride may be ours, this doctrine might contribute to peace. But if, as many were naturally tempted to assume, the pride was the other man's, then this doctrine could be used to reinforce hostility towards him.

This sense of scandal was often crucial to theologically-minded members of society. There were many who were not so minded: for them, the important assumption was that neither the State nor the households and families which composed it could subsist in any sort of security unless buttressed and guaranteed by religion. That many people thought this is widely known, but why did they think it? Such beliefs had been held for a long time, but in Protestant England they were strengthened by the increasingly literal use of the Old Testament. The concept of the Church involved in this pattern of thought is of course an old one. What is new is the reinforcement of this concept of the Church by its closer identification with the nation, and this identification of the Church with a single political community makes Old Testament parallels more directly relevant.

[1] Felix Raab, *The English Face of Machiavelli*, London 1964, 109, 123, 125, 131 n. 2, 162, 209 n. 2.

[2] *Newes from Hell, Rome and the Inns of Court* (Thomason E. 133), London 1642, 1–12. For a more serious ascription of a desire for division to the Devil, see Stephen Marshall, *Meroz Cursed*, London 1642, 37. Calamy quoted Cyprian to the effect that it was worse to divide the church than to sacrifice to an idol: *An Indictment against England Because of her Self-Murdering Divisions*, London 1645, Title Page.

[3] *Sermon Against Contention, Sermons or Homilies*, London 1638, 142. Since the Church was the bride of Christ, for its members to commit spiritual infidelity was spiritual whoredom and adultery.

[4] John Dod, *A Remedy Against Private Contentions*, London 1610, 10, 7–8.

One of the constant arguments of the Henrician reformers was that Church and State could not have two heads, for they were one and the same body of men. The same people, with the same head, are assumed to constitute both Church and State.[1] As Hooker said: 'there is not any man a member of the Church of England, but the same man is also a member of the commonwealth; nor any man a member of the commonwealth, which is not also of the church of England'.[2] It was easy to deduce from this position that the attempt to withdraw from the Church of England constituted an attempt to withdraw from the commonwealth: for Eliot to attack the Papists as 'members of the body of this land who have studied to be incorporate with others'.[3] In contrast to France and Holland, where a tendency developed to define the nation by its opposition to Spain, in England religion came to be part of the very definition of a nation.[4] One of the arguments for union with Scotland was that the two countries had the same religion, and therefore were a nation. Favour, the old Puritan vicar of Halifax, listed three reasons why the English and the Scots constituted a nation: they had a common frontier, similar speech and manners, and the same religion. James I listed the same three reasons why England and Scotland might be made a nation, and Baillie in 1640 expressed the hope of obtaining a conformity of religion between them, 'and by it a most hearty nation of the kingdoms'.[5] When this belief was combined with Nicholas Fuller's belief that 'we being now the people of God, the Jews being cut off',[6] it was easy to give all the Old Testament material

[1] See, for example, Stephen Gardiner, *De Vera Obedientia*, ed. P. Janelle, Cambridge 1930, 117.

[2] Hooker, *Of the Laws of Ecclesiastical Polity*, VIII, i. 2. On the influence of the Old Testament, first as a source, and then as a means of making old ideas both more literal and more national, see P. R. L. Brown, op. cit., 114, and J. Lecler, op. cit., i. 7, 31, 70. One of the Scottish canons of 1635 threatened excommunication to those who denied that the king had the same authority in ecclesiastical causes that godly kings had among the Jews: Heylin, *Cyprianus Anglicanus*, Dublin 1719, iv. 35.

[3] *Negotium Posterorum*, ed. A. B. Grosart, London 1881, i. 70. He also said division in religion 'wrongs divinity', and 'dissolves all ties and obligations, civil and natural'.

[4] D'Avaux, The French Ambassador to the United Provinces, claimed in 1644 that 'the names of Catholic and Hollander can go together. It is possible to be an enemy of the King of Spain without being a Protestant': P. Geyl, *The Netherlands in the Seventeenth Century*, London 1961, i. 143.

[5] A. G. Dickens, 'Writers of Tudor Yorkshire', *Transactions of the Royal Historical Society* (5th series 13, 1963), 72–3: *Basilikon Doron*, *Political Works of James I*, ed. C. H. MacIlwain, Cambridge Mass. 1918, 51: R. Baillie, *Letters and Journals*, ed. Laing, Edinburgh 1841, i. 278. These passages do not say quite the same thing, but the variation is probably due to difference in dates.

[6] Faith Thompson, *Magna Carta*, Minneapolis 1948, 260. For many Puritans, this sense of being the chosen people, that, as Job Throckmorton put it, 'the Lord hath vowed himself to be English' (J. E. Neale, *Queen Elizabeth I and her Parliaments*, London 1957, ii. 170) was a profound source of comfort. One of their persistent fears was that if they corrupted their worship. God would deprive them of their status as chosen people, as he had deprived the Jews. This is the meaning of the frequent allusions to the danger of the golden candlestick being removed. See E. Calamy, *Eli Trembling for Fear of the Ark*, Oxford 1663, 15; W. Perkins, *The Idolatry of the Last Times*, *Works*, Cambridge 1605, 811; Peter Smart, *The Vanity and Downfall*, Edinburgh 1628, 38; and Sir John Wray, in Rushworth, *Historical Collections*, III, i. 240–1.

on idolatry, blasphemy and error a direct application to English politics, and some of that material is very rich.

The lack of secular doctrine of obligation, either political or social, was a more serious cause for concern. Most gentlemen, masters, husbands or fathers, not to mention kings, wanted to preserve a sense of obligation to the social order (or some part of it), and could rarely see how this could be done but by religion. The belief that authority was legitimate because it was ordained of God was not confined to holders of what Figgis chose to classify as the doctrine of divine right: it was, as Professor Owen Chadwick says, 'common ground to anyone who used his Bible'. That all power is of God was a *cliché* to which both Whitgift and Rutherford could subscribe, and, as Roger Manwaring said, 'there is no power, unless it be given from above'.[1] Against this background, no theory of obligation could be effective unless it relied on the proposition that men (and women) were bound to obey *because* God commended it.

A government with overwhelming military force may survive without a generally accepted theory of obligation, though few have wished to make the attempt. But Tudor and Stuart governments were conscious of their lack of coercive and investigatory powers, and correspondingly felt the greater need for a theory of obligation. The standard point that fear was not enough to rely on was true: if obedience were not of conscience, it was unreliable. As Hooker said: 'men fearing God are thereby a great deal more effectively than by politic laws restrained from doing evil; inasmuch as those laws have no farther power than over our outward actions only, whereas unto men's inward cogitations, unto the privy interests and motions of their hearts, religion serveth for a bridle'.[2] The emphasis on the need for witnesses to believe they would suffer spiritual penalties for breaking oaths was perhaps in inverse proportion to the chances of detecting perjury. Charles I was quite right in maintaining that 'if the pulpits teach not obedience, the king will have but small comfort of the militia'.[3]

Country gentlemen were often more aware of the need for a theory of obligation in their families and households than in the State. It was not only in Shakespeare's plays that women were hard to subject as thoroughly as convention demanded. Gouge, giving a standard exposition of the subjection of women to their husbands, provoked unforeseen indignation

[1] Owen Chadwick, *The Reformation*, London 1964, 391. Figgis was discussing 'the divine right of kings in its completest form', which is not the same subject as divine right: see J. N. Figgis, *The Divine Right of Kings*, Cambridge 1914, 4. Whitgift, *Works*, iii. 588; S. Rutherford, *Lex, Rex*, London 1644, 21; R. Manwaring, *Religion and Allegiance*, London 1627, i. 8.

[2] Hooker, op. cit., v. ii. 3. On oaths, see Christopher Hill, *Society and Puritanism in Pre-Revolutionary England*, London 1964, 382–419. It may be doubted whether the growth of cynicism about oaths (as distinct from objection on grounds of content to any individual oath) had any particular connexion with Puritanism.

[3] W. Haller, *Liberty and Reformation in the Puritan Revolution*, New York 1955, 66. The statement is from a private letter to Henrietta Maria in 1646. On preachers as a means of controlling the Elizabethan north, see C. Hill, 'Puritans and the Dark Corners of the Land', *T.R.H.S.* (5th Series, no, 13, 1963), 79.

among his parishioners, and became known as a woman-hater.[1] Whitgift struck a sensitive spot when he said: 'the rule of obedience, that is betwixt the magistrate and the subject holdeth betwixt the husband and the wife, the father and his child, and master and the servant. Therefore, measure thou the obedience to the magistrate, as thou wouldest they should perform it unto thee'.[2] Manwaring believed the State's troubles were because men in youth had not been 'subdued with any reverence or godly fear towards their superiors'.[3] One of the few passages in Edwards's *Gangraena* which is emphasised by a marginal hand argues that if a toleration were granted 'they should never have peace in their families more, or even after have command of wives, children, servants'.[4] The desire for a generally accepted theory of obligation was a social, as well as a political fact.

The simplest theory of obligation in use was that of Romans xiii, 'the powers that be are ordained of God'. The subject, wife, child or servant obeys the immediate superior because in doing so he or she is obeying God, whom all are bound to obey. In the words of Ponet's gloss, 'neither is that power and authority which kings, princes, and other ministers of justice exercise only called a power; but also the authority that parents have over their children, and masters over their servants, is also called a power: and neither be the parents and masters the power itself, but they be the ministers and executors of the power, being given unto them by God'.[5] This theory of obligation was useless unless inferiors could identify obedience to their superiors with obedience to God: the theory is not merely primarily, but solely religious.

Some politicians attempted to use other doctrines of obligation. Some Parliamentarians deduced obligation from the mutual acceptance of law by king and people. Pym, as a cautious politician, never quite committed himself to this proposition: he allowed his hearers to pick it up as a subliminal suggestion.[6] Yelverton, in 1607, could safely be more explicit: 'ire sub lege is allegiance.'[7] This sounds like the ground for a secular theory

W. Gouge, *Domestical Duties*, London 1626, Ep. Ded. Authority in the family and in the State were supposed to be essentially of the same type, and division in either caused alarm. Calamy asked the City, 'Would it not be a sad thing to see twelve in a family, one of them a Presbyterian, another an Independent, another a Brownist, another an antinomian, another an Anabaptist, another a Familist, another for the Prelatical Government, another a Seeker, and the tenth it may be an atheist, the eleventh a Jew, and the twelfth a Turk?': *The Great Danger of Covenant-Refusing and Covenant-Breaking*, London 1645, 37. The State, moreover, regarded heads of households, as well as local officials, as subordinate ministers of its authority. See the instructions about Paul's churchyard in 1631 in Rushworth, *Historical Collections*, III, i. 91.

[2] *Works*, iii. 590.

[3] *Religion and Allegiance*, London 1627, ii. 5.

[4] T. Edwards, *Gangraena*, London 1646, i. 156. The significance of the marginal hand is that Edwards thought this should be selected by preachers as one of the arguments likely to persuade their hearers.

[5] John Ponet, *A Short Treatise of Politike Power*, 1566, Sig. C. 5.

[6] Conrad Russell, 'The Theory of Treason in the Trial of Strafford', *English Historical Review*, lxxx (1965), 42; see above, p. 101.

[7] *Parliamentary Diary of Robert Bowyer*, ed. D. H. Willson, Minneapolis 1932, App. 380.

of obligation, but it was not: the lawyers were too keen to show that their subject had a theological base. Bagshaw claimed that a conflict between the common law and the canon law was between 'the law of God' and 'the law of the Pope'.[1] Coke said that 'without question the law is sprung up from a divine mind, and this admirable unity and consent in such diversity of things proceeds from God, the fountain and founder of all good laws and constitutions'. He maintained that in law all infidels are perpetual enemies, with whom there can be no peace, and that in English law a pagan cannot have any action at all.[2] Hooker's Thomism led from different origins to a similar conclusion: 'of law there can be no less acknowledged than that her seat is the bosom of God, her voice the harmony of the world'.[3] If law is itself deduced from religion, then obligation based on law is simply based on religion at one remove.

Contractual, as well as legal, theories of obligation could not stand without a religious basis. Contracts were not usually modern free contracts, but covenants: three-cornered agreements between men and God. Any success in wringing consent out of the diversity of men's wills was because they had consented to the will of God. As Gauden and Edwards argued, error is so various that it is always opposed to other errors as well as to truth, and so any search for consent would fail if not based on truth.[4] Calamy said: 'you shall find in Scripture, that when a church, state or person divided itself from God by sin, God suffered it as a punishment to be divided from itself by faction'.[5] Truth alone provided the unity needed to make and keep a contract. And any theory of contract demanded that subjects and ruler should contract to preserve true religion: if there were disagreement on what this meant, the contract would be inoperable. Once the contract had been made, there had to be some obligation to obey it. The obligation which Hobbes found in 'the terror of some power', Hooker and Morton found in the divine right of the ruler established by contract: 'unto kings by human right, honour by divine right is due'.[6] Without religion, there would be no sanction to ensure that contracts or covenants were obeyed any longer than the parties chose. Contractual theories of obligation, too, were not thought effective without religion.

The most comprehensive doctrine of obligation was that of the Great Chain of Being. There is no need to describe this doctrine, or rather set of

[1] E. Bagshaw, *Two Arguments*, London 1641, 25. He said that 'matters of religion, and of our laws . . . like Hippocrates' twins, they live and die together': Rushworth, *Historical Collections*, III, i. 26–7.

[2] C. Hill, *Intellectual Origins of the English Revolution*, Oxford 1965, 255: Coke, 7th Report 17 (Calvin's Case).

[3] Hooker, op. cit., I, Conclusion 8.

[4] John Gauden, *The Love of Truth and Peace*, London 1641, 41; Edwards, *Gangraena*, London 1646, i. 18.

[5] *An Indictment*, London 1645, 32. He said the only way to end divisions was to find God again.

[6] Hooker, op. cit., VIII, ii. 6; J. W. Allen, *English Political Thought 1603–60*, London 1938, i. 491. Neither legal nor contractual theories of obligation were common before 1640: almost all ideas of obligation were based on Rom. xiii, either directly or through the Great Chain of Being.

assumptions, in detail, since it has already been described by A. O. Lovejoy, E. W. M. Tillyard, and W. H. Greenleaf.[1] It was, however, perhaps more widely held, and capable of more various interpretations, than Dr. Greenleaf suggests.[2] As a doctrine of obligation, it was useful because it was one of interdependence, not merely of authority: all authorites in the Great Chain of Being held their station and power, not independently, but for the good of their inferiors, and subject to their superiors. As Gouge said: 'they that are superiors to some, are inferiors to others . . . The master that hath servants under him, may be under the authority of a magistrate. Yea, God hath so disposed every one's several place, as there is not any one but in some respect is under another, and all under the king. The king himself is under God, and his word delivered by his ambassadors'.[3] It is only in this last clause that Gouge goes beyond unquestioned assumptions. Obligation, in the Great Chain of Being, is by interdependence: it 'hath in it the properties of a natural body, wherein no members can be happy in an abstracted sense, but as parts conjoined with the whole: because every part had besides the near relation to the whole subsistency in it, which is the foundation of any other good it receives. And so consequently the good or gain of the whole is the gain of every member, and whatever tends to the dissolution of the whole, cannot but be destructive to the parts'. This, said Marshall, 'is a mere prevailing argument than reason can make, it is ground in nature, which must prevail with all'.[4] The force of obligation is that every person, to keep their own station safe, must respect that of their superiors: were the pattern of order destroyed, they as beneficiaries from order would lose as much as everyone else. The kingdom, the body, and the family were supposed to correspond, and therefore the theory produced was of family and moral, as well as political, obligation. Cawdrey said that 'a household is as it were a little commonwealth, by the good government whereof, God's glory may be advanced, the commonwealth, which standeth of several families, benefited, and all that live in that family receive much comfort and commodity'. He says, too, that a householder should have 'a church in his house'.[5] Lord Vaux, the optimistic recusant

[1] A. O. Lovejoy, *The Great Chain of Being*, Cambridge, Mass. 1936; E. W. M. Tillyard, *The Elizabethan World Picture*, London 1943; W. H. Greenleaf, *Order, Empiricism and Politics*, London 1964.

[2] Dr. Greenleaf suggests that these ideas were identified with the cult of royal authority. They could be so identified, but they could also be used for very different purposes, as when Pym, addressing the Lords in January 1642, drew from a standard Great Chain comparison between the body politic and the human body the conclusion that 'diseases of the brain are most dangerous': Rushworth, *Historical Collections*, III. i. 510.

[3] W. Gouge, *Domestical Duties*, London 1626, 3. He said that 'even the highest governor on earth is called a minister, for the good of such as are under him'.

[4] Stephen Marshall, *Meroz Cursed*, London 1642, 19.

[5] Robert Cawdrey, *A Godly Forme of Household Government*, London 1600, 13 and Ep. Ded., Sig. A. 2. To those who thought such instruction too much effort, Cawdrey offered the argument that they would, therefore, have more honest and diligent servants, and more obedient children. He said it was the solution for all those who complained of bad servants, since servants did not do their duties well unless they did them for God's sake: ibid., Sig. A. 4, pp. 39–40.

peer who 'did claim his household to be a parish by itself' was not being entirely frivolous.[1] Calamy asked: 'shall a master in a family have power to put away a servant that is tainted with a gross opinion, and yet not be called a tyrant over that servant's conscience . . . Is not the kingdom the magistrate's house and family?'.[2]

The Great Chain was a doctrine of order, but cannot be understood as one of order alone. Order, unredeemed by co-operation, was disliked, and would have been hard to enforce. Order was supposed to be accompanied by harmony, which, on the Platonic pattern, existed *because* everyone was in their right place, and doing the work belonging to them. As Manwaring said, 'order gives to every thing its proper place, and so procures, and preserves, rest and quiet thereunto'.[3] This harmony depended on the exercise of authority in a co-operative spirit, for the good of those below, and in respect for those above, the spirit of the prayers for different sorts and conditions of men in the Edwardine Primer. Sandys said: 'we bear not up ourselves: God doth bear up all; and each man is or should be a stay to bear up others. We are all members of one body; and we know we have need one of another. The hand cannot want the help of the toe, though the least and lowest member'. Without unity, such harmony was impossible: 'of this unity and conjunction of men agreeing in the truth ariseth that brotherly concord whereof St. Paul . . . saith "be like minded, having the same charity". Where dissent in religion is, there can hardly be consent in love'.[4] Without this consent in love, the benefit to be gained by obligation disappeared. This emphasis on unity as a necessary condition of authority existed in civil, as well as religious questions. One of the most consistent features of the treatment of delinquents is the demand that they should sign a submission: Strafford and Laud were indeed said by one observer to have made their offence worse by defending themselves.[5] Where there is no peaceful machinery for changing the government, some unity of purpose is a practical necessity. William Cecil, according to his contemporary biographer, thought that 'all must not be like, some must rule, some obey, and all do their duties to God, and the church, like good pastors and teachers in every function. He held there could be no government where there was division; and that State could never be in safety where there was toleration of two religions. For there is no enmity so great as that for religion, and they that differ in the service of God cannot agree in the service of their country. Church and State: they rest secure on order and

[1] John Bossy, 'The Character of Elizabethan Catholicism', *Crisis in Europe*, ed. Trevor Aston, London 1965, 225.

[2] *An Indictment*, London 1645, 38.

[3] Op. cit., ii. 8.

[4] Sandys, *Works*, London 1841, Sermon xx, 392; Sermon v, 97. He continues: 'for there can be no agreement between Christ and Belial, the light of one and the other's darkness . . . such as are not of one true religion with us, their profession may be friendship, but their practice is deceit'.

[5] *The Judges' Resolution: Also the Manner of Judge Berkeley's Being Enlarged out of Priso* London 1642, 3.

degree'.[1] Order and degree, in fact, depended on men's acceptance of them, and this acceptance depended on unity.

Thus the Great Chain was in two ways a religious doctrine of obligation. The consent it needed was unattainable without unity, a unity to which religious division was the most frequent threat. And the doctrine itself is a religious one: the Chain existed because it was God's creation, it was united because God was its one head, and all its members' ultimate loyalty was to God. Without strong support from religion, the Great Chain too would have been useless as a doctrine of political or social obligation.[2]

Fear of the consequences if this doctrine were to become useless was in turn strengthened by the prevailing assumptions of the natural wickedness of man, which though particularly strong among those of a Calvinist theological persuasion, was not confined to them. Hooker thought that 'laws are never framed as they should be, unless presuming the will of man to be inwardly obstinate, rebellious and averse from all obedience unto the sacred laws of his nature; in a word, unless presuming man to be in regard of his depraved mind little better than a wild beast'.[3] Preston said all fellow-feeling for others sprang from religion: 'every man is a member of the Old Adam, and therefore in a sense he is born a dead man . . . you know a dead member hath no sympathy with the rest, but a living member hath a fellow-feeling'.[4] It was widely thought that all social and moral sense was in the last resort religious. The notorious Lord Audley, who was accused of having a homosexual affair with his page, and then of assisting him to rape his wife, was quoted by counsel as a fair example of what might happen when the force of religion was gone. 'And when men once habituate themselves unto evil, no marvel if they fall into any sin. Also, he was constant in no religion, but in the morning would be a Papist, and go to Mass, and in the afternoon a Protestant, and hear a sermon. He believed not in God, he feared not God, he left God, and God left him to his own wicked way, and then what might not he run into'. Edwards also listed becoming a Sodom among the fates that loss of religious sanctions would bring upon England.[5] One of Falkland's anonymous opponents thought that 'no error can fall, even in a point which seemeth wholly speculative, but soon it breedeth a practical effect, or rather defection, in Christian behaviour'.[6] This analysis, whereby moral, as well as political, obligation

[1] J. Hurstfield, 'Church and State: the Task of the Cecils', in *Studies in Church History*, ed. G. J. Cuming, London 1965, ii. 124. I would like to thank Professor Hurtsfield for a number of helpful comments.

[2] One of the interesting problems is why there was so much concern with obligation during this period, but it is a problem which has more possible solutions than can usefully be discussed here.

[3] Hooker, op. cit., I, x. i.

[4] '*The New Life*', *Sermons Preached Before His Majestry*, London 1630, 28.

[5] Rushworth, *Historical Collections*, II, i. 99; Edwards, op. cit., ix. 120. Edwards listed a Sodom alongside a Münster. Sodomy was one of the curses which smote the Israelites when they forsook God.

[6] 'An Answer to the Lord of Falkland's Discourse of Infallibility', 10–11, in Lucius Cary, Lord Falkland, *Discourse of Infallibility*, ed. Triplet, London 1651.

was held to depend on religion, completes the picture whereby the whole of society was thought to be sanctioned by religion, and helps to explain some of the hysterical visions of what might happen if this sanction were removed. The real measure of the universality of these assumptions is the refusal to tolerate atheists. Père Lecler has only been able to discover two authors who were willing to tolerate atheists, Dirck Coornhert in Holland, and Roger Williams in New England.[1] At the Oxford Act in 1602, it was maintained that it was impossible for anyone to be simply an atheist,[2] but the commoner position is that 'promises, covenants and oaths, which are the bonds of civil society, can have no hold upon an atheist'.[3] The debate about the rights of atheists was not joined in Tudor and Stuart times: it was provoked by Mill *On Liberty* and the election of Bradlaugh.

All that these propositions go to show, however, is that the stability of society depended on religion: they do not show why it should be supposed that it depended on everyone holding their religion in the same form. The beliefs demanded for social stability were not what were called 'school-points', but the basic elements of Tudor and Stuart Christianity: obedience unity, the sanctity of oaths, morals, charity and avoidance of pride. Could it not be recognised that this stability could follow from other creeds than one's own?

The answer appears to be that it often was recognised, but only in so far as other forms of religion were regarded as true and sincere. Those who argued a latitudinarian case normally did so, not on the ground that religious unity was unnecessary, but on the ground that the different denominations were united in all basic points, and therefore religious unity already existed between them. Their case, then, is not fundamentally different from that of other protagonists of religious unity: they only have a different definition of that wherein unity consists. Bishop Williams, when asked why as an undergraduate, he had found Overall his favourite lecturer, said it was because, after expounding any doctrine, Overall always indicated to his hearers how far they could safely dissent from his conclusions, without breach of Christian unity.[4] This is the exact opposite of the Jesuit Knott's position, that 'any the least difference in faith cannot stand with salvation on both sides'.[5] Jeremy Taylor thought the solution was 'to be united in that common term, which as it does constitute the church in its being such, so it is the medium of the communion of Saints, and that is the Creed of the Apostles, and in all other things an honest endeavour to find out what proofs we can, and a charitable and mutual

[1] J. Lecler, op. cit., i. 486.

[2] Faculty of Theology. In Vesp. Aegidii Thompson: 'an quisquis possit esse simpliciter atheos' -neg'. *Register of the University of Oxford*, ed. Andrew Clark, Oxford 1887, II, i. 203. I would like to thank my wife for this reference.

[3] Locke, *Letter Concerning Toleration*, ed. Gough, Oxford 1946, 154. Locke is here speaking for his contemporaries.

[4] Hacket, *Scrinia Reserata*, London 1693 i. 11.

[5] *Charity Maintained*, 1638, Preface. Knott continued: 'So must they also believe we cannot be saved, if they judge their own religion to be true, and ours to be false'.

permission to others that disagree from us in our opinions'.[1] This is the approach which relies on the concept of 'fundamentals', and its weakness is exposed by John Hales's circular definition of fundamentals as 'those things where in all men can agree'.[2]

The difficulty in agreeing on a definition of fundamentals was only one of the smallest obstacles to this approach. One of the largest was the savage Puritan denigration of will, and of what they called 'will-worship'. Perkins thought that only acts directly and explicitly commanded by God deserved the name of worship, and that all others devised by men were not merely will-worship, but idolatry.[3] By this definition, Christianity consisted chiefly of submission to a series of known plain, scriptural demands. The distinction between fundamentals and non-fundamentals was destroyed. Whatever God commanded was fundamental: its breach was rebellion. As Calamy put it, 'there is no sin simply little: there is no little God to sin against'.[4] A breach of unity in small things was, therefore, as fundamental as in great ones, and to permit it would be to open the floodgates to human invention: to authorise man to rebel against God, and all rebellions, like all treasons, were total.

Reformation epistemology was another obstacle to this latitudinarian approach. The Reformers were not fighting against unity or authority, but simply for truth. They needed a true authority to replace the pope, and this was, and must be, the Scriptures: Tyndale said God's word was our judge, and not the pope. But it was and had to be an article of faith that the words of this judge were clear: that Scripture could not readily be misinterpreted. The *Homilies* maintained that 'presumption and arrogancy is the mother of all error: and humility needeth to fear no error. . . . Therefore the humble man may search any truth boldly in Scripture without any danger of error'. Rutherford, asked how men could decide controversies that the Scripture did not evidently decide, replied: 'there is nothing that the Scripture hath left simple, and in itself controversal. The Scripture has determined of all things contained in it, whether fundamentals or not fundamentals: only in regard of our dulness and sinful blindness some things are controverted'. Puritans were particularly sensitive to any suggestion that there could be sincere dispute about the meaning of Scripture. Prynne called the proposition that Scripture was hard to understand a 'corrupt popish point', and one of the errors which particularly disturbed Edwards was that 'to read Scripture in English to a mixed congregation without present expounding it, is dangerous, and worse than to read it in Latin; for in Latin, as it doth no good, so it doth no

[1] H. R. McAdoo, *The Spirit of Anglicanism*, London 1965, 69.

[2] W. K. Jordan, *History of Religious Toleration*, London 1936, ii. 405–6.

[3] W. Perkins, *A Golden Chaine, Works*, Cambridge 1605, 106 (sic.) sc. 109. He added: 'man not regenerated hath freewill to do only that which is evil, none to do good'. On will-worship and idolatry, see ibid., 814. He said those who set up a devised worship set up also a devised God.

[4] *Englands Looking Glasse*, London 1642, 28.

harm'.[1] This devotion to the idea that truth is self-evident overflowed from the direct interpretation of Scripture into other points of debate. Edwards, for example, said he intended to make no attempt to confute the errors he listed, and hoped the mere naming of them would be sufficient confutation, and Pym, having accused Laud of shutting up the gates of heaven and opening the gates of hell, was able to conclude: 'I shall need to say no more: these things are evident, and abundantly known to all'.[2]

This unwillingness to allow debates which might cast doubt on the plainness of fundamental truths produced some interesting effects on the notion of fair practice in trials. Prynne, for example, was prepared to go to great lengths to collect references to prove that papists bowed to the altar, but by comparison, he made little attempt to prove that it was wrong to bow to altars.[3] In England, there was a unique interaction between puritan emphasis on certainty and the obviousness of Scripture, the closer identification of Church and State following from many of the arguments used to justify the Royal Supremacy, and the suggestion of a new Israel which both these assumptions helped to make respectable. This continuous interaction is one reason why the case for religious unity was harder to challenge than in many other countries.[4]

Such emphasis on the obviousness of truth inevitably produced doubt, or even denial, of the sincerity of opponents. Such denials raised the question of the erroneous conscience: it was impossible to claim liberty of conscience for dissenters if no erroneous conscience could be regarded as a genuine conscience. For many people, conscience was not a product of the workings of reason, which might or might not be erroneous, so much as an innate idea of the type later attacked by Locke, or simply submission to Scripture.[5] Laud, compressing much of the religious unity case, maintained: 'it is impossible in any Christian commonwealth that the church should melt, and the State stand firm. For there can be no firmness without law; and no laws can be binding, if there be no conscience to obey them: penalty alone could never, never, do it. And no school can teach

[1] *Exhortation to the Reading of Holy Scriptures*, ii. in *Sermons or Homilies*, London 1938, 7; S. Rutherford, *A Free Disputation Against Pretended Liberty of Conscience*, London 1649, 24; Prynne, *Canterburies Doome*, London 1646, 244; Edwards, op. cit., i. 19. Rutherford said that 'we must judge false spirits to be false spirits, not because they agree not with ours (that is the calumny of libertines) but because they swerve from the word of truth, though we be not infallible, as the Apostles were'. He thought the alternative was that we must 'die in no belief at all': op. cit., 119–20.

[2] Edwards, op. cit., i. 4; Rushworth, *Historical Collections*, III, i. 201.

[3] Prynne, *Canterburies Doome*, London 1646, 64. In 1637, Prynne himself had been taken *pro confesso* as a result of a similar refusal to admit that the crucial points could be open to dispute.

[4] The powers of the Old Testament kings were frequently quoted in support of the royal supremacy, but if the kings were Old Testament kings, the preachers could claim to be Old Testament prophets. Marshall told the Commons that 'my duty this day is to do that which Jeremy did': *Reformation and Desolation, or the Symptoms of a Kingdom To Which God will by No Means be Reconciled*, London 1642, 18.

[5] For a vivid definition by Luther of conscience as submission to Scripture, see J. Lecler, op. cit., i. 149–50 and 157–8.

conscience, but the church of Christ'.[1] Hooker regarded the desire to achieve unity in one true religion as an innate idea: 'the generality of which persuasion argueth that God hath implanted it by nature, to the end it might be a spur to our industry in searching and maintaining that religion, from which as to swerve in the least points is error, so the capital enemies thereof God hateth as his deadly foes, and without repentance, children of endless perdition'.[2] Rutherford was particularly explicit on this question of conscience: 'the conscience doth neither bind potentially, nor actually, but is a mere reporter, a messenger and an official relator of the will and mind of God to us, and all the obliging power is from the word. . . . Understanding, information and indictment of conscience doth not add any actual obligation to the word that it had not before, it is only a reporter. . . . We say that conscience at its best is but *regula regulata*, not *regula regulans*, nor ought it to have the throne of God, for God is only *regula regulans*'. 'Conscience is considered by divines as a principle of our acting in order to what the Lord commandeth us in the law and the Gospel'. By this definition, an erroneous conscience is no conscience at all.[3] Perkins, while recognising the possibility of an erroneous conscience, thought its possessor would be damned either for following it or for not following it, and among his hearers many were probably less willing to believe an opponent had an erroneous conscience than that he had a 'seared conscience . . . which doth not accuse for any sin at all'.[4] Rutherford rightly maintained that the argument that men should be allowed liberty to follow their supposed consciences was capable of dangerous extension. If a heretic claimed a conscience to believe heresy, so a murderer might claim a conscience to commit murder, and he as much as the heretic was punished for following his conscience. Neither could be pardoned because they claimed liberty of conscience. If liberty of conscience were sufficient ground for the heretic to claim impunity, it would be sufficient for the adulterer and murderer too. Where would this end? 'Conscience is hereby made every man's rule, umpire, judge, Bible and his God, which if he follow, he is but at the worst a godly, pious, holy heretic, who feareth his conscience more than his God, and is to be judged of you a saint'. The comparison between heresy and adultery and murder was

[1] Sermon iv (1625), in *Works*, Oxford 1847, i. 112.

[2] Op. cit., v. i. 3.

[3] *A Free Disputation Against Pretended Liberty of Conscience*, London 1649, 133–5. He said (Preface) that if this doctrine of liberty of conscience were given play, 'the mind, an absolute sovereign princess, can no more incur guiltiness in its operations about an infinite sovereign God, and his revealed will, by this lawless way, than fire can in burning . . . be arraigned of any breach of the law'. He thought (104) that heretics were 'willingly ignorant' and quoted the Epistle to Titus that they were 'self-condemned by their own heart' (107). 'When any in ill blood deny such truths, as that there is a God, and parents are not to be loved we all say, such do sin, and offer violence to their conscience . . . such go near to put off humanity'.

[4] *A Discourse of Conscience*, ed. Thomas F. Merrill, Nieuwkoop 1966, 42, 68. Perkins thought conscience a part of the understanding, but regarded it also as the direct judgment of God: *Works*, Cambridge 1605, 617, 619. He also thought of conscience as a set of innate ideas: ibid., 620, 622.

often made, because it was hoped that the wickedness of one act was as clear as that of the others. One of Edwards's stories shows how some unexpected people might be affected by this sense of the obviousness of errors, combined with concern for their families. One Nichols, visiting an Independent congregation in Stepney who were devoted to the idea of toleration, preached that all lies came out of the mouth of God, together with equally provocative doctrines, whereupon:

'Some of them said this was not to be endured, and they said among themselves what a sad thing it would be to have their own children and wives drawn away; and it was propounded whether in such a case a man ought not to keep his wife and children from such a one; and it was answered a man was king in his own family, to rule and govern; and it was reasoned thus by some in the company, if one man may keep out such a one, whether some families living near together may not join to keep out such a one, and so whether a whole town might not join to keep away such a one: and it was answered yes; and then it was replied, if a whole town might, why not a whole country, and so a whole kingdom, but upon these words there was a little pausing and suspending'.[1]

One of the consequences of these assumptions and attitudes was that it was easy to refuse to admit the sincerity of opponents, or, if such admission became inescapable, to regard them, not as fellow-Christians disagreeing in inessentials, but as enemies of God and, therefore, of society. These beliefs were incompatible with the assumption that other Christian groups could be tolerated because they shared all necessary unity. Atheists were outside any unity, and polemicists frequently described opponents as papists and atheists in the same breath.[2] D'Ewes professed that 'I could not tell whether Dr. Cousens did not mean to bring in heathenism, as well as Popery.'[3] Heylin said of the early Puritan lecturers: 'nor were they raised so much out of care and conscience, for training up the people in the ways of faith and piety, as to advance a faction, and to alienate the people's minds from the government and form of worship here by law established'.[4] It was a standard part of propaganda to speak of opponents acting, not from conscience, but from 'pretended conscience', and it was a short step from this to saying they were acting from antichristian, vicious or subversive motives.[5] A man who had convinced himself of this could happily ignore pleas for liberty of conscience. And if his opponents lacked true conscience, they lacked the minimum of religion necessary to make them

[1] Edwards, op. cit., i. 79.

[2] Francis Marbury, in M. Maclure, *The Paul's Cross Sermons*, Toronto 1958, 79; *News From Ipswich*, 1637, 2. For a discussion of the authorship of *News From Ipswich*, see W. M. Lamont, *Marginal Prynne*, London 1963, 38. The question is probably still open.

[3] *Journal of Sir Symonds D'Ewes*, i (ed. Notestein), New Haven 1923, 458.

[4] Heylin, *Cyprianus Anglicanus*, Dublin 1719, 6. For an amusing example of the same process applied by papists to Protestants, ibid., 71.

[5] For one of the more hilarious examples of this process, see [Giles Calfine,] *A Fresh Bit of Mutton for those Fleshly-Minded Cannibals that Cannot Endure Pottage*, London 1642 (Thomason E. 149).

good citizens. Such accusations of insincerity are constant, and one must sometimes wonder how seriously they were taken. It is true that even D'Ewes may occasionally admit that a Roman Catholic believes his case,[1] but such exceptions did not prevent the charges of insincerity from influencing the general climate of thought. Such suggestions are frequently comforting to their holders, and for a man tempted to persecution awareness of opponents' sincerity needs to be very strong before, in the heat of passion, he remembers it and is restrained by it. In the *Histriomastix* trial, it was easier for the judges to take it as unquestionable that stage plays were lawful, and confine their argument to the offence committed by those who falsely proclaimed the opposite. And, as Laud said when dealing with the Scots, if the pretence of conscience were admitted in opposition to the government, soon every government action would fall foul of someone's conscience.[2] These assumptions of insincerity could also sanctify prejudice: most heated debaters are tempted to believe their opponents are insincere, because the stupidity of their case is so clear. The epistemology of many early reformers gave doctrinal authority to these prejudices: it was not a point of conscience to resist prejudice, but to indulge it.

Another consequence of this epistemology (or frequently also of papalist epistemology) is the belief that in all differences one side must be damned by error which goodwill and humility could easily have prevented. Julius Palmer, a Marian martyr, was told by the examining sheriff of Berkshire: 'I perceive, Palmer, one of us twain shall be damned; for we be of two faiths, and certain I am there is but one faith that leadeth to life and salvation'. But Palmer said 'I hope that we shall both be saved'. To the question how could that be, he replied, that as he himself had been called at the third hour, at the age of 24 years, so he trusted that the sheriff would be called at the eleventh hour.[3] If all differences were fundamental, Protestants were led to consider papists, not as misguided Christians, but as akin to the infidels. Henry Parker thought 'we ought not to look upon them as the primitive Christian did the Jews, but as the Jews did the heathens, for the Jewish religion had been true, and was rather altered than abolished, and that in accidents, rather than substance; and so we must not hold of the Popish schism'.[4]

It was argued that if Papists should be regarded as infidels, marriages should not be made with them, an argument addressed with ironic eloquence by James I to his infant son.[5] Sandys touched Elizabethan prejudices by describing marriage with one who was not 'of the household of God, professing one true religion with us' as 'disparagement'.[6] By this

[1] *Journal of Sir Symonds D'Ewes*, ii (ed. Coates) New Haven 1942, 14.

[2] Rushworth, *Historical Collections*, II, i. 398, Laud to Traquiir, 11 September 1637.

[3] Foxe, *Acts and Monuments*, ed. S. R. Cattley, London 1839, viii. 217.

[4] Henry Parker, *The Altar Dispute*, London 1641, 33. I would like to thank Mr. N. J. Tyacke for this reference.

[5] *Basilikon Doron, Political Works of James I*, ed. C. H. MacIlwain, Cambridge, Mass. 1918, 35.

[6] Edwin Sandys, *Sermons*, P.S., 325.

parallel to the Jews' attitude to the heathen, many more Old Testament texts were given political application. Prynne applied the texts against marriage with the Canaanites or other idolatrous nations to Charles I's marriage with Henrietta Maria.[1] It is true that theological infidelity was not thought of as an excuse for ending an existing marriage, though Perkins argued that attempted conversion by an infidel spouse should be met by Lysistrata tactics.[2] Many Old Testament texts restricted dealings with outsiders. Perkins argued that we were sharing the sin of the enemy by trading in the goods of spiritual warfare, frankincense, wax or cloth to be used in the service of idols. There is a remarkable sense of priorities involved in some of these arguments. Marshall says: 'such a man was upright with God: the meaning is, all his days he sustained God's worship. And yet let me tell you some of their moralities were no better than they should be. Asa in the text was a choleric passionate man, and covetous in his old age, yet because he went through-stitch in the reformation of religion, Asa's heart was said to be upright with God all his days. With this God useth to cover all their infirmities as it were with a veil.[3]

The problems that religious division created for governments were often more practical. One was simply that it produced trouble. The *Homilies* said religious disputes led to tavern brawls,[4] and Hooker remarked that religious divisions tended to be more heated than others, 'forasmuch as coldness, which in other contentions may be thought to proceed from moderation, is not in these so favourably construed'.[5]

But the toughest problem was still that of political obligation. The standard position, from which Ponet and Goodman were rare deviationists, involved a reconciliation of Romans xiii, 'the powers that be are ordained of God', and Acts v. 29, 'we ought to obey God rather than man'. It is not as widely recognised as it should be that every bishop, and even James I, agreed that when a subject was given a command contrary to God's command, he must refuse to obey it.[6] Laud, having arrested Walker for a sermon on Acts v. 29, was accused of punishing him for saying we should obey God rather than man. Laud replied: 'no man doubts but it ought to be so, *when the commands are opposite*'.[7]

Trouble arose when, though both government and subjects thought God's will was clear, some subjects nevertheless thought the government's commands were contrary to God's. They had, of course, to disobey such commands. And though their resistance was bound to be passive, Prynne

[1] Prynne, *Hidden Workes of Darkeness*, London 1645, 1. Prynne did not invent this argument: see Cawdrey, op. cit., 315.
[2] *The Idolatry of the Last Times*, *Works*, Cambridge 1605, 839; *A Golden Chaine*, ibid., 33.
[3] *A Sermon*, London 1641, 27.
[4] *Sermon Against Contention*, *Sermons or Homilies*, London 1938, 141.
[5] Op. cit., v. Dedication 5.
[6] *Trew Law of Free Monarchies*, *Political Works*, ed. C. H. MacIlwain, Cambridge, Mass. 1918, 61.
[7] Cobbett, *State Trials*, iv. 374.

showed that the limits of passive resistance were very wide ones[1]: to Charles, the resistance was more obvious than the passivity. Sibthorpe, though as ready as anyone else to admit that subjects must disobey commands contrary to God's, was also prepared to say: 'rulers are only a terror to the wicked, but for the praise of them that do well. But they that resist, it is a sign that they esteem them a terror, and expect no praise from them, and consequently they are wicked, and not well doers'.[2] To insinuate falsely that the government's religion was wrong was highly dangerous: it was an incitement, at best to a campaign of passive resistance and bitter discontent, and at worst, to rebellion. It is striking that though subjects were told endlessly that they must not rebel if false religion were enforced, it was widely expected that, in fact, they would rebel.[3] Laud, at the second trial of Prynne, asked the king rhetorically: 'what safety can you expect, if you lose the hearts of your people? And how can you retain their hearts, if you turn their religion into superstition?'[4] In 1605 the judges were consulted about the offence of Puritans who submitted petitions to the king suggesting that his subjects would be discontented if he did not subscribe to them, 'whereto all the justices answered, that it was an offence fineable at discretion, and very near to treason and felony in the punishment. For they tended to the raising of sedition, rebellion and discontent among the people'.[5] The reactions to the punishment of Prynne, Burton and Bastwick in 1637 illustrated this danger; they were fêted along the route to their places of imprisonment, and at the execution, men soaked their handkerchiefs in the blood, to collect relics. As Strafford commented, 'a prince that loseth the force and example of his punishment, loseth withal the greatest part of his dominion'.[6] Such incidents help to explain the importance attached by governments to outward conformity: a man who could outwardly conform, thought the service, if erroneous, not so damnable that he need incur martyrdom by opposition to it, and therefore as being within

[1] Prynne was sincere in his repeated protestations that he believed in nothing more than passive resistance. See W. M. Lamont, *Marginal Prynne*, London 1963, *passim.*

[2] R. Sibthorpe, *Apostolike Obedience*, London 1627, 13. This could be an ever acuter dilemma in families. John Brinsley maintained that 'for a woman to engage herself to a church without her husband's consent was an infringement of her divinely ordained duty of submission', but a woman who refrained from attending a meeting because her husband restrained her was told that there were limits to a husband's authority, and she must come unless restrained by force. So long as both beliefs were current, families without religious unity might become unmanageable: K. V. Thomas, 'Women and the Civil War Sects', in *Crisis in Europe*, ed. Trevor Aston, London 1965, 332–3.

[3] Lancelot Gobbo's is probably a typical sample of the type of behaviour expected in this situation: 'and in my conscience, my conscience is but a hard kind of conscience, to counsel me to stay with the Jew. The fiend gives the more friendly counsel: I will run, fiend: my heels are at your commandment': *Merchant of Venice*, II. i. 30–2.

[4] *Works*, Oxford 1847, VI. i. 38.

[5] S. Barton Babbage, *Puritanism and Richard Bancroft*, London 1962, 121. On the theory of treason involved, see Conrad Russell, 'The Theory of Treason in the Trial of Strafford', *E.H.R.*, lxxx (1965).

[6] *Cal. S.P. Dom. 1635–7*, 332. Sir Kenelm Digby, who was in the process of conversion to Catholicism, ended his account: 'you see how prone men are by nature to reverence the relics of martyrs'. Garrard to Strafford; Strafford to Laud: Knowler, *Strafford Letters*, London 1739, ii. 85, 119.

the limits of minimal Christian unity. The distinction involved in this emphasis on outward conformity was by no means entirely an unprincipled one.

All governments thought it was one of their ends to enforce true religion, and were, therefore, the more justified in doubting the loyalty of potential victims of this enforcement. As Pym said: 'it is the end of government that virtue should be cherish'd, vice suppressed'.[1] There is no need to multiply examples to show that it was commonly thought it was the government's duty to enforce truth and suppress error: the Royal Supremacy, if nothing else, demanded it. Hooker, or the *Homilies*, for example, thought it was the ruler's duty to attempt to bring about his subjects' salvation,[2] and Sandys used Ezekiel iii. 18 ('if thou speakest not to warn from his wicked way, his soul will I require at thine hand') in setting forth the responsibility of a bishop.[3]

These beliefs created a vicious circle. Men who thought the government's religion was false might in any case find it hard to remain loyal subjects, but they found it harder for the prospect of being 'lovingly corrected'.[4] Gauden hoped to find peace by 'exemplary punishing those that are the perturbers of our peace; justly troubling those that have troubled Israel, as Joshua to Achan. Thus seek peace and pursue it, by pursuing those that would rob us of it'.[5] Whenever subjects denounced the government's religion, the measures taken against them for fear of rebellion made it more likely that their passive resistance would become active. Ashurst, in 1648, discussing the fears of those who might be ruled by a Leveller Parliament, said: 'which doubts and fears will increase, if the supreme power be wholly put into the hands of a party who differ from them in principles of religion and civil government, and they have no visible security beforehand to enjoy religion and their liberties . . . it is to be feared they cannot but look upon themselves as under oppression'.[6] So long as governments assumed that enforcement of true religion was among their duties, so long the belief that subjects of a contrary religion were disloyal had the quality of a self-fulfilling prophecy.

It was largely because of this connexion between religion and obligation that the Venetian Ambassador in France, in 1561, could say that on changes or divisions in religion alteration of government necessarily follows.[7] Many people feared arbitrary government, and the desire to

[1] Rushworth, *Trial of Strafford*, 667.

[2] Hooker, op. cit., VIII. i. 4; *Sermon of Charity*, ii, in *Sermons or Homilies*, London 1938, 69. The *Homilies* argue that if rulers do not try to bring their subjects to salvation, they love neither God nor those whom they govern, 'as every loving father correcteth his natural son when he doeth amiss, or else he loveth him not'.

[3] *Sermons*, P.S., 333.

[4] See above, n. 2.

[5] John Gauden, *The Love of Truth and Peace*, London 1641, 29.

[6] W. Ashurst, *Reasons Against Agreement with a late printed Paper*, London 1648, 5. The paper in question is the *Agreement of the People*.

[7] Surian to the Doge, *Cal. S.P. Ven. 1558–1580*, nos. 228, 272. I would like to thank my wife for these references.

avoid it was an extra reason for clinging, while possible, to religious unity. This connexion between alteration of religion and alteration of government became obsessive during Charles I's reign, and it has a long and complicated series of roots. One is the belief that since division of religion causes so much disturbance, where it exists, the government must have force and arbitrary power, or fail to control the tumult. Catherine de Medici's experience could do nothing but strengthen this belief. Strafford repeatedly told the king that so long as a large proportion of the Irish were papists, it would be folly to think of disbanding the Irish army,[1] and Heylin remarks on the king's failure to protect Laud that Laud might have learnt a lesson from the duke of Somerset, who did not attempt to alter religion until he had got an army into his hands, ostensibly to fight the Scots.[2] It was true that if religious division made political obligation ineffective, government must then be arbitrary and dependent on force, or else could not exist.[3] By contemporary standards, Prynne was not being entirely absurd in maintaining that Ship Money was wanted for the setting up of idolatry.[4] Alternatively, if government in time of division failed to become arbitrary, it might degenerate into democracy, a fear which afflicted as unexpected a character as bishop Hooper.[5] La Boétie, in France, expressed this fear more lucidly than many English thinkers:

'When people realize that they are not bound to obey their natural superiors in matters of religion, they exploit this principle, which itself is not bad, and draw the conclusion that they only have to obey their superiors in things that are good in themselves; they then claim to judge for themselves what is good, what bad, and in the end convince themselves that there is no law but their own conscience, which for the majority means their own ideas and imaginings, and sometimes anything they want'.[6]

Religious division could also produce alteration of government by creating a large body of discontented people who could be drawn on as potential supporters by ambitious men: the obscure story of Hamilton's supposed conspiracy in 1631 would seem to illustrate this process.[7] Or alteration of

[1] Strafford to the king, 31 March 1637, 15 August 1637; Coke to Strafford, 5 September 1637: Knowler, op. cit., ii. 60, 92, 103.

[2] Heylin, *Cyprianus Anglicanus*, Dublin 1719, v. 57. This reads remarkably like an admission of Parliament's main charge against Laud, that he had been trying to alter religion.

[3] It was often supposed that any ruler of false religion must be a tyrant. This position was reached in a number of ways, but the chief appears to be the normal Jesuit syllogism: tyrannies and monarchies are to be distinguished in terms of the end for which they use their powers: a chief end of government is to enforce true religion: *ergo* a ruler whose religion is false is acting against his proper ends, and is a tyrant. And the common picture of a tyrant was far less moderate than Aristotle's: he was supposed to be likely to commit all possible vices. For an example of this syllogism, see Sir John Eliot, *The Monarchy of Man*, ed. A. B. Grosart, Chiswick 1879, 14, 21–2 and 79.

[4] *Hidden Workes of Darkenes*, London 1645, 196.

[5] *Later Writings of Bishop Hooper*, P.S., 84.

[6] J. Lecler, op. cit., ii. 169.

[7] Lord Rea's appeal of treason against David Ramsey: Rushworth, *Historical Collections*, II. i. 114–15. The point was made more generally by Hooker (op. cit., v. Dedication,

religion, if undertaken by the government, could produce alteration of government simply as a practical necessity: religion was guaranteed by law, according to constitutional forms, could not be altered without consent of parliament. Such consent was unlikely to be forthcoming, nor was parliament faced with alteration of religion likely to vote much money for the maintenance of government. A king who wanted to alter religion would therefore have to find enough ordinary revenue to rule without parliament.[1] Or, according to another interpretation, the king, failing to manage parliament, was offered a supporting faction by those who feared parliament because they did not share its religion.[2] Loss of religion might also make government arbitrary by depriving it of those settled and known rules which prevented it from being a mere expression of the ruler's will.[3] Ponet thought alteration of government was connected with religion because tyranny was one of the punishments God inflicted on a country which corrupted its religion.[4] All these were refinements on a current *cliché*, which reinforced the belief that religious divisions were dangerous.

Why did so many Englishmen maintain this belief in the dire consequence of religious toleration, although the French, the Dutch and the Poles had some measure of toleration, and yet their States survived? One reason was dislike of being asked to adopt foreign practice. Dr. Stoye's list of continental travellers shows a dearth of members of the parliamentary opposition, and when returned travellers quoted continental practice in parliamentary debates, they were often howled down. It is, perhaps, more important that travellers knew well that other countries had not achieved toleration without bitter civil dissension.[5] Grateful Englishmen, amazed at their own internal peace, often ascribed it to the survival of some religious conformity. Sandys said: 'what stirs diversity of religion hath raised in nations and kingdoms, the histories are so plain, and our times in such sort have told you, that with farther proof I need not trouble your ears'. Other nations, he said, expected utter ruin and desolation: 'in the meanwhile we sit still under our vine; every man in peace may quietly follow his vocation. God hath not dealt with all nations as he hath dealt with us, the least nation of all'.[6] After the French wars were over, those who wanted evidence of the dire consequences of religious division need

7): 'there are hereby so fit occasions ministered for men to purchase to themselves well-willers by the colour under which they oftentimes prosecute quarrels of envy or inveterate malice'.

[1] Rous, in *Old Parliamentary History*, ix. 197, and Rudyerd, in Rushworth, *Historical Collections*, III. i. 25. The Long Parliament's fears of alteration of religion and of arbitrary government were closely interconnected, and the interconnection may help to make both more intelligible.

[2] See C. Hill, *Society and Puritanism*, London 1964, 15.

[3] 'It is the antichristian voice of the Pope, sic volo, suc jubeo'. Grindal's refusal to suppress the prophesyings: Strype, *Grindal*, 572.

[4] *A Short Treatise of Politike Power*, 1556, Sig. A. 3.

[5] J. W. Stoye, *English Travellers Abroad*, London 1952, 172, 96–7.

[6] Sandys, *Sermons*, P.S., 47, 61.

only look at the Thirty Years' War.[1] Moreover, in France and Holland, some degree of alteration of government was supposed to have happened. France was frequently regarded as a seat of arbitrary government, and Holland as a haunt of dangerous democracy.[2] Both facts encouraged Englishmen the more to thank God that they were not as other men were.

These were mainly political arguments: the argument that sin and false worship must be avoided because God punished them on earth could be an argument of sheer survival. Here, too, the influence of the Old Testament was crucial: whether God had gone out with the armies of Israel depended always on the faithfulness of their worship, and such passages as Deuteronomy xxvii, which was used in the Commination service, were very powerful indeed. Earthly punishment for sin might take many forms, but these divided into two main types: internal dissolution by the breaking of the ligaments of society, and the direct stroke of God's punishment. Hooper regarded sedition as the punishment for evil doctrine, and then plague as God's visitation to punish sedition.[3] One of the clearest expressions of this distinction was made by Laud: he said that there were two ways in which a State might melt: 'one is great and multiplied sin. To sin is to melt, and drop away from all foundation in virtue, all steadiness in justice. And here a State melts inwardly, there is little seen as yet. The other is God's punishment for these sins'.[4]

This doctrine reinforced the case for religious unity, because the sins punished, whether by plague, disaster in battle or civil war, could include not only the performance of false worship, but its toleration by others. Sandys and Rutherford both argued that travellers who taught false religion should be excepted from the rules of hospitality, lest the whole house or country be punished.[5] The standard quotation was from Gratian: 'whoever does not prohibit an evil which he could prohibit, commands it'. Preston rightly said this was a rule his hearers would all know.[6] And in the Old Testament, false worship, and especially idolatry, had most often received this punishment. Of all the arguments for religious unity, this need to avoid earthly punishment for sin was repeated most often.

[1] The point is not whether the Thirty Years' War was a religious war, but whether Englishmen thought it was, which they did. See Holles, in Rushworth, *Historical Collections*, II. i. 370. There was certainly awareness of the devastation the war had caused: Calamy chose the inauspicious time of February 1642 to thank God that 'England hath been like Noah's Ark, safe and secure, when all other nations round have been drowned with a sea of blood'. But, at the same time, he warned the Commons that 'the nature of man is prone to censure Germany and Ireland as horrible sinners above others', and warned them that if they did not reform religion, God's love might be withdrawn from them, and England would share the same fate: *God's Free Mercy*, London 1642, 17–18.

[2] On the idea of arbitrary government in France, see Conrad Russell, art. cit., 43. On Holland, Marchamont Nedham, in Joseph Frank, *The Beginning of the English Newspaper*, Cambridge, Mass. 1961, 195.

[3] *Later Writings of Bishop Hooper*, P.S., 79, 166.

[4] Sermon iv (1625), in *Works*, Oxford 1847, i. 96.

[5] Rutherford, *A Free Disputation*, 176; Sandys, *Sermons*, 266. Sandys referred to 'such as are of no religion, of no church, godless people, some papists, some Arians, some libertines'.

[6] *The New Life, Sermons Before His Majesty*, London 1630, 50.

It is sometimes hard to know how seriously to take this doctrine, since it came too easily to people's lips to be always the product of very serious thought. But it followed logically from a Calvinist view of providence, and constant repetition often passes an idea into the stock-in-trade of a society so effectively that it influences its members in ways of which they may not be aware. This is particularly true of a society's stock of familiar stories, and of these two of the commonest were that of Achan (Joshua vii) and Phinehas (Numbers xxv). Achan had taken of the forbidden spoil of Jericho, and Israel's armies were defeated until Joshua detected Achan, and stoned him to death. The Lord's favour then returned to Israel, and they were victorious. Phinehas was faced with a plague, because the Israelites had committed whoredom with the idolatrous daughters of Moab. Finding a Moabitish woman with child in the camp, he ran her through the belly with his sword, and by this act of zeal the plague was stayed. When Marshall thanked God that we still had a 'sprinkling of Phinehazzes', parliament knew what he meant.[1] The way such ideas were taken for granted is illustrated in the letters of Lady Harley. Her son Edward, at Oxford, had been ill, and Lady Harley, in an otherwise typical maternal perturbation, wrote that the crucial thing was for Edward to find out what sins he had committed, so that the Lord might cease to correct him.[2]

Such fears could influence cynical and secular-minded people. As the *Homilies* said, if we were such worldlings that we did not care for the eternal judgments of God, we could still lose our crops and good in this life, 'which we as worldlings seem only to regard and care for'.[3] The counterpart of this doctrine was that the practice of true religion was a cause of worldly success, or that worldly success proved true religion. Sir Dudley Carleton, in Holland during the Arminian controversy, could not see why they should not wish to 'preserve that form of doctrine without change or alteration, the fruits whereof appear in their prosperity beyond man's discourse'.[4] The admission of false doctrine within the realm was an economic, as well as a theological, imprudence.

[1] *Reformation and Desolation*, London 1642, 40. This sermon was preached at a fast: fasts were the normal way of averting such divine punishment by humiliation, and one of the government's perpetual concerns was to stop the organisation of unofficial fasts by private men, carrying the suggestion that members of the kingdom must humiliate themselves to avoid punishment for the sins of the government. See Bancroft's visitation articles at Wells, S. Barton Babbage, op. cit., 333, the case (or rather one of the cases), of Charles Chauncey, *Cal. S.P. Dom. 1635–7*, ccclxi, no. 67; Laud's complaints to the bishop of Aberdeen, in 1635, Rushworth, *Historical Collections*, II. i. 315; the Scottish canons in 1635 and the Kentish Petition of 1642 in Heylin, *Cyprianus Anglicanus*, Dublin, 1719, iv. 35 and v. 33.

[2] *Letters of Lady Brilliana Harley*, Camden Soc. 1st Series, no. lviii, ed. T. T. Lewis, London 1853, 47, These ideas also influenced the type of inquest which was held after a disaster. See Matthew Newcomen, *A Sermon Tending To Set Forth the Right Use of Disasters*, London 1644, *passim*. He preached on the story of Achan in Joshua vii.

[3] *Sermon of the Right Use of the Church*, i. in *Sermons or Homilies*, London 1938, 169–70. In this case, the disasters are threatened for the sin of not going to church.

[4] *Letters of Sir Dudley Carleton*, ed. Hardwicke, London 1757, 113. These attitudes shed a somewhat different light on some of the passages identifying Puritanism and prosperity:

continued

This set of assumptions also had the effect of sanctioning the anti-politic temperament: 'seek ye first the kingdom of God, and all these things shall be added unto you'. This temperament is of course common to all centuries, but the sanction which much current theology gave to it made it harder to argue against, and helped its holders to come nearer to the seats of power than they have been able to do in many other periods. Moreover, those who scorned expediency went to greater lengths than others in order to enforce religious unity.

One important theme which cannot be properly treated in the space available is the doctrine of the Visible Church. Christ's promises had been made to his Visible Church, and power to minister the Sacraments effectively, for example, could only pass down through a continuously Visible Church. This is why it became an important question whether the Visible Church had continued through the Lollards, or in the more official form preferred by the Laudians. For many people, who could not accept Hooker's argument that the Visible Church was made up of many parts, not all of which were equally sincere and sound,[1] the belief that one's own Church was part of the Visible Church necessarily implied that all others were outside it, and therefore damnable. People who held this position could not believe that the different types and Christians were united in fundamentals: others were outside the Church, if not Antichrist, and the true Church could have no peace with them.[2]

Latitudinarians or tolerationists usually conceded that the other side might be right: that there was no infallible knowledge that they were committing errors. For many people, this concession was intolerable. An admission that opponents might be right involved the admission that one might oneself be wrong, and therefore sanctioned doubt, scepticism and anxiety. Rutherford, attacking Goodwin's idea of 'new light' produced a satirical Independent prayer: 'grant that thy Holy Spirit may bestow upon my dark soul more sceptical, conjectural and fluctuating knowledge, to know and believe things with a reserve, with a leaving of room to believe the contrary tomorrow of what I believe today'. This, he said, would destroy 'settled and fixed knowledge, and a well-rooted faith of truths to believe them without a reserve or a demur', and turn the Word of God into a 'nose of wax', which could give us no certain guidance.[3] Rutherford felt that any supporter of toleration could not understand the true nature of faith. Calvin warned his followers not to be certain of election, but in practice many later Puritans were, and this certainty was their strongest fixed point of comfort. Perkins thought that 'every man to

continued
the identification was often made simply because Puritanism was thought to be right, rather than because it was then supposed to be a doctrine with any specific commercial content.

[1] Op. cit., III. i. 4.

[2] *Register of the University of Oxford*, ed. Andrew Clark, Oxford 1887, II. i. 204.

[3] *A Free Disputation*, 81–3. He said such a doctrine would lay a blasphemous charge on the Holy Ghost, as having written the Scriptures in such a way that we could gain no certainty from them.

whom the Gospel is revealed, is bound to believe his own election, justification, sanctification, glorification in, and by Christ'.[1] To destroy this was to destroy their hope and strength, and if they admitted that their opponents might be right, and therefore that they, and not their enemies, might be rebelling against God, they lost their saving faith.[2] Many thought such concessions threatened the foundations of society and the Reformation, as well as their own trust in salvation. It was a large concession to ask a man to make.

Finally, the religious-unity arguments were fortified by the generally accepted terms of debate. If unity was good, and division bad, a debater's first aim had to be to present himself as the friend of unity, and his opponents as its enemies.[3] Henry VIII's Act Against Papal Authority claimed that the pope should be rejected because he was responsible for the interruption of 'unity, love, charity, concord and agreement'.[4] The whole of the debate between Jewel and Harding was dominated by the attempt to expose each other as enemies of unity.[5] Edwards protested of the Independents that 'what themselves are most faulty in, that they will charge upon others, the Presbyterian ministers and people as making division, as breaking the peace, and causing misrules, tumults, as being guilty of persecution, when as 'tis evident to all the world they are most faulty in all these particulars'.[6] The only sure guarantee of unity was truth: 'the bond of unity is simple verity', as Jewel said, paraphrasing Ephesians iv.[7] Therefore, the enemies of truth were the enemies of unity. Heylin thought an important reason for enforcing conformity between England, Ireland and Scotland was that the Papists made it a major debating point that his Majesty's three kingdoms, under one Royal Supremacy, had three several confessions, and Whitgift wrote to Burghley in 1584: 'assure yourself that the papists are rather grieved at my doings, because they tend to the taking away of their chief argument; that is, that we cannot agree among ourselves, and lack unity; and therefore are not of the church'.[8] So long as writers and readers in the constant theological controversies assumed that those who could prove themselves the friends of unity won the debate, it was hard to get outside the terms of debate altogether, surrender the points at issue, and question how far or in what way unity was actually desirable or necessary. It was easier, and in the

[1] W. Perkins, *A Discourse of Conscience*, ed. Thomas F. Merrill, Nieuwkoop 1966, 19–20; *Register of the University of Oxford*, II. i. 198, 199, 201 and 205.

[2] Rutherford (*A Free Disputation*, 13–14) thought the doctrine that there were no distinctive marks of saving grace 'subverts the faith'.

[3] Calamy argued that division encouraged the king's supporters, and that as the willingness to divide the child showed the false mother, so the willingness to divide the church showed its false child: *An Indictment*, 14, 18.

[4] 28 Hen. VIII cap. 10.

[5] Jewel, *Works*, P.S., ii. 608, 622–3.

[6] Edwards, op. cit., 63–4.

[7] Jewel, op. cit., ii. 623.

[8] Heylin, op. cit., iv. 17; Whitgift, *Works*, P.S., iii. 603.

short term more productive, to stay within the terms of debate which were generally understood, and argue about where the blame for the dangers to unity was to be placed.

12

The Parliamentary Career of John Pym, 1621-1629

On the morning of 27 November 1621, two members of the House of Commons caught Mr Speaker's eye together, and the man who sat down was John Pym.[1] This incident is symbolic of the early career of Pym, who, both in the House of Commons and outside it, was a surprisingly inconspicuous member. In the amply reported Parliament of 1621, he is known to have delivered 37 speeches and one report. The figure should be compared with 62 speeches by William Mallory, 336 speeches by Sir Robert Phelips, and 447 speeches by Sir Edward Coke. Even among these 37 speeches, the majority were brief procedural interventions, only noticed by a minority of the diarists. Even his later friend Sir Thomas Barrington appears not to have known who he was, and reported him under the most inappropriate name of 'Mr Pope'.[2] In a Parliament which proliferated committees on such a scale that leading members were literally unable to fulfil their commitments, Pym was only named to 13 committees. It only took one man, not the whole House, to name a member to a committee. For that reason, one may wonder whether a man who was named to so few was a rather friendless man. When he was named to his first committee, after four weeks, he took home one of

I am grateful to the Central Research Fund of the University of London for grants for purchase of microfilms and other expenses, and to the Trustees of the Bedford Settled Estates, Sheffield University Library and Lord Delamere, The Trustees of the James M. Osborn Collection, Beineke Library, Yale University, and the Yale Center for Parliamentary History for permission to quote from copyright material in their possession.

1. Diary of John Hawarde, Wiltshire RO, Ailesbury MSS. (unnumbered and unfoliated), 27 Nov. 1621. *Commons' Debates in 1621* (hereafter cited as *1621 Debates*), ed. W. Notestein, F. H. Relf and H. Simpson (New Haven, 1935), III, 460; V, 215. Pym had been much irritated by a similar incident earlier in the session. He recorded that 'that interruption ceasing', the debate was resumed: *ibid.*, IV, 196–7.
2. *Ibid.*, III, 190; *C J*, I, 612.

its papers and kept it, apparently as a souvenir.[3]

In this, as in many other ways, Pym was a very untypical member of the Commons. To a purist, of course, any individual member is by definition untypical, yet Pym is much more untypical than most. It is therefore the more unfortunate that, because of his importance 20 years later, he is more often used as a 'typical member' than most. This is misleading because the subjects on which he is most often quoted as typical of his fellow-members – his attitudes to recusants, Spain and the Duke of Buckingham – are in fact among the subjects on which the consistency of his views is most nearly unique. All remarks in this essay are meant to apply to Pym alone, unless otherwise stated.

One of the most unusual things about Pym is his lack of a county community. Professor Barnes, Professor Everitt, Dr Hirst, Dr Morrill and others have rightly taught us that to study a seventeenth-century M. P., we need to see him in his local context. It is perhaps Pym's greatest peculiarity that he is an exception to this rule: when he spoke of his country, he did *not* mean his county. Indeed, it is an open question which his county was. What used to be thought to be his single appearance as a J.P. has now vanished before the scrutiny of Mr Richard Cust.[4] In his approach to the work of a Westminster legislator, he was immune from the restraining influence of local office. He belonged to no local community, enjoyed no local power base, and appears to have been uninfluenced in the House of Commons by any ties of localist sentiment.

He was born in Somerset, where his rather scanty hereditary estates were, but before he reached the age of four, his mother's second marriage took him out of the county. He was brought up in Cornwall, in the home of his step-father, Sir Anthony Rous. Kinship counted for as much in Pym's loyalties as neighbourhood counted for little, and his friendships with members of the Rous family lasted till his death, when his step-brother Francis Rous was one of his executors.[5] His wife, Anne Hooke of Bramshott in Hampshire, was a collateral of the Rous family,[6] and gave him tenuous contacts in yet a

3. Somerset RO, Pym MSS. no. 152. The document in question is a licence granted by Mompesson to an inn at Wingham in Kent. It is possible that Pym was named to the committee on the Masters in Chancery by his feoffee to uses Sir Edward Wardour. Some of the criticism of them arose from the case of Morgan *v.* Bowdler and Meggs, in which Wardour had a considerable personal interest.
4. R. P. Cust, 'A list of commissioners for the forced loan of 1626–7', *BIHR*, LI (1978), 202–8. Pym's nomination as a Forced Loan Commissioner was in Hampshire.
5. There is no known copy of Pym's will. Our knowledge that Rous was one of his executors is from Sheffield University Library, Hartlib MSS. 7/32 (Dury to Rous). For what may be a list of Pym's executors see Somerset RO, Pym MSS. no. 259. They are Oliver St John, Sir Benjamin Rudyerd, John Crew, Francis Rous, Anthony Nicoll and Alexander Pym.
6. PRO, PROB 11/70/f.293. I owe this reference to the late Miss Evelyn Gore.

third county. In 1607, this Hampshire contact was reinforced by his appointment to the only office which exercised a significant influence on his outlook: that of Receiver of Crown Lands for Wiltshire, Hampshire and Gloucestershire. Yet even as a receiver, he appears to have felt that his real loyalties were to the Exchequer, rather than to the counties in which he worked. The Pym who claimed in 1626 that 'the custom of the Exchequer is the law of the kingdom, for so much as concerneth the revenue', was showing the real centre of his loyalties. Chamberlain, with his usual thumbnail accuracy, characterized him as 'one Pym, a receiver'.[7]

The implied social sneer is an important part of this characterization, for in local society, Pym was definitely not 'county'. When he came of age, he appears to have tried to establish himself in Somerset, and failed. He was still trying in 1621, when he gave enthusiastic support to attempts to restore the parliamentary representation of Ilchester and Minehead,[8] but he never even secured appointment as a Somerset commissioner of sewers. One minor Somerset gentleman was bound for him when he became a receiver, and another was one of his feoffees to uses in 1614.[9] With these two exceptions, Somerset gentlemen are conspicuous by their absence from lists of his non-parliamentary contacts. During the 1620s, he made a second attempt to establish himself as a country gentlemen, this time in Hampshire, which seems to have been his base for most of the decade. This attempt was equally unsuccessful. By 1630, he seems to have abandoned it, and was living in the parish of St Andrew's, Holborn. By 1638, he had taken refuge in ideologically congenial company, and was living in what Clarendon called 'a kind of classis' in the house of his friend Richard Knightley of Fawsley in Northamptonshire.[10] This, then, was a man who offended against the most sacred canon

7. *L J*, III, 615. *Letters of John Chamberlain*, ed. N. E. Mc.Clure (Philadelphia, 1939), II, 412. See also Clarendon's description of Pym, *History* (1732 edn), I, 185: 'always a man of business, being an officer in the Exchequer, and of a good reputation generally, though known to be inclined to the Puritan faction'.
8. *1621 Debates*, IV, 201; *C J*, I, 572; n. 2 above.
9. Somerset RO, Pym MSS. no.s 139–146; PRO, E 159/430, m.56. I am grateful to Mr David Thomas for this reference.
10. Clarendon, *History*, I, 183. Pym's letter in *CSPD*, 1637–8, 571, says he is about to return to the country 'where I have been the most part of these two years last past'. The dating of Pym's letters in Sheffield University Library, Hartlib MSS. 31/3, appears to show that 'the country' here means Northamptonshire. I am grateful to Dr Charles Webster for drawing my attention to these letters. On one of the rare occasions when Dorothy Pym gave an address in a letter to her brother Charles, she wrote from Fawsley. James M. Osborn Collection, Beineke Library, Yale University, Pym Box, Family Letters, no. 5. Some of the likely members of this gathering may be shown by the list of trustees chosen by Knightley when he

of Tudor and Stuart respectability: he had no fixed address.[11] He was, then, able to be uniquely his own man in his contributions to debate in the House of Commons.

Why did Pym fail to establish himself in county society? Part of the answer must be the smallness of his estate, and perhaps also his recklessly long leasing of it. His estate only gave him a marginal claim to be a J.P., yet both his father Alexander and his younger son Charles supported the dignity of a J.P. on the same estate. Perhaps, then, Pym's county failure was in part social. He was a good and expeditious man of business, yet somewhat lacked the light touch. His surviving letters appear to be more single-minded in their concentration on the business in hand than those of any other contemporary except Robert Cecil. In all his adult life, he is only known to have made one joke, and even that was perhaps not meant to be funny. In his diary for 1621, reporting the debate on whether Oxford or Cambridge should be mentioned first in the bill of subsidy, he wrote: 'all those that had been of either University inclined to that place of which they were. But such as had been of neither remained indifferent and were only swayed by reason. So that, upon question, the precedence was appointed to Oxford'. Even here, being a careful man, Pym felt compelled to add: 'confirmed by order'.[12] Except for his loyalty to Oxford, he appears to have been almost devoid of non-functional interests. It is no ground for surprise that a letter about racing should turn out not to be written by John Pym, but by someone else of the same name.[13] Even in the Pym papers, the letter from a Somerset neighbour saying: 'I long to vent my passion for my horses on you which you may furiously expect',[14] could only have been written to its actual recipient, his younger son Charles. When Pym's daughter Dorothy set her heart on a pair of second-hand virginals, which she hoped might be cheap because they were going out of fashion, her request did not go to her father. It went, as such requests do, to the real seat of power, to 'my solicitor general, a pretty preferment I tell you for a

converted his impropriations into a trust for John Dod, vicar of Preston Capes. They were Saye and Sele, Sir Nathaniel Rich, John Hampden, John Crew, John Pym and Christopher Sherland. On the deaths of Rich and Sherland, they were replaced by Edward Bagshaw and Sir Arthur Haselrig: Northamptonshire RO, Knightley MSS. no.s 36, 38, 40, 42, 45, 107. It was to Knightley's house that John Preston retired to die: P. S. Seaver. *The Puritan Lectureships* (Stanford, 1970), 265; Birmingham Reference Library, Coventry MSS., Commissions, no. 258, 16 Nov. 1639.

11. PRO, SP 14/134/90. I am grateful to Lynda Price for this reference.
12. *1621 Debates*, IV, 144–5.
13. BL, Add. MS. 40, 629, f. 128.
14. C. J. Sawyer and Co., Catalogue no. 155, no. 102, Francis Luttrell to Sir Charles Pym, March 15, 1660/1. I am grateful to Messrs Sawyer's for permission to quote from their sale catalogue. Many of the originals from this sale cannot now be found.

young lawyer': it went to her brother Charles.[15]

It was likely to be difficult for a man with so few local roots to secure election to the House of Commons. His first two elections, for the Wiltshire boroughs of Calne in 1621 and Chippenham in 1624, appear to be due to his position as receiver. He sat for Chippenham as the candidate of the corporation franchise, and his chances of future election to the Commons seemed to be severely threatened when the committee of privileges quashed his election in favour of that of Sir Francis Popham, the candidate of the wider freeman franchise. Pym contested this case with passion, and continued to contest the principle of it after he had waived his own election and decided to sit elsewhere. Dr Hirst has shown that he believed in the corporation franchise, but this is not enough to explain why this was one of the rare occasions in his parliamentary career when he made a fool of himself. In the words of Hawarde's diary, having made his election, and now being no party 'he was permitted not only to sit at the committee (of privileges) but heard at large with much favour to say what he could. He was very large, but to very little purpose, in so much as Mr Brooke said he had delivered a great deal of false doctrine'.[16]

It appears to be the lesson of the Chippenham case that Pym could not count on election to the Commons without the assistance of a patron. It was fortunate for him that it coincided with the appearance of a patron able to offer him a regular seat. He was Francis, second Lord Russell of Thornhaugh, who bought up the estates of the bankrupt Earl of Bedford in 1617, and succeeded to his title in 1627.[17] Bedford supplied him with a regular seat, and he never looked elsewhere. Even in 1640, it is doubtful whether he could have secured a seat without the help of a patron. In Bedford (as he will be called for convenience throughout this essay) Pym was fortunate to have acquired a patron who was almost as literal-minded as he was, and one who did very little to limit Pym's freedom of action. Bedford appears to have had an even more insatiable appetite for exact information than Pym, and Pym's chief service to him seems to have been supplying copies of his Commons' diaries, which Bedford read and annotated with scrupulous care.[18] The

15. Yale University, Osborn Collection, Pym Box, Family Letters, no. 5 (undated: *c.* 1635–41). See Sawyer's Catalogue 155, no. 69 for another request to Charles Pym for virginals, this time from Pym's youngest daughter Katherine. Diary of Sir William Spring, 25 Feb. 1624: I am grateful to the Yale Center for Parliamentary History for allowing me to use a transcript of this diary. D. M. Hirst, *The Representative of the People?* (1975), 83, 198–9, 233, 234.
16. Diary of John Hawarde, Wilts. RO, Ailesbury MSS., 9 March 1624.
17. PRO, C 142/435/118.
18. BL, Add. MS. 26, 637 (1621); Bedford MSS. 197 (1625). Add. MS. 26, 639, though not annotated, consists of extracts from Pym's diary for 1624, and comes from a collection which appears to have once been in Bedford's possession.

acquisition of a patron in the Lords doubtless strengthened one of Pym's deepest reflexes, which was to encourage the House of Commons, in moments of crisis, to turn for good correspondency, and indeed for rescue, to the Upper House. However, since this tendency was already apparent in Pym in 1621, before there is any evidence that he enjoyed Bedford's patronage, Bedford cannot be credited with creating it, but only with reinforcing it.[19]

There are a number of occasions on which the two men can be shown to have worked together, such as the impeachment of Manwaring. On one occasion, their collaboration appears to have averted a potentially serious dispute between the Houses. On 3 March 1626, the House of Lords set up a committee, including Bedford, to complain of a breach of their privileges by the House of Commons in sending for the Duke of Buckingham without asking leave of the Lords. The next morning Pym, apparently briefed on what was happening in the Lords, drew attention to what appears to have been a genuine error in the *Commons' Journal*, and said that they should take the chance to correct a further error by the clerk in claiming that they had 'sent for' Buckingham before they received any message from the Lords. Pym's fiction was duly accepted by all parties to the dispute (including the clerk).[20] One of the most successful examples of Pym's tendency to turn for rescue to the House of Lords concerned the arrest of Digges and Eliot, later in the Parliament of 1626, for words spoken at a committee of both Houses. Pym proposed that all members of both Houses who were present should make a protestation that Digges and Eliot had not spoken the words with which they were charged. Bedford's readiness to make the protestation as soon as it was put before the Lords suggests that he may have been involved in the planning of it, and it was successful: Digges and Eliot were released.[21]

Yet, though it is possible to show many instances of common action between two like-minded people, it is surprisingly hard to show any case of Pym accepting a 'line' either from Bedford, or from his other noble patron, the Earl of Warwick. Pym's persistent, if vain, support for bills to legalize the militia supported a cause strongly backed by Bedford as lord lieutenant of Devon, but there is no reason to doubt that they also represented his own

19. *1621 Debates*, III, 331, II, 399–400, III, 353. In the case of Floyd, Pym's concern appears to have been to preserve the rights of the Commons as prosecutors, rather than as judges: IV, 361, III, 287–8.
20. *LJ*, III, 514; Diary of Bulstrode Whitelocke, Cambridge University Library, MSS. Dd 12–20, 12–21 and 12–22 (hereafter cited as Whitelocke Diary); 12–20, fos. 51v, 46v; *Letters of John Chamberlain*, II, 629; BL, Add. MS. 40, 089, fos. 38r–44v, 157v.
21. Whitelocke Diary, 12–22, f. 12v; *LJ*, III, 627; *Debates in the House of Lords 1624 and 1626*, ed. S. R. Gardiner (Camden Soc., n.s. XXIV, 1879), 196–200; *HMC*, Buccleuch MSS., III, 292.

conviction.[22] Perhaps the clearest case of Pym following a patron's line is in his strong support of the private bill to settle the estate of the Earl of Devon, to whom Bedford was a feoffee to uses.[23] On the impeachment of Buckingham, an issue on which people were particularly keen to seek the protection of patrons, Pym followed Bedford's line of speaking against the duke from the beginning, rather than the more cautious waiting game played by Warwick, yet there is no evidence that he needed Bedford's prompting to do so.[24] There is, indeed, one example of Pym's freedom of action being unhampered by his patron's evident disapproval. In his first draft for the 1625 petition on religion, Pym proposed the reform of impropriations, to allow impropriators to be charged to pay higher maintenance to their vicars. Bedford, in his copy of Pym's parliamentary diary, wrote in enormous capitals, 'NO'. Yet Pym's activity in trying to reform impropriations appears to have been undiminished.[25] On the whole, seventeenth-century patrons appear to have operated a political 'whip' only on issues which personally concerned themselves, or on issues where it was necessary for like-minded men to seek safety in numbers and in combined tactics. The Earl of Devon's private bill and the impeachment of Buckingham may serve for examples of the two types of issue.

There were two obsessive themes which ran through the majority of Pym's speeches in the 1620s, and Bedford was largely in agreement with one of them, and wholly in agreement with the other. The two themes, which, appropriately, were the subjects of Pym's first two speeches in the Commons, were the purity of the true religion, and the sanctity of the king's revenue. Pym was, from the beginning of his parliamentary career, one of those who believed the world was a perpetual struggle between the forces of good and evil, of Christ and Antichrist, a battle in which there was no resolution short of final victory.

22. Diary of Sir William Spring, 16 April 1624; Northants. RO, Finch-Hatton MS. 50, f.65r (Pym's diary); *CJ*, I, 768. *Commons' Debates in 1628*, ed. R. C. Johnson, M. F. Keeler, M. J. Cole and W. B. Bidwell (New Haven, 1977) (hereafter cited as *1628 Debates*), III, 617. BL, Stowe MS. 366, f.276r; Bedford MSS. XI (i), 158–63. On the Manwaring case, Bedford was on the committee to take depositions, and copied part of Pym's speech into his commonplace book: *ibid.*, 1258; *LJ*, III, 846.

23. Diary of Sir Richard Grosvenor, Trinity College Dublin MS. 612 (hereafter cited as Grosvenor MS. 1628), 10 June; PRO, PROB 11/154, fos. 37–8; *1628 Debates*, III, 10n.

24. Whitelocke Diary, 12–20, fos. 65v–64v; *Lords' Debates* (ed. Gardiner), 115; *HMC*, Buccleuch MSS., III, 272; Bedford MSS. XI (i), 56–8, 177.

25. Bedford MSS. 197, f.15r. Bedford's objection could be to the proposal to allow owners of impropriations to make them presentative by deed: his capitals are too large to allow precise statements about where he intended to place them. Bedford was equally unsympathetic to the pleas of Hoby and Rich for silenced ministers. On this issue also Pym appears to have been unhampered by his patron's objections. For Pym's further concern with impropriations, *1628 Debates*, III, 7–8, 10; *CJ*, I, 924.

Evil, in the form of popery covert and overt, was constantly present, and 'the remedies of this contagious and dangerous disease we conceive to be of two kinds, the first to consist in strengthening our own religion, the second to the weaking [*sic*] and abating of theirs'.[26] Pym, partly because he was so nearly immune from the countervailing pressure of good neighbourhood, was able to approach the task of hunting out corrupt and popish religion with a single-mindedness which was shared only by Richard Knightley in Northamptonshire and Sir Thomas Posthumus Hoby in Yorkshire. In this hunt for the forces of evil, he seems to have been particularly on the watch for those who would 'divide us among ourselves, exasperating one party by the odious and factious name of Puritans'. This was the occasion of his maiden speech, an attack on a church papist member of the Commons called Shepherd, who had opposed the Sabbath bill on the ground that it was a 'Puritan' bill. Shepherd annoyed the Commons, but enraged Pym. He held Shepherd guilty of an offence 'against the state, which is the highest object that civil offences can reach unto'. Only Pym thought his offence was '*generale generalissimum*, against the flourishing estate of the kingdom', or that 'such small seeds of tumult and sedition grow up into great dangers, even to the overthrow of states'. He showed very clearly one of the distinguishing marks of his creed, the belief in the universality of evil: 'nothing', he said 'is so apt to multiply as evil'. 'Sins against God are infinite in respect of the object, because they offend an infinite Majesty'. This attempt to divide protestants, he thought, could threaten the overthrow of the state by breeding boldness in the 'common adversary'. He wanted Shepherd expelled, imprisoned during pleasure, fined £100, and exempted out of the general pardon. In 1621, this speech did not catch the mood of the House, and no less a pair of recusant-hunters than Sir Edward Seymour and Sir James Perrott condemned it as 'too violent'. To Pym's obvious disappointment 'the sentence consisted only of his expulsion'.[27] Thus, in his maiden speech, Pym set out what was to become one of his lifelong themes. In 1624, he tried unsuccessfully to have the town of Liverpool punished for contempt for electing a non-communicant, but unconvicted, papist as a member of Parliament. He wanted attacks on papists to be directed at church papists as much as at formal recusants, and stressed that they should consider 'those who by their practice show what they are, as well as those that are convicted'. He wanted to root out popish office-holders, especially deputy lieutenants.[28] The extent to which this determination overrode

26. *Commons' Debates in 1625*, ed. S. R. Gardiner (Camden Soc., n.s. VI, 1873) (hereafter cited as *1625 Debates*), 20. The references to 'contagious and dangerous disease' should be read in the light of the fact that they were written during the 1625 plague. I am grateful to Mr P. D. Lake and Mr R. I. Moore for discussions of these points.
27. *1621 Debates*, IV, 62–5, V, 499–502. For Shepherd's reputation as a papist, see W. R. Prest, *The Inns of Court under Elizabeth I and the Early Stuarts* (1972), 184.
28. Bodl., Tanner MS. 392, fos. 40v, 50v, 77v; BL, Add. MS. 18, 597, f.109v.

considerations of immediate political advantage is nowhere more clearly shown than on 3 May 1626, the day after the Commons had decided to transmit their charges against Buckingham to the Lords. On that day, he tried to ensure that the list of recusant office holders presented by the Commons should include the Earl of Arundel, one of the chief supporters of the impeachment, on the ground that he had three recusant servants.[29] There is no need to multiply examples of this kind.

If the gravest crime in Pym's political calendar was that of destroying the purity and the unity of true religion, the second gravest crime was that of defrauding the king of his lawful revenue. This was the offence for which he attacked Sir Giles Mompesson. His attack was almost confined to Mompesson's patent for concealed Crown lands. Others attacked Mompesson for oppressing the subjects: Pym's attack on him was almost entirely confined to the charge of defrauding the king. The wording of Mompesson's patent on concealments allowed him to find as concealed all lands which were not in charge before the auditor of the Exchequer: 'by pretence whereof, he hath gone about to pass some parts of forests, which are not in charge; no more are houses of access, divers ancient castles, other houses, grounds, and woods reserved for his Majesty's own use'.[30] This theme is even clearer in the Parliament Roll text of the declaration in which the concealments charge was ultimately presented to the Lords. In this Pym, to put it no higher, had a very big hand. This declaration draws heavily on Pym's knowledge of Exchequer procedure. For example, the declaration expresses outrage at Mompesson's power to pass land which had been encroached upon; 'herein he may gain things of great and unknown value from his Majesty and thereby dismember most of his Majesty's manors'. Inquisitions to find the value of concealed land could be taken at unsuitable places (for example, inquisitions of land held of the manor of East Greenwich were taken *at* East Greenwich). The values of the inquisitions were accepted even if they showed a lesser value than the lands had formerly yielded to the Crown, and since Mompesson's particulars were made out by the king's remembrancer, the auditor was unable to exercise any control on the finding of lands at under values. The wording of his grant had enabled him to find lands as being concealed which were legitimately in charge in the Pipe Office, and even to acquire some parts of the entailed lands.[31]

This speech shows detailed knowledge of royal revenue, and a serious concern with reforming it: it shows the Pym of whom it has been well said that the

29. *CJ*, I, 853; Grosvenor MS. (1626), 3 May. Grosvenor establishes Pym's personal responsibility, and gives a figure of only two servants.
30. *1621 Debates*, IV, 110–1, V, 260; *CJ*, I, 530.
31. PRO, C 65/185. This declaration was the work of Hakewill, Clement Coke and Pym. Pym's diary (*1621 Debates*, IV, 140) describes it as a declaration in writing made by Mr Hakewill, but does not say whether it was the declaration or the writing that was made by Mr Hakewill.

Excise is his most enduring memorial. It is, moreover, a concern which is constant throughout Pym's career. This accountant's mind enabled him, alone among the Commons, to see material for a proper legal charge against Buckingham in the case of the prize ship *St Peter*. When Pym heard that the duke's men had removed a number of bags of gold and silver from the ship, he wanted to know 'by what warrant they delivered the money of the King or the Frenchmen to the Duke'. It is the same administrative Pym who complained, in the impeachment of Buckingham, of the reprising of bailiffs' fees in lands granted to the duke. He complained of exchanges between the duke and the Crown, whereby the duke, he said, was enabled to cut down woods, enfranchise copyholders and make new leases, and then surrender the land back to the Crown at an unchanged rent. Pym referred approvingly to the fact that under the civil law 'public treasure was held in the same reputation with that which was dedicated to God and religion' – perhaps the strongest image a man of Pym's outlook could employ.[32]

This is a man who carries more credibility than the rest of the Commons when he claims that 'the Commoners aim not at judgement only, but at reformation'. In this speech, he proposed an Act of Resumption of Crown lands, and also that lands should be entailed upon particular titles, so that the Crown should again benefit from land coming in by escheat. In revenue and supply debates, Pym showed that he was as good as his word. He was prepared to delay supply for the impeachment of Buckingham and for the Petition of Right, but with these two exceptions, every speech he made on subsidies was in favour of giving the largest possible number of subsidies in the shortest possible time, in order, as he put it on 3 May 1626, 'that the bounty of the subsidy may give the King occasion'. On 19 April 1628, he collaborated with Digges and Rich in throwing out a bill for the royal manors of Bromefield and Yale, because the bill was drafted with insufficient care for the royal revenue. In 1626, he prefaced his first attack on the duke with a proposal for 'a select committee to consider of the king's estate and revenues . . . that we may with the Lords . . . take a course for the enabling of the King and preventing danger.' It was the same financial realist who intervened in the 1626 project for a West India Company, to fight the king of Spain on £200,000 a year, with a calculation that the rigging alone for the required ships would cost £120,000.[33]

He was, then, a man for whom the state's service took priority over everything except God's service. Where a man has two such obsessive themes, it is natural to ask whether they were in any way connected with each other. In such matters as the valuation of recusants' estates, there is a direct, but ultimately superficial, connection. Is there a deeper connection between the two obsessions? In the reign of James, it seems that perhaps there was. Pym's views

32. Whitelocke Diary, 12–20, f.53v; Grosvenor MS. (1626), 1 May; *L J*, III, 615.
33. Grosvenor MS. (1626), 3 May; *1628 Debates*, II, 570: Whitelocke Diary, 12–21, f.129v.

of foreign policy were those of Sir Francis Walsingham and John Foxe: 'your Majesty is the chief head and defender of those who profess the reformed religion, and . . . another prince is the head of the popish religion'.[34] The monarchy, had a divine purpose, which was incompatible with popery. For this divine purpose, the monarchy enjoyed divine right:

> As God, together with the being of things, had infused into them certain special qualities and instincts, aptest for the preservation of that being, so, by a kind of proportion and resemblance, it might be said, that the state of monarchy, which is the perfectest state of government, doth breed in the hearts of all princes certain inclinations and affections, apt to preserve monarchies . . . every prince desireth (touching human dependency) to be within his own dominions, as God is in the world; that all power and favour should be derived from him, all services dedicated to him. This independancy upon others is broken in all that party adhering to the church of Rome, by their subjection to foreign ecclesiastical jurisdiction.

In the true tradition of Foxe's cult of the Christian Emperor and of the Act of Supremacy, he thought that popery was incompatible with monarchy, and incompatible in part because of 'the popularity of them, against which in itself all kings have a kind of repugnancy'.[35]

The king, then, ruled by divine right: 'the image of God's power is expressed in your regal dignity'.[36] But the English monarchy enjoyed divine right for a purpose: the purpose of warring against God's enemies. For this purpose, the monarchy was too weak. Pym the financial realist was well aware that the monarchy lacked the resources for the task allotted to it by Pym the religious enthusiast. On 27 November 1621, he commented on possible plans for a Continental land war: 'that this war must be supplied by money, wherein we are too weak for the King of Spain'.[37] Seeing so fundamental a defect, Pym was of course committed to rectifying it. The bounty received by the Duke of Buckingham he thought the more dangerous because it was had in time of war, 'when there appears great wants and hazards of the kingdom, for the provision of the navy, and guard of the seas in his own charge, the kingdoms threatened

34. E. Nicholas, *Proceedings and Debates in the House of Commons in 1620 and 1621* (1766) (hereafter cited as Nicholas), II, 235.
35. Nicholas, II, 238. It must be stressed that this is an *ex parte* text, as the reference to 'your' Majesty illustrates. It was written out by Pym for submission to the king. However, Pym left in the most offensive matter, including the reference to the king's 'wariness of his own person'. The passage quoted here has a close enough resemblance to the texts in *1621 Debates*, II, 463, V, 222 and VI, 327 to suggest that it is not dramatically different from what he delivered in the House. Diarists frequently skipped divine right imagery, treating it as so much padding.
36. M. Judson, *The Crisis of the Constitution* (Rutgers, 1949), 18; Nicholas, II, 234.
37. Nicholas, II, 219; *1621 Debates*, IV, 442.

with invasions, and potent enemies'.[38] The security of the monarchy, then, was essential to the security of religion.

So long as Pym was certain he lived under a protestant prince, his themes could be reconciled. In 1624, when war against Spain was being prepared, reconciling them was a simple work of piety and patriotism. In the subsidy debate, he said that 'we have made one step from the greatest danger that ever threatened us God grant we relapse not again' and moved to grant the full sum of six subsidies and twelve fifteenths which the king was requesting and to agree on the particulars at a committee of both houses.[39] On 2 March he seconded a motion by Digges 'to give thanks to the Lords for the correspondency between the Houses, to the prince for his favour and constancy to religion, to the King for accepting our advice in so great a work, and that he will declare himself to the world, and that there may be through the kingdom a general thanks to God for his gracious favour herein' – a speech recorded in the more secular glass of Hawarde's diary as 'Mr. Pym *al* no purpose'.[40]

For the whole of James's reign, Pym retained his confidence that he was living under a protestant prince. He might often think that James was asleep at his post, and that 'his Majesty's . . . royal disposition is not yet bent to that which we desire'. It might be necessary to explain to James that, in believing he could avoid popish plots by lenity in executing the recusancy laws, he had, literally, failed to understand the nature of the beast: 'for having gotten favour they will expect a toleration, after toleration they will look for equality, after equality for superiority, and after superiority they will seek the subversion of that religion which is contrary to theirs'. Pym seems to have been pleased with this sentence, since he got it copied into the Commons' petitions on religion in both 1621 and 1625.[41] Yet he always thought James was a protestant. It was, after all, hard to regard the man who had been on the throne on the fifth of November 1605 as an agent of the international popish conspiracy. Moreover, as Pym often remembered, James had spent 'upwards of sixty pages' proving the pope to be Antichrist. It might be advisable to protect James, as it had been advisable to protect the equally misguided Queen

38. *LJ*, III, 614.
39. Spring Diary, 19 March 1624: also BL, Harleian MS. 6383, f.105r; PRO, SP 14/166, f.92r; Cumberland RO, diary of Sir John Lowther, 19 March 1624. I am grateful to Professor Robert E. Ruigh for drawing my attention to this diary.
40. Bodl., Tanner MS. 392, f.19r; Wilts. RO, Hawarde Diary, 2 March 1624.
41. *1621 Debates*, II, 463; Nicholas, II, 264; *1625 Debates*, 19. By 1625, the last clause no longer referred to the subversion of the true religion, but to 'the extermination both of us and our religion'. The 1625 petition, drafted by Pym and Sandys, also repeated Pym's charges of 1621 about the 'popularity' of papists. The same phrases were repeated by Sir Robert Grosvenor in his charge to the Cheshire electors in 1624. It is not clear whether Grosvenor is quoting from Pym or from the petition quoting from Pym (Cheshire RO, Grosvenor MS., 2 Feb. 1623/4). I am grateful to Richard Cust for this reference.

Elizabeth, by reviving the Bond of Association, to ensure that offices were held by those who were loyal both to religion and the king's person. Yet even if Pym did not believe James was well cast in the role of godly prince, he did not believe he was beyond the reach of a prompter. Thus he was enabled to work with the grain of the political system in which he lived, and to regard a Parliament as an agent, not for the fruitless task of trying to coerce a king, but for the more congenial and practicable one of persuading him: 'herein lies the principal part of our labour, to win the King, for he is the first mover, from whence all the prosperity of this and other affairs of Parliament must be derived'.[42]

This belief was crucial to the views of the Jacobean Pym about the nature and function of a Parliament. His was the administrative view of Pym the receiver, the view of a man of business almost untouched by Cokeian legalism. On 7 December 1621, he said that 'the liberties and privileges of the House are but accessory, and bills are the end of a Parliament. And therefore he would not that the end of preserving our liberties should hinder the end for which we came hither'. On 18 December he repeated the same point: 'moved to settle the good bills and articles now in agitation, and then if we have any more time to spend it about our privileges, for that thother are *magis principale*'.[43] His diary also gives the impression that in 1621 he did not want, either to start a privilege dispute, or to enter into any detailed foreign policy debate. He noted that the first attempt to make an issue of the restraint of Sir Edwin Sandys was 'well passed over' by the House, and the speech of Sir George Hastings, the only attempt at a really detailed discussion of foreign affairs, is dismissed in the words 'here were interposed some unseasonable motions'.[44] By contrast, he recorded the contents of bills in unusual and valuable detail, and showed himself much concerned about such practical points as whether it should be possible to convict a drunkard on the unsupported oath of his drinking companion.[45] Yet he showed a readiness to leave things to administrative action which his colleagues sometimes found surprising. For example, he seems to have offended Coke and Alford by maintaining that James's proclamation condemning the patent for alehouse recognizances was a sufficient condemnation of the patent, without the support of an Act of Parliament.[46] A week

42. *1621 Debates*, IV, 448 (Pym's diary). The fact that Pym's diary comes to a sudden halt at this point could be held to indicate a fear that his labours to 'win the King' were proving unsuccessful.
43. Nicholas, II, 297; *1621 Debates*, VI, 244. For a sharply different version of the speech of 7 Dec. see *1621 Debates*, VI, 229.
44. The conclusion of Pym's speech of 27 Nov. was that they should vote additional supply 'without any mention of the war' and go back to bills: *1621 Debates*, IV, 441, 439, 443.
45. Northants. RO, Finch-Hatton MS. 50, f.8v.
46. *1621 Debates*, III, 44. Pym said the proclamation which took it away was good, 'which was not denied, all the house saith'.

later, he persuaded the House to throw out a bill to move a court leet on one of Sir William Brereton's manors, on the ground that the king could, if it pleased him, perfectly well do this without an Act of Parliament, and therefore it was not worth passing one.[47]

His attitude to parliamentary privilege appears to have been strictly functional, immune from the element of self-importance which was so essential a part of the subject in the minds of Coke and Phelips. He objected to the banning of discussion, and to the imprisonment of members, yet when he saw a privilege dispute beginning, he wished 'to cast balm to heal the wound, not to make it wider'. In 1626, Coke, who was claiming to be a member in spite of being a sheriff, claimed parliamentary privilege in a lawsuit. Pym commented: 'our privileges given us [*sic*] as in respect of our attendance: if we have forbore his attendance we may forbear his privilege'. In 1628, when Phelips objected to the king's message asking them to have no Easter recess, Pym asked 'cannot we accept a motion from his Majesty as willingly as we do from a member of this House?'[48] As late as the end of May 1628, Pym was still arguing in a way which convinced Sir Edward Coke he did not have the root of the matter in him. The Commons were debating Monson's revival of Lepton's patent for a monopoly of engrossing bills and processes in the Council of the North. Pym agreed to the condemnation of the patent because he thought the monopoly of engrossing bills a grievance because Monson was unskilful in it, yet he insisted on dividing the House to prevent a condemnation of the monopoly of making processes. He said: 'as for the process it is in the king to erect a court, shall not he that erects the court appoint who shall make the process'? Coke claimed that this speech showed that Pym did not understand the statute of Monopolies.[49]

All these views on the nature and function of a Parliament were inoffensive to the monarchy, even if offensive to Coke or Alford. Under James, there is no evidence, except on the single subject of impeachment, that Pym had any wish to change the place or function of Parliament in the state. Parliament, like other things, was to be made, as far as possible, an efficient instrument of business. This committed Pym to a concern with efficient procedure, to a dislike of time-wasting debate,[50] to the voting of sufficient supply, and to the dispatch and efficient drafting of bills. In the words of Hawarde's law French: 'Mr. Pym will no bill sans order. Private bills in le morning'.[51] Under James, there is nothing which justifies classifying him as in any sense a member of a parliamentary opposition.

47. Nicholas, I, 344.
48. Grosvenor MS. (1626), 8 June; *1628 Debates*, II, 403. See also the instructive case of Sir Simeon Steward, *ibid.*, III, 136.
49. BL, Add. MS. 36, 825, fos. 414r, 416r; Grosvenor MS. (1628), 30 May.
50. It is interesting to contrast the reports of Pym and Barrington for 28 May–4 June 1621, and of Pym and Dyott for 11 Aug. 1625. See also the comments on Coke and Seymour, *1625 Debates*, 71, 121.
51. Wilts. RO, Hawarde Diary, 23 Feb. 1624; *CJ*, I, 716.

If this is the case, it is necessary to explain why he was imprisoned after the 1621 session. The real reasons for the 1621 imprisonments may not have been the same as their ostensible grounds.[52] The ostensible grounds for Pym's imprisonment appear to have concerned his speeches of 27 and 28 November. It is possible to look through these speeches, and find passages which might have given offence. The proposal to revive the Bond of Association, the proposal for the king to employ a commission drawn from both Houses to execute the recusancy laws and a reference to the king's 'wariness of his own person' might all have given offence.[53]

Yet it is worth looking at the comment of a sensitive contemporary writing without hindsight, even from a week later. On 1 December Chamberlain commented: 'I have heard extraordinary commendation of a neat speech made by one Pimme, a receiver, wherein he laboured to show that the King's clemency, justice, bounty, facility, peaceable disposition and other his natural virtues were by the adverse party perverted and turned to a quite contrary course; and though he were somewhat long in the explanation of these particulars, yet he had great attention, and was exceedingly commended both for matter and manner'.[54] It is hard to believe that Chamberlain or his informants had so little capacity to recognize an offensive speech. It is therefore worth wondering whether Pym had done anything which might have encouraged the duke or any other councillor to give exaggerated reports of his speech to the king. He had: there is one thing that all those punished after the 1621 Parliament had in common: they were all on the short list of members who had impeded Buckingham's plans and endangered his security by taking up the case of Lepton and Goldsmith. In this case, Pym's contribution had been one of the most effective. It was his immediate motion to seal their studies and search their papers which had made the whole case possible.[55] If this is the cause, the duke and not the king was largely responsible for Pym's imprisonment. The imprisonment does not appear to have soured his attitude to the king, nor to have alienated him from the Court as a whole. He was released on the intercession of Bedford's friend Lord Treasurer Cranfield, who required his

52. C. Russell, 'The examination of Mr Mallory after the Parliament of 1621', above, chap. 4, pp. 113-20. The issue is discussed further in my article, 'The foreign policy debate in the House of Commons', above, chapter 3, pp. 91-112, and in my book, *Parliaments and English Politics 1621–9*, chapter II.
53. Pym had been given a warning before his speech of 28 Nov. (*1621 Debates*, IV, 448). The only possible occasions for this warning are his speech of 27 Nov., in which he proposed to vote supply unconditionally and go back to bills, and his speech on Lepton and Goldsmith on 24 Nov. See *1621 Debates*, III, 462, II, 464, VI, 206–7; Nicholas, II, 219, 236.
54. *Letters of John Chamberlain*, II, 412.
55. *1621 Debates*, III, 439. There is a significantly full text in Nicholas, II, 201, which would have been available to the Duke.

services on official business.[56] In 1624, he made no attempt to support the making of a privilege issue out of his imprisonment, and even opposed the very limited motion of Mallory, that in future the clerk, who appears to have been the Council's informant, should not set down a man's name to a motion. Unlike many of his leading parliamentary colleagues, he seems to have never made any attempt to come to terms with the duke, but until the death of James, there was apparently nothing else to disqualify him from using his administrative talents as a holder of high office.

Pym's eagerness to develop the process of impeachment cannot be held to have disqualified him as a candidate for office. If it were a disqualification, it would have ruled out many of the Council, led by Pembroke, Arundel, the duke and the Prince of Wales. It was Pym, well before any other member, who formed a clear picture of what later became the recognized procedure of impeachment, with the Commons as prosecutors and the Lords as judges, and it was in the impeachment of Manwaring, in 1628, that he first turned this picture into fact.[57] The Commons, he thought, should be responsible for what he called 'the inquisition of the fact', the Lords for judgment, and the king for its execution. As he put it, 'the high court of Parliament is the great eye of the kingdom to find out offences and punish them'. It was a task which was to be undertaken in collaboration with the king, not in opposition to him: 'for execution, left to the king wholly, who hath the sword'.[58] For this reason, impeachment in the 1620s was not a suitable weapon to secure ministerial responsibility. It is, as we have recent cause to remember, possible to use the power of pardon to frustrate the purpose of an impeachment. Pym was well aware of this fact, and had no idea of making any use of impeachments without the king's consent. Indeed, many of the numerous delinquents he pursued were much too small to be put through the cumbrous process of an impeachment. Instead, the king was to be petitioned to take the necessary action against them.

That Pym's aim was not ministerial responsibility is perhaps best shown by listing the delinquents he attacked, most of whom could not by any stretch of imagination be called ministers. They are Shepherd, Mompesson, Sir John

56. National Register of Archives, Sackville MSS. ON 8746, 867 and 277: I am grateful to Professor Roy Schreiber for these references. See also *HMC*, 4th Report App., 312–3. Bedford was Cranfield's sponsor when he took his seat in the Lords in November 1621: *L J*, III, 163.

57. *1621 Debates*, III, 264, 287–8, IV, 361 and other references; C. G. C. Tite, *Impeachment and Parliamentary Judicature in Early Stuart England* (1974), 51, 175–6 and other refs. On the impeachment of Manwaring, *L J*, III, 847; *Debates in the House of Lords*, ed. F. H. Relf (Camden Soc., 3rd ser. XLII, 1929), 219. The key point in control of an impeachment prosecution was control over the production of witnesses. Pym achieved this in part by selecting witnesses some of whom were members of the Commons: House of Lords RO, Braye MS. I, f.67.

58. *1621 Debates*, III, 30, II, 303.

Bennet (a corrupt probate judge), Floyd, Lambe and Cradock (two corrupt officials of ecclesiastical courts), Lepton and Goldsmith, Dr Anian, president of Corpus Christi College, Oxford, who was charged with bribery, buggery and disparagement of preaching, Simon Dormer, a Popish schoolmaster, the town of Liverpool, Richard Montagu the Arminian, Bishop Harsnett of Norwich, Buckingham's client Edward Clerke (for rude words about Sir Edward Coke), Cleydon and Lewis (two more popish schoolmasters), the Duke of Buckingham, More and Dyott (for ill-advised speech in the House of Commons), Boyd, a projector, and John Cosin the Arminian. In 1628, Pym had a new list: Baber, recorder of Wells, Walter Brooke, who had carried a young woman beyond seas, where she suffered a fate worse than death (by becoming a nun), Burgess, vicar of Witney, who had made rude remarks about puritans, the deputy lieutenants of Cornwall, Roger Manwaring, William Welby, deputy lieutenant, Edmund Sawyer auditor of the Exchequer, and the Countess of Buckingham. In 1629, he added Aleyn, who had made rude remarks about puritans, Lord Lambert, who had illegally levied militia rates, and Bishop Neile.[59] Of these, only the cases of Buckingham and Neile really raise issues of ministerial responsibility. On the cases of Cranfield and Bacon, Pym remained silent. Pym's attacks on these delinquents, like the attacks of earlier parliaments on Mary Queen of Scots, were not meant to hinder the monarchy: they were meant to help it. Yet they do show the extraordinary force of Pym's zeal for rooting out delinquents: if the members of the 1620s were to be nicknamed along the lines of Sir John Neale's famous 'choir', Pym would indubitably be classed as 'Pym the prosecutor'.

Under James, Pym's rather excessive loyalty was in a tradition which had been well established in the days of Sir Francis Walsingham and Sir Walter Mildmay. If he had more concern for the king's safety than the king himself, they had had more concern for the queen's safety than she had herself. If he thought the king allowed some men to hold office in the Church who were less godly than they should be, Walsingham and Mildmay had thought Queen Elizabeth did the same. James's attitude to Abbot could even be compared favourably to Queen Elizabeth's attitude to Grindal.

For Pym, the confidence that he lived under a protestant prince was rapidly destroyed during the first three years of the reign of Charles I. The cause of the destruction was the rise of Arminianism. It is perhaps a significant coincidence that the rise of Arminianism happened at exactly the same time as Pym began to acquire some knowledge of the inner workings of the Court. Before he was taken up by Warwick, Pym had enjoyed an exceptional ignorance of Court affairs. Most leading members had their Court contact: Pym, except for what appears to have been a purely business contact with Cranfield, did not. The Pym who, in 1621, had believed that a royal proclamation was a sufficient

59. In some of these cases, notably those of Aleyn and Lambert, Pym's interventions were procedural, and their tactical object is not certain.

security for the abolition of a monopoly was showing a naïveté which only ignorance could explain. For such a man, the discovery that the Court was not always what it seemed was likely to be a shock at any time. When this shock merged with the shock of the rise of Arminianism, the reverberations lasted the rest of Pym's life.

Dr Tyacke has identified Pym as the leader of anti-Arminian feeling in the Commons,[60] and similarly, the rise of Arminianism should be identified as a watershed in Pym's career. For Pym, who had been a friend of John Preston before his election to Parliament,[61] the belief in predestination and election was one of the central and defining points, not of puritanism, but of international protestantism.[62] This belief runs through the whole of his circle of friends: every surviving will we have from a friend of Pym or from a member of the Rous family asserts, with dogmatic clarity, its certainty of its author's own election.[63] For Pym, predestination was the doctrine of the Church of England because it was so laid down by law. It was laid down in the Thirty-Nine Articles and the Book of Homilies, both of which were confirmed by Act of Parliament. For Pym, then, an assault on predestination was an assault on protestantism, an assault on law, and an assault on the position of Parliament within the state. Above all, it was an attempt to subvert the state, both by depriving it of that religious unity without which it could not function, and by destroying that unity between king and people without which no government could be other than arbitrary.

Dr Tyacke emphasizes the far-reaching re-definition of 'puritanism' attempted by the Arminians, and this appears to have been one of the points which offended Pym most. The Committee of Religion reported, possibly in Pym's words, in 1625: 'if Puritans be so bad, it were good we knew them. But

60. N. R. N. Tyacke, in C. Russell (ed.), *The Origins of the English Civil War* (1973), 121, 135.
61. John Preston, *A Funeral Sermon on Mr. A. Upton* (1619), dedicated to Pym.
62. BL, Add. MS. 36, 825, fos. 470r–471v. See also his explicit contrast between Arminianism and 'our religion', *Commons' Debates in 1629*, ed. W. Notestein and F. H. Relf (Minneapolis, 1921) (hereafter cited as *1629 Debates*), 112. Dr Tyacke remarks: 'for many people in the early seventeenth century the basic issue between Protestantism and Catholicism was that of divine determinism versus human free will': Russell, *Origins*, 128. See also C. Russell, *The Crisis of Parliaments* (1971), 216–7. Pym appears to have been uncertain whether the Arminians actually were papists: in 1643, he accused the bishops of introducing 'Arminian or papistical ceremonies, whether you please to term them, there is not much difference': *A Declaration or Vindication of John Pym, Esq.* (1643), 5.
63. E.g. PRO, PROB 11/116/f.199 (William Pym); PROB 11/137/f.508 (Anthony Rous) and PROB 11/181/f.386 (Richard Knightley). The only exception is Pym's mother, who seems to have believed she was predestined to damnation: C. Russell, 'The wardship of John Pym', above, chapter 9, pp. 150 and n. 22, 160

Mr Montague leaves this uncertain, for by his opinion we may all be Puritans. Mr Ward and Mr Yates are Puritans, and yet these are men that subscribe and conform'. In Pym's words in 1628:

> He seems to make a difference between the church in foreign parts and the church of England. As for his charge of sedition, it is clear by dividing the kingdom under the name of Puritans, labouring to bring his Majesty in jealousy with his subjects and to stir up others in hatred against such. First he lays the name Puritans upon the King's subjects that are dutiful and honest subjects in truth. At the first this word was given to them that severed themselves from the church, but he says there are Puritans in heart and Puritans in doctrine, as of predestination and reprobation. Also this division and aspersion is new, and under this name he comprehends some of our bishops. Also he labours to bring these persons into dislike with his Majesty as dangerous persons.[64]

Pym was the first member of the Commons to take up the issue of Arminianism, in 1624, yet it appears that his initial reflex was to look for help to authority. He believed that James's warrant for the printing of Montagu's first book had been procured 'without his privity, as it should seem', and after James's death, he showed an entire, and justified confidence in the readiness of Archbishop Abbot to put down the new doctrine if he could. Alarmed though he was, Pym seems to have continued to believe for some time that he was dealing with 'boldness of private men', which, with the aid of the House of Lords, could be duly put down by authority.[65] The idea that the centre of popery was actually at the English Court was one so dreadful that it seems to have taken Pym a long time to absorb it. He took part in the attack on the duke, yet he did not attack the duke's religion. It was Sherland, not Pym, who accused the duke of being the patron of a semi-Pelagian semi-popish faction.[66] Pym thought the duke had brought the state into danger of 'final destruction' by exhausting its revenues, but in May 1626, he does not yet appear to have thought that the duke was an agent of international popery. The realization that Arminianism was being securely, openly and knowingly supported from within the Court appears to have come to him during the campaign to elect the duke chancellor of Cambridge University. On 3 June 1626, he said 'that a member of the Lords' house went to Cambridge to solicit this business for the Duke, with the consent of some others who have been agents to utter Montague's book, as

64. *1625 Debates*, 49; BL, Add. MS. 36,825, f.471r. See also Francis Rous, *Testis Veritatis* (1626), 105–7. Contrast the lack of any immediate fear of idolatry in Francis Rous, *Oil of Scorpions* (1623), 108–10.
65. *1625 Debates*, 46, 47, also his significant seconding of Fleetwood's motion of 8 Aug., *ibid.*, 140–1.
66. The correct order of speeches was established by Tite, *op. cit.*, 198n., and the correct division between the speeches is according to *L J*, III, 610–6.

Dr Cosins and Mr Mason have explained themselves about this that it may be to perfect a conspiracy to bring in Arminianism'.[67] For Pym, this speech appears to have been the crossing of the Rubicon, the moment at which the notion that the Court harboured a 'popish and malignant party' was born.

When Parliament reassembled in 1628, the Pym who came back to Westminster had changed as fundamentally as the Church of England. He had also suddenly become a frequent speaker. Over a third of all Pym's speeches during the 1620s were made in the Parliament of 1628. He had also suddenly acquired an intense concern with questions of law and liberties, on which his previous silence had been so complete as to be deafening. As Hexter said, 'Pym's love of the law had about it a certain quality of intermittency'.[68] His support for the Petition of Right was enthusiastic, vocal and unyielding, and in stating it, he began the enunciation of a rapidly developing body of political ideas. He used the concept of the birthright: 'a man as soon as he is born is born into the world, not into a prison'. He became one of the surprisingly few vocal adherents of Coke's doctrine of the ancient constitution: 'we are upon the point of imprisonment. Sir Edward Coke can say much and tell you what a plain right the subject enjoys. Nay the conqueror himself though he conquered the kingdom he conquered not the law.'[69] He later claimed that William the Conqueror had obtained the Crown by composition with the people.[70] He was so eager to reject notions of arbitrary power and reason of state that he came perilously close to denying the Scriptural text 'render unto Caesar the things that are Caesar's':

> And though he would not presume to expound a place of Scripture, yet as an historical observation he desired their Lordships to remember that the Jews were at that time a conquered nation, and so for their laws persons and estates subject to the absolute power of the Romans who were the conquerors, whereby this case is far different from the case of this kingdom, which hath been always free and hereditary.[71]

Pym's new cult of the law and the ancient constitution was not meant to diminish the monarchy: king and law were, for him, coeval and interdepen-

67. Grosvenor MS. (1626) 3 June; Whitelocke Diary, 12–22, f.33r.
68. J. H. Hexter, *The Reign of King Pym* (Cambridge, Mass., 1941), 194–5. See also his clash with Selden in 1629 about whether the Lambeth Articles and other formulations not confirmed by law could properly be regarded as 'public acts of the church'. *HMC*, 13th Report App VII, 64, 68; *1629 Debates*, 119–20.
69. *1628 Debates*, III, 77, II, 106. On most topics, the body of explicit political ideas material in parliamentary debates before 1628 is small. After 1628, these debates circulated in numerous manuscript copies and some printed extracts.
70. BL, Add. MS. 36,825, f.495r. Also fos. 493v–494r, 506r–v.
71. *Ibid.*, f.498v. It is impossible to be certain that Pym taxed the Lords' patience with the whole of this script. Yet the report to the Lords by Coventry seems to be an accurate précis of the whole speech: House of Lords RO, Braye MS. I, fos. 60–67. See also *C J*, I, 919.

dent. As he put it, 'we are subject to a kingly power with an established law'. Both, in their turn, rested on the law of God, the ultimate source of all authority: 'no king, no council, no judge, either by God's law or man's, can lay imprisonment without cause, which not at his pleasure, but originally in the party himself'.[72]

Yet, even in the middle of his new cult of law, Pym had too much appreciation of the facts of political power to believe that it was possible to use the law as a coercive force to bind the king. On one offer to confirm liberties in general words, he commented: 'we have it already and it has been broken already', and significantly went straight on to express his deepening concern about martial law.[73] Pym was well aware that the king possessed soldiers, and that *inter arma silent leges*: 'these heads are most considerable, the unlawfulness of these men, the forced contributions, the exemption of them from law, the superinducing of an unlegal authority, the uselessness of them, and the jealousness and religion of them'.[74]

Pym was well aware that the king could not be forcibly controlled by law: the law was an instrument for proceeding against lesser mortals, and, if the king so chose, one of the greatest guarantees of the love and loyalty of his subjects. In the debate of 6 May about whether to take the king's word for a confirmation of their liberties, Pym's objection was not to taking the king's word: in the last resort, he knew there was no other security. His objection was that the king had not said the right word:

> the King's word were enough if we knew how far he meant to express that word. A comfort to us to hear the King. If he understood the laws, he would not err. We have a greater tie on him, at his coronation, in his conscience. If the King should say that he is better satisfied in the law than he was the last year, and apply it to our business, I should rely upon it. But I hear not the King say that we shall have no more imprisonments for loans, nor that his name shall not be used in such like; that it shall not be pretended to be matter of state when it is not so.[75]

It would seem clear on chronology alone, even without the aid of logic, that it was the rise of Arminianism which first persuaded Pym that the rule of law was in danger. Yet, believing it was in danger, he did not become less eager to supply the king with money. He moved that 'the King may not lose Tonnage and Poundage, nor yet take it against law', and offered to 'settle it in as ample ways as ever any of his predecessors enjoyed it'. He said the same in 1629, claiming that voting Tonnage and Poundage was the only way to 'sweeten the

72. *1628 Debates*, III, 102, 156–7, 162.
73. *1628 Debates*, III, 102 (also 97, 107).
74. *Ibid.*, II, 367.
75. *Ibid.*, III, 281–2. See also 276, 286: 'the King's word can add no obligation to the oath he took at his coronation'.

business with the King', and that by comparison with the liberties of the kingdom, 'the privilege of this House is but a mean matter'.[76]

In trying to 'sweeten the King', Pym was trying to preserve something which was, for him, bigger than the law, though it was interdependent with it. He was trying to prevent something akin to what Locke was later to call 'the dissolution of society'. A threat to the principle of government was more than simply a threat to the rule of law: 'there are some laws which are co-essential and con-natural with government, which being broken, all things run into confusion'.[77] For Pym, the greatest threat came from what he saw as the making of a division between the king and the people. Without unity all the circumstances which made a rule of law possible would be lacking. The destruction of unity was a task Pym believed had been begun by the Arminians, and he saw it carried on most dangerously by Roger Manwaring, a clergyman who had preached that the Forced Loan was due by the law of God, and that those who refused it were, as he put it 'temporal recusants'.[78] Pym was well aware of the danger which arose if such arguments were put to the king while parliaments were not adequately supplying him, and took the occasion to remind his hearers once again of the need for a greater permanent endowment for the Crown. Yet, if the king would have practical excuse for listening to Manwaring, this merely appeared to make his insinuations more dangerous. Pym accused him of 'a wicked intention to avert his Majesty's mind from calling of Parliaments', and when he thought of what would happen if there were no Parliaments, it was, significantly, their function in rooting out offences of which he thought first: 'If Parliaments be taken away, mischiefs and disorders must needs abound without any possibility of good laws to reform them; grievances will daily increase without opportunity or means to redress them, and what readier way can there be to distractions betwixt the king and people, to tumults and distempers in the state than this?'.

This threatened the grounds of political obligation: 'he hath acted the part of the Romish Jesuits, they labour our destruction by dissolving the Oath of Allegiance taken by the people, he doth the same work by dissolving the oath of protection, and justice, taken by the King'. It was an attempt to corrupt 'his Majesty's conscience, which is the sovereign principle of all moral actions'. In one of his most revealing phrases, Pym said that if taxation should

76. BL, Stowe MS. 366, f.276r; *1629 Debates*, 156–7, 222–3.
77. *LJ*, III, 615. In this speech, and in his attack on Manwaring, Pym feared what Locke, in the last chapter of his *Second Treatise*, called 'the dissolution of government'. The loss of religious unity threatened 'the dissolution of society', which was the more irreparable fate of the two. See C. Russell, 'Arguments for religious unity in England 1530–1650', above, 181-9, 195-200.
78. There is no evidence that Manwaring was an Arminian. The speech in *1628 Debates*, II, 92, if it is Pym's, suggests that Pym believed him to be one.

cease to be by consent, the subjects would lose the means 'by any act of bounty or benevolence to ingratiate themselves to their sovereign'. It was, as he put it, an attempt to alienate the king's affections from his subjects. He claimed, as he was to claim again in the trial of Strafford, that the like offence had never before been committed. He thought that Manwaring was doing no less than dissolving the ancient constitution, a dissolution which he thought threatened the king as much as it threatened the subjects.[79] There is an ominous warning in the description of Manwaring's doctrine as 'spiritual poison offered to the ear of the king, appropriating omnipotency to princes. Where we note the grace of the king, not to be taken up by these immodest terms: Herod, consenting to the blasphemy etc, was eaten up of worms'.[80]

Pym's speech to the Lords on Manwaring came early in the miserable week between the king's first and second answers to the Petition of Right. In the next two days Pym first began the remonstrance debate by moving, through his tears, for the doors to be locked, and 'then added the state of Ireland for matter of religion. Many companies soldiers there commanded by popish recusants'.[81] In this picture of an army in Ireland which may be employed here to reduce this kingdom, we are suddenly within measureable distance of the Pym of 1640. It is, then, no surprise to read, in Oliver St John's obituary tribute to Pym that, about 1630, 'fearing that popery might overgrow this kingdom', he intended to make 'some plantation in foreign parts, where the profession of the Gospel might have a free course'.[82] St John was undoubtedly right in the priority he gave to religious over constitutional issues in Pym's intellectual make-up. Pym was not much interested in the privileges of Parliament, and even the rule of law perhaps mattered to him more because it guaranteed the true religion in England than for any other reason. When Pym accused Montagu of laying the charge of puritanism upon 'conformable persons', it was law which gave him the measure of the degree of conformity he regarded as acceptable.[83] For him, the rule of law without the security of true religion could never be more than the most tenuous form of security. Law, for him, was a measure of the mutual obligation of king and people to each other, and without unity in religion, such a sense of mutual obligation would be quickly replaced by something approaching Hobbes's

79. BL, Add. MS. 36,825, fos. 490v–510r *passim*. See also C. Russell, 'The theory of treason in the trial of Strafford', above, 92-3, 101-3, 105-7.
80. *1628 Debates*, III, 410 (Pym's report to the Commons of 14 May. This passage was delivered to the Lords by Pym's assistant Francis Rous.
81. BL, Stowe MS. 366, f.218v; J. Rushworth, *Historical Collections* (1659), I, 609–10; BL: Stowe MS. 366, f.223r; Add. MS. 36,825, f.450r and also 451r.
82. BL, Add. MS. 31,116, f.99v. I am grateful to Professor V. Pearl for this reference. It is worth remembering that in 1643, Pym claimed to be defending 'the orthodox doctrine of the church of England': *A Declaration or Vindication* (1643), 4.
83. See Pym's speech on the subscription bill, *1628 Debates*, III, 515, 519, 520, 522 (text of bill, *ibid.*, 459). Also BL, Add. MS. 36,825, f.470r–v.

state of war. Without a common body of belief, he believed there could be no consent, no law, and no liberty. It was this common body of belief which he believed to have been destroyed by the Arminians. Was it a self-fulfilling prophecy in which he said, in April 1626, that 'the raising of a division or distemper in religion doth often meet in this *tertio*, to ruin the body of the church and state'?

If Pym was making self-fulfilling prophecies, it was not an activity in which he and his friends could claim a monopoly. It is equally arguable that Laud was making a self-fulfilling prophecy when he said, also in 1626:

> 'they, whoever they be, would overthrow *sedes ecclesiae,* the seats of ecclesiastical government, will not spare (if ever they get power), to have a pluck at the throne of David. And there is not a man that is for parity, all fellows in the church, but he is not for monarchy in the state. And certainly either he is but half-headed to his own principles, or he can be but half-hearted to the throne of David.

In 1626, Pym was no more genuinely in favour of 'parity' than Laud was in favour of 'popery'. These two growing fears present a mirror image to each other, and came to enjoy a curious interdependence, each being necessary to validate the other. Francis Rous's fear of popish frogs out of the bottomless pit is curiously similar to Richard Montagu's fear of puritan 'allobrogical dormice'. Throughout the reign of James, this mutual commerce of fear had been soothed by the near-certainty that nothing very dramatic was going to happen. In 1625, the accession of a young and energetic king brought these mutual fears to a point where they became uncontrollable. As Laud remarked, 'break unity once, and farewell strength'.[84]

Dr Tyacke is indubitably right that in starting the chain of events it was Charles and Laud who were the innovators.[85] The gulf between the Pym of 1624 and the Pym of 1628 shows how quickly a shrewd observer reacted to them. It is worth remembering that both Clarendon and the Grand Remonstrance, from their very different points of view, firmly claimed that the origins of the crisis of 1640–2 should not be sought any further back than the accession of Charles I.[86] When we find that, as early as 1628–9, John Pym was already looking back to the days of King James, the man who had proved the pope to be Antichrist and upheld the decrees of the Synod of Dort, the man who had censured Vorstius and condemned Cowell,[87] it is time for us to wonder whether what they tell us three times is true.

84. *1625 Debates,* 179 (Report of 17 April 1626); W. Laud, *A Sermon Preached on Monday the Sixt of February* (1625), 40, 9. Cf. R. C. Richardson, *Puritanism in North-West England* (1972), 174–6.
85. Tyacke, in Russell, *Origins,* 143.
86. Clarendon, *History,* I, 3; S. R. Gardiner (ed.), *Constitutional Documents of the Puritan Revolution* (1906), 206–9.
87. *1625 Debates,* 183; BL, Add. Ms. 36,825, fos. 506r, 509v, 472v; *1629 Debates,* 20.

IV

THE ROAD TO WAR

13

The British Problem and the English Civil War

The study of the English Civil War has so far created more problems than it has solved. The tendency of much recent research has been to show England before the Bishops' Wars as a society not sufficiently divided or polarized to make the war easily explicable. Professor Elton, indeed, has been moved to say that 'some of us wonder whether there really was a civil war since its famous causes have all disappeared'.[1]

It is perhaps a consolation, if not a help, to find that this sense of bewilderment at the Civil War was shared by some of those who lived through it. Sir Thomas Knyvett, in 1644, wondered whether 'the best excuse that can be made for us, must be a fit of lunacy'. In June 1642, Lord Wharton, an active enough Parliamentarian to be in a position to know, wrote to the Chief Justice Bankes, who was with the King at York, to ask what they were quarrelling about. He said those he knew at Westminster were not disloyal, and those who were with the King at York 'wish and drive at an accommodation'. 'How is itt then, hath all this kingdome noe person prudent enough according to theyr affections to prevent the ruine coming upon us; or is itt want of industry, or is itt the wantonness of some few interested or unprovided people to pull downe more in one day, then the rest can build upp in yeares? Or is itt a judgement upon us immediately from the hand of God, for which no naturall or politique reason can be given?'[2]

This is a revised and expanded version of an inaugural lecture delivered at University College, London, on 7 March 1985. I would like to thank Peter Donald for numerous discussions of Scottish matters, and also my Yale pupils, notably Martin Flaherty, David Venderbush and Jim Wilson, who helped to stimulate my interest in matters British. The research for this article was done with assistance from the Small Grants Fund of the British Academy.

[1] G.R. Elton, 'English National Selfconsciousness and the Parliament in the Sixteenth Century' in *Nationalismus in Vorindustrieller Zeit,* Herausgegeben von Otto Dann (München, 1986), p. 79.

[2] B. Schofield (ed), *The Knyvett Letters* (Norfolk Record Society, 1949), xx, 133. I would like to thank Miss Ann Brophy for this reference. G. Bankes, *Corfe Castle* (1853), pp. 132-33.

Since the last of Wharton's explanations is not open to us, or at least not in our professional capacity, we are bound to supply a logical answer to his question. It does not help that both the types of explanation favoured over the past 40 years, based on long-term constitutional conflict and on long-term social change respectively, appear to have suffered irretrievable breakdown: we have to begin all over again.[3] There seem to be four possible ways of attempting the task.

One would be to say that we have not found long-term causes of the Civil War because there were none to find: that the war was the result of a short-term failure to solve a political crisis, together with the need to supply retrospective justification for actions taken in the heat of the moment. I am supposed in some quarters to have adopted this position already, and have been credited in one recent publication with having 'abolished the long-term causes of the Civil War'.[4] This report, like that of Mark Twain's death, is grossly exaggerated. Unlike some colleagues, I see no *a priori* impossibility in this type of explanation, but it remains highly improbable. It should be adopted, if at all, only on the application of Sherlock Holmes's law: 'when you have eliminated everything else, what remains, however improbable, must be the truth'. Since we are very far from having eliminated everything else, this approach remains premature.

A second approach, which I would associate with Peter Lake, Richard Cust and Ken Fincham,[5] would argue that the appearance of an undivided society is deceptive, and rests on the fact that a high proportion of our surviving sources were either addressed to the Privy Council, or written in fear of an accident to the posts. This approach contains much truth: it appears that in this period the private letter is often a less free-spoken medium than the Parliamentary speech, but it will take some time for us to be sure how much truth it contains. It is clear that there were significant divisions of opinion in England before the Bishops' Wars, and it seems clear that the effect of the Bishops' Wars was to exacerbate divisions which did exist, rather than to create others which did not. Yet it remains permissible to wonder how long these divisions, like fault-lines in rocks, might have remained latent if not subjected to the hammer-blows of outside intervention.

The third approach, which this article is designed to investigate, would argue that we have not found the causes of the English Civil War because the question involves trying to discover the whole of the explanation by examining a part of the problem. The English Civil War is regularly discussed as if it were a unique event, but it was not: between 1639 and

[3] This was written before the publication of J.P. Sommerville, *Politics and Ideology in England 1603-40* (1986). The book has not caused me to change this judgment, but it has convinced me that it needs more defence than can be offered here.

[4] Christopher Haigh, *The Reign of Elizabeth I* (1985), p. 19.

[5] Peter Lake, 'The Collection of Ship Money in Cheshire', *Northern History,* 1981, xvii, 71. Kenneth Fincham, 'The Judges' Decision on Ship Money in 1637: the Reaction of Kent', *Bulletin of the Institute of Historical Research*, 1984, lvii, 230-36. Richard Cust's book on the Forced Loan is at present in the press.

1642, Charles I faced armed resistance in all three of his kingdoms. In England and Ireland, civil war and resistance were simultaneous, but in Scotland five years elapsed between resistance in 1639 and civil war in 1644. This seems to be, not because Scotland was a less divided society than England or Ireland, but because the King of Scots, while resident in London, had so little power and patronage that he found the gathering of a party more uphill work in Scotland than in either of his other kingdoms. Charles appears to have regarded the absence of civil war in Scotland in 1639 as a political failure of his own, and his judgment deserves to be taken seriously.[6]

The tendency of dissidents in each kingdom to try to make common cause with sympathisers in the others ensured that the English, Scottish and Irish troubles could not remain three isolated problems: they triggered off a period of repeated intervention by the three kingdoms in each other's affairs, including Scottish intervention in Ireland in 1642, Scottish intervention in England in 1640, 1643, 1648 and 1651, and on a smaller scale, Irish intervention in England in 1643. This list is accompanied by a list of might-have-beens of which Strafford's supposed threat to use the Irish army is the most famous. Though the might-have-beens are not facts, the political hopes and fears they engendered are facts, and often influenced people's conduct. This period of acute British instability came to an end only with the English conquest of Scotland and Ireland in 1649-51.

When three kingdoms under one ruler all take to armed resistance within three years, it seems sensible to investigate the possibility that their actions may have had some common causes. We will not find them in constitutional development, for their constitutional structures were profoundly different. We will not find them in their social systems, for they were even more different: a social history of Britain in the early seventeenth century would be a stark impossibility. However, there are two obvious types of cause which are common to all three kingdoms. One is that they were all ruled by Charles I. It is perhaps fair to paraphrase Lady Bracknell, and so say that 'to lose one kingdom might happen to any king, but to lose three savours of carelessness'.

The other thing all three kingdoms have in common is that they are all parts of a multiple monarchy of three kingdoms. We now know, thanks to a large body of work, that the relations between multiple kingdoms were among the main causes of instability in continental Europe, and Professors Elliott and Koenigsberger have been asking for some time whether the rule which applies across the Channel also applies in Britain.[7] This article is intended to suggest that the answer to their question is 'yes'.

Thanks to them and many others, we now know a good deal about the normal flashpoints in multiple monarchies. They include resentment at the

[6] *Calendar of State Papers Domestic 1639*, Vol ccccxvii, nos. 3, 26, 65; Vol ccccxviii, no. 50.
[7] J.H. Elliott, 'The King and the Catalans', *Cambridge Historical Journal,* 1953. H.G. Koenigsberger, *Dominium Regale and Dominium Politicum et Regale: Monarchies and Parliaments in Early Modern Europe* (London, 1975).

King's absence and about the disposing of offices, the sharing of costs of war and the choice of foreign policy, problems of trade and colonies, and the problems of foreign intervention. All these causes of difficulty were present in Britain. It is particularly interesting that Secretary Coke, probably in 1627-28, drew up a plan for a British version of Olivares' union of arms, and that the Scots in 1641 were demanding the right to trade with English colonies,[8] Yet these issues are surprisingly peripheral: it is possible to find them if we look for them, but only in Anglo-Irish relations between 1625 and 1629 does one of them (in this case the cost of war) become a central theme.[9] The absence of wars for much of the period between 1603 and 1640, and the overwhelming preponderance of the English revenue over those of Scotland and Ireland both contribute to this comparative silence.

This leaves only one of the normal causes of trouble within multiple kingdoms, that caused by religion. This one issue alone accounted for almost all the difficulties between the kingdoms of Britain between 1637 and 1642, and it caused enough trouble to leave very little room for any others. Some of the trouble seems to have arisen from the fact that religion for Charles, like arms for Olivares, was the issue on which he chose to press for greater uniformity. In Britain, as in the Spanish monarchy, it is the issue on which the centre demanded uniformity on which the liberties and privileges of the outlying kingdoms are most loudly asserted.

The rare cases in Europe of multiple kingdoms with different religions do not suggest that the British reaction is disproportionate. One case is that of France and Béarn, where Louis XIII, discovering, to his dismay, that he was King of the Protestant kingdom of Béarn (part of Henri IV's old kingdom of Navarre), decided to invade it and suppress it, even at the risk of war with Spain.[10] The most famous case of multiple kingdoms with different religions is that of Spain and the Netherlands, and that produced disturbances on the same scale as the British. Britain, moreover, offered the peculiar and illogical combination of difference of religions with a theory of authority in two kingdoms (or, as Charles believed, in three) vesting authority in the king as supreme head of the church. A British king who presided over different religions thus offered a built-in challenge to his own authority, something which Charles I was never likely to accept with equanimity. Though there are other cases in Europe in which one king presided over two religions, I am aware of none in which a single king presided over three. Moreover, Britain appears to be a unique case of multiple kingdoms all of which were internally divided in religion, and in all of which there existed a powerful group which preferred the religion of one of the others to their own. Perhaps the problem we ought to be trying to solve is not why this situation produced an explosion under Charles, but how James succeeded in presiding over it for 23 years without one.

[8] SP 16/527/44: BL Stowe Ms 187, ff. 51a, 57b.

[9] Aidan Clarke, *The Old English in Ireland* (1966), pp. 28-60. Also W. Knowler [hereafter Knowler], *Strafford Letters* (1739), I, 238.

[10] J. Russell Major, *Representative Government in Early Modern France* (New Haven, 1980), pp. 449, 474.

The capacity of religion to cause political trouble in the seventeenth century did not just arise from the actions of zealots, though there were plenty of those. It was more serious than respectable conventional or governmental opinion accepted that it was its duty to enforce truth, and to repress error. The case for religious unity was such a conventional cliché that, as the Scottish Commissioners in London put it, it was accepted by 'sound...politicians'. It was the sound politicians' intellectual assent to many of the zealots' propositions which led them into actions which caused trouble. In the Scots Commissioners' words 'we doe all know and professe that religion is not only the mean to serve God and to save our owne soules, but it is also the base and foundation of kingdomes and estates, and the strongest band to tye the subjects to their prince in true loyalty'.[11] Conversely, as they said, 'the greater zeal in different religions, the greater division'. They even invoked Bede's account of the Synod of Whitby to support the proposition that it was unwise to allow the existence of different religions within the same island. In this, if in little else, the Covenanters agreed with Charles I.

Charles, at some date not later than 1633, and possibly as early as 1626,[12] decided to drop a match into this powder-keg by setting out to achieve one uniform order of religion within the three kingdoms. The task was the more necessary for the fact that Charles's interpretation of the English religious settlement, and especially of the 39 Articles, made the gap between the three churches appear considerably wider than it had done under James. Under James, it had been as true in a British as in an English context that Calvinist doctrine served for a 'common and ameliorating bond'[13] between those who disagreed about many other things. When Charles broke this 'common and ameliorating bond' between the churches, he not only widened the gap between them, but also offered a handle to his critics. It became possible for them to challenge Charles, as Pym did, through praise for the Irish Articles of 1615, or, as Peter Smart of Durham did, by publishing material highly critical of English authorities in Edinburgh.[14] It was, perhaps, essential to the survival of Charles's and Laud's Arminian innovations in England that Scotland and Ireland should

[11] National Library of Scotland [hereafter NLS] Advocates' Ms 33.4.6, ff. 142a-146b.
[12] F. Larkin, *Stuart Royal Proclamations* (Oxford, 1983), II, 90-3. I would like to thank Dr N.R.N. Tyacke for this reference. Knowler, I, 187. I would like to thank Martin Flaherty for this reference.
[13] C. Russell (ed), *The Origins of the English Civil War* (1973), p. 121.
[14] *Proceedings in Parliament 1628* edited by Robert C. Johnson, Mary Frear Keeler, Maija J. Cole and William B. Bidwell (New Haven, 1977), iv, 261, iii, 515; S.R. Gardiner (ed), *Debates in the House of Commons in 1625* (Camden Society New Series VI, 1873), p. 181. Peter Smart, *The Vanities and Downfall of the Present Churches* (Edinburgh, 1628). I am grateful to Dr Tyacke for drawing my attention to the significance in this context of the citations of the Irish Articles against Charles's Arminian tendencies.

cease to provide anti-Arminian Englishmen with a much more attractive alternative model. It was perhaps for this reason that Charles seems to have employed Laud as a sort of Secretary for ecclesiastical affairs for all three kingdoms. As early as 1634, Laud complained to Wentworth that 'I was fain to write nine letters yesterday into Scotland: I think you have a plot to see whether I will be *universalis episcopus,* that you and your brethren may take occasion to call me Antichrist'.[15] This attempt to make the three kingdoms uniform in order to protect Charles's changes in England was bound, to heighten theological resistance, to provoke fears that they were being dragged at English chariot wheels, being made, as Baillie put it, 'ane pendicle of the dioces of York',[16] and to encourage those Englishmen who resisted Charles's changes to rely on Scotland and Ireland for assistance in doing likewise.

Laud and Wentworth were both committed to this policy of uniformity between the kingdoms, which Wentworth even carried to the length of recommending that Scotland be governed by the English Privy Council as a dependency of England. Yet they both feared that, in his zeal to implement this policy, Charles did not see how difficult it was. In 1634, Wentworth wrote to Laud that 'the reducing of this kingdom (Ireland) to a conformity in religion with the church of England is no doubt deeply set in his Majesty's pious and prudent heart, as well in perfect zeal to the service of the Almighty as out of other weighty reasons of state and government' but, he added, in a typical Wentworth phrase, to do so without adequate preparation 'were as a man going to warfare without munition or arms'.[17] It is a warning to which Charles should have paid attention.

In trying to impose a uniform religion on Britain, Charles had to work through three very different legal and constitutional systems. Scotland was not in any way legally dependent on England, and it was of some importance to many Scots that in 1603 the King of Scots had inherited England, and not vice versa. The English Privy Council had no *locus standi* on Scottish matters, and even in 1639, between the Bishops' Wars, the Earl of Northumberland, who was a member of the Council Committee for Scottish affairs, was reduced to complaining that he knew no more of Scottish affairs than if he were at Constantinople.[18] The Committee for Scottish Affairs could advise on how, or whether, to use English military force to enforce the King's Scottish policy, but if any of them believed the policy itself to be mistaken, they had no authority to say so. Scotland had

[15] Knowler, I, 271. Laud was making fun of the 'Jonnisms' he associated with Wentworth's supposedly 'Puritan' upbringing in Cambridge.

[16] Robert Baillie [hereafter Baillie], *Letters and Journals*, edited by D. Laing (Bannatyne Club, Edinburgh, 1841), I, 2 (further references are to Vol I unless otherwise stated). Also Nicholas Tyacke, *Anti-Calvinists* (Oxford, 1987), pp. 230-34.

[17] David Stevenson, *The Scottish Revolution* (Newton Abbot, 1973), p. 100 (Knowler, II, 190-92); Knowler, I, 187. I would like to thank Martin Flaherty for this reference.

[18] *Historical Manuscripts Commission: De L'Isle and Dudley*, VI, 366, Kent Archive Office [hereafter KAO], U 1475 C.85/2.

its own Privy Council, its own Parliament, and its own law. The Scottish Privy Council could govern so long as it was allowed an effective form of devolution, but whenever the King of Scots chose to form policy from London, his Scottish Council found it was not easy to advise him from Edinburgh. Scotland also had its own form of church government. It had bishops, but what authority they might have, and how that authority might be related to that of a General Assembly, were to an extent matters of opinion. There was a widespread Scottish sentiment which held that the only ultimate source of lawful authority was the General Assembly, what Alexander Henderson called the 'representative kirk of this kingdom'. For such men as Laud, who protested during the Glasgow Assembly that 'for a national assembly, never did the church of Christ see the like', such theories were more than offensive: they were incomprehensible.[19] A pure Ullmanite ascending theory of power was equally beyond the comprehension of Charles, who believed, with little obvious justification, that he was supreme head of the Church of Scotland.[20] At the Pacification of Berwick, the Covenanters were faced with the task of explaining to Charles that he did not have a negative voice in a General Assembly as he did in an English Parliament, and he simply did not understand what they were talking about.[21] Moreover, Charles was offended by Scottish liturgical practice, as well as by Scottish doctrine and discipline. In 1633 when he went to Edinburgh to be crowned (eight years late) he insisted on using the English liturgy wherever he worshipped. In the *Large Declaration* of 1639, after he had officially abandoned the new Service Book, he complained of the 'diversitie, nay deformitie, which was used in Scotland, where no set or publike form of prayer was used, but preachers and readers and ignorant schoolmasters prayed in the church, sometimes so ignorantly as it was a shame to all religion to have the Majestie of God so barbarously spoken unto, sometimes so seditiously that their prayers were plaine libels, girding at sovereigntie and authoritie; or lyes stuffed with all the false reports in the kingdome'.[22] It perhaps highlights the difficulty in communication which difference of religion might cause that the way the Scots would have expressed the same point was that they did not have a reading ministry.

[19] John Leslie, Earl of Rothes [hereafter Rothes], *A Relation of Proceedings Concerning the Affairs of The Kirk of Scotland from August 1637 to July 1638*, edited by James Nairne (Bannatyne Club, Edinburgh, 1830), pp. 45-6, 5. Scottish Record Office GD 406/1 Hamilton MSS no. 547 [hereafter Hamilton MSS].

[20] For the claim to the royal supremacy in Scotland, see the Scottish canons, Laud, *Works,* V, 586. For Laud's belief that such authority was inherent in all sovereign princes, as it had been in the Kings of Judah, see Baillie, II, Appendix p. 434. For a rare attempt to justify Charles's claim in Scottish law and practice, see John Rylands Library, Crawford MSS 14/3/35, probably dating from the Pacification of Berwick. I am grateful to the Earl of Crawford and Balcarres for permission to use these MSS, and to Dr J.S.A. Adamson for bringing them to my attention. For the case Charles appears to have been discussing, see B. Galloway, *The Union of England and Scotland 1603-1608* (Edinburgh, 1896), p. 87. See also *Stuart Royal Proclamations,* II, 91.

[21] Hamilton MSS M. 1/80. For the case for believing the supremacy was *jure divino,* and not founded on the municipal laws of any kingdom, see SP 16/288/88.

[22] Gordon Donaldson, *The Making of the Scottish Prayer Book of 1637* (Edinburgh, 1954), pp. 42-3. *A Large Declaration* (1640), pp. 20, 16.

The existence of three kingdoms also created opportunities to fish in troubled waters, and these opportunities were much used. Any group who lost a round in their own kingdom could always make common cause with their sympathisers in another, and call in another kingdom to redress the balance of their own. The Scottish Arminians, who were very heavily dependent on English backing, were the first to learn this lesson, and only time prevented them from holding all the best bishoprics and deaneries in Scotland. The English Parliament learned it second, and the Irish Parliament, relying on the English Parliament for its remonstrance against Strafford, learned it third, but it was perhaps Charles who learned it most thoroughly. In May 1641, after the failure of the Army Plot, Secretary Vane expected Charles to settle with his English Parliament, 'there being in truth no other [course] left'.[42] In saying this, Vane merely revealed his ignorance of Charles's Scottish policies. Since 3 March 1641, Charles had been committed to a growing intrigue with Montrose which was designed to create a Scottish party to counterbalance the one at the disposal of his opponents, or (as in the event happened) to induce the Covenanters to withdraw from England before he could succeed in this attempt.[43]

Charles's opportunity came from growing hostility to the Covenanters inside Scotland. One of the major surprises of this work has been finding how strong this sentiment was. In the spring of 1641, it had reached the point at which the liturgy against which the Scots were fighting was being used inside the Scottish army.[44] Other things, such as Montrose's increasing jealousy of the power of Argyll, are the sort of thing which is part of the price of power. So are Scottish resentment at such things as the prohibition of salmon fishing on the Sabbath, or the occasion on which Baillie denounced his patron from the pulpit because at a wedding there was among the lords 'more drink than needed'.[45] The stages of Charles's intrigues with anti-Covenanter Scots are obscure, stretching through the plot of Napier, Keir and Blackhall,[46] the Incident in October 1641, and an abortive plan of May 1642 to secure Scottish intervention against the English Parliament.[47] The consistent theme underlying the details is Charles's desire to build a party of anti-Covenanter Scots, and to use that party to redress the balance of English politics. The schemes he began in 1641 were the ones he pursued until he pulled them off in 1648, and lost his head for it. The point which is immediately relevant to the origins of the English Civil War is that it was Charles's hope of breaking the Anglo-

[42] SP 16/480/20.

[43] NLS Wodrow Ms fol. 65, ff. 65a, 72a-b. For the hardening line towards the Scottish Commissioners in London which accompanied this switch, see *LJ*, iv, 175.

[44] NLS Advocates' MSS 33.4.6, ff. 119a, 121b.

[45] Baillie, II, 6-7, 34-5.

[46] S.R. Gardiner, *History of England* (1893), IX, 395-98, NLS Wodrow Ms fol. 65, nos. 12, 17.

[47] This abortive plan was perhaps more important in Charles's strategy in 1642 than has been appreciated. See Gardiner, X, 203, and Stevenson, pp. 248-49. See also *RPCS*, VIII, 255-63, 264-65, *Letters of Henrietta Maria*, edited by M.A.E. Green (1853), pp. 53, 60, Hamilton MSS 1653, 1723, 1753, 1760, HMC *Buccleuch*, I, 298, and East Riding RO Hotham MSS DD/HO/1/4.

Scottish alliance which encouraged him to believe that Vane was wrong in insisting that he must settle with his English subjects. It is worth remembering that in September 1641, Charles did succeed in breaking the Anglo-Scottish alliance, and it was only the outbreak of the Irish Rebellion which kept the English Parliament in being from then on.

The existence of three kingdoms also provided dissidents with an alternative model, and thereby contributed to polarising the politics of all three. The English godly, who for so long had had to be content with half a loaf, found that having a Scottish army to press their demands had an intoxicating effect. When Burges, at the opening of the Long Parliament, preached on the delivery of Israel from Babylon by an army coming from the north, it was impossible to mistake his meaning.[48] As Baillie put it, 'God is making here a new world', and the reaction of many of the English godly was 'gramercies, good Scot'.[49] The opportunity encouraged D'Ewes to hold forth on the proposition that the English and the Scots were one nation, except for the Hebrideans, who were Irish, and to propose the setting up of a committee for the abolishing of superstition.[50] When the Root and Branch Bill passed in the Commons, Nehemiah Wallington commented 'Babylon is fallen, is fallen'.[51]

The polarizing effect of such utterances was because these men's hopes were other men's fears, and the fears tended to be expressed in the form of appeals to anti-Scottish sentiment. The Scots gave a particularly good opportunity for this when they asked for a euphemistically named 'Brotherly Assistance' of £300,000. Hyde's friend Thomas Triplett, who was pouring a stream of anti-Scottish sentiment into Hyde's ear from Newburn onwards, reported a rumour that the money for the Brotherly Assistance was to be raised by fining Alderman Abell the wine monopolist, 'and so lett Abel pay Cain'.[52] Gervase Holles, in the House of Commons, said the Scots might be our younger brothers, but, like Jacob, they were stealing our birthright—an image liable to boomerang on him.[53] The Earl of Bristol, the chief English negotiator, was surely not choosing his words at random when he described the Brotherly Assistance as a 'viaticum' for the Scots.[54] This anti-Scottish feeling grew steadily through the summer of 1641, and the emotions which led to Civil War were very near the surface when Sir Robert Harley reported that Sir William Widdrington had been overheard saying that he looked forward to the day when any member calling the Scots 'brethren' would be called to the bar.[55]

[48] C. Burges, *The First Sermon* (1641), p. 6.
[49] Baillie, p. 283. The poem to which Baillie refers is in *Diary of John Rous,* edited by M.A.E. Green, Camden Society, (1886), cxvi, 110-11, and NLS Advocates' MSS 33.1.1, XIII, no. 69.
[50] W. Notestein (ed), *Journal of Sir Symonds D'Ewes* (New Haven, 1923), p. 320, BL Harl Ms 163, f. 10a.
[51] Nehemiah Wallington, *Historical Notices*, edited by Rosamond Ann Webb, I, 171. His text, *Rev* 18.2, describes the downfall of the Beast. See also Paul S. Seaver, *Wallington's World* (Stanford, 1985), p. 164.
[52] Bodleian Ms Clarendon 10, no. 1514.
[53] Yale University Beinecke Library, Osborn Shelves b 197, f. 40b.
[54] Maija Jansson (ed), *Two Diaries of the Long Parliament* (Gloucester, 1984), p. 18.
[55] BL Harl Ms 163, f. 696b.

Ireland, by contrast, was not an independent kingdom, but, like Massachusetts or Virginia, a semi-autonomous dependency of the English Crown. Under the King, the Dublin administration was headed by a Lord Lieutenant, Lord Deputy or Lord Justices (the title varying according to the status of the holder). He and his Irish Privy Council were answerable to the English Privy Council, which could, and sometimes did, discuss Irish affairs. There was also an Irish Parliament though the operation of Poynings' Law firmly subordinated it to the English Privy Council. The English Parliament, before 1640, was not normally regarded as having any standing in Ireland: in British terms, the English Parliament was as much a local assembly as the Cortes of Castile.[23] In religion, there was an established Protestant Church of Ireland, run by Archbishop Ussher along lines acceptable to St John or Brereton, and to many of the increasing numbers of Scots settled in Ulster. Outside the Church of Ireland, the Catholic majority, handicapped by a formidable series of legal disabilities, enjoyed an intermittently Nelsonian blind eye.

Irish affairs also suffered from a threefold division of race. The New English, Protestants who usually controlled the government in Dublin, were English settlers who had arrived since the Reformation. For them, the key problem was always how to stop Ireland being Irish, an aim which became more and more closely identified with Protestantism and with a policy of plantation. The 'mere' or native Irish were excluded from the political nation, though with an apparently increasing number of exceptions. The pigs in the middle of Irish politics were the Old English, descendants of pre-Reformation English settlers, and often either Catholics or church-papists. The key to the Old English creed seems to have been the belief that it was possible to be a gentleman first, and a Catholic second. As owners of a third of the profitable land in Ireland, they felt increasingly threatened by the policy of plantation. The Earl of Ormond, threatened by one such scheme, commented that he was the first Englishman to be treated as if he were Irish.[24] He was not the last: in 1641, one of the rebels marked the great watershed in Irish history by describing them as the 'new Irish'.[25]

It is no wonder that the complexity of these arrangements enmeshed Charles in many things for which the simplicity of his original plans had left no room. It is also important that though there was a Privy Council for each kingdom, there was no institutional equivalent of the Spanish Council of State, which could advise on issues affecting all three. Laud and Wentworth, or on occasion Hamilton and Lennox, might give British

[23] This was the conventional view, but in *Calvin's Case* it had been argued that the Parliament of England could bind Ireland by express words: Coke, *Seventh Report,* 17. For the conventional view, stated by the Earl of Leicester, probably when about to take up appointment as Lord Deputy, see K.A.O. De L'Isle and Dudley MSS, Z 47. I am grateful to Blair Worden for drawing my attention to this uncalendared portion of the collection and to Viscount De L'Isle and Dudley for permission to quote from his family papers.

[24] *New Irish History,* edited by T.W. Moody, F.X. Martin and F.T. Byrne (Oxford, 1976), III, 242.

[25] Aidan Clarke, 'Ireland and the "General Crisis" ', *Past and Present* 1970, p. 81.

counsel, but only when the King asked for it. On most British issues, Charles, like the classic medieval tyrant, was without counsellors.

Charles's attempt at British uniformity was begun in Ireland, where some sharp political infighting between Lord Deputy Wentworth and Archbishop Ussher appears to have ended in a draw.[26] He was nearly 'surprised' by an attempt by Ussher's friends to secure confirmation of the Calvinist Irish Articles of 1615, but managed to secure Irish confirmation for the English 39 Articles. The attempt to set up an Irish High Commission was successful, and the attempt to impose new Irish canons produced a long battle between Ussher and Bishop Bramhall, Laud's chief Irish ally. Taken together with Laud's remark that there was no need to introduce the English liturgy because the Irish had it already, the programme sounds remarkably like the one which was tried out in Scotland from 1635 onwards.

It may have been the need to compromise with Irish resistance which moved Charles and Laud to act with so little consultation in Scotland. They consulted some of the Scottish bishops, who belonged to that faction in Scotland which welcomed moves towards uniformity with England. The use of proclamation, however, bypassed all the normal machinery of consultation. The Scottish canons appeared almost without warning, and though the new Prayer Book was expected, when ministers were commanded to buy it and use it, there were no copies available and none of them had yet seen it. The attempt to produce the Scottish Prayer Book as a *fait accompli,* however, cannot be regarded as a success.

It is fortunately unnecessary to recount the narrative of Scottish resistance to the Prayer Book: for the moment, it is the British implications which concern us. Two stories will perhaps help to illustrate them. Both tell of Covenanter conversations with the King's commissioner the Marquess of Hamilton. In one, the Covenanters explained that the Reformation of England was 'verrie farr inferior to the Reformatione of Scotland'.[27] This was an idea Charles could not allow to get loose in England. It also helps to explain why the Scots, who had had to admit to junior partner status in so much, clung so obstinately to the belief in the superiority of their Reformation, and so helps to explain their policy in England in 1640-41, when the boot was on the other foot. The other story describes how Hamilton told the Covenanters that his instructions allowed him to remove the Scottish canons and Prayer Book, but not to condemn anything in them 'which might reflect against any public order or any thing practiced, or allowed by my Lord of Canterburie and his followers in England or elsewhere'.[28] This story illustrates, both one of Charles's reasons for sticking to his guns, and the likely consequence for England of a Covenanter victory. The Covenanters' response, according to Baillie, was to insist that the doctrines be condemned because so many in their own church held them. Superb organisation and the King's absence enabled the

[26] Knowler, I, 212, 298, 329. I would like to thank Martin Flaherty for these references.
[27] Rothes, p. 144.
[28] Baillie, p. 120.

Covenanters to claim to be much more representative of Scottish opinion than in private they ever believed themselves to be. We can see here the possibility of the anti-Covenanter opening which became crucial to Charles's Scottish policy in 1641 and beyond.

Charles first planned to invade Scotland with an Irish force under the Earl of Antrim, head of that clan who were Macdonnells in Ireland and Macdonalds in Scotland.[29] In doing so, Charles turned Argyll and his clan into devout Covenanters, since Antrim's chief motive had been to secure possession of lands in dispute between him and the Covenanters. As Baillie reflected, the ways of Providence were indeed strange.[30]

Charles finally decided to play his trump card of English intervention, and, to cut a long story short, lost at the battle of Newburn, on 28 August 1640. This was the day on which the apple was eaten: for some 14 years from Newburn onwards, the kingdoms were involved in each other's affairs with a daily urgency which had not been seen since the days of Edward I and Robert and Edward Bruce. When Hamilton told the Covenanters, shortly before war began, that if Charles turned to English intervention, he doubted if he would ever see peace in this kingdom again,[31] he spoke little more than the truth: he was executed in 1648 for leading a Scottish intervention in England on behalf of Charles I.

There is no sense, in an article of this type, in attempting a blow by blow narrative of the period from Newburn to the Civil War. It seems more sensible to examine the ways in which the affairs of one kingdom impinged on those of others.

The first way was by direct control, exemplified by the Scots in the 12 months after Newburn. They had an occupying army in Northumberland and Durham, while their commissioners negotiated a peace treaty in London. It was the Scots who dictated that Charles should call an English Parliament, since they refused to negotiate with any commissioners who were not appointed by King and Parliament, or to accept any treaty not confirmed by an English Parliament.[32] As Secretary Vane said in reporting this demand to Secretary Windebank, 'by this you may judge of the rest'. It was thus Scottish intervention which created an English Parliament, and which made a crucial contribution, by involving it in the treaty negotiations, towards giving it a share in executive power. It was also the Scots, by deliberately prolonging the treaty for the sake of their English friends, who made the first contribution to turning it into a Long Parliament.

The second way in which the kingdoms influenced each other was by direct copying. The Queries of the Irish Parliament appear to be a copying of the Petition of Right,[33] while their attempt in 1641, to impeach their Lord Chancellor, the Lord Chief Justice, Bishop Bramhall and the

[29] The suggestion of using Antrim appears to have originated with Hamilton. Hamilton MSS, 10,488, Hamilton to Charles, 15 June 1638.
[30] Baillie, pp. 192-94.
[31] Rothes, p. 137.
[32] SP 16/466/36, 467/5; BL Harl Ms 457, ff. 3b, 4a, 6b, 8a.
[33] SP 63/260/7.1; *C.J. Ireland,* I, 174ff.

Laudian Provost of Trinity College, Dublin, was surely an imitation of what the English parliament was busy doing to Strafford. The committee they sent to negotiate with Charles in 1641 was empowered to act as a recess committee if there were a dissolution.[34] This was a Scottish idea, copied by the Irish and only subsequently by the English. The oath of Association of the Irish rebels in 1641, beginning 'I A.B. doe in the presence of Almightie God', is a copy of the English Protestation of May 1641, with a few intriguing alterations. The oath is taken in the presence of all the angels and saints, as well as Almighty God, the qualification 'lawful' is omitted from the things they engage to do in defence of religion, and the word 'Protestant' is at all points replaced by 'Catholic'.[35] Perhaps the Irish Rebellion was the greatest copying of them all. One of its leaders, arrested at the beginning of the rebellion, was asked what he was trying to do, and replied: 'to imitate Scotland, who got a privilege by that course'.[36] In England, the Triennial Act followed, at the Scots' suggestion, a Scottish Act to the same effect,[37] and the proposals of 1641-42 that the Parliament should choose the great officers, were consciously borrowed from the Scottish settlement of September 1641.[38]

It is also possible to regard the Scots' drive to impose Scottish uniformity on England as a copying of what the King had been doing to them. Baillie said that they had 'good hopes to get bishops' ceremonies and all away and that conformitie which the King has been vexing himself and us to obtaine betwixt his dominions, to obtaine it now, and by it a most hearty nation of the kingdomes'.[39] It was also the Scots, first and foremost, who insisted on the death of Strafford, whom they regarded as the one Englishman unwilling to accept the verdict of Newburn as final. As the Scots painstakingly explained, using arguments almost comically like those used by Charles in 1639, they could not guarantee their own domestic security except by imposing profound changes on the domestic politics and religion of England.[40] They found, as Charles had done before them, that such attempts created considerable resentment.[41] It was these efforts by the Scots, and notably their paper of 24 February, which prevented Pym and his allies from reaching a peaceful settlement with the King, since a settlement which did not remove the Scottish army would be no settlement, and not worth reaching.

[34] *C.J. Ireland,* I, 165.
[35] Bodleian Ms Carte 2, f. 137b.
[36] *LJ,* iv, 415.
[37] BL Stow Ms 187, ff. 9b, 41a. SP 16/471/22 shows the Scots pressing for such an Act in England, in order that any future disputes between the kingdoms should be considered in Parliament.
[38] H.B. Wheatley (ed), *Diary of John Evelyn* (1906), IV, 95, 97, 98.
[39] Baillie, 278.
[40] NLS Advocates' MSS 3.4.6, ff. 145-6; David Stevenson, *The Scottish Revolution* (Newton Abbot, 1973), pp. 218-21. The Scots' paper of 24 February is in BL Stow Ms 187, ff. 38-9, and Thomason Tracts 669 f. 3(4). It is worth remark that the Ms version is in Scottish spelling, and the printed version in English spelling.
[41] *LJ,* iv, 216; BL Harl Ms 6424, f. 55a. NLS Advocates' MSS 33.4.6, ff. 130, 133. Edinburgh University Library Ms Dc 4.16, ff. 93a-94a.

The Scots' paper of 24 February 1641 demanding the Presbyterianising of England and the death of Strafford, gave this body of feeling its opportunity for organised expression. The debate on this paper on 27 February, according to D'Ewes, 'raised one of the greatest distempers in the House that ever I saw in it'.[56] This debate marks the appearance of two-party politics in the Commons. The study of this and other debates bearing on the Scots shows that who spoke for and who against the Scots provides a better predictor of allegiance in the Civil War than any other issue, even Root and Branch or the Militia Ordinance. This fact is surely not purely coincidental. Charles was perhaps justified in accusing the Scottish negotiators in London of trying 'to stir up his people of England, and make a division between him and his subjects'.[57] Whether or not they tried, they certainly succeeded.

In the relationship between the three kingdoms, any rapprochement between two of them had a billiard-ball effect on the third, and for most of the first half of 1641, it was Ireland which came out third. The Scottish-Parliamentary alliance aimed, in the ominous phrase of the petition of the 12 peers, at 'the uniting of *both* your realms against the common enemies of the reformed religion'.[58] Ireland was a likely victim of any such unity. We are fortunate to have an early Irish reaction to this anti-popish drive. John Barry, an Irish Officer in the King's English army, reported that the Parliament had taken orders to cashier all popish officers, 'and among the rest myself. They call out bitterly against us, and begin to banish us out of town, and remove us from court; what will become of us, I know not, but we are in an ill taking at present.' Barry resented the imputation of disloyalty: 'Sir, I was never factious in religion, nor shall ever seeke the ruine of any because he is not of my opinion'.[59] For him and many like him, the imputation was to become a self-fulfilling prophecy.

Barry was one of those who saw the increasing co-operation between the English Parliament and the Scots an opportunity for increasing co-operation between the Old English and the king. In the spring of 1641, Charles was negotiating with an Irish Parliamentary Committee at the same time as he was negotiating with the Scots, and their demands were to an extent alternatives. The main thing the Irish committee wanted was confirmation of the Graces, a set of royal concessions of the 1620s of which the key one was itself copied from England. It would have applied to Ireland the English Concealment Act of 1624, making 60 years' possession of an estate a valid title to it. In England, this merely stopped an unscrupulous way of raising money. In Ireland, it would have had the much

[56] *D'Ewes* edited by Notestein, p. 418; *Two Diaries of the Long Parliament,* pp. 12-13.

[57] NLS Advocates' MSS 33.4.6, f. 129a. See also NLS Wodrow Ms Quarto 25, f. 117b, describing how the Scottish preachers in London were ordinarily invited to preach publicly to great auditories, and Surrey RO (Guildford) Bray MSS 52/2/19(8), Nicholas to Charles, 8 August 1641, reminding Charles 'what invoncenience pmitting the Scots comrs. to be in towne and treate hath beene to yet mats. affaires, and what a disturbance their daily presence did give to ye government'. I am grateful to Dr J.S.A. Adamson for drawing my attention to this important group of Nicholas Papers.

[58] SP 16/465/16 [my italics].

[59] HMC *Egmont,* I, 122.

more far-reaching effect of putting a stop to the policy of plantation. For this reason, it caused great alarm to the government in Dublin. When Charles confirmed the Graces, on 3 April 1641, he forged an alliance with the old English, but he also forged another, between the Lords Justices in Dublin and the English Parliament.

During 1641, many Irishmen came to realise that the greatest threat to their liberties came, not from the English king, but from the English Parliament. When the Parliament had set out to impeach Strafford for his conduct as Lord Deputy of Ireland without having any jurisdiction in Ireland they set out on a slippery slope. At first, they were very cautious, dealing with Irish petitioners by recommending, requesting and referring, but such caution could not last.[60] They were finally pushed over the edge by a series of cases of which the most important was that of Henry Stewart, the Don Pacifico of the British Civil Wars. Henry Stewart was an Ulster Scot, imprisoned by Wentworth for refusing to take an oath renouncing the Scottish Covenant, and the Scottish negotiators were demanding that those who imprisoned him should be punished. As a result, the English House of Lords summoned the whole of the Irish Privy Council to appear before them as delinquents. This was too much, and the Irish Privy Council and Parliament immediately protested.[61]

In denying that Ireland was subject to the English Parliament, the Irish were up against the Scots, who repeatedly assumed that it was. They also had to eat a number of their own words, dating from the anti-Strafford phase in which the Irish Parliament had been busy claiming the liberties of Englishmen, and trying to make common cause with the English Parliament. Like many later Whigs, they hoped that the English Parliament gave more weight to its rhetoric about law and liberty than to its rhetoric about anti-popery, and they realised their mistake too late. If they faced subjection to an English Parliament in which they were not represented, they would be reduced to the unambiguous status of a colony, and with a Parliament as anti-popish as the English, the prospect was not inviting. In December 1641, when the Old English decided to throw in their lot with the Irish rebels, they accused the Lords Justices of having conspired 'to make this realm totally subordinate to the jurisdiction of the Parliament of England'. They said it was their aim 'to preserve the freedom of this kingdom without dependency of the Parliament or State of England'.[62] Thus, the Irish Rebellion was a reaction to changes in the power structure in England, brought about by Scottish intervention, which in turn had been provoked by attempts to impose English religion on the Scots, lest the Scots might set an evil example to English dissidents. There can be no better illustration of the fact that this subject does indeed have an Athanasian complexity.

* * *

[60] *D'Ewes* edited by Notestein, pp. 3, 100-2, 224; SP 63/258/51. 53, 68.
[61] House of Lords Main Papers, 9, 17, 30 July 1641. For an attempt by the Irish bishops to involve the English Parliament in Irish affairs, see SP 63/274/44.
[62] J.T. Gilbert, *History of the Irish Confederation* (Dublin, 1882), I, 251, 289.

This article has been intended to test two different, but not incompatible hypotheses. One is the hypothesis that when there are rebellions in three highly disparate kingdoms, one possible cause is the King who provides the most conspicuous common factor between them. This case appears to contain much truth. It is not given to historians to make controlled experiments, but the study of Charles I in a Scottish, an English and an Irish context is perhaps less remote from a controlled experiment than most things we are able to do. Variables, of course, are not eliminated, and it is particularly important that the Charles who handled the English crisis had already handled and suffered from the Scottish. Yet the man who appears in all three stories is perhaps more totally the same than, in such different situations, he should have been. The same convictions, the same imaginative blind spots, and the same defects in political methods, show up in all three situations. One constant characteristic is Charles's refusal to accept that he was bound by the limits of political possibility. His determination, during 1638, to force the Scots to give up the Covenant appears to have been immune to any advice that this was something he simply could not do. As Traquair reported to Hamilton in July 1638:

> I find nothinge sticke with his majestie so much as the covenant, he have drunk in [sic] this opinion, that monarchie and it can not stand together; and knowing the impossibilitie of haveinge it renderit upp, you may easily conjecture what will ensue if the king continue but a few days more of that mynd...If I was wearied in Scotland, my heart is broke heir, since I can see no possibilitie to satisfie our masters honor, so deeply doth he conseave himself interessed, as the country from ruine.

When Hamilton, in September 1638, advised Charles how to gain a party for the Glasgow Assembly, 'his answer was, that the remedy was worse than the disease'.[63] This is surely the same man who believed, in January 1641, that he could enjoy the services of Pym as Chancellor of the Exchequer together with those of Juxon as Archbishop of York.[64] The King emerges, not only as a man who had difficulty in recognising the limits of the possible, but also as one who, when he did recognise them, was liable to conclude that peace could have too high a price. This is the same King who told Hamilton, in December 1642, that, win or lose, he would make no more concessions in the English Civil War, and would rather live a glorious king, or die a patient martyr.[65] He is perhaps an example of E.M. Forster's Law, that the tragedy of life is that one gets what one wants.

He also emerges in the Scottish and English stories as a man with a real allergy to Puritanism in all its forms. In many places, this prevented him from facing facts. His repeated promises to the Scots that there would be no 'innovation' in religion seem to have been made in all sincerity, and in blissful ignorance that they appeared to many of his honest subjects to

[63] Hamilton MSS 718, 719.
[64] HMC *De L'Isle and Dudley*, VI, 366; KAO U 1475 C 114/7.
[65] Hamilton MSS 167.

contradict the policies he was then pursuing.[66] This is the same king who emerges from the tangled story of the English Arminians and the 39 Articles. This allergy also seems to be the main explanation for his obstinate, and apparently sincere, insistence that the Scottish troubles were not about religion at all, since he was unable to absorb that many Scots sincerely believed him guilty of innovation.[67] This blindness to the force of Puritanical conviction does not seem to have made it easy for him to handle a force whose very existence he was incapable of admitting.

Charles also emerges as a King subject to the political failing of saying 'never', and then retreating, thereby encouraging his subjects to believe that they could always press him harder, and he would retreat further. From the Petition of Right to the execution of Strafford, this habit handicapped Charles of England, and it is equally apparent in his handling of the Scottish service book. It was the Earl of Nithsdale, not the most conciliatory of his Scottish advisers, who reproved him for this habit: 'it would have been better to refuse them at the first, and better to grant what they ask with a seasoning to resent, then still to give ground'. As Hamilton explained after the Pacification of Berwick, this habit made life very difficult for Charles's servants. 'Those particulars which I have so often sworne and said your matie would never condiscend to, will now be granted, therefore they will give no credit to what I shall say ther after, but will still hope and believe, that all ther desires will be given way to.'[68]

It was a political style which tended to advertise the fact that concessions were made unwillingly and under duress. In instructing Traquair for the 1639 Scottish Parliament, he commented on the Act for abolishing episcopacy/: 'we consent to this act only for the peace of the land, and in our own judgment hold it neither convenient nor fitting'. He then told Traquair to publish this opinion. At the same time, he reassured the Archbishop of St Andrews that 'you may rest secure, that tho perhaps we doe [erased] may [inserted] give way for the present, to that which will be prejudiciall both to the church and our government, yett we shall not leave thinking in time how to remedy both'. In September 1640, Loudoun commented that the King's actions 'beget a suspition that his matie doth not yet intend a reall peace'.[69] It is not surprising that Pym and Saye should have come to share this suspicion, and should have formed a desire to institutionalise Charles's concessions so thoroughly that he would be unable to reverse them. There is no reason to suppose Pym and Saye paid as much attention to the history of the Irish Graces as they did to that of the Scottish bishops, but had they done so, the story could only have strengthened a belief that Charles's concessions had to be bound in

[66] *Cal SP Dom 1639,* Vol ccccxviii, no. 50; *RPCS, VIII, 3-4; Rothes, pp. 98-9; Baillie, pp. 25, 43.*
[67] *A Large Declaration* (1640), pp. 1-16.
[68] Hamilton MSS 883, 948.
[69] Hamilton MSS 1031, 1030, 1218.

chains.[70] We are dealing with a king who invited resistance in all of his three kingdoms, and got what he was asking for.

Yet this stress on blame for Charles will not serve to eliminate the other major theme of this article, that the relationship between the three kingdoms itself, and not merely its mishandling, was a major cause of instability in all three of them. That Charles's English regime was in the event brought down through military defeat at the hands of the Scots is a point too obvious to need labouring. What perhaps needs saying is that this is not the intervention of a random factor like a stroke of lightning, but the results of a long-term difficulty in securing religious unity between Charles's three kingdoms. Charles's decision to impose the Scottish liturgy was not taken out of the blue, and 'folly' is not a sufficient explanation for it. It was the result of a long-standing conviction, known to Wentworth and Laud by 1634, that there must be a closer union in religion between Charles's dominions. The underlying thinking emerges in Laud's insistence, in 1633, that English *and Scottish* soldiers and merchants in the Netherlands should be compelled to use the English liturgy, or in his otherwise Utopian objective of sending a bishop to New England.[71]

It is clear that Charles was well aware that his Scottish policy had English implications. To take one example among many, in 1639, he would agree to Traquair, as commissioner, assenting to an Act of the Scottish Parliament declaring episcopacy contrary to the constitutions of the kirk of Scotland, but not to one calling it 'unlawful':

> If I doe acknowledge or consent that episcopacie is unlafull in the kirk of Scotland, though as you may have sett it downe in your consenting to the act, the word unlafull may seem to have only a relation to the constitt. of that kirke, yet the construction there of doth runn so doubtfull, as that it may too probably be inferred, that the same callin is acknowledged by us to be unlafull in any churches of our dominions.[72]

The political realism of a concern for unity in religion between the three kingdoms is perhaps best illustrated by the fact that Charles shared it with the Scottish Covenanters, with Pym and with James. The political danger of the objective is also illustrated by the fact that Charles shared it with all these people, and by the fact that no two of them were pursuing unity in the same religious position. The inherent difficulty of the situation has perhaps been masked by James's success in pursuing union in religion between the kingdoms so slowly, and so much by stealth, that Dr Galloway has even been moved to question whether he had the objective at all.[73] James's pursuit of episcopacy in Scotland was conducted by so many small stages, over such a long period of time, that there was no one moment at

[70] See my article, 'The British Background to the Irish Rebellion', **below, ch. 15, pp. 263-80.**
[71] Laud, *Works,* VI, i, 23; H.R. Trevor-Roper, *Archbishop Laud* (1940), pp. 157-62. See also S.R. Gardiner, *History of England,* viii, 167.
[72] Hamilton MSS 1031.
[73] B. Galloway, *op. cit,* pp. 86-9.

which it was obvious that its opponents should stand and fight. The process of reconciling moderate Presbyterian ministers to episcopacy stage by stage looks remarkably like the policy of separating moderates and extremists described for England by Dr Fincham and Dr Lake.[74]

Taken by itself, or even together with the Five Articles of Perth, James's commitment to Scottish episcopacy need not show that he was working towards unity between the three kingdoms. It looks much more likely that James had the objective when his commitment to Scottish episcopacy is taken beside his commitment to Calvinist doctrine for England and Ireland. From 1603 onwards, many Scots recognised an adherence to Calvinist doctrine as an essential ground for unity between the churches,[75] and James's policy seems to have been to build up a church with Scottish doctrine and English government. The choice of George Abbot to consecrate his Scottish bishops puts his policy in a nutshell.[76]

The difference between James and Charles, then, was not in the objective of unity between the three kingdoms, but in the theological position from which they pursued that objective. Charles pursued it from a position which markedly increased the number of influential Englishmen who preferred the Scottish model to their own. Also, Charles did not pursue unity, as James had done, by shifting each kingdom a little bit towards the others, but by shifting Scotland and Ireland towards that interpretation of the English settlement which, of all others, made it most remote from the Scottish and Irish churches. Charles's Arminian stance may have been barely sustainable as an English one, but it was certainly beyond the bounds of the possible as a British one.

It was by involving the Scots in English politics that Charles created that vital ingredient of a major political crisis, a serious rival power centre to himself. Over and over again, the Scots, by changing the bounds of the possible in England, drew Charles's critics to attempt what they would not otherwise have risked. The petition of the 12 peers, for example, had been discussed between Englishmen and Covenanters for a year before it surfaced.[77] It is not a coincidence that it ultimately did surface when the Scots crossed the Tweed, and was immediately reported to Edinburgh.[78] Indeed, Hamilton had warned Charles, as early as June 1638, of the opportunity a Scottish war would give his English critics:

[74] Kenneth Fincham and Peter Lake, 'The Ecclesiastical Policy of King James I', *Journal of British Studies,* 1985, xxiv, 169-207. W.R. Foster, *The Church Before the Covenants* (Edinburgh and London, 1975), pp. 12, 16, 18, 20, 22, 26, 29.
[75] Galloway, pp. 6, 43; Foster, p. 2.
[76] Foster, p. 29.
[77] Hamilton MSS 985. The story emerged from a rash Covenanter boast to Traquair, and was relayed by Traquair to London.
[78] NLS Advocates' MSS 33.1.1, no. 28. I am grateful to Dr T.I. Rae for drawing my attention to this Ms. The Petition of the 12 Peers was reported together with the City petition, which was prepared jointly with it. For a text of the City Petition, see Yale University Beinecke Library, Osborn Shelves b. 197, f. 9v.

> the conquering totally of this kingdome will be a difficult worke, though ye were sertain of what assistans ingland can give you, but it faires me that they will not be so forwardt in this as they ought, nay that there are some malitious spereites amongst them thatt no souner will your bake be turned, bot they will be redie to dou as we have doun heir, which I will never call by a nother name than rebellioun.[79]

For such 'malitious spirits', for whom Burges and Marshall may serve as fair examples, and for those to whom they preached, Scottish intervention in England could serve 'in working up their hearts to that indispensable pitch of heavenly resolution, sincerely to strike through a religious and invoiable covenant with their God'.[80] It was Scottish intervention which turned the programme of 'further reformation' for which the Long Parliament Fast preachers were spokesmen, into practical politics.

Yet, by the very act of turning 'godly reformation' into practical politics, the Scots also presented Charles with an opportunity to recruit an English party. It is no coincidence that Falkland and Sir Frederick Cornwallis long before they were royalist MPs had been anti-Scottish volunteers in the First Bishops' War,[81] for it was anti-Scottish feeling, and fear of the 'further reformation' the Scots brought with them, which provided the cement between Charles and his new royalist allies of 1641. Falkland probably spoke for them all when he commented on the Scots' Brotherly Assistance that it was an English proverb not to look a given horse in the mouth, and he wished it were a Scottish one too.[82]

In this situation, Charles reacted with more than usual shrewdness. He appreciated that it was the Scots who conferred power on his English opponents, and from the beginning of the Long Parliament onwards, his strategy was designed to divide Pym and his group from their Scottish allies. For the first few months of 1641, Charles's terms for settlement, the preservation of episcopacy and the life of Strafford, were precisely those which would have the effect of separating the English Parliamentarians from their Scottish allies. From March 1641 onwards, he pursued the same objective by another method, and aimed, by Scottish concessions, to remove the Scots from English politics. In the autumn of 1641, when he exacted promises of non-intervention in English affairs from Argyll and Loudoun as part of his Scottish settlement, he appeared to have succeeded.[83]

It was at this point that the Irish Rebellion drove Charles back onto the mercy of his English Parliament. The Irish Rebellion, like the Bishops' Wars, is regularly discussed as if it were a random intervention of an outside factor, like a stroke of lightning. In fact, it was not. It was the very measures taken to draw England and Scotland together which had forced England and Ireland apart.[84] It was demonstrated that one of the most

[79] Hamilton MSS 327.1.
[80] C. Burges, *The First Sermon,* Ep.Ded.
[81] *Cal SP Dom 1639,* Vol ccccxvii, nos. 85, 92.
[82] Bodleian Ms Rawlinson D.1099, f. 22b.
[83] Hamilton MSS 1585, 1586.
[84] See my article, 'The British Background to the Irish Rebellion', below, ch. 15, pp. 263-80.

Athanasian characteristics of the British problem was the way in which avoidance of one error led straight to the perpetration of another. For the second time, it was failure to handle the British problem successfully which led Charles to failure in England. Perhaps the point on which we should really be pondering is that it took five years of continuous British crisis to drive the English body politic to the point of Civil War. This might perhaps suggest that, in spite of all the strains to which it had been subjected, the English social fabric of 1637 was still very tough indeed.[85]

It is part of the Athanasian quality of this subject that Charles's kingdoms provided three independent stories, as well as one combined one, and it is worth asking what were the peculiarities of each kingdom as they emerge from comparison. The order in which the kingdoms resisted Charles was Scotland, Ireland, England, and it seems that this may represent more than a chronological progression. Though the Irish troubles proved after 1649 to be more long-lasting, there are more senses than one in which the Scottish troubles may be regarded as the *primum mobile* of the British. The Scots, from the beginning showed none of that extreme hesitancy at the idea of resistance which characterised the English. Through Knox and Buchanan, they could draw freely on a tradition of resistance theory, which was subject to none of the taboos which inhibited it in England. With their ascending theory of power in a kirk which was 'ane perfect republic'[86] they were better equipped than the English with a rival ideology to that of Charles I. Over and over again the key measures and ideas of the English Parliament, the Triennial Act, the notion of treason against the realm, or the election of the great officers in Parliament, turn out to have been anticipated in Scotland.

By contrast, the peculiarity of England is that, of Charles's three kingdoms, it was the one in which the King gathered the largest party. Since it was the kingdom in which Charles lived and the source of nine-tenths of his revenues, it is not surprising that he found it the easiest kingdom in which to gather support. Moreover, it was for his vision of the Church of England that Charles offended the Scots, and it is not surprising that the Church of England, like the Tory party after it, found more support in England than in the rest of Britain. The gravity of the English Civil War, when it came, was that it resulted from an even division of opinion: in no other kingdom did Charles muster the support of nearly half the kingdom. England experienced trouble, not because it was the most revolutionary of Charles's kingdoms, but because it was the least. Baillie was quite entitled to his observation that 'a gloom of the King's brow would disperse this feeble people, for any thing yet we see, if the terror of God and us afrayed not their enemies, if help from God and us did not continue their courage'.[87]

[85] For a very different route to a similar conclusion, see John Morrill and J.D. Walter, 'Order and Disorder in the English Revolution' in *Order and Disorder in Early Modern England* edited by A. Fletcher and J. Stevenson (Cambridge, 1985), pp. 137-65.
[86] The phrase is from *Reasons for a Generall Assemblie* (Edinburgh?, 1638), STC 22,054 Sig B.1.
[87] Baillie, 283.

14

Why did Charles I call the Long Parliament?

At first sight, it might appear a superfluous exercise to explain why Charles I called the Long Parliament. Like so many other decisions of his, it may perfectly well be explained on grounds of necessity. After the battle of Newburn, on 28 August 1640, Charles faced the combination of a victorious invading army of Scots in front of him, and an empty treasury and public disaffection behind him. The Privy Council in London were advising him that they lacked the power to force any further supplies of men or money.[1] Moreover, since the line of the Tees is not defensible, Charles's forces had no secure line of defence behind which they could re-group. If Charles could not fight without a Parliament, he could not negotiate without a Parliament either, since the invading Scots were insisting that they would not consider any peace treaty unless it were confirmed by an English Parliament.[2] Since Charles had so little choice in the matter, it is perhaps necessary to say why his decision to call a Parliament needs explanation.

The decision to call a Parliament was not a substitute for a policy, but a choice of forum in which to pursue one. To explain events in any Parliament, it is necessary to understand the purposes the Crown called it to serve. Did Charles call the Long Parliament in order to retreat from the Scottish war on the most face-saving terms possible, or in order to gain English support for a renewed attempt to enforce the Scottish Prayer Book? Did he intend the calling of the Parliament as a cosmetic gesture to enable him to continue his English policies, or did he accept the advice of his Privy Council that the top priority was 'the uniting of your Majesty and your subjects together, the want whereof the Lords conceive is the source of all the present troubles'? This memorandum of the Privy Council appears to have begun the scheme for Charles to broaden the basis of his regime by taking some of his critics into his Council.[3] It is important to know whether, when the Parliament met, Charles appreciated that any such scheme would involve significant changes in his policies. Did Charles intend to make a virtue of necessity, and announce an about-turn in policy, or did he mean to hold what the French Ambassador, before the Short Parliament, called a 'Parlement à sa mode', an assembly which would virtuously rubber-stamp what he intended to do anyway?[4]

In the country at large, the decision to call the Long Parliament was one of the most popular decisions Charles ever took. This was in part because of attachment to Parliaments *per se*, a sentiment which had always been strong, and which Ship Money and the Bishops' Wars appeared to have

[1] *Clarendon State Papers* ii 97-8. (Public Record Office) S(tate) P(apers) 16/466/1 and 5 appear to be rough notes for parts of this document. I would like to thank Professor Caroline Hibbard for reading and commenting on an earlier draft of this article.

[2] S.P.16/466/36,467/5,469/62.

[3] *Clarendon State Papers*, *ubi supra*.

[4] P.R.O. 31/3/71, p. 154.

strengthened.[5] Yet the enthusiasm for a Parliament was not merely about the chance to have a meeting: it was also because conventional wisdom associated the calling of Parliaments with specific policies which were more likely to find support in Parliaments than outside them. The petition of the twelve peers is a good example of this association. Among these policies, Dr Hibbard has mentioned alliance with France, hostility to Spain and criticism of the Laudian church as policies pro-Parliamentary Councillors were likely to associate with the calling of a Parliament.[6] By 1640, this list should include abandonment of the Scottish Prayer Book and the end of the Scottish Wars. Before the Short Parliament, George Wyllys, writing to his father in Connecticut, found the prospect of a Parliament 'gives many hopes of better times and a thorough settlement of a peace with the Scotts'.[7] Before the Long Parliament, Rossingham reported to Conway that 'we are all mad with joy here, that his Matie does call his Parliament, and that he puts the Scotch business into the hands of his peers, who, the hope is here, will make peace upon any condicions'.[8] The Parliament was so widely welcomed partly because it was thought to symbolize a decision for peace with Scotland. It is then important, in judging Charles's relations with the Long Parliament, to know whether he understood or shared the symbolism associated with its calling.

The story begins with the English defeat at Newburn, on 28 August 1640. This rapidly led to a decision to summon a Great Council of Peers, which met at York on 24 September 1640. Charles announced his decision to call a Parliament in his opening speech to the Council of Peers. The Parliament was called for 3 November, leaving the statutory minimum of forty days between the issue of the writs and the meeting of the Parliament.

After the defeat at Newburn, the King seems to have remained determined to continue fighting,[9] while a group of Privy Councillors, among whom Secretary Vane is the best documented, became more and more articulate in their determination to get out of the war on the best terms possible. By 20 September, the peace faction on the Council appeared to have prevailed, and Vane reported to Roe that 'for ventringe all of a day, I conceive there is no danger of that'.[10]

During the period before the meeting of the Council of Peers, the Privy Council twice discussed the possible calling of a Parliament. The first time, in the week of Newburn, it discussed whether to call a Parliament or a Council of Peers. The rival arguments were those of Dorset and Cottington. Dorset's view was that since a Parliament would happen anyway, the Council rather than the peers should get the credit for advising the King to call it. Cottington's advice, which prevailed, was to let the peers take the responsibility for advising Charles to call a Parliament.[11] The

[5] Anthony Fletcher, *The Outbreak of the English Civil War* (New York and London, 1981), pp. 1-2; Esther Cope, *The Life of a Public Man: Edward, First Baron Montagu of Boughton* (Philadelphia, 1981), pp. 160-167, and Kenneth Fincham, (*BIHR* forthcoming).

[6] Caroline Hibbard, *Charles I and the Popish Plot* (Chapel Hill, 1983), p. 21.

[7] George Wyllys the younger to George Wyllys the elder, 8 April 1640, *Wyllys Papers*, Connecticut Historical Society, vol. 21, p. 9. The younger Wyllys had returned from Connecticut in order to sell the family land in England.

[8] S.P. 16/468/86. See also P.R.O. 31/3/72, p. 269 for the French ambassador's belief that the calling of the Parliament implied peace with Scotland.

[9] S.P. 16/466/28, 467/28, 467/101.

[10] S.P. 16/467/120.

[11] S.P. 16/466/11 and 12.

second time, on 16 September, the Privy Council explicitly advised a Parliament, apparently on the motion of Arundel and Laud. This advice had reached Charles by 18 September, but Vane still reported that 'I doe not finde in his Matie yett any certaine resolution for the same'.[12]

Six days later, the King had not merely taken his decision, but announced it. Vane, whether by inside information or by a lucky guess, foresaw the decision before it was announced.[13] There is no reason to suppose the decision was known to anyone else before it was made public. Indeed, there is some evidence that it was *not* known to some key people before it was made public. In deciding to call a Parliament in exactly forty days from his announcement, Charles put the Lord Keeper and the Clerk of the Crown under considerable pressure to issue the writs promptly. In his speech to the Council of Peers, Charles, using the past tense, claimed that he had 'already given order to my Lo. Keeper to issue the writs instantly'.[14] Charles's use of the past tense appears to be incorrect. The Lord Keeper's instruction to the Clerk of the Crown to send out the writs instantly, and to remember to date them that day, is written on the bottom of a list of commissioners chosen to negotiate with the Scots. These commissioners were not chosen till the afternoon after the King's speech. With this letter, Vane sent a message from the King asking for the Queen to be told of the decision for a Parliament, so it would appear that she too had no advance knowledge of the decisions.[15]

Charles, as he said, took the decision to call the Long Parliament 'of my selfe'. In this, it was like many of Charles's major decisions: he had taken advice, but the final decision was a solitary one, and the thoughts which led to it were not shared with anyone. It is, then, necessary to explain Charles's decision, not in terms of the advice he received, but in terms of his own words and actions. The speech in which he announced the decision shows that, at this date, he had not seen any connection between calling a Parliament and making peace. It is a thoroughly belligerent speech. He told the peers they had been called because of sudden invasion, and 'this being our condicion at this tyme, and an army of rebells lodged within this kingdome, I thought it most fitt to conforme myselfe to the practise of my predecessors in like cases, that with your advice and assistance wee might iointly proceede to the chastisement of these insolencies, and securing of my good subjects'. At the time Charles announced the decision to call a Parliament, he saw it in conjunction with a desire to continue the Scottish war.

That afternoon's debate in the Council of Peers might have done something to show Charles that he was following two incompatible policies. It was begun by a motion by Bristol to enter into treaty with the rebels. According to Vane, 'most lords' believed they had it in their power to make peace, and this should probably be interpreted as meaning that they wished to do so. The peers' choice of commissioners to negotiate with the Scots strengthened the impression that they were opposed to the war. About half the commissioners chosen were signatories of the petition of the twelve peers, and none of them was a known supporter of the war.

[12] S.P. 16/467/75 and 101.
[13] S.P. 16/467/135.
[14] For this and subsequent quotations from the King's speech at York, see S.P. 16/468/1.
[15] S.P. 16/468/16 and 22.

Vane, emboldened by the pacific sentiment around him, plucked up courage to tell Windebank that 'I told you so', and said that the Councillors going south at the end of the Council would tell Windebank 'many good passages' in which 'the Earl of Bristol hath spoken much and freely'.[16]

This impression of 'a free and frank exchange of views' is strengthened by the official communiqué of the Council of Peers. This document, signed by 57 peers for the benefit of potential lenders in the City of London, is drawn up in careful antiphonal phrases which seem designed to give full weight to both sides in a debate. The antiphonal phrases perhaps represent a debate inside the committee responsible for drafting the letter, which consisted of Strafford, Finch, Manchester, Bristol, Hertford, Bedford, North, Goring, Littleton, Bankes and Vane. The peers said they were treating for:

> such an accommodation as may tend to the honner of his matie and ye perfect union of both kingdomes; wherein as wee rest most assure that his Matie will bee no way wanting in his grace and goodnesse to listen to the just and reasonable demands of his subjects of Scotland; so, if they shall insist upon terms dishonnerable for his Matie and ye English nation to condiscend unto, wee should all hold our selves obliged in honner and duty to preserve and defend this kingdome from all invasions and spoyles by any kind of enemy whatsoever.[17]

These exchanges with the peers might have marked the point at which Charles was persuaded to abandon the Scottish war, and the antiphonal phrases might have been intended to save the royal face. Yet, though the communiqué alone might have borne such an interpretation, it will not bear it when seen in the context in which Charles placed it. For Charles, it seems that 'terms dishonnerable' meant anything which conceded more than the Pacification of Berwick, in which Charles had refused to abandon either the Scottish Prayer Book or Scottish episcopacy.[18] If these were Charles's objectives, then, whether Charles knew it or not, they were ones which could not be achieved without war.

The impression that Charles gave this communiqué a hard line interpretation is strengthened by the words in which Windebank, who had not been at York, but was in close contact with the King, reported it to Hopton in Madrid. Windebank's version was this:

> if they [the Scots] will accept of such conditions for theire return into Scotland as shalbe thought fitt, they will have an offer of such made unto them: but if they shall refuse such reasonable and fayre conditions, they are to be pursued by

[16] S.P. 16/468/23, 39, 83. The Venetian Ambassador claimed that *all* of these 16 commissioners had declared themselves in favour of the Scots, and were 'equally zealous' for the calling of a Parliament. The assertion is not now verifiable, but it is probably only a slight exaggeration. *CSPV 1640-2* p. 86, 2/12 October 1640.

[17] West Devon Record Office, Drake of Colyton MSS 1700/M CP 17: Alnwick MSS vol. 15, British Library Microfilm no. 286, f. 98 r-v. I am grateful to His Grace the Duke of Northumberland for permission to use these MSS. The word 'communiqué' may sound anachronistic, but I can think of no other accurate description of the type of document involved. Hardwicke State Papers, London 1778, ii 213. All the other documents in this section of the Hardwicke collection are from genuine originals in State Papers. It appears probable that this is a perhaps imperfect transcript of Sir John Borough's original notes, and that the original has disappeared from State Papers between 1778 and the making of the *Calendar*.

[18] S.R. Gardiner, *History of England* (1893), ix 209: David Stevenson, *The Scottish Revolution* (Newton Abbot, 1973), p. 211. *Hardwicke* S.P. ii 220-223.

> force as traitors....If either this money be leavied, or the nobility will continue firme to his Maty for the repulsion of the Scotts, there is no doubt but this black storme wilbe dispersed[19]

The most interesting word in this report is the verb 'continue'. The record of what happened at York has never looked to anyone else as if the peers were 'firme to his Maty for the repulsion of the Scotts'. If Charles had got this impression, he must have treated attempts to preserve the minimum appearance of courtesy as expressions of support for a possible resumption of the war. If so, he was desperately deluded. It is also hard to remember, reading Windebank's confident phrases, that he was making plans for a *defeated* army.

It appears, then, that Charles came south to meet his Parliament still believing that he could impose on the Scots terms resembling those which had originally provoked the war, and that he would enjoy public support for resuming the war if the Scots did not meekly agree to such terms and make themselves scarce. Maybe, as Clarendon suggests, he had become convinced that a Parliament would be more sensible of his honour than the commissioners who were negotiating at Ripon. As Charles put it in the Council of Peers on 6 October, he hoped it would be 'a shock of Parliament to give invaders or rebels money'. At moments during this day's debate, Charles seems to have been trying to get the Council of Peers to support resuming the war rather than accept the Scots' financial demands in the Treaty of Ripon. He asked 'whether better to give rebels money or to stop them?' and 'whether to give them any thing, or remove them by force'.[20] As Clarendon also suggested, Strafford was still prepared to think of resuming the war.[21] Strafford contained his anti-Scottish feelings until the Scots' financial demands were made known, and then began to argue, with the accuracy of a self-fulfilling prophecy, that 'to grant them any dishonourable terms, he will first die'. On 17 October he quarrelled sharply with Lord Keeper Finch, who had called it a 'hopeful treaty'. Under extreme pressure from Bristol, he reluctantly conceded what the King would not concede, that he 'would not answer for the success' of a battle. He did, however, offer to bring over the Irish army at two days' notice, if he were given shipping. It is in these last debates at the Council of Peers that Strafford, as he in part foresaw, ensured that he would be cast as a scapegoat for the Scottish war. For whatever reason, Charles seems to have been quite unable to imagine that a Parliament, faced with a rebellious and invading army, could have any reaction but a desire to get it out again. It is possible to understand Charles's bewilderment, since English willingness to back a Scottish invading army against their own king is a somewhat startling phenomenon. Yet, bewildered, and even outraged,

[19] Bodleian Library, MSS Clarendon, vol. 19, no. 1437, 1 October 1640. In citing Clarendon MSS, I have used the piece numbers from the Ogle and Bliss Catalogue, rather than folio numbers. The money to which Windebank refers was to be borrowed by the peers from the City of London to keep the King's army together until negotiations were completed. It was not intended to finance a resumption of war. A week earlier, on 24 September, Windebank had told Hopton that the rebels must be chased out, and the only way to do *this* was judged to be the speedy calling of a Parliament. *Ibid* no. 1430.

[20] *Hardwicke S.P.* ii 241-6.

[21] Edward, Earl of Clarendon, *History of the Rebellion* (Oxford, 1732), I 159. Hardwicke S.P. ii 246-7 (6 October), 264, 266 (12 October), 279, 280 (17 October), 284, 287, 288 (18 October). For the King answering Bristol's questions by maintaining that the army was strong enough to fight, see *ibid.* 230 (28 September).

though Charles may have been entitled to be, after the debates at York, his belief that he could gain Parliamentary support for resuming the war cannot be classified in terms less harsh than a flight from reality.

When the Parliament met, on 3 November, Charles began by telling them that if what he had said about the Scots to the Short Parliament had been believed, none of this trouble would have happened, 'but it is no wonder that men are soe slow to believe that soe great sedition should be raysed upon so little ground'. The belief that the Scots had rebelled on a 'little ground' is a somewhat startling one. For agenda, Charles said he would not mention the 'support' he was justly entitled to expect, since there were at that time 'twoe points merely considerable. First the chasing out of the rebells, and the other is the satisfying your just grievances'.[22]

This speech seems to have caused some surprise, since two days later, Charles came back to 'explain myselfe'.[23] He repeated that the Scots were rebels, but said that since he was in treaty with them, they were his good subjects too. He said he hoped the treaty would have been concluded by this time, but, after his attempts to give a soothing impression, concluded with the words: 'I doubt not but by your assistance I shall make them know their dutyes or by your assistance make them returne whether they will or noe'. Between the two speeches, Charles had made a tactical retreat. In the first speech, he proposed war. In the second, he offered the Scots the chance to avoid war by withdrawing and conceding most of the points in dispute, with the threat of war to follow if they did not do so. It is a retreat which probably seemed less significant to others than it did to Charles.

It seems clear, then, that Charles called the Long Parliament in the hope of getting Parliamentary support to resume the war against the Scots. In this, he had made a grievous misjudgement of the public mood. In taking his decision, he was following his own counsel. He had, in the main, concealed his intention from his Councillors, and seems to have regarded his lonely decision to call a Parliament as an appeal, over his Councillors' heads, to a wider public from which he had expected a greater concern for his honour. Moreover, he expected, in a way reminiscent of 1628, that the Parliament would tackle the Scots *first*, before dealing with the domestic situation. What Charles meant by *just* grievances there is no source to tell us, but his use of the phrase in 1626 and 1628 suggests that he placed considerable limiting force on the adjective. The Privy Council, on hearing of the decision to call a Parliament, had assumed it was to be followed by an announcement of the abolition of Ship Money,[24] but when the Parliament met, no such plan was in evidence. There was counsel available to Charles to tell him that he could not expect a Parliament to take action against the Scots before they had dealt with their own frustrations. On 22 October Northumberland wrote to his brother-in-law Leicester:

[22] Neither of Charles's opening speeches is noted in the *Journals*: see n. 33 below. The speech of 3 November survives in House of Lords Main Papers, 3 November 1640, S.P. 16/471/13 and Bodleian Library MS Clarendon vol. 19, no. 1446. There are verbal variations of no great apparent significance between these texts. I have used the House of Lords text on grounds of provenance.

[23] House of Lords Main Papers, 5 November 1640.

[24] S.P. 16/468/17, undated Privy Council notes in the hand of Edward Nicholas. These must be dated between 24 September and 3 November 1640, and the editors of the *Calendar* are probably right in assigning them to the earlier part of this range.

untill we have setled those points that were in agitation the last Parlament, wch was matters of religion, proprietie of goods, and libertie of person, and peradventure some others, we shall hardly bring the Parlament to any resolution that may free us from this army of rebells.[25]

This, as the event showed, was a more accurate assessment of the situation than Charles's own, but it represented a line of policy which, every time he had the choice, he rejected.[26]

The House of Commons almost totally ignored the agenda Charles had proposed for them. There was just one moment when they paid attention to the type of arguments Charles wanted them to discuss. This was on the morning of 10 November when Sir William Widdrington, knight of the shire for Northumberland, delivered a petition about the distress of the occupied county of Northumberland. This, if anything, should have been the cue for the sort of patriotic anti-Scottish reaction Charles expected. In the course of his speech, Widdrington, like Charles, called the Scots 'invading rebels'. Immediately, Holles and Glyn moved that he should either explain himself or be punished. Widdrington, somewhat ambiguously, said he 'called them no more rebells seing his Majestie called them otherwise', and the matter was allowed to drop with a note that his words were 'ordered to be entred in the Journal as language disliked by the House'.[27]

The Widdrington case raises the question of the exceptional silence of the anti-Scots in the second half of 1640. Charles was right that there was still a considerable body of anti-Scottish sentiment in England, and it can still be found in private letters. Young Richard Dyott, for example, regarded the twelve peers as, in effect, in collusion with the enemy.[28] Hyde's correspondents Archdeacon Marler and Thomas Triplett (admittedly both clergy) continued to express anti-Scottish sentiments.[29] Why did these not surface in public until very much later in the Long Parliament? It is possible that the fact of Widdrington deterred others who might have wished to speak to the same effect. Free speech in the Long Parliament, as Gervase Holles, Digby, Palmer and Dering were all to discover, was somewhat selective.

However, it is more important that from the battle of Newburn onwards, there were two different lines of criticism of the Scottish war. These lines started from ideologically different positions, but led to practically similar conclusions. For Denzil Holles and Glyn, criticism of the war was based on the fundamentalist assumption that the Scots were right. There is no reason to suppose that the whole country had suddenly been converted to this very Calvinist view. Its strength can only be assessed on later evidence, but on that, it looks as if it appealed to about half the House of Commons. The other line of criticism, with which Vane, Arundel, Northumberland and Bristol should be associated, involved no objection of principle to the

[25] Kent Archive Office, U 1475/C.44. I am grateful to Viscount De L'Isle and Dudley, VC.,KG., for permission to quote from these papers.

[26] Caroline Hibbard, *op. cit.* p. 227.

[27] *The Journal of Sir Symonds D'Ewes*, vol. I, Ed. W. Notestein (New Haven, 1923), pp. 20, 531. *Commons' Journals* II 25. See also Sir John Holland's speech of 9 November which appears to follow the York communiqué, D'Ewes, *op.cit.* p. 16.

[28] Staffs. R.O. Dyott MSS, D 661/11/1/5. (7 September 1640).

[29] Bodleian Library MSS Clarendon, vol. 20, nos. 1506, 1514, 1528. See Triplett's suggestion (no. 1514) that Alderman Abell's fine should go towards paying the Scots, 'and so lett Abell pay Caine'. (The Scots were requesting a 'Brotherly Assistance'.)

Scottish war. To these critics, the war was wrong because it had failed.[30] It had proved, as the Privy Council pointed out on 3 September, unduly divisive in English politics. Moreover, because it had ended in defeat, it had left the King in a very dangerous situation from which he could only extricate himself by cutting his losses and unambiguously making peace. The key spokesman for this case was Bristol. As he put it in the Council of Peers on 26 September 'if his Majesty were in case, it were best to bring them on their knees. But now, considering their strength, Newcastle and the two provinces taken, we must now speak of the business, as to men that have gotten these advantages'. On 12 January 1641, Bristol outlined the case for the treaty to the Lords. He said many might think it a dishonour to relieve an invading army, but it was not so 'as the case now standeth'. He said the nation 'could hardlie be brought to this condicon, were it not for want of unitie and discord amongst ourselves'. He regarded the restoration of unity as an essential preliminary to the recovery of the nation's honour.[31] People of this stamp were never pro-Scottish, but the time when they rallied to an anti-Scottish line was in the spring of 1641, when it became apparent that the Scots were endeavouring to interfere in an *English* settlement.[32] It was this line of criticism, that the policy needed to be abandoned *because* it had failed, which moved most of those on whom Charles might otherwise have relied for ideological support. Charles had no excuse for being unaware of this line, since it was widely held within his own Privy Council.

It was Charles's failure to understand that most of his potential friends had been convinced by this case that left him so startingly isolated in November 1640. This isolation had profound political consequences in his relations with the Parliament. When the Long Parliament met, they, and many of the Privy Council too, were looking for symbols of Charles's willingness to abandon the policies with which Laud and Ship Money were associated, since the conventional wisdom of November 1640 was that, right or wrong, these policies had ceased to be viable. The longer such a change of policy was put off, the bigger the symbols needed to convince members that it was being undertaken would grow. The later Charles's concessions came, the bigger they would need to be.

It is a crucial misfortune for all concerned that it was not until early December that Charles was convinced it was necessary for him to make peace with his Scottish subjects and make concessions to his English ones. In the first month of the Parliament, when such a policy would have been easiest to follow, there was a deafening silence from the King. This silence did much to establish the Parliament as a sort of alternative government, paying the armies and negotiating with the Scots while they waited for the King to wake up to the true situation. This royal inability to perceive the true situation did much to begin the Privy Council's and the Long Parliament's habit of carrying on government as if the King were incapacitated. When someone wanted to look at his speech of 5 November,

[30] For Northumberland's views see K.A.O. U 1475 C 85/3 (7 November 1639) and C 44 (22 October 1640) on the Scots, and *ibid.* C 2/42 (7 May 1640) and C85/17 (18 June 1640) on the impracticality of the war.

[31] *Hardwicke S.P.* ii 225: Bodleian Library MS Dep. C.165 (Nalson Ms 13), 12 January 1640/1. See also *H.M.C. 10th Rep.* VI, p. 137.

[32] For an early attempt to rally anti-Scottish sentiment, led by Hyde, Capel, Strangeways and Hopton, see the debate of 27 February 1641. D'Ewes, *op. cit.* pp. 417-8.

threatening war against the Scots, it is no surprise to find that Secretary Vane, as a good servant, claimed to have 'lost' it.[33] In the growth of the tendency to push the King into a back seat, and in the ultimate failure to reach a settlement between him and the Long Parliament, this month's delay before Charles could believe the evidence of his own ears may have a greater importance than it has ever been given.

[33] *H.M.C. De L'Isle and Dudley*, VI 370-1. Vane had lost the clerk's original, and it was claimed that 'no other copie can be had'.

15

The British Background to the Irish Rebellion of 1641

'By the blessing of Almighty God, these troublesome storms and tempests are ending in a peaceable calme, which doubtlesse cannot but produce a happy union, soe much now desired by both nations'.[1] The author of this remarkable piece of optimism was Secretary Vane, writing to Roe on 22 August 1641, and it may help to spotlight the British significance of the Irish rebellion. Since our stock-in-trade as historians is what happened, it is only in our lighter moments that we can deal in might-have-beens. What we are entitled to do, though, is to point out what did happen, even if it lasted only a few weeks. Among such things, the brief period of euphoria among Charles I's advisers between 17 August and 29 October 1641, is a conspicuous example, for as far as anyone could see at the time it was soundly based.

Charles, in August 1640, had come into a crisis which was caused by the invasion of the Scots, and when he finally induced the Scots to withdraw he appeared, by having ridden out the cause of the crisis, to have succeeded in riding out the crisis itself. He still had a parliament at Westminster, and was bound not to dissolve or prorogue it without its own consent. However, the members had been there quite long enough for most of them. When Charles left for Scotland, in August 1641, he left behind, at the request of the house of lords, the general pardon whose passage should have marked the end of the session.[2] His latest reports from Westminster told him that a full settlement of tonnage and poundage was ready, so he could expect an adequate revenue according to a new book of rates. With a significant plague epidemic gathering strength in London, the Commons were unlikely to show great determination to resist a suggested prorogation.[3] Nicholas, on 12 October, told the king that Mr. Pym and others, 'wished rather that they should sit here at Westminster and dye here together, but I believe Mr. Pym will find few (besides those of his juncto) of that opinion'.[4] As Nicholas constantly reminded Charles, nothing but his speedy return from Edinburgh was needed to bring his English troubles to an end. It was the outbreak of the Irish rebellion which brought

[1] Public Record Office, SP 16/483/81, Vane to Roe, 22 Aug. 1641. See also SP 63/260/16, 16/483/94 and Surrey Record Office (Guildford), Bray MS. 52/3/9(2). I am very grateful to Dr. John Adamson for this last reference, and for commenting on a draft of this article.

[2] House of Lords Main Papers, Parchment Box 178: *Lords Journals*, iv. 345–6, 365; *Commons Journals*, ii. 183; British Library, Harley MS. 163 fo. 730; *Nicholas Papers*, ed. G. F. Warner (Camden new ser., xl, l, lvii, 3rd ser., xxxi, 1886–97), i. 6–7; but also Brit. Libr., Sloane MS. 3317 fo. 33.

[3] Scottish Record Office, Hamilton MSS. G.D. 406/1/1397 and 1411; P. Slack, *The Impact of Plague in Tudor and Stuart England* (1985), pp. 146, 193 and other refs. The plague of 1641 was not a major epidemic, but it was among the most serious of the minor ones.

[4] Surrey R.O., Bray MS. 85/5/2(4), Nicholas to the king, 12 Oct. 1641. I am grateful to Dr. Adamson for this reference.

this brief period of euphoria to an abrupt end, and put the British crisis back on the boil.

There has hitherto been a tendency (in which this author has been an offender himself) to treat the Irish rebellion as a sort of *diabolus ex machina*, an irrelevant interruption to a political process which was merely English, or at most Anglo-Scottish. The object of this article is to ask whether that assumption was correct: to ask whether there is in fact a British dimension to the Irish rebellion. Was it, in fact, not an irrelevance at all, but a reaction to events many of which were taking place in London and Edinburgh? It is only if the answer to this question is 'yes' that the conciliar euphoria of August to October 1641 can genuinely be shown to have been based on an illusion.

This article is designed to investigate the events of a period slightly shorter than a year, from the passage of the remonstrance of the Irish house of commons on 7 November 1640, to the outbreak of the rebellion on 22 and 23 October 1641. To what extent should the events of that year be seen as part of a general British crisis? Before discussing them, it is necessary to explain briefly the workings of Irish society and government. Irish society was conventionally divided into three groups. The first, the New English, were Protestant settlers whose interest in Ireland dated from after the Reformation. They tended to be the dominant influence in the government in Dublin, and to be dedicated to the task, as they put it, of 'civilizing' the Irish. This process involved getting the Irish to adopt English religion, language, law, dress and other customs. It was only in periods of real crisis, such as the one after the outbreak of the rebellion, that leading New English figures such as Cork would utter the creed that 'the only good Irishman is a dead Irishman', but they did think the Irish were better dead than adherents of the Scarlet Woman.[5] Protestant ascendancy and personal profit were the two non-negotiable items in the New English creed. The second major group was that of the Old English, or, as Roger Moore preferred to call them, the 'new Irish'.[6] The Old English were English by descent, but had normally been settled in Ireland since before the Reformation. To say the Old English were Catholic would be an exaggeration, since some of them, of whom the earl of Ormond was the most conspicuous, were both Protestants and members of the Irish council. The religious position of the Old English is perhaps best expressed by saying it raises all the same ambivalences as the religions of the House of Howard. Some were downright Catholic, some were downright Protestant, many were church-papist, and some were uncertain, neutral or doubtful. In 1640, the Old English owned a third of the land in Ireland, and as Catholics and men of property, they were liable to be pulled two ways by any threatened polarization of Irish society. It was perhaps the central item of the Old English creed that it was possible to be a gentleman first, and a Catholic second, and it was only so long as they could hold to that belief that the position of the Old English remained tenable. In particular, if plantation schemes threatened Old

[5] Brit. Libr., Egerton MS. 80 fos. 31–4, Cork to Warwick, 25 Feb. 1642. For Cork's rather more relaxed attitudes to the Irish before the rebellion, see N. Canny, *The Upstart Earl: . . . Richard Boyle, 1st earl of Cork, 1566–1643* (Cambridge, 1982), pp. 29, 35, 126, 127 and *passim*.

[6] J. Nalson, *An Impartial Collection of the Great Affairs of State* (2 vols., 1682–3), ii. 543–4.

English security of tenure, their desire to see themselves as members of the Irish establishment would become impossible. Ormond, when threatened with losing some of his land to a plantation scheme, protested that he was the first Englishman to be treated as if he were Irish:[7] he was not the last. The third group, the 'mere Irish', or 'natives', are by far the most inaccessible to historians. It is tempting to follow Roger Moore's belief that they were always ready for rebellion at a moment's notice,[8] but the destruction of the rebel archives at Kilkenny has made this belief almost entirely unverifiable.

In Irish government, the ultimate authority was the king, whose authority was largely delegated to a lord lieutenant or lord deputy in Dublin. At the beginning of our period, Strafford was lord lieutenant, and since he was in the Tower, Christopher Wandesford was acting as his deputy. On Wandesford's death in December 1640, executive power in Dublin devolved on two lords justices, Sir William Parsons and Sir John Borlase, both New English and dedicated believers in Protestant ascendancy. Since Leicester, who succeeded Strafford as lord lieutenant, never set foot in Ireland, Lords Justices Parsons and Borlase remained in control of the Irish executive for the whole of the period with which we are concerned. To advise them, they had an Irish privy council based in Dublin. Both the lords justices and the council reported to the English Secretary of State and to the English privy council, which was, under the king, the ultimate authority in Irish matters. However, the English privy council knew very little about Irish affairs, and, by controlling the flow of information to Westminster, the lords justices could often hope to manipulate the authorities in England.

For legislation, the Irish council depended on an Irish parliament, and though the Irish council was subject to the English council, the Irish parliament was emphatically not subject to the English parliament.[9] In British terms, the English parliament was a municipal body, with no authority outside the borders of England. On the other hand, by the operation of Poynings's Law, the Irish parliament was firmly subordinated to the English privy council. According to Poynings's Law, no Irish bill could pass into law without first being transmitted for the approval of the English privy council. According to Strafford's interpretation of Poynings's Law, only the Irish privy council had the right to transmit bills for English approval. Any bill amended in the course of its passage through the Irish parliament had to be re-transmitted for further English approval. Strafford and his predecessors had relied further on other devices, such as packing, *quo warrantoes* and the proxies of Englishmen holding Irish peerages, to keep the Irish parliament in a considerable

[7] *A New History of Ireland*, ed. T. W. Moody, F. X. Martin and F. J. Byrne, iii (Oxford, 1976), p. 242.

[8] Nalson, ii. 545.

[9] See Kent Archives Office, U 1475/Z 47 (De L'Isle and Dudley MSS.) for a statement of the constitutional position by the earl of Leicester, possibly on his appointment as lord lieutenant. Ireland, he said, was 'not appertaining to the state of England, only annexed to the Crown in propriety and the heirs thereof'. Therefore, he said, 'it belongs to the king and not to the parliament and ought to be governed by the king and not by the parliament'. In other words, its constitutional status was like that of the Channel Islands and the Isle of Man. I am grateful to Dr. Blair Worden for this reference, and to Viscount De L'Isle and Dudley, V.C., K.G., for permission to quote from his family papers.

state of subordination. If ever any parliament has stood in need of a Notestinian winning of the initiative, it was the Irish parliament in 1640.

On the departure of Strafford for England, it seems that this was precisely what they achieved. This was the easier for the fact that Strafford, as Aidan Clarke put it, had managed 'with impartiality',[10] to alienate every interest in sight. Much of this was by quite needless provocation. For example, when Strafford held the inquisition which found the king's tenure for the plantation of Galway, he stayed in the earl of Clanricarde's house because it was the only house of sufficient quality in the neighbourhood. What he did not need to do was to add insult to injury by turning his horses into Clanricarde's grass which was about to be cut for hay, and lying on Clanricarde's best beds in his riding boots.[11] After Strafford's departure, even the Irish privy council admitted that a particularly liberal general pardon was needed, because the people were fearful 'after such a government as we have of late had heere'.[12]

On 7 November 1640, the Irish house of commons suddenly broke free from their shackles, and passed a remonstrance condemning the government of Strafford lock, stock and barrel. They passed this remonstrance without one single speech of debate. When reproached for having done so, their committee explained that a member was on his feet, ready, as they believed, to call them into the presence of Lord Deputy Wandesford to be adjourned. Like Sir John Eliot in 1629, they had to pass their remonstrance immediately and by acclamation. It was, of course, no use sending grievances against Strafford to the scrutiny of Wandesford, so they took a leaf out of the Scottish book in appointing a committee to go to London to represent their grievances direct to the king. The element of imitation of the Scots is even clearer in their decision that the committee should retain authority to represent the House in the event of a recess, and authority to represent 'the commonalty of Ireland' in the event of a dissolution. The membership of the committee shows how completely Strafford had broken down the normal groupings of Irish politics. The first two names were Sir Donagh McCarthy, a native Irishman, a Catholic, and a future Irish rebel, and Sir Hardress Waller, a New English settler, a devout Protestant, and a future New Model colonel and regicide.[13] The Irish Lords, though equally angry, were more deliberate, and did not succeed in appointing their committee before the recess. The recess did not defeat them, however, and the Lords then in town named four of their number to go to London.[14] When the House reassembled, it conferred retrospective legitimation on their actions. Strafford, it seemed, was the only Englishman ever to break down the religious divide in Irish politics.

In this sudden outburst of parliamentary activity, the desire to imitate the

[10] A. Clarke, 'The policies of the "Old English" in parliament, 1640–1', *Historical Studies*, v (1965), 85–102, at p. 88.

[11] 'A discourse between two councillors of state', ed. A. Clarke, *Analecta Hibernica*, xxvi (1970), 161–75, at p. 170.

[12] P.R.O., SP 63/259/45, Irish privy council to Vane, 1 July 1641.

[13] *Commons Journals, Ireland*, i. 162–5; P.R.O., SP 63/258/64.

[14] *Lords Journals, Ireland*, i. 142, 148, 149–51, 152.

English parliament was very prominent and very explicit. The Irish remonstrance claimed that the people of Ireland were 'for the most part derived from British ancestors, [and] should be governed according to the municipal and fundamental laws of England'. As the Irish committee put it, 'albeit your majesty's kingdom of Ireland hath beene and is governed by the greate charter and the laws and customs of that kingdome, yet many things have beene and daylie are don amisse by your majesty's ministers there, contrary to ye said great charter and other lawes and statutes of the land'. Lord Lambert, in the Irish house of lords, explicitly demanded that they should have a full general pardon like the one they had in England.[15] Like the Americans after them, the Irish were to find that when colonials laid claim to the liberties of England, they ran into problems in their relations with the English parliament, but in the heady days of the winter of 1640–1, everything was swept along before the demand for the rule of law. If there is anyone who still believes the old whig canard that Catholics are in some way less legalist or less constitutionalist than Protestants, an hour or two's reading of the Irish *Commons' Journals* for 1641 would provide a healthy corrective.

The common ground uniting both Houses in the Irish parliament in 1640 was that they were men of property, and it is no coincidence that the rule of the law was most stressed in the areas where it led to the protection of property. To take one paradigm issue, when the previous session of the parliament had voted subsidies, Strafford had arbitrarily introduced the lump sum assessment system, later introduced by Pym in England, by which each county was bound to raise a certain sum. As the gentry of the Pale explained, both here 'and in England whence we have our laws', subsidies were imposed by authority of an act of parliament, and Strafford could not alter them simply by a ruling of the privy council. This, they said, was against 'the common law of England, our birthright', and vested unlawful power in the council board 'according to the manner of France, impositions at will and pleasure'.[16]

In their specific complaints, the Irish Houses provided the case which later became the heart of the first eighteen articles for the impeachment of Strafford, that he exercised an arbitrary government over the lives, liberties and estates of the king's subjects. To take one example among many, the charge that Strafford had said the Irish were a conquered nation, which became article 3 of his impeachment, rested on a petition presented by Gormanston and Kilmallock for the committee of the Irish house of lords in London:[17] 'the Lord Lieutenant to impart a slavish opinion said they were a conquered nation, and must expect laws as from a conqueror'. In testifying to this article, Gormanston, Catholic Old English, and with an uncle serving the king of Spain in the Netherlands, appeared side by side with Cork, the New English planter and admirer of William Perkins. Both helped to make Strafford the first victim of British justice.

[15] *C.J. Ire.*, i. 162; P.R.O., SP 63/258/64; *L.J. Ire.*, i. 154.

[16] P.R.O., SP 63/258/33.

[17] *Ibid.*, SP 63/258/73, 70.2. For the frank resting of the king's title on conquest, see Bodleian Library, MS. Carte 1 fo. 139 (prosecution of the Galway jury) and Kent A.O., U 1475/Z 47, Leicester on the constitutional status of Ireland.

So long as Strafford was the prime target, the Irish committee in London could work, both with the English parliament, and with the Scottish commissioners, who were in London at the same time. Indeed, the Irish house of commons had appealed, with no sense that they were calling in a Frankenstein, to the English house of commons to help to get their remonstrance presented to the king.[18] In the queries of 16 February 1641, the biggest constitutionalist manifesto of the Irish parliament, they were still claiming that they were 'to be governed only by the common law of England and statutes in force in this kingdome'.[19] When they decided to impeach their lord chancellor and lord chief justice, they were forced to make the even more specific claim that English precedents were binding in Ireland, and that they had 'received their laws from England'.[20] So far, their purposes suited the Scots and the English parliament well enough.

It was altogether a different matter when the Irish committee began to negotiate on their major single demand, which was for confirmation of the Graces. The Graces had been granted by the English government in 1628, in return for the financing of an Irish army which was to help in the wars of the sixteen-twenties.[21] They should be seen as part of Secretary Coke's plan for a British Union of Arms.[22] When peace was made, the English government had bowed to pressure from the New English, who did not like arming Catholics, and withdrawn the Graces. The Irish parliament was asking for them back again.

Among the Graces, one was more important than all the rest put together, and this was the one which extended to Ireland the English Concealment Act of 1624, which enacted that sixty years' possession should confer a good title against the Crown. In England, this act had merely conferred freedom from the activities of speculators, projectors and extortioners prying into defective titles. In Ireland, it would have conferred this, but much more as well, for it would have put a stop to the whole policy of plantation, which was the ark of the New English covenant. Since the days of Sir John Davies, early in James I's reign, the English had held that any Irish landowner could only have title if he could show a proper feudal tenure, by which the land was, mediately or immediately, held of the Crown. Those who could do this attracted wardship, and those who could not were liable to lose their lands, which would then be planted with English or Scottish settlers. To Lord Justice Parsons, who was master of the Irish court of wards, this policy had its own attractions. To the Irish privy council, there were many other reasons for defending plantation. Feudal tenures were vital to keeping up Irish revenues, and also, they argued, to establishing a legal dependency on the king. They guaranteed religion and 'civility' (the English code-word for Anglicization) and ensured that the lands concerned 'cannot in point of interest come into the hands of the Irish'. They had produced more societies of Protestants than all the kingdom besides, and above all,

[18] Clarke, 'Policies of the Old English', p. 90; Brit. Libr., Egerton MS. 1048 fo. 13.

[19] P.R.O., SP 63/260/7.1.

[20] *C.J. Ire.*, i. 191. This claim was to be forwarded for support to the *parliament* of England.

[21] On the Graces, see A. Clarke, *The Old English in Ireland, 1625–42* (1966), pp. 47–9, 86–8 and *passim*.

[22] P.R.O., SP 16/527/44. I would like to thank Mr. Andrew Thrush for valuable discussion of this document.

'ther was noe way to reduce this kingdom to the English lawes and obedience of the Crowne, and to free England of the perpetuall charge therof, but only a full conqest, or a politique reformation, by plantations'.[23] If it was the New English view that the purpose of plantations was to make Ireland safe for Protestants, it was a logical Old English or Irish response to see the Graces, by stopping plantation, as making Ireland safe for Catholics. In the climate of 1641, this was a very much more divisive issue than the condemnation of Strafford. It seems to have divided the Irish committee in London itself. On 8 March 1641, John Barry reported that Burke and Plunkett, who represented the Catholic faction on the committee, were believed to have private access to the king 'by means of my Lord Cottington and some others well wishers (as they conceave) of ye Catholique partie', and to have well disposed him to the performing of all the Graces. This can hardly have been pleasing to a future New Model colonel like Sir Hardress Waller, and it is no surprise to learn from Barry that other members of the committee were defending plantations, both for the revenue to which they could give rise, and 'the cheifest and mayne reason of all the propagation of the Protestant religion, in those partes', which was held to be very necessary for the safety and improvement of the kingdom.[24] It is not difficult to see that in March 1641, an issue like this had more than purely Irish significance. The basis of the Anglo-Scottish *rapprochement* that Pym and others were asking Charles to undertake would have been a closer union of the two realms against Popery in all its forms. It would involve, in the words of the Petition of the Twelve Peers, 'uniting of *both* your realms against the common enemies of the reformed religion'.[25] It is not fanciful to see behind this demand, as the Irish rebels did, a demand for the reduction of Ireland to a mere dependency of England, rather than an independent kingdom, and it is certainly not fanciful to see it and the granting of the Graces as two contradictory and mutually exclusive policies. If Charles were to attempt to grant the Graces, he would be likely to provoke a demand to subject Ireland to the English parliament. He was also likely to increase the desire of the Scots to interfere in Ireland: they had been saying since 1638 that they wished the king's subjects in England and Ireland would take the same covenant as they had, for it would be much to the king's advantage, and a greater tie of their fidelity.[26] They were already championing the Ulster Scots who had been punished by Strafford for refusing to renounce the Covenant, and if they had the opportunity to

[23] *Ibid*., SP 63/258/93.

[24] Brit. Libr., Additional MS. 46924 fo. 209r–v. I am grateful to Dr. Adamson for this reference.

[25] P.R.O., SP 16/465/16, my italics. For Irish awareness of the implications of this petition, see 'A discourse between two councillors', p. 171: 'the petition exhibited to his majesty . . . by the southern lords praying that his majesty would be graciously pleased to accord to the pacification then in treaty, to the end that both the kingdoms might be united against the common enemy of the reformed religion, the copy of which petition coming to the hands of the Irish, was more apprehended by them, than anything those in Ireland could contrive, and truly I believe was one principal cause of their taking arms'. This is a work of confederate propaganda coming from Kilkenny in 1642, and deserves attention. From an Irish point of view, perhaps the most ominous thing in the Petition of the Twelve Peers was their patent belief that Charles ruled over two kingdoms, and not three.

[26] John Leslie, earl of Rothes, *A Relation* (Bannatyne Club, xxxvii, 1830), p. 122; Scottish R.O., Hamilton MS. G.D. 406/1/M88. See also *Acts of the Parliaments of Scotland*, v. 300 for the Covenanters' determination to make an issue of the religious rights of Scots living outside Scotland.

object, they were not likely to take quietly an attempt to make Ireland safe for Catholics. The Scots tended to concede England's superior claims to an interest in Ireland, but in the somewhat provocative form of supposing that Ireland was subject to the *parliament* of England, referring casually to 'the parliament of England within quch [*sic*] is included the kingdome of Ireland'.[27]

At the same time, in the context of the trial of Strafford, it was easy to remember that the first time the Graces had been granted, they had been granted in return for the raising of an Irish Catholic army. Charles certainly remembered this, and in a letter of 16 January, now lost, asked the Irish council to investigate the possibility that the Irish parliament might undertake the financing of the new Irish army. He appears to have got a dusty answer to this suggestion,[28] but as late as 28 March 1641, the king still hoped to keep the Irish army on foot.[29] Since it was perfectly plain that the king could not reach a settlement with the Scots or with the English parliament if he kept the Irish army on foot, the king's determination to do so must be held to cast doubt on how far he ever wished for any such settlement. His negotiating position in London was that he wanted to keep it on foot until the Scottish army was disbanded,[30] but what appears in the Irish state papers is a desire to make the force permanent. It was not any desire to settle with his English parliament that made Charles ultimately decide to abandon the Irish army. Up to the beginning of the Long Parliament, the Irish army had been financed out of the English exchequer, but after November 1640, this was impossible: if the army were to be kept up at all, it would have to be financed from Irish sources. The Irish privy council, in their letter of 10 April, made it clear to Charles that this could not be done. Their letter was referred to an English council committee, which advised simply that since Charles could not maintain the army, he had better disband it.[31] It was only by coincidence that this decision was taken the same weekend as the king agreed to execute Strafford.

The issue of the Graces, then, involved a great deal else as well as Irish policy. It is probably not a coincidence that when Charles issued a signet letter, on 3 April 1641, saying he would grant the Graces, he was in the process of committing himself to the Army Plot, and rejecting the Protestant strategy that Pym and the Scots were urging on him. Ironically, it was the anxieties of the Irish parliament which prevented the king's concession of 3 April from finally settling the matter of the Graces. The Irish had been granted the Graces once, and had lost them, so they wanted the new concession embodied in the security of a statute. They at first suggested avoiding the requirements of Poynings's Law by using an ordinance of the two Houses recorded in the parliament roll instead of a statute (thereby giving

[27] Scottish R.O., PA 7/2 fo. 78v; Brit. Libr., Stowe MS. 187 fo. 54v. See also Brit. Libr., Harley MS. 163 fo. 597, where D'Ewes refers to Ireland 'which kingdom they always understand under the title of England'.

[28] P.R.O., SP 63/258/70.

[29] *Ibid*., SP 63/258/85. It seems that an offer was made by some of the 'Connacht men' to finance the army for a year, but nothing came of it (*ibid*., SP 63/258/96).

[30] *Journal of Sir Symonds D'Ewes*, ed. W. Notestein (New Haven, Conn., 1923), pp. 229–30; Brit. Libr., Add. MS. 6521 fos. 65, 68; *Journal of D'Ewes*, pp. 350, 482.

[31] P.R.O., SP 63/258/70 and 85, 63/274/21 and 22. For the payment of the Irish army out of the English Exchequer, see P.R.O., E 405/285 fo. 143.

the English parliament a useful idea).[32] In the end, however, they seem to have decided they needed a statute. This meant bills had to be transmitted to the English privy council under Poynings's Law, and an opportunity was created for second thoughts. That opportunity was skilfully exploited by the Irish privy council.

Since the Irish council seem to have been less than certain that Charles shared their devotion to the Protestant interest in Ireland, the issue they increasingly concentrated on was the loss of Irish revenue caused by concessions already implemented or in the pipeline. On this, they had a very strong case: the rule of law, as so often, had turned out to be very largely a means of diminishing the king's profit. As Sir Adam Loftus, the vice-treasurer, wrote to Secretary Vane, 'in truth the times will not now admit of the former harsh and strickt way'. He explained that that and the abatement of the book of rates, as demanded by the Irish parliament, were producing a considerable fall in the value of the customs. The lords justices explained to Vane, in somewhat *ex parte* language, that there were numerous attempts to defraud the king, and the officers were fearful of complaints to parliament if they tried to do anything about it, while they themselves dared not interpose the king's authority, as other governors had done, lest they diminish it.[33] This changed atmosphere, together with some of the specific concessions Charles made, produced a fall in almost every type of revenue. The drop in the subsidy, when Strafford's lump sum system of assessment was abandoned, was truly startling. A subsidy for the whole kingdom dropped from £40,000 to £12,000. In County Cavan, it dropped from £1,250 to £204, in County Limerick from £1,630 to £236, and in Dublin, rather more under the council's eye, from £1,300 to £826.[34] Respite of homage, which the Irish parliament had said to have been too rigorously assessed, fell from £622 a year to £242. Revenue in the wards dropped from £8,251 in 1639 to £5,897 in 1640.[35] A subsidy of the nobility, another subject of parliamentary protests, fell from £885 to £590.[36] The customs in 1639 had brought in £51,874, and in the first half year of 1640, they brought in £18,519, equivalent to an annual rate of £37,039.[37] The revenue from the tobacco monopoly was likely to stop altogether. All this information is known to us because the Irish council made it available to the English council in loving detail. They reminded the king that, by depriving himself of future plantations, he was ruling out the obvious way of remedying the situation. Though the Irish council did not ask Charles to reverse his decision on the Graces, they proposed that he should adopt the principle known to Ronald Reagan as 'linkage': he should make the bills to confirm the Graces wait on equivalent concessions by the Irish parliament to bring the king's revenue up to what it had been before. Otherwise, as they constantly reminded the

[32] P.R.O., SP 63/259/9, 60 and 61, 63/274/9; *An Argument delivered by Patricke Darcy, Esquire* (Dublin, 1764), p. 60. For the signet letter, see *C.J. Ire.*, i. 211–12 and P.R.O., SO 3/12 fo. 142. For an earlier use of the words 'ordinance of parliament' in Ireland, see Scottish R.O., Hamilton MS., G.D. 406/1/803, Strafford to Hamilton, 24 March 1640.

[33] P.R.O., SP 63/259/46, 26, 1.

[34] *Ibid.*, SP 63/273/8 and 9.

[35] Bodl. Libr., MS. Carte 1 fos. 319, 321.

[36] P.R.O., SP 63/260/8.

[37] *Ibid.*, SP 63/258/89.

English, Ireland would have to become, as it had been under James, a net charge on the English exchequer. In the circumstances of July 1641, this was something no English government could contemplate.[38] When the English privy council conducted a full hearing of the Irish grievances, on 16 July, they conceded the majority of them, but imposed two specific conditions which very much have Charles's personal stamp. One was that 'his Majestie's revenue and profitt . . . be no way lessened', and the other was that 'the clergy must not lose any part of their legitimate livelihood'.[39] With these principles, they spelt out a long series of specific measures they wanted the Irish parliament to adopt.

With this decision, the fate of the Graces was probably sealed. The Irish parliament was to be adjourned on 7 August, and the necessary bills would have had to leave London by the last week of July, at the very latest. When the Irish committee left London, arriving in Dublin on 6 August, they did not have the bills to confirm the Graces with them. The decision to withhold the Graces, at least for another session, was effectively taken by the time the Irish committee left London, and it should probably be blamed on the effective lobbying of the Irish privy council on the issue of revenue.

However, at the twelfth hour, Charles was presented by the house of lords with an opportunity to blame the parliament for the withholding of the Graces, and he took it with both hands. To understand how he came to be given this opportunity, it is necessary to go back to the beginning of the trial of Strafford, and to follow events from the point of view of the English parliament. It had always been difficult for the English parliament to impeach Strafford for his doings in Ireland without claiming that Ireland was under their jurisdiction. For much of the last quarter of 1640, they were walking a tightrope, which they occasionally slipped off.

On 6 November, the first day of business, Pym's attempt to set up a committee for Irish affairs raised a dispute: 'in the debate, itt was moved that Ireland had parliaments to retrieve theire own grievânces. But the generall opinion was that they might be heard here for a writt of error ther lies in the King's Bench here much more a redress in parliament'. Pym skilfully evaded the issue of jurisdiction by diverting the debate into an argument about whether Irish suitors had power to come to Westminster if they chose.[40] On 15 November, the Commons rashly 'required' Radcliffe and King to come as witnesses in the trial of Strafford. The king, reacting as he regularly did when he saw an infringement of his authority, but did not want to make an immediate issue of it, got them off the hook by summoning Radcliffe and King on his own authority.[41] On 28 January 1641, the grand committee for Irish affairs was more cautious: it dealt with a case by *recommending*

[38] P.R.O., SP 63/259/63 and 26.1, 63/260/12; *Nicholas Papers*, i. 4–6, 20–1.

[39] *Calendar of State Papers, Ireland, 1633–47*, pp. 317, 319 (Privy Council Register, xii, pp. 1–47). For another concession requiring a statute which did not appear, see T. C. Barnard, *Cromwellian Ireland* (Oxford, 1975), p. 32.

[40] Palmer's diary, Cambridge University Library, MS. Kk vi 38 fo. 7 (6 Nov. 1640); *Journal of D'Ewes*, p. 3; *C.J.*, ii. 21. See also Cambridge Univ. Libr., MS. Kk vi 38, reverse end (undated notes, possibly for the trial of Strafford): 'Ireland a distinct dominion but being by conquest may by expsse. wordes be bounde by parliaments here'.

[41] P.R.O., SP 63/258/51 and 52: *Journal of D'Ewes*, p. 31; *C.J.*, ii. 27–8.

the petitioners to the lords justices for speedy relief.[42] The issue remained a flashpoint, especially when witnesses were needed, since the temptation to require them to attend was likely to become irresistible. Since Irish suitors continued to go to Westminster in the hope of reversing unfavourable judgments, the issue continued to arise. On 3 March 1641, the Irish house of lords received a warrant from Lenthall requiring the bishop of Ardagh to attend at Westminster on the suit of one Teige O'Roddy, and they refused him leave to go. They instructed their committee in England to raise the issue with the king, and Lord Maguire, a later leader of the Irish rebellion, moved to go into committee of the whole to consider the matter further.[43] The English parliament left this case alone until 25 June and then 'because it might breed a long dispute', referred it to the parliament of Ireland in order to save charge, thereby pointedly refraining from waiving the claim to jurisdiction. In June 1641, Sir John Clotworthy the Ulsterman proposed that the Root and Branch Bill should apply to Ireland.[44]

The case which brought this issue of jurisdiction to a head was the case of Henry Stewart, who has some claim to be considered a British Problem in his own right. Henry Stewart was an Ulster Scot, who had been imprisoned by Strafford for refusing to take an oath renouncing the Covenant. The house of lords in London could not let the case drop, since the Scots were demanding punishment of those responsible for imprisoning him as part of the terms of the peace treaty.[45] As a result, the house of lords bravely issued an order commanding almost the whole of the Irish privy council to appear before them as delinquents. This was too much, and even Lord Justice Parsons, the chief friend of the English parliament in Ireland, sent in a vehement protest. The Speaker of the Irish parliament did the same,[46] and on 4 August 1641, these protests were placed before the house of lords. The Lords decided they had to make an issue of this, and set up a committee to search records of Ireland's dependency on this kingdom. More seriously, they sent Essex, Manchester, Bristol and Saye to see the king to ask him to stay the Graces until this matter was settled. The king, as argued before, must have already decided to stay the Graces, but seized the chance to pass the buck with distinction. He told the Lords the next day that he would agree to stay the Graces at their request, until this matter was settled. Temple, writing to Leicester, the new lord lieutenant, expressed the New English view by saying this might be a great advantage to the king's service in Ireland.[47]

From a native Irish or Old English point of view, however, what had happened was much more alarming. There had been encroachments by the English parliament before, but now a formal claim to jurisdiction had been made and enunciated. Moreover, that formal claim to jurisdiction had been linked with a

[42] House of Lords Main Papers, 28 Jan. 1641.

[43] *L.J. Ire*., i. 174–6.

[44] *C.J.*, ii. 187; Brit. Libr., Harley MSS. 163 fo. 737, 5047 fo. 36.

[45] Brit. Libr., Stowe MS. 187 fo. 54v.

[46] House of Lords Main Papers, 9, 27 and 30 July 1641; P.R.O., SP 63/259/66.

[47] *L.J.*, iv. 339, 342, 345, 348, 353; Brit. Libr., Harley MS. 6424 fo. 87v; Kent A.O., U 1475/C 114/2; Temple to Leicester, 5 Aug. 1641 (Hist. MSS. Comm., *De L'Isle and Dudley MSS*., vi. 407).

move for the denial of the Graces, exactly as the Protestant interest in Ireland was demanding. From an Irish point of view, what had happened had all the ingredients of a Protestant plot. Moreover, even if there were no immediate Protestant plot, members of the Irish committee who had been in London could see well enough for themselves what would be the likely consequence of rule over Ireland by an English parliament in which men like Pym and Saye were the dominant spirits. By so skilfully evading responsibility for withholding the Graces, the king had left open the possibility of an Anglo-Irish axis, with the Irish Protestants and the parliament on one side, and the king and the Old English on the other. When the Irish rebels maintained that the parliament was drawing the prerogative out of the king's hands to disenable him from granting those graces he was always inclinable to grant, they were falling victims to a highly skilled royal propaganda plant.[48]

Did the king do more than this to encourage the Old English and the Irish to support him against the Protestant ascendancy in London and Dublin? Many scholars, from S. R. Gardiner to Caroline Hibbard, have believed that he did. They have believed that the Irish rebellion was the result of a royal plot to gain control of the members of the disbanded Irish army for possible use against the English parliament. This view has received the support of no less an Irish scholar than Aidan Clarke, with whom an Englishman cannot lightly disagree.[49] The principal agent of this plot is supposed to have been the earl of Antrim, second husband to the former duchess of Buckingham, and the main source on which it has rested is a confession made by Antrim to the victorious Cromwellians in 1650. According to Antrim, he was acting as Charles's agent to recruit soldiers from the former Irish army for possible service against the English parliament, but 'the fools' (the phrase is Antrim's) jumped the gun and started independent action.[50] It is a plausible story, and worth considering. On the other hand, Antrim's confession is not a sufficient source to carry the story on its own: he was speaking nine years after the event, and to English regicides who badly needed to be justified in the eyes of the public for what they had done. Antrim was telling his audience what they wanted to hear, and his confession should not be believed unless contemporary confirmation can be found.

There is a lot of peripheral supporting evidence which can be used to back up this story. Antrim was in Dublin on 23 October, the day on which the rebels had decided to seize the Castle.[51] Moreover, the rebels would have been able to arm themselves. When the army was disbanded, their arms were put back into store in Dublin. Shortly afterwards, Charles appointed Kirke, his personal gentleman of the

[48] Bodl. Libr., MS. Carte 2 fos. 217–18.

[49] S.R. Gardiner, *History of England, 1603–42* (10 vols., 1896–1901), x. 49–52 and nn.; C. M. Hibbard, *Charles I and the Popish Plot* (Chapel Hill, N.C., 1983), pp. 179–80, 197–8, 213–14; Clarke, *Old English in Ireland*, pp. 156–65.

[50] R. Dunlop, 'The forged commission of 1641', *Eng. Hist. Rev.*, ii (1887), 527–33. It is worth remarking that the commission accuses the English parliament of appointing governors, commanders and officers at their pleasure. This would seem to suggest that in the form in which it survives, the commission was written after the passage of the militia ordinance. The text of the commission in Bodl. Libr., MS. Dep. C 174 (Nalson MS. 21) no. 2, is endorsed 'read 15 of March 1642'.

[51] P.R.O., SP 63/260/33, Archibald Steward to the king, 28 Oct. 1641.

robes, clerk of the ordnance in Ireland—a somewhat improbable appointment.[52] If Charles wanted to use the disbanded Irish soldiers as a private force of his own, he could have armed them without the assistance of the Dublin council. When Vane told Ormond to disband the army, he told him to begin by disbanding 4,000 out of 8,000.[53] All these are supporting evidence, but they are no more: the delay in disbanding could have been no more than desire to delay things till some more money was available. So far, we have *Hamlet* with a fine supporting cast, but without the prince. It is necessary to look at what was happening to the Irish army on disbandment. By a proposal which originated with Pym's Irish ally Sir John Clotworthy,[54] it was decided to get them out of harm's way by shipping them off to serve the king of Spain, who was desperate for men. The council committee which recommended disbandment accepted this proposal in order to reduce the risk of tumults. The question is whether Charles genuinely attempted to implement this proposal. On this, the best witness seems to be the Spanish ambassador, who was watching like a hawk for any attempt to interfere with his levies, and the Spanish ambassador, though a deeply suspicious man, appears to have held the king innocent of any attempt to interfere with the shipment of the troops out of Ireland. He put the blame on Saye, Brooke and a member of the Commons he said was called 'John Pis'. He said these people had originally been in favour of the proposal, but had turned against it when they began to hope that Charles might declare war on Spain in the Palatine interest. Reading between the lines of the Spanish ambassador's dispatches, it seems that one significant reason why the troops were still in Ireland when the rebellion broke out was Madrid's delay in dispatching money. Another, and more important, reason was that the house of commons, on Pym's initiative, made ship-owners take bonds not to transport Irish soldiers to Spain. The French ambassador appears to have had good reasons for treating the Five Members as his 'friends'.[55] John Barry, one of the Irish captains who later joined the rebellion, was still expecting to go to Spain only seven weeks before it broke out, and bound himself to the Spanish ambassador in £1,500 to go.[56] There is

[52] *Cal. S.P. Ire. 1633–47*, p. 328. He is described as 'Henry' Kirke, but since he is said to be of the robes, George is likely to be intended. Antrim, in his confession, said the men were to be armed out of the store at Dublin (Dunlop, p. 528). This was not, however, Kirke's first attempt to obtain an Irish office (G. E. Aylmer, *The King's Servants: the Civil Service of Charles I, 1625–42* (1961), pp. 346–7). I am grateful to Dr. Adamson for this reference.

[53] Bodl. Libr., MS. Carte 1 fo. 383. Modern work on military history should lead us to think that disbanding an army by stages, in order to wait for money, is less abnormal than the suspicion attached to this letter would suggest. On the raising of money to disband the army, see P.R.O., SP 63/259/3, 24 and 31; *ibid.*, SO 3/12 fos. 149v and 150. On 19 July, the lords justices proposed to sell off army surplus, and there is no record to suggest that they were discouraged (*ibid.*, SP 63/259/59).

[54] *Journal of D'Ewes*, p. 347.

[55] *Wild Geese in Spanish Flanders, 1582–1700*, ed. B. Jennings (Dublin, 1964), pp. 330–55 at pp. 354–5. On 15 Aug., Cardenas noted interference by the queen, but he may well have been right in believing she was acting in the French interest. Cardenas also appears to have been right in seeing the Palatine interest behind the opposition to Spanish recruitment in Ireland. See the speech by the Palatine agent Sir Richard Cave, Brit. Libr., Harley MS. 163 fo. 878v; also *ibid.*, fo. 865v; P.R.O., HCA 30/854 (I am grateful to Dr. David Hebb for this reference); *ibid.*, PRO 31/3/73 fo. 10.

[56] Brit. Libr., Add. MS. 46925 fos. 137–9.

no evidence here that Charles tried to use the disbanded soldiers for rebellious purposes.

Nor do Antrim's letters for the months in question show the confidential accomplice of the king portrayed in his confession. In June and July 1641, when the conspiracy was supposed to be taking place, Antrim was writing suppliant letters to his friend Hamilton, asking for a captaincy for one of his relations, and begging for a reduction in his subsidy assessment. He plaintively asked Hamilton to try to get the king to read his letters. Antrim may have been a clever man, but he is unlikely to have set up a blind so unflattering to himself.[57] It is a more serious objection to the story of a royal plot that July and August 1641 are the very last time when it would have been in Charles's interest to undertake such a plot. He thought he was just about to get rid of the English parliament peaceably with its own consent, and had no need whatever to stir up a hornets' nest by attacking it with an Irish army. It seems improbable that Charles encouraged the Irish rebellion, because at that moment it was not in his interest to do so. He might have wanted to employ Irish soldiers in Scotland, for help in any trouble arising out of the Incident, and, interestingly, the Irish rebels themselves believed there was a possibility the disbanded Irish army would be used in this way.[58] But if Charles wanted to raise troops to fight against Hamilton, Antrim, who was a close friend of Hamilton's, is about the last Irishman he would have employed to do so.

We are, then, driven back in explaining the rebellion on the rebels' own propaganda, and on one solitary confession by Lord Maguire, who was captured in a cockloft in Dublin on the day the rebellion began. According to Maguire, Roger Moore, who seems to have been the moving spirit behind the rebellion, had been planning it since January 1641. He was relying on the disbanded Irish army, and also on support from Owen Roe O'Neill, who commanded a regiment in the Spanish service in Flanders.[58] Owen Roe ultimately arrived, but late, because the Spaniards had put him in the glasshouse for a breach of military discipline.[59]

The confession and the rebel propaganda all show three themes, every one of which has a British dimension. The first is a desire for liberty, and especially for liberty of conscience, in which there was a very strong imitative element. One captured rebel said they did it 'to imitate Scotland, who got a privilege by that course'.[60] Another pamphlet, in a carefully barbed phrase, claimed that they were 'no more rebels than other subjects who took up arms against the king, and yet had very good quarter'. Lord Maguire, in his confession, struck the same note: he said Roger Moore and his fellows told him that it was 'for religion, and for to procure

[57] Scottish R.O., Hamilton MSS. G.D. 406/1/1355, 1356/2x and 1389. On 19 July, Antrim had received no reply to his letter to the king of 4 June. His request to take over Lord Raby's company was refused (P.R.O., SO 3/12 fo. 141v). In Sept. 1642, Antrim was facing a summons from Charles to answer charges of complicity in the rebellion. If Charles had been Antrim's accomplice, this would have been a daring charge (Scottish R.O., G.D. 406/1/1778). Early in Dec. 1641, Antrim assured Charles of his opposition to the rebellion (P.R.O., SP 16/486/66).

[58] Nalson, ii. 546.

[59] P.R.O., SP 77/31 fo. 154v, De Vic to Vane, 29 Nov. 1641 (? O.S.). This drastic action for what De Vic believed to be a small breach of military discipline might suggest that the Spaniards shared the Irish belief that Owen Roe had been negotiating with Richelieu.

more liberty for their country, as did (they say) of late Scotland'.[60] In this demand for liberty of conscience was included a demand for the Irish to be no longer treated as second-class citizens. In an interesting peace mission undertaken by Lord Dillon of Costello, the Catholic lords and gentry for whom he was speaking asked for repeal of all statutes against the Catholic religion, and 'a charter of free denizen in ample manner for ye meere Irish'.[61] In this theme, the imitative element is surely clear enough. If there were any doubt, it would be removed by the rebels' Kilkenny oath, which is a straight parody of the English Protestation, practically unaltered save for the insertion of 'all the angells and saints in Heaven' after 'almightie God'.[62]

The second theme is fear for the Catholic religion, based on observation of what was happening in the other kingdoms of Britain. As Lord Dillon's mission put it, 'the papists are severely punished (though they be loyall subjects to his majestie) in the neighbouring countries, which serves them as beacons to look unto their own country'.[63] This fear of the spread of anti-Catholicism often took the form of fear of a Scottish invasion: 'that the English and Scots combined and joined in a petition to his majestie to bee licensed for to come into Ireland with the Bible in one hand and the sword in the other, to for to plant their Puritan, anarchical religion among us, otherwise utterly to destroy us'.[64] According to Maguire's confession, 'a great fear of suppressing religion was conceived', and he said this was why the Irish parliament began to oppose the plan to take the ex-soldiers out of the kingdom.[65] If the Scots invaded to enforce uniformity on Ireland, they would be needed. In the light of a number of the Scots' statements, this fear that they might attempt to root out popery in all the king's dominions was by no means irrational.

The more sophisticated rebels, among whom Roger Moore was conspicuous, linked this fear for the extirpation of Catholicism with English parliamentary claims to authority over Ireland. When urging Maguire to join the rebellion, he told him that

> the welfare . . . of the Catholick religion, which, he said, undoubtedly the parliament now in England will suppress, doth depend on it: for, said he, it is to be feared, and so much I hear from every understanding man, the parliament intends the utter subversion of our religion.[66]

Pym would have been hard put to it to plead not guilty to this charge. Indeed, the archbishops and bishops of the Church of Ireland, alarmed by the number of

[60] *L.J.*, iv. 415; 'A discourse between two councillors', p. 173; Nalson, ii. 551; see also R. Bellings, *History of the Irish Confederation*, ed. J. T. Gilbert (7 vols., Dublin, 1882–91), i. 236.

[61] P.R.O., SP 63/260/37; Gardiner, x. 46n., ix. 383–4. For another copy of this letter, with signatures, see Bodl. Libr., MS. Dep. C 164 (Nalson MS. 12), pp. 5–6. There are 26 signatures, all Farralls. It is possible that Dillon's mission, rather than Antrim's confession, represents the line of Charles's Irish planning. Dillon's was a bridge-building, rather than a rebellious, mission, but had been kept secret from the Irish council, who would not have approved of it.

[62] Bodl. Libr., MS. Carte 2 fo. 237.

[63] P.R.O., SP 63/260/37 and 38.2.

[64] Bellings, ii. 4; see n. 25 above.

[65] Nalson, ii. 546; *C.J. Ire.*, i. 276–7.

[66] Nalson, ii. 544.

Catholics who appeared in public in 1641, were inviting the English parliament to take authority in Ireland in order to suppress them.[67] In another formulation, more precise if not much less chilling, the rebels protested that 'the parliament of England, being of opinion that the statutes in England shall bind the natives of this kingdom contrary to lawe, and the liberties and freedome of this kingdome, wee cannot expect better measure att their hands than those of England'.[68] Perhaps the best formulation was by Viscount Gormanston, the man who had objected to Strafford saying the Irish were a conquered nation. In a private letter to the earl of Clanricarde, unsuccessfully urging him to join the rebellion, he said:

> it was not unknown to your lordship how the Puritan faction of England, since, by the countenance of the Scottish army, they invaded the regall power, have both in their doctrine and practice laid the foundation of the slavery of this country. They teach that the laws of England, if they mention Ireland, are without doubt binding here, and the parliament has wholly assumed the management of the affairs of this kingdom, as a right and preheminence due to it. And what may be expected from such zealous and fiery professors of an adverse religion, but the ruine and extirpation of ours.

To the native Irish, such fears tended to lead to a generalized anti-English panic. To Gormanston, who was Old English and the senior viscount in Ireland, they led to a defence of the Irish parliament: Clanricarde, he said, was 'too noble to subject the merits of your ancestors, and the estate which you derive from those that have made way to it over the bodyes of their enemies, to be subject to the dispose of any other parliament than our owne'.[69] It is a voice an American of 1776 would have understood.

This story surely shows that the Irish rebellion was not an irrelevance to the concerns of England and Scotland, but a very direct, and indeed logical, reaction to them. It shows how far religious passion was a dry rot in the body politic, spreading across national boundaries like dry rot through walls. And it should also show that, even if it could have been made operable across St. George's Channel, the settlement for which Pym and Argyll were working could not have been implemented without upsetting the peace of Ireland. For Charles, who was the only person bound to take a British view of the problems of 1640/1, the Irish consequences of such a settlement alone could have been a sufficient ground for refusing it. It simply was not possible to give head to the amount of anti-popery gathering in England and Scotland, without letting it spread to Ireland, where such men as Parsons and Cork were ready to welcome it with open arms. As Lord Mountgarret, an Old English rebel, wrote to Ormond, 'it hath been a principal observation of the best historians that a whole nation, how contemptible soever,

[67] P.R.O., SP 63/274/44, asking the lords justices to second their suit to the parliament of England.

[68] Bellings, ii. 5.

[69] *Ibid.*, i. 255–6. It seems painfully clear that when Gormanston objected to Strafford calling Ireland a conquered nation, he did so, not because of any doubt whether conquest could confer title, but because he believed he was one of the conquerors and not one of the conquered.

should not bee soe incensed by any prince or state, how powerfull soever, as to bee driven to take desperate courses, the event whereof is uncertain and resteth only in the all-guiding power of the Omnipotent'.[70] With the 'best historians', we should now concur.

[70] Bellings, ii. 2. The only one of the 'best historians' named by Mountgarret is Commines.

16

The First Army Plot of 1641

ON 11 May 1641, Maurice Wynn reported that 'some plott or other' had been discovered to the Commons.[1] The vagueness of his reaction seems to have been characteristic of much assessment of the army plot ever since. There is a general sense that there is enough smoke to make it probable that there is some fire, but we are not extremely clear who plotted with whom to do what. This is, in part, because of a very justifiable caution. It is felt that Charles I's plots, like his grandmother's lovers, are capable of growing in the telling, especially when the tellers are people to whom belief in popish conspiracy comes with eagerness distressing to a modern ear. Pym and Hampden's later readiness to exploit such mare's nests as the Beale plot at crucial moments in the debate on the Grand Remonstrance adds further to the wariness with which plot stories from the Long Parliament are treated.[2] Wariness is an entirely justified reaction with any Long Parliament plot, but wariness may stop short of incredulity. Above all, a belief that plots should not be taken on trust is no substitute for an examination of the sources.

The key source consists of the body of depositions presented to the Commons in Nathaniel Fiennes' report from the Close Committee on 14 June 1641. These depositions were subsequently published as part of the propaganda war of 1642,[3] and have normally been used in their printed version. The provenance of this printed version, as part of the paper war of 1642, has not added to its credibility. However, it is not necessary to rely on the printed versions. The original MSS, signed by the deponents on each sheet, survive, and are divided between the Braye MSS and the Nalson MSS, now in the Bodleian. There are a very few discrepancies between the printed and manuscript versions. The last page of Goring's deposition does not now survive, but the fact that the surviving MS differs from the printed version only in the sort of trivial errors which normally arise in transcription suggests that this is an accident of survival rather than any nefarious interference with the sources. There is only one interesting piece of information in

[1] National Library of Wales, Wynn of Gwydir MSS, no. 1685.

[2] *Journal of Sir Symonds D'Ewes*, ed. W. H. Coates (New Haven 1942) (hereafter '*D' Ewes* (C), pp. 148, 149, 151, 167.

[3] *C.J.* ii 573. All subsequent references are to vol. ii.

the manuscript depositions which has been suppressed in the printed version. This information, which is crossed out in the MS itself, is that Henry Jermyn had been seen visiting his laundress at three in the morning. It was not only Jermyn's reputation as a dandy which might have made the Parliament doubt whether his motives on this occasion were primarily political.[4] We are perhaps dealing here with a reminder that this was still a struggle between gentlemen.

These depositions, though they are known through the report which presented them to the Commons, were in fact taken, as the signatures on them prove, by the Lords' committee for examinations, which enjoyed the advantage over the Commons of being able to administer an oath. It consisted of Bath, Essex, Warwick, March, Saye, Wharton, Paget, Kimbolton, Howard of Charlton and Howard of Escrick with Attorney General Herbert and Serjeant Glanvill to take the examinations.[5] The majority of these, with some significant exceptions, such as the deposition of Sir William Balfour, Lieutenant of the Tower, are confessions of the minor conspirators. We have another confession by the Earl of Northumberland's brother Henry Percy, which was not taken by the committee, but was extracted from Percy by his brother in return for a blind eye to his escape. This confession exists in two versions, one in Northumberland's papers, and the other printed in London in the summer of 1641.[6] The difference between the two versions is disappointingly small, and consists mainly in the greater clarity of the second.

Confessions as evidence have their limitations, and it is fortunately possible to check them against some other sources. The best of these is a series of letters, now in State Papers, addressed to Northumberland and Conway by Sir John Conyers, Lieutenant General of the Horse, who had a ringside view of the plot developing, and did not like what he saw. This can be supplemented by a limited amount of record evidence in the State Papers, the Signet Office docket book, and the Queen's accounts in the National Library of Wales. There is a very

[4] Bodleian Library MS dep. C. 165 (Nalson MS 13) item 9 *C.S.P.D. 1633–4*, vol. ccxxxviii, no. 35 examination of Eleanor Villiers: 'he never promised her marriage, for she loved him so much that she never asked him'.

[5] *L.J.* iv 235 (subsequent references are to vol. iv unless otherwise stated). The peculiarity of this committee is that it contained no bishops. This need not be a statement of political hostility, since the committee's work could be regarded as coming close to the giving of judgements of blood.

[6] Alnwick Castle MSS vol. 15 (British Library Microfilm 286) f. 223a–b. I am grateful to His Grace the Duke of Northumberland for permission to examine these MSS. The MS is not in Henry Percy's hand, but in that of someone who was in England on 11 May (see below n. 85). There is no name on it, but the description of the occasion when 'Goring and I' went to see the King makes the identity clear. Percy's public confession is in SP 16/481/41.

limited amount of correspondence between the conspirators in the papers of William Legge, Lieutenant General of the Artillery, now in Stafford Record Office. In addition, the Scottish Commissioners in London and Newcastle and the French ambassador had enough interest, and a close enough view, to count as first hand sources on a number of points.[7] Fortunately, it seems to be possible to cross-check enough points to decide how far the confessions should be believed.

During the early months of 1641, the King's main English objectives were to preserve some form of episcopacy, and to save the life of the Earl of Strafford. During the weeks before the army plot began, the King had learnt painfully that he was unlikely to achieve these objectives by merely political means. In the third week of February 1641, prospects had looked brighter for a settlement than they did in any other week of the Parliament. The passage of the Triennial Act and the first subsidy bill, on 15 February, were rapidly followed by the appointment of seven new Privy Councillors on the 19th. Most of these new Councillors immediately made token gestures in favour of Strafford, and Charles, by his own subsequent confession, believed that preferment would lead them to drop their opposition to episcopacy also.[8] What Charles hoped, the Scots feared, and for a few days, it seemed as if the Parliamentary-Scottish alliance which had brought Charles to his knees was about to break.[9]

This optimism was shattered by the publication of the Scottish paper of 24 February, demanding the death of Strafford and the abolition of episcopacy in England, and by the refusal of the Parliamentary leaders to condemn this paper in the hard-fought debate of 27 February. The King's disappointment can be measured by the depth of his anger: in Johnston of Wariston's words, 'the king hes run stark mad at it'.[10] What Charles learnt in the two weeks after 24 February was that he could not settle with his critics on any terms he would find acceptable. Instead, he began plans to fight back. On 3 March 1641, in conversation with Walter Stewart, he committed himself to the intrigue with Montrose, designed to end Covenanter control of Scotland, which was to culminate in the Incident.[11] In

[7] The French ambassador's main informant was the Earl of Holland, who became Lord General in the middle of April, but he also enjoyed numerous sources in the queen's household, including Father Philip, the queen's confessor.

[8] *His Majesties Declaration* (12 Aug. 1642) BL, E. 241(1) p. 517. On the behaviour of the new Privy Councillors, see Staffs. R.O. D 1778/1/i/14, O'Neill to Legge, 23 Feb. 1641. I am grateful to the Earl of Dartmouth for permission to use his family papers.

[9] Robert Baillie, *Letters and Journals*, ed. D. Laing (Bannatyne Club, Edinburgh, 1841–2), i. 305–6 (hereafter cited as '*Baillie*').

[10] David Stevenson, *The Scottish Revolution* (Newton Abbot, 1973), 219. I hope to discuss this matter at length elsewhere.

[11] National Library of Scotland, Wodrow MS Fol. 65, f. 72a–b.

England, the issue of episcopacy was one on which he could afford to wait while Hyde, Digby, Culpepper, Strangeways, Bristol and Williams harnessed a growing anti-Scottish reaction to his service. On the issue of Strafford, he could not afford to wait, and it was precisely at the moment when this realisation was becoming urgent that growing discontent in the English army in the north presented Charles with a golden opportunity to exploit.

The English army felt that its honour had been wounded by the defeat at Newburn, and it had already suffered a hiatus in its pay caused by the City's reluctance to lend money until it had procured the execution of Goodman the priest. It was also suffering severe disciplinary problems because of absence of martial law, and the soldiers' deep sense of the hostility of civilian justice to the military. Conyers warned Conway on this subject on 13 February, adding that 'I would I had stayed at Bredae'.[12] On top of this already simmering discontent, the City now decided to withhold loans of money for *both* armies until they had justice on the Earl of Strafford.[13] This move caused severe problems in both armies, and made the competition between them for what money was available even more acute than it was before. This competition became urgent in the Parliamentary debate of 6 March. The House was about to send a sum of money to the English army when it received a demand for money from the Scots, backed by a threat to advance further if they did not get it. On the motion of William Purefoy and Secretary Vane, the House diverted £10,000 from the English to the Scottish army. This vote appears to have produced an explosion of anger among the English army officers in the House. Strode found Willmott and Ashburnham 'much discontented' in Westminster Hall: from such conversations the House took alarm at what it had done. They were too late: Henry Percy, another army officer highly discontented, had been sent to see the King as a one-man deputation on the Algiers pirates, and he enjoyed the opportunity to share his discontent with the King.[14] The real lesson of the day was that the Commons were vulnerable to military pressure.

On 20 March the English army officers submitted a memorial of

[12] Public Record Office, State Papers (hereafter SP) 16/477/26 (also 12 and 54). I am grateful to Dr Ronan Bennett for a helpful discussion of the attitudes of civilian courts to soldiers.

[13] SP 16/477/46: Valerie Pearl, *London and the Outbreak of the Puritan Revolution* (Oxford 1961), 198–207. I have not added significantly to Professor Pearl's account of this episode.

[14] *Journal of Sir Symonds D'Ewes*, ed. Wallace Notestein (New Haven, 1923), 448–52 (hereafter *D'Ewes(N)*). BL Harleian MS 163, f. 837a (Strode speaking on 13 Aug. 1641).

their discontents to the Lord General. 'First', they said, 'wee complayne as gentlemen that by the long neglect of sending our paie wee have bene enforced contrary to our disposicions, and the qualities of our former lives, to oppresse a poor countre, and live upon the curtesie and at the discretion of strangers, which both they and wee are weary of'. They complained that their former address by way of petition had found no credit and brought no remedy, touched in passing on the 'perverse endeavours' of those who crossed their proceedings, expressed a desire to recover their military honour, and complained of judges 'unexperienced and not practiced in our way and profession' beseeching the Parliament to preserve them from those that would impose such innovations on them.[15] This letter was brought to London by a junior officer called Captain James Chudleigh, and from his arrival in London, on 21 March, the army plot took off. Chudleigh first met William Davenant the poet, who told him it was 'a matter of greater consequence that he imagined', adding that 'the Parliament was so well affected to ye Scotts, as yt there was no lyklihood the army should have satisfaction so soone as they expected it'. Davenant then put him in contact with Henry Jermyn and Sir John Suckling. Jermyn asked to show a copy of the army letter to the Queen, and asked if he might bring Chudleigh to see her. Chudleigh very properly refused the second request, saying it was the task of Lord General Northumberland, to whom the letter was addressed, but he does not tell us his response to the first. Suckling told him the King would be well pleased if the army would receive Goring as their Lieutenant General.[16]

Meanwhile, it seems, Henry Percy had begun a second conspiracy, involving himself, Commissary Willmott, Captain Pollard, John Ashburnham, Sir John Berkeley and Daniel O'Neill. This group, according to Pollard, began meeting 'about the beginning of Lent', which was on 10 March. This is a group of minor courtiers and junior army officers (Henry Percy was Master of the Horse to the Prince, and Daniel O'Neill a Gentleman of the Privy Chamber extraordinary).[17] The key common factor of this group seems to be that four of the six were among the limited group of army officers who were also members of Parliament, and at least three of those four were present and indignant at the debate of 6 March. The key to the thinking of this group was the desire to imitate the Scots: they had seen the Scots able to bend the Parliament by petitions with the sword behind them, and

[15] House of Lords Main Papers, 20 March 1641.

[16] House of Lords Record Office, Braye MSS 2 147v. A clumsy passage in this testimony is the result of a correction to eliminate hearsay.

[17] SP 16/480/14: PRO LC5./134, p. 300.

intended to see whether what the Scots could do, they could do better.[18] Henry Percy arrived at their first meeting with the heads of a petition already drawn. It asked to preserve the bishops' functions and votes, that the Irish army should not be disbanded until the Scots were too, and that the King's revenue should be improved 'to that proportion was formerly'. Pollard confessed that 'what was meant by the king's revenues, I understand not, unless how to improve it'. Even without Pollard's testimony, it would be possible to doubt whether these articles originated spontaneously with those who were offering them. These articles so much measure royal preoccupations that it seems highly likely that the articles Henry Percy brought to the first meeting came from the king. There is only one of the king's major preoccupations missing, and this may be because the conspirators had cold feet about it and rejected it. Willmott and Ashburnham both insisted that they had not agreed that anything should be done towards the saving of Strafford; or, Willmott added, to the prejudice of the Parliament. Had they felt otherwise, it is likely that we would have known Percy's petition with four heads and not with three. This sounds a law-abiding picture, and it is one Charles later admitted to in relation to the second army plot, saying that 'the commanders and officers of the army had a mind to petition our Parliament, as others of our people had done'.[19]

While Henry Percy was organising his petition, Jermyn, Suckling, Davenant and probably Goring were organising a more far-reaching plan to take control of the Tower and bring the English army southwards. These two were always described by the conspirators as a single plot. The king, probably on 29 March, organised a meeting which was meant to bring these two conspiracies together. This meeting brought together Percy, Willmott, Pollard, Ashburnham, O'Neill and Berkeley from one conspiracy with Jermyn and Goring from the other. Percy's company appear to have refused a request to admit Suckling. It is perhaps in their accounts of this meeting that the conspirators' accounts need to be read with most caution, since they were all concerned to establish that the more shocking propositions came from somebody else, preferably somebody safely abroad. In particular, Percy and Goring, who turned state's evidence, may have been more deeply implicated than their own confessions suggest. On the other hand, the fact that when the plot became public, at the beginning of May, Jermyn, Suckling, Davenant and Percy fled before anyone had accused them is itself evidence for thinking that they were more deeply implicated than those who stayed behind.

[18] Bodleian MS dep. C. 165, ff. 30–41: SP 16/481/41.
[19] *L.J.* 667.

According to Goring, he was recruited for this meeting through a preliminary approach from Jermyn and Suckling. They took him to see the Queen, who in turn took him to see the king. 'His Majesty asked him, if he was engaged in any cabale concerning the army: to which he answered, that he was not: whereupon his Majesty replied, I command you then to joyne your self with Percy and some others, whom you will find with him'.[20] The King did not attend the subsequent meeting in Percy's chamber, which seems to have been a difficult one. Without necessarily accepting that Willmott, Ashburnham and Percy were quite as holier than thou as their subsequent accounts suggest, we may believe that what they heard gave them cold feet. Pollard said that 'we were afraid to know their proposicions', and that Willmott and Ashburnham had argued that the bringing up of the army to London would lead to 'inconveniences' to king and subject. Ashburnham, by contrast, said that at this meeting he never heard of bringing the army to London, but admitted there were 'some extravagant discourses' so wild they were dissented from. He supplied no particulars of what these discourses were.[21] Percy, in his confession from abroad, said Jermyn and Goring were considering 'a way more sharpe and high, not having limits either of honour or law'. Percy's original manuscript confession, now in Northumberland's papers, is a little franker on this point, though hard to use because the burning of the edge of the paper has destroyed some key words. He said 'there was an intention to ——[1 word] the army and to putt it in a posture of being able ——[2 words] of beeing willing to interpose in the proceedings ——[2 words]'. He concludes 'this I thought unlawfull' to interpose in the proceedings of the House.[22] Goring denied responsibility for the propositions of bringing the army south and taking the Tower, but admitted they were put forward by Jermyn.

It is at least agreed that there was considerable dissension at this meeting, and Percy tells us that he and Jermyn, as representatives of the two rival designs, went to see the King, who told Jermyn and his fellows that 'these ways were vain and foolish, and (he) would think of them no more'.[23] It seems probable that the King said this, and that it was what he wished Percy and his fellows to believe, but it is not what happened. A full understanding would involve an ability to explain why there were two plots. It is possible that this is simply an example of the difficulties conspiracy suffers through secrecy. It is also

[20] Braye MSS 2, f. 158 ff.

[21] Bodl. MS dep. C. 165, ff. 14–41. Ashburnham appears to contradict himself.

[22] SP 16/481/41: Alnwick MSS vol. 15, f. 223b. There is an intriguing suggestion in the last line of the Alnwick confession that Percy may have told Northumberland about the plot before his flight.

[23] SP 16/481/41.

possible, however, to see them as having been initially the king's plot and the queen's plot. Percy's plan for army petitions represented something the king was prepared on a later occasion to admit to having done, whereas by contrast he always vehemently and totally denied any involvement in any plan to bring up the army. This interpretation would turn the king's command to Goring to join himself with Percy into an attempt to merge the queen's wilder plot into his own more responsible plot. It would involve believing that the king spoke truth when he told Goring and Percy that 'these wayes were vain and foolish, and (he) would think of them no more.'

This interpretation solves some difficulties, only to create others. It explains the two plots, and the king's conduct, but it does not explain why the more serious plot managed by Jermyn and Suckling was not brought to a halt by the king's ostensible veto. The plan to bring the army south continued at least for another week, and when Chudleigh came back from the army on 4 April, Suckling took him to report to the king. It would be possible to explain this by saying that Chudleigh had already left for the army before Goring and Percy spoke to the king, and that orders countermanding the plot waited for his return from the north. According to Chudleigh's testimony, he stayed in London eight or nine days from his arrival on 21 March. This would mean he left on the 29th or 30th. Since we do not know how long after the meeting of 29 March Goring and Percy reported to the King, it is impossible to tell which event happened first. It is then possible to explain the failure to stop the plan to bring the army south without disbelieving the king. It is a more serious difficulty that the king's disavowal, as reported by Percy, applied equally to the plan to bring the army south and to the plan to take the Tower. The plan to take the Tower we know he continued, operating through Suckling. On this point, his disavowal must be taken as for public consumption only. Since we must disbelieve half the disavowal, I am inclined to disbelieve the other half, and regard the king as a full participant in the plan to bring the army south.

At this point, Goring chose to impart 'the mayn of the business', though not the particulars, since he had taken an oath of secrecy, to his brother-in-law Lord Dungarvan, then to the Earl of Newport Master of the Ordnance, and finally to Bedford, Saye and Mandeville.[24] From the first week of April onwards, the army plot was conducted in full view of the House of Commons. On 6 April the Commons voted, in the first use of a form of words which was to have a long, if not honourable, history during 1642, that no one was to move the king's army or the Yorkshire trained bands 'without special

[24] Goring's deposition, as above.

order of his Majesty, with the advice and consent of both Houses of Parliament'.[25] The fact that this very public notice did not bring the Army Plot to a halt is one of the most intriguing facts about it.

On the same day, Conyers gave warning of a meeting of officers at Boroughbridge, which had taken place on 3 April, though he said he could not find out what had happened at it. He also gave warning of a plan to make Goring Lieutenant General, and gave warning that neither he nor Astley would serve under him. He asked, if Goring should come to the army, for leave to come to London to tell his story.[26] Fortunately, we have other descriptions of the Boroughbridge meeting. Colonel Vavassor said Chudleigh said that the Parliament had taken great offence at the letter of 20 March, that those who had written it would be questioned for it, and that there was small hope of money for the present. He also brought them a letter ready drafted, addressed to Goring, saying that if the king should appoint him Lieutenant General, they would be willing to receive him. Chudleigh confirms the story of the letter asking for Goring to be Lieutenant General, and says he brought it back to London on 4 April, with the signatures of Colonels Vavassor and Fielding and a few others, and that Suckling brought him to kiss the King and Queen's hands. He also spread a report that the Earl of Newcastle was to be their general, and that the King would pawn his jewels to get them pay. His handling of the meeting was not inconsistent with the advice Suckling had given him, that the army 'did undiscreetly to show their teeth, except they could bite'.[27] Shortly afterwards, another officers' meeting was organized at York, at which they were offered a ready drawn declaration 'of their readinesse to serve his Majesty', 'but not findinge any great cause for it, it was after torne'.[28] It is, perhaps, not fanciful to hear a lack of enthusiastic support behind these words. It looks as if the failure of the York and Boroughbridge meetings dampened the plans to bring the army to London.

When Chudleigh returned from Boroughbridge, on 4 April, he brought a letter to Goring from some of the officers, offering to serve under him as Lieutenant General. Not finding Goring in London, Chudleigh took this letter to Suckling, who in turn took it to the king,

[25] *C.J.* 116 and other refs. For the origins of this resolution, see B.L. Harl. MS 164, f. 951b. Stapleton and Holles who moved it, regarded it in part for the protection of the Scots. See also SP 16/479/27.

[26] SP 16/479/13, 13.1, 19, 88. No. 88, which is an extract taken from a letter by Conyers not now in State Papers, says that Percy, as well as Holland and Goring was expected at the army. This probably means that Chudleigh or his colleague Sergeant Major Willis told the officers so, but it need not follow that we should believe them.

[27] Braye MSS 2, ff. 147–9. Depositions of Chudleigh and Col. Vavassor.

[28] *ib.* f. 151, deposition of William Legge.

'and afterwards brought him to kiss ye kg. and queenes hands'. 'Within a day or two', the letter was returned to Chudleigh, who took it on to Goring at Portsmouth. On 4 April the plan to bring the army southwards was still alive. By 9 April, when a new Lord General was appointed, it was dead.[29] This timing is compatible with two explanations for calling off the plan to bring the army south. It could represent the king's first chance to bring Chudleigh (and his wife) into line. It could simply represent a recognition, which the evidence would warrant, that the Boroughbridge meeting had not shown enough support to make the design a practical possibility. What seems clear is that the plan to bring the army south did not advance further after 4 April. When a new general was appointed to replace Northumberland, who had malaria, it was not the hard-liner Newcastle, but the much more flexible Earl of Holland, whose appointment had been proposed on 29 March by Percy. Nothing more was heard of some of the rumours spread by Chudleigh and others, of the Prince's going to the army, of French support from Frenchmen around London, or of 1,000 horse financed by the clergy.[30] A rumour continued to circulate through April that the King had sent money to the army, and might go to the army in person, but there is no secure provenance for this rumour.[31] There is only one more suggestion of bringing the army south, in an ambiguous letter from Sir John Berkeley to Legge, written on 1 May.[32] The plan to bring up the army was a genuine plan, but one which failed. Since the Boroughbridge meeting, at which the plan was definitely still in progress, came after Charles's assurance to Henry Percy that he would think of the plan no more, it seems overwhelmingly probable that it was lack of support in the army, rather than Charles's own moral scuples, which brought

[29] SP 16/480/9.

[30] Chudleigh's deposition, ff. 147–8. The plan to make Newcastle general was discussed at the London meeting, but Willmott, Ashburnham and Pollard denied that these other propositions had been discussed there. Chudleigh's suggestion that Newcastle would feast the troops in Nottinghamshire, where his estates were, raises the possibility that the army might have been moved far enough south to cause alarm, but not far enough to burn its boats.

[31] *Calendar of State Papers, Venetian 1640–42*, pp. 142, 145; *H.M. Twelfth Report* (2), 280.

[32] Staffs. R.O. D 1778/1/i/18, Berkeley to Legge, York, 1 May 1641. This letter deserves quotation in full: 'Deare Will, I have ordered my officers to meete me at Doncaster, and therefore cannot stay. I have performed what was agreed on last night, you know there hath been many occasions of our delay but none from me although I of all men were most excusable if I had, being told by Capt. Palmes that I was mistaken if I thought the rest did not discent as much as he: then which in my judgement nothing could be more. However as I have not been backward heretofore so I will not be for the future in any honourable resolution that shall be approved on by such persons so itt be undertaken roundly and heartily and so you may assure all or any of them from thy Jo. Berkeley'.

the plan to a halt. It is the scuples of the army, unpaid and angry as they were, which are truly impressive evidence of the instinctive constitutionalism of the English.

What undoubtedly continued after the first week of April was the plan to secure Strafford's escape and gain control of the Tower. Sir William Balfour Lieutenant of the Tower, 'our good kind countrieman', as Baillie called him,[33] was unwilling to agree to any such suggestion. He remained unwilling even when Strafford, three or four days before his death, offered him £20,000 and a good marriage for his son to agree to it.[34] If Strafford could be got out of the Tower, his brother Sir George had a ship waiting down river ready to get him away. On one occasion, Strafford and Sir George Wentworth were overheard making plans for an escape. Elizabeth Nutt, wife of a merchant of Tower Street, confessed in an examination on 4 May[35] that she and two other women had gone into the Tower to peep through the keyhole in the hope of seeing Strafford, 'and they then peeping through the keyhole and other places of the dore to see the said Earle did heare him and the other partye conferring about an escape as they conceived, and saying it must be done when all was still and asked the said partie where his brothers shippe was—and doubted not to escape if something which was saied concerninge the Lieutenant of the Tower were done, but what was, as also where they might bee in twelve hours, they could not know by reason that when they talked further off they could not perfectly heare'. Like Sir William Balfour, I find this testimony convincing: the refusal, in spite of palpable frustration, to make up what they could not hear carries conviction. Mrs Nutt also, more questionably, heard the Earl say 'that if this fort could bee safely guarded or overwritten for three or four months there would come aid enough'.

The problem, then, was to gain physical control of the Tower without alerting everyone by going through the ritual of dismissing Balfour. This task was undertaken by Sir John Suckling, in collaboration with an officer from Strafford's Irish army called Captain Billingsley.[36] On Easter Eve 24 April, Billingsley, in the name of Sir John Suckling, approached a certain John Lanyon to recruit him for mercenary service for the King of Portugal, telling him that the king's leave for him to quit royal service could be procured, and he should bring as many cannoneers as he could. Unfortunately for Suckling

[33] *Baillie* i. 282, Balfour's deposition, Braye MS 2, f. 156 r–v.

[34] BL Harl. MS 163, f. 500a; *L.J.* 229–30.

[35] Braye MS 2, f. 144 r–v. This was not taken by the Lords' committee for examinations, but by Balfour and Newport as Lieutenant and Constable of the Tower. In acting as Constable, Newport was twenty-four hours premature.

[36] Bodleian Library MS Carte 1, f. 182v.

and Billingsley, Lanyon went to check the story with the Portuguese ambassador, who said that they were very willing to have men, but that he knew nothing of Suckling or Billingsley, and had given them no commission to raise men. After this, Lanyon seems to have avoided turning up at meetings with Billingsley, and received nothing more from him than an offer to buy arms.[37] Others seem to have been less cautious than Lanyon, and by the end of April, Billingsley had a hundred men in his service. These were more than enough to overpower the forty Yeoman Warders of the Tower, and Balfour viewed them with an alarm which can only have been increased when Strafford told him it might be dangerous to refuse to let them in. On 3 May Balfour's resistance was supported by a petition to the House of Lords, from the citizens, who kept a very close watch on what happened at the Tower. The Lords immediately sent Essex, Hamilton and Holland to the king to ask him to withdraw Billingsley's men. There can be no better evidence of the intensity of Charles's determination to save Strafford than the fact that, even at this late date, with the plot in effect discovered, and the weight of the Lords against him, he still demurred. It was reported that 'upon discourse between him and the Lieutenant of the Tower concerning the great concourse of people that resorted about the Tower, his Majestye did think fitt for the better preserving the munition in the Tower, to putt 100 men under the commande of Captain Billingsley into the Tower to garde the munition, but if any jelousie should arise by puttinge those 100 men, his majestie is willing to heare whate advice their lordships will give him in it'. This reply provoked the Lords to send an immediate further deputation, consisting of Pembroke, Bath, Essex, Hamilton, Warwick, Bristol and Saye, 'humblie to desire his majestie' that Billingsley's men should be immediately discharged. Before the deputation returned, the Lords ordered Newport to go and take command of the Tower.[38] The next day, Newport reported smugly from the Tower that 'Suckling and his desines are discovered, and I am assured he will pay for it if he stay by it.' He added, with even greater smugness, that the Lords had sent him to take command of the Tower, the King was making him Constable, and 'I have behaved myself so well, I am trusted by both'.[39] For all his smugness, Newport's condemnation of Suckling should be taken seriously.

Even this defeat did not bring the king and queen to a halt, and

[37] Braye MS 2, f. 146 v–r (*sic*) (Lanyon's deposition).

[38] Paul Christianson, 'The "Obliterated" Portions of the Lords' Journals', *E.H.R.* xcv (1980), 346–8. I have taken the liberty of changing Professor Christianson's reading of 'Lord Chancellor' on p. 347, since there was no such officer at the time. 'Lord Chamberlain' appears a more probable reading. Original Journals, vol. 16, p. 222.

[39] Staffs. R.O. D 1778/1/i/21.

the plan to send the queen away to Portsmouth, which Goring had fortified with her money, persisted for several days longer. This plan had been some time in gestation. Henry Browne, the queen's servant, testified on 6 May that he had packed up all the queen's plate the week before Easter (18–25 April),[40] and his testimony may have had something to do with the Lords' decision, on the same day, to send Bristol and Holland to the king to stay the queen's journey.[41] It was the day *after* this appeal, Saturday 7 May, that the French ambassador found the queen's carriages waiting at the door, and her most precious things all packed up. He implored the Bishop of Angoulême to stop her, saying flight would only hasten the dangers she feared, to which Angoulême replied undiplomatically that he agreed, but the queen would not listen.[42] He sent the ambassador to see Father Philip, whose letter of the previous day appealing for French help had been intercepted, and is now in State Papers.[43] He decided, after a long conversation, that Father Philip had a hand in the queen's decision. It was only two hours later that he learnt that the queen had changed her mind. What the queen's objectives were is not clear. It may be that the king simply wanted her out of the way, in the hope that he might then be able to refuse to sign the attainder bill without fear for her safety, but the fact that she was withdrawing to a place newly fortified and in the direction of France was bound to make people fear the worst.

The Parliamentary committee which investigated the plot claimed that the plot also included a plan to obtain French help. This was not true, but the king and queen had only themselves to blame for the spreading of the story, since they and their allies had industriously circulated it. The queen had in fact wented to obtain help from France, and had been spreading the rumour that she would go to France, presumably to get help, ever since February. Richelieu, in March, had told the queen bluntly that such a visit would be '*mal à propos*', and warned her that '*en telles occasions qui quitte la partie le perd*'. He advised the queen '*de se donner un peu de patience, jusques a' ce que le mal qui la presse soit sur son retour*'.[44] This advice annoyed the queen so

[40] Bodleian MS dep. C 165, no. 9.

[41] *L.J.* 236.

[42] PRO 31/3/72, f. 552 r–v.

[43] SP 16/480/18.

[44] PRO 31/3/72, p. 458, but see *ib.* pp. 460–2 for the emasculated official form which this advice was transmitted to the Queen. For the deliberate circulation of the rumour, see *ib.* p. 416 (Jan. 28/Feb. 7), when the French ambassador reported that it was thought she hoped to inspire some jealousy in the Parliament. See also *Baillie* i. 295, PRO 31/3/72, pp. 423–4, 435, 436, *H.M.C. De L'Isle and Dudley* vi. 386 and Kent Archive Office U 1475/C 114/7. I am grateful to Viscount De L'Isle and Dudley, V.C., K.G., for permission to quote from his family papers. For the Queen's anger at Richelieu's response, see PRO 31/3/72, pp. 465, 482.

much that she started the rumour that she was going to go to Ireland instead.[45] The French ambassador, on 7 May, industriously circulated a denial of French intervention through Holland,[46] but Jermyn, Suckling and others had circulated it enough to make it hard to kill. It is also doubtful, in spite of the French ambassador's optimism, whether the Parliamentary leaders really wanted to kill it. There is an endorsement on Father Philip's intercepted letter of 6 March, which suggests that on this one issue, they were behaving in the way royalist propaganda has always attributed to them. There are two notes on the dorse of this letter. One says '*pca 25 Junii*', presumably meaning that it was read in the Commons on 25 June, when the impeachment of Father Philip was discussed. The other reads 'fit to be read. To incense the French'.[47] This can only mean a desire to increase French irritation with Charles and Henrietta Maria for claiming French help when they knew it was not available. If members knew that this letter would incense the French, they knew that the charge it was sustaining was not true, and were spreading a false accusation in the hope that mud would stick. They were clearly quite capable of behaving in this way: it is only the fact that the King happened to be guilty on the other charges which meant they did not need to. Another item which gave rise to misplaced alarm was the delivery of new guns at the Tower in the first week of May: the order had been placed in the aftermath of Newburn.[48]

There is further evidence of the King's complicity. During the weeks when the army plot was in gestation, he granted annuities to Percy, Willmott and O'Neill. The week of Henry Percy's flight, facing a potential treason charge, he altered Percy's grant from a grant to him direct into a grant to feoffees to his use, thereby ensuring that a conviction for treason would not make Percy lose it.[49] In June, reports were circulating that the king wished to bring back Jermyn and Percy, and in the autumn Jermyn, jointly in survivorship with his father, was granted the Keepership of Hampton Court Park. It is a small

[45] *C.S.P. Ven. 1640–2*, p. 127.

[46] PRO 31/3/72, p. 554.

[47] SP 16/480/18. It is not clear why a House of Commons document is now in State Papers.

[48] PRO (Kew) WO 55/455 (26 Sept. 1640). This order carries a note that Browne's men were to be paid extra wages because of the need for haste. Payment is noted on 20 April 1641. For the order of 10 Dec. for new gun platforms for these guns, PRO WO 49/72, 10 Dec. 1640 (payment 8 May 1641). For the original desire to fortify the Tower after Newburn see SP 16/464/45 and 466/2 and 11, and Bodleian MSS Clarendon 1418 and 1423.

[49] PRO SO 3/12, ff. 142 v, 144 v: SP 16/480/48 and 15.

grant, but one not normally made to exiled traitors.[50] During the Civil War itself, many of the plotters, notably Jermyn, Willmott, Ashburnham, Berkeley, Goring and O'Neill showed every sign of remaining in favour. In August 1641 the King intervened to secure the payment of O'Neill's pension out of the Irish hanaper.[51] Lunsford, who had been involved on the fringes of the meeting at Boroughbridge, was clearly still in the King's favour in December. A final and unexpected witness in favour of the genuineness of the plot is Edward Nicholas, in his history of the Long Parliament, where he says that Jermyn and Goring, and interestingly, also Percy and Willmott 'advised—how the English army might be assured to the King, and if it pleased him, to be persuaded to march southward'.[52] He is a man who is not likely to have repeated the charge lightly.

Another question worth thought is where the money came from. Some of it was raised by a method of delightful simplicity. There was a regular procedure for officers whose pay was in arrears to jump the queue by getting a warrant to receive their back pay directly from Uvedale in London, instead of waiting in the queue to receive it at York. Many innocent people used this procedure, but those taking advantage of it also included Goring, Ashburnham and Chudleigh, who again used the cover story of mercenary service for the King of Portugal. This money, though, is unlikely to have gone far.[53] The report, circulated by the Venetian ambassador, that the king sent money down to the army at York, cannot be confirmed,[54] but since the Treasurer of the Chamber's accounts and the Privy Purse accounts do not survive, the lack of evidence is not conclusive. What is rather more suggestive is the note by Sir Richard Wynn the Queen's Receiver that on 24 March 1641, £1,300 was issued into the queen's own hands. Once it was in her own hands, it no longer needed to be accounted for, and could be spent without creating any further record. It should be said that this is not the only sum issued into the queen's own hands: there is a regular issue at the end of the year for New Year's Gifts, and an unusual one in 1642 to do with the repayment of the loan the queen had made for the Bishops' Wars. However, the entry about the loan is noted in Wynn's warrant book for what it is. There is no such note for the payment of 24 March, but instead a most unbureaucratic note that the receipt was 'written with the

[50] Bedfordshire Record Office St John MSS J 1382. PRO C. 233/5, f. 87v.

[51] PRO SO 3/12, f. 169v. See PRO Wards 9/431, f. 387v for the payment of Willmott's pension.

[52] BL Add. MS 31954, fo. 184a.

[53] SP 16/480/11 (Chidley) and 41 (Goring and Ashburnham).

[54] *C.S.P. Ven. 1641–2*, p. 142.

Queen's own hand'.[55] Combined with Chudleigh's testimony that the queen had sent Goring money for fortifying Portsmouth, this is very nearly conclusive.

It is also necessary to ask the question Professor Hibbard has often asked me: how are we to interpret plotting conducted as much in public as Louis XIV's dressing? From 6 April onwards, if not earlier, the plotters should have known that the House of Commons was alert to their activities. Billingsley's activities around the Tower were plain for all the citizens to see. There is no sign that Goring, for all his public leaking, ever suffered any significant royal disfavour, nor that Willmott ever lost the king's confidence for the indiscreet remark, on 19 April, on the floor of the Commons, that all the army officers were sent for to the army very suddenly.[56] This question should be considered alongside the question why Goring chose to leak the plot almost as soon as he was embarked on it. The chronology does not seem to make it easy to explain Goring's leaking in the terms suggested in his deposition, of pique at not being made Lieutenant General, since his appointment as Lieutenant General was still on the cards at Boroughbridge, several days after he had leaked the plot. It is possible that Goring, like Willmott and Ashburnham, gave evidence out of genuine shock at what he had been asked to do. It is true that it is dangerous to underestimate the constitutionalism of any Englishman in 1641, not excluding the army plotters, but it is not easy to regard this as the sole explanation of Goring's conduct. It would square a good many circles if we were to consider the hypothesis that Goring leaked the army plot because the king asked him to. The whole pattern of the politics of 1640–42, for Pym as much as for Charles, is the pattern of the use of threat to force compliance. In almost every example of this process, the initial object of the exercise was not to carry out the threat: it was to achieve the compliance. The lengthy prehistory of the Grand Remonstrance is a classic example of this process. So is the lengthy prehistory of the militia ordinance, first threatened by Pym on 23 June 1641.[57] So is the lengthy prehistory of the attempt on the Five Members.[58] It is only when the deployment

[55] National Library of Wales, Wynnstay MSS vol. 165 p. 10 (Wynn's book of poundage); vol. 173 pp. 12–13 (Wynn's warrant book). The warrant book records £1,400 not £1,300 as delivered into the Queen's hands. I am grateful to Professor Caroline Hibbard for drawing my attention to these MSS. The brief of Wynn's annual account, SP 16/484/48, shows £9,500 as delivered into the Queen's own hands. Of this, £4,200 is not accounted for in the poundage book or the warrant book. In December 1641, when Balfour was offered £3,000 to leave his place at the Tower, the money was channelled through Sir Richard Wynn. *D'Ewes*(*C*) p. 330.

[56] *C.J.* 123.

[57] Bodl. MS Rawlinson D 1099, f. 86a.

[58] See my *The Fall of the British Monarchies 1637–1642* (forthcoming).

of these threats failed to induce any compliance that it became necessary to carry them out. The Civil War itself is the ultimate example of this history of the called bluff. This, perhaps, is the pattern into which the army plot should be fitted. It was Charles's primary objective to save Strafford who had trusted in him, and bishops, who had been entrusted to him. It is likely that Charles believed, as he may have believed as late as the summer of 1642, that the mere threat of force, as soon as he could get it to be believed, would be enough to bring the recalcitrant into line. In the reign of Henry VIII, this assumption would almost certainly have been correct. It is the real peculiarity of the reign of Charles I that throughout it, the threat of force increased, instead of diminishing, the recalcitrance of his opponents.

This is something many of the plotters seem to have appreciated better than their leader. Suckling, in his anonymous memorandum of February or March 1641, told the King there was no other way to preserve his ministers but by being first right with his people. He advised Charles that 'it will not be enough for ye kinge to doe what they desire, but he must doe something more, for yt will showe ye heartiness, I meane by doeinge more, the doeinge something of his owne, as throwing away things they call not for'. He added pointedly that 'to make itt appeare perfect & lasting to ye kingdome, it is necessary ye Queene really joine'.[59] Henry Jermyn, too, had been deep in the settlement negotiations of February 1641, even to the extent of trying to make money out of Leicester's desire for office, by selling himself, literally, as the man who got him the job.[60] There is only one among the whole list of plotters of whose thinking this desire to secure compliance by the threat of force is characteristic, and that is Charles I himself. Even if the direct evidence did not lead to a belief in Charles's own involvement, the design so much bears his hallmark that the burden of proof must rest on those who would suggest that he was not responsible.[61]

This suspicion can only be strengthened by the suggestion that the army plot may have had a Scottish dimension, since the king was alone among the conspirators in having the *locus standi* to have a Scottish policy. Such a dimension clearly existed in the second army plot of July 1641, which was in many respects a pale carbon copy of

[59] SP 16/478/82. Gardiner, who is usually accurate on the Army Plot, is at his most Gladstonian in commenting on this memorandum; *History of England*, ix. 311–2 (1893).

[60] *H.M.C. De L'Isle and Dudley*, VI 367, 382.

[61] Scottish Record Office, Hamilton MSS G.D. 406/1, 1437 and other refs.

the first. When Daniel O'Neill, from the king, lobbied Sir Jacob Astley with plans to move the army southwards, Astley made the obvious objection that 'they must fight with the Scotts first and leave them before they could move southward', to which O'Neill replied 'what if the Scotts could be made neutrall'?[62] If Charles had such a design in the spring of 1641, he at least had material to work with. The City's withholding of money until the death of Strafford had the ironic effect of disabling the Scots as a fighting force, and had contributed substantially to their retreat from the paper of 24 February.[63] Their impatience to finish their business and go home was growing more intense, and was being expressed with an increasing eloquence.[64] They were, moreover, vulnerable to royal attempts to intrigue behind their backs in Scotland. They had been well aware from the beginning that the Covenanters were very far from representing a united Scottish nation, and that the anti-Covenanter cause needed only leadership to make itself effective. They were aware that Montrose, who was one of the leading commissioners with the army at Newcastle, had had a supposedly secret correspondence with Charles since 1639.[65] The beginning of negotiations, on 3 March, with Montrose's allies on a plan which appeared to lead to Montrose's supporters getting the leading Scottish offices may well have been meant as a threat to the Covenanters in the same way as the army plot was meant as a threat to the English, to induce them to adopt a more compliant negotiating posture. The Covenanters were well aware of the strength of what Baillie called 'our unfriends' about Charles.[66] When Charles, on 21 April, told the Scottish Commissioners he meant to come to Edinburgh to complete the treaty, he was raising both hopes and fears: he appealed to the hope that his presence at Edinburgh might signal a greater willingness to make concessions, but also to the fear that it might give him a greater opportunity to pursue the policies he ultimately adopted in the Incident, of spiking the Covenanters' guns by doing a successful deal with their Scottish opponents.[67] The carrot and stick character of Charles's policy is highlighted by the fact that, shortly after starting his intrigue with Montrose, he tempted the Covenanters with the one concession which would have made Montrose's strategy impossible: an agreement that the Scottish great officers and Council should be appointed from a list of nominees made

[62] Astley's deposition 29 Oct. 1641, Braye MS 2, ff. 203–4.
[63] National Library of Scotland, Adv. MS 33.4.6, ff. 132v, 134r.
[64] *L.J.* 231, BL Harl. MS 457, f. 72r and Stowe MS 187 f. 63r.
[65] Scottish Record Office, Hamilton MSS G.D. 406/1/878 and 1096.
[66] *Baillie* i. 350; Edinburgh University Library MS D.c.4.16., f. 89v.
[67] National Library of Scotland, Adv. MS 33.1.1 vol. XIII no. 80: David Stevenson, *op. cit.*, 223.

by the Scottish Parliament.[68] He was, in effect, offering the Scots control of their own affairs in return for the end of their meddling in English affairs: the same offer he made to Loudoun and Argyll in the autumn. The withdrawal of the Scottish army from England was an essential condition of any such offer.[69] At the same time, he was threatening, through rumours spread by the Earl of Holland, to use the Irish army against the Scottish if the Scots should fight to secure the death of Strafford.[70] If Charles hoped in April, as he did in July, that the Scots could be made neutral, his hope was not unrealistic: he had put a lot of intelligent effort into securing it. This aspect of the plot was less reported than the others, since the English Parliament lacked the authority to investigate it, but all the clues suggest that it was probably as genuine as the rest.

In the event, the army plot did nothing but defeat all those objectives for which it had been undertaken. It contributed significantly to the death of Strafford, and Strafford's own final letter, 'I beseech your Majesty, for prevention of evils which may happen by your refusal to pass this bill',[71] is plain advice to the king to give up the plot. If Gardiner's date of 4 May is correct, this letter was written the day after Billingsley had failed to gain admission to the Tower, and probably immediately after Elizabeth Nutt had revealed his plans to escape. If so, Strafford probably had little choice in the matter. The circulation of stories about the Irish army during April must have contributed to the Lords' willingness to convict Strafford on that charge, and Strafford can hardly have benefited from the fact that the story of Billingsley's designs on the Tower broke, by Charles's timing and not by Pym's, on the day before the third reading of the Attainder Bill.

Among Charles's potential moderate supporters, the army plot caused a deep dismay. On 3 May Sir John Culpepper, probably the King's most distinguished supporter in the Commons, moved 'for the remonstrance, and peticion of rights to be forthwith read, and then to goe to the Lords and by that we may try the affeccion of the kinge, and that if we should be dissolved, that we might be found doeinge the service we were hither sent for'.[72] Sir Thomas Roe, the Stuarts' Greek chorus, was even more eloquent: 'the tydes returne with every

[68] Harl. MS 457, ff. 77r, 80r: National Library of Scotland, Wodrow MS Quarto 25, f. 160v. It is worth noting that this offer was not made at a formal meeting of the negotiators, but at a private meeting between Charles and the Scottish Commissioners.

[69] Hamilton MSS, GD 406/1/1585 and 6.

[70] PRO 31/3/72, fo. 513 (8/18 April). This rumour is unlikely to have helped towards Strafford's acquittal on the Irish army charge.

[71] S. R. Gardiner, *op. cit.* ix 362 and n.

[72] BL Harl. MS 477, f. 28r.

season, but obedience will be long lame, if ye Parlament every way restore it not'. He hoped for things to improve, but added 'if not I shall envy those that perish with honour than they yt outlive the honour and peace of their countrye'. Roe spoke with feeling, since he had been turned out of the great cabin in his ship by the fleeing plotters, who 'soldier-like, mean to live upon their quarter'.[73] Since Roe, on diplomatic service, possessed the only exemption to the order stopping the ports, it was an obvious move for the fleeing plotters to batten on him. It is, of course, possible that Roe also spoke with fuller information than is available to the rest of us.

The bill against the dissolution of the Long Parliament, without which the Civil War would have been nearly impossible, was another consequence of the army plot. Sir John Culpepper was not alone in fearing that the plot involved a plan to dissolve the Parliament, and when Black Rod came to the Commons to summon them to hear the King's speech, on 1 May, he soothed fears by saying 'fear not, I warrant yow'.[74] The need for security for payment of the armies was an important motive for the Act against Dissolution, but it can hardly be a coincidence that it was passed at the height of a major dissolution scare. Moreover, the need for security for the armies is unlikely to explain the Commons' success in totally rejecting a Lords' amendment to restrict the life of the bill to two years.[75] The disbandment of the Irish army, announced on 7 May, looks like another reaction to the army plot, but curiously, it is not: it is simply a belated acceptance that there was no longer the money to keep it together.[76]

The Protestation, on the other hand, patently is a reaction to the army plot. The proposal for an oath of association was moved by Marten, Wray, Harley and Perd, in the middle of the debate on the plot, and the preamble of the Protestation itself sets out what it is: a declaration of readiness to resist a royal *coup d'état*.[77] At the same time, it was something the Scottish party had failed to obtain in more settled times: it was, as Baillie put it, 'I hope in substance our Scottish Covenant'.[78] The Protestation achieved this synthesis by weaving the army plot together with the 'designs of the priests and Jesuits and other adherents of the see of Rome', and reiterating the case Pym

[73] SP 16/480/26.

[74] BL Harl. MS 163, f. 512a.

[75] *C.J.* 138–40, BL Harl. MS 477, ff. 43r, 45v, 47r. It is intriguing to imagine the course of the Civil War if this amendment had been carried.

[76] SP 63/274/21 and 2.

[77] S. R. Gardiner, *Constitutional Documents of the Puritan Revolution* (Oxford repr. 1979), 155–6.

[78] *Baillie* i. 351.

and Rous had been repeating since 1628, that the subversion of the fundamental laws was being attempted because the fundamental laws were an obstacle to the introduction of popery.[79] This was in part an attempt to assimilate the unacceptable to a familiar context, symbolised by Tomkins' motion on 10 May to search the cellars.[80] It is in part also a result of the necessary conventions of seventeenth century political speech. Leading members knew perfectly well, in the first week of May 1641, that what they were facing was a royal plot. Idiom did not permit them to say so, so they had to find a code method of describing it. It cannot have done Charles any good that the code word for 'royal plot' became 'popish plot'. This sort of displacement aggression may also help to explain why, in the weeks after the plot, there was a sudden turning on the bishops from people not all of whom would have been expected to be their natural enemies. Perhaps the most intriguing example of this process is that crusty old anti-Puritan Sir John Conyers. On 28 May, he wrote to Conway that 'I feare so longe as the bishops have any power the church of Ingland will hange toward that of Roome, and will never be aright settled to the true service of God'.[81] On June 14 Baynham Throckmorton, a future royalist, was saying he hoped to hear of the 'the turninge out ye bishops altogether since now there is no other remedy for cure of the disease'.[82] In this way, the army plot presented the godly with numerous unexpected allies.

Perhaps the biggest contribution the army plot made to the coming of civil war was in the contribution it made to convincing respectable members of the House of Lords that true loyalty might take the form of taking authority, and especially military authority, out of the king's hands. The decision, on 3 May, to send Newport to take command of the Tower before he had the King's consent was the first such decision, and it led to others. Also on 3 May, the Houses sent Mandeville to secure Portsmouth and Earle to secure the trained bands of Dorset. The resemblance to the Houses' actions over Hull a year later is very close. The two Houses asked Charles to change the Lords Lieutenant in Yorkshire, Dorset and Hampshire, appointing Essex instead of Strafford in Yorkshire, and Salisbury and Southampton in addition to Cottington and Richmond in Dorset and Hampshire. On 7 May the Lords called in the trained bands of Wiltshire and Berkshire to secure Portsmouth, while instructing those of Sussex and Dorset to

[79] Caroline Hibbard, *Charles I and the Popish Plot* (Chapel Hill, 1983), 194–6.
[80] BL Harl. MS 163, fo. 544a.
[81] SP 16/480/73.
[82] Bristol Record Office, Smyth of Long Ashton MSS, no. 136(e). 'Cure of' is an interpolation in the MS.

remain in readiness.[83] On 7 May there was also an almost unique example of a proclamation issued on the 'advice' of the House of Lords.[84] On 8 May the committee for the defence of the kingdom directed the Lord Admiral to give command of ships to 'men of trust.' The Lords seem to have believed in the first two weeks of May 1641 that the kingdom was on the edge of an immediate civil war, as they told Charles not too obliquely on 11 May. In reply to the king's final request for a reprieve to Strafford, the Lords told him that his wish could not be 'without danger to himself'.[85] This story does not only illustrate the danger of civil war at the beginning of May 1641. It also illustrates two very deep seventeenth century political assumptions. One is the Lords' view of themselves as a government-in-waiting, ready to take over authority whenever the king could not cope. In this line, their measures of May 1641 foreshadow much of what they did during 1642. The other assumption it illustrates is that whenever the body politic was divided to the point of danger, the king was thought to have a special responsibility for making the concessions necessary to restore unity. It was not only the king who had used the threat of armed force to get his way in English politics: his opponents, in alliance with the Scots, had done so quite as much as he had. Yet, because more was expected of kings than of ordinary mortals, the king suffered for it in a way his opponents never did. Above all, the army plot left many responsible politicians with a feeling that politics were too important to be left to kings. Since this was an assumption Charles could not share, it ultimately became one against which he had to fight.

[83] *L.J.* 238, 241 and 235–246 *passim*; *C.J.* 135. The Lords Lieutenant asked for were duly appointed: PROC 231/5, ff. 447, 450, 451.

[84] *Stuart Royal Proclamations*, ed. James F. Larkin (Oxford, 1983), ii. 742–3.

[85] Alnwick MSS vol. 15 (BL Microfilm 286), f. 221; *L.J.* 245, Original Journal, vol. 16, p. 24.

V

EPILOGUE

17

The Catholic Wind

This essay was written for a collection called *For Want of a Horse: Choice and Chance in History*, edited by my former Yale colleague John Merriman. It seemed, then, an obvious invitation to imagine that a major historical event had turned out differently. I at first contemplated writing a piece assuming Charles I's victory in the Civil War, but, to my surprise, decided that I could not be certain any long-term development would have been different if he had won it: his victory might have been just as pyrrhic as the Parliament's was.

I then contemplated the possibility of James II's victory in 1688, and found the resulting piece startlingly easy to write. What is written here masquerades as an extract from a well-known twentieth century textbook discussing James's victory. This extract states no 'fact' from before 1688 which I do not believe to be correct, and it is therefore an exercise in applying a different optical perspective to a constant body of events. It is startling how well the new perspective fits.

It is not in the nature of such imaginative work to prove that James II might have defeated William in 1688, but I hope it will make us pause for some time before we make the opposite assumption.

To contemporaries, the 'Catholic Wind' of November, 1688 appeared nothing less than providential. Right across the spectrum, from the Scottish minister who complained sourly that God had turned Papist, to the triumphant *Te Deum* with which King James restored Westminster Abbey to the faith in which it had been founded, it was taken for granted, both that the wind was God's judgement on the disputes of Protestant and Catholic and that it was the wind which had settled who would retain the English throne. Yet to us, conditioned as we are to somewhat more sophisticated explanations, such a stress on the significance of the short-term and the accidental must savour of what the French call *l'histoire événementielle*. It comes more naturally to us to look on developments of this magnitude as the product of more deep-seated, and more long-term, forces. To us, it appears an exercise in historical myopia to suppose that in 1688, the ultimate triumph of Catholicism and absolute monarchy in England could still have been in doubt. Their triumph is the result of long-term trends which were already well-established, and which, moreover.

were very far from confined to England.

If one trend in seventeenth-century Europe is clearer than any other, it is the decline of Parliaments and representative assemblies. To say that English Parliaments were on the way out is to say no more than that they were subject to the same forces of historical change that operated in France, Spain, Savoy, Sicily, Naples, and many other parts of Europe. Where we have a trend that affects the whole of Europe from Ireland to Poland, it is hard to argue that a mere chance like the direction of a wind might ever have exempted England from its operation. It was already clear well before 1688 that Parliament in England was a body without a future.

Indeed when one looks at the essentially medieval character of these assemblies, it is difficult to see how they could have been expected to survive far into the modern world. An assembly that had started life as a gathering of the King's feudal tenants-in-chief clearly had no place in the post-feudal world. It is not just that they were disorderly assemblies, in which, as James I of England once said, 'there is nothing heard – but cries, shouts, and confusion.' It is not just that their inveterate localism was surely incompatible with the needs of a modern state. It is surely more significant that the forces of social change had led to a situation in which they had outlived their usefulness. Medieval representative assemblies had been, in their very essence, *occasional*. They had been called when the King wanted what, in medieval terminology, was called an *extraordinary* supply of money. In the seventeenth century, to regard war as extraordinary surely savoured of out-of-date utopianism. Wars, which happened on a regular basis and continued from one year to another, could not be financed by reliance on occasional and extraordinary assemblies. With an enemy at the gate, normal rules of law are usually suspended. That is why in the face of the recurrent emergencies created by continual warfare, representative assemblies and taxation by consent were abandoned all over Europe for the medieval anachronisms that they were. England, insular as always, was slow to fall into line, but since warfare, of all things, most constantly crosses national boundaries, it was hard to see how one country could remain insulated from its effects.

It is equally difficult to see the ultimate triumph of English Catholicism as due to any accidental or short-term factors, for here again there is a trend visible all over Europe, and it is hard to see why England should have been immune. By about 1620, Protestantism was clearly 'over the top': it was not winning new converts, and, even more important, it was not generating new ideas. Richelieu, sensitive as ever to the tide of events, had chosen the right moment to roll back the Protestant tide. Wherever any exception can be found to the rule that Protestantism was not generating new ideas, it is in a development, like Arminianism in Holland or Laudianism in England, which allowed it to creep back towards the intellectual universe it left. The poetry of the period is a memorial to the failure of Protestantism to develop any important appeal to the imagination. As Milton, one of the last great intellects of a dying creed, put it, Protestantism 'found no end, in wand'ring mazes lost.' Protestant theology in the middle seventeenth century is increasingly inward looking, engaged in more and more careful examination of its theological entrails. The names associated with new thinking, like St. Charles Borromeo or St. Francois de Sales, are consistently those of Catholics.

The decline of English Protestantism from 1688 onwards merely underlines the extent to which, ever since the reign of Henry VIII, it had depended on the force of official favour to keep it going. The dogged resistance English Catholics had kept up through their darkest days had surely served to show where spiritual vitality really lay. Those Protestant ministers who talked constantly about the 'seductive' force of Catholicism surely recognized that they were fighting a force, spiritual and psychological, against which they could manage no more than a rear guard action. The persistence, in many contexts, of communal ritual for which Protestantism could find no room surely shows that there was one, at least, among the major functions of religion that it was totally unfitted to discharge. It is not only among theologians that the new ideas belong to Catholics. If we look at people of real distinction, at Galileo, Kepler, Rubens, or Inigo Jones, to name but a few, it is remarkable how consistently, often in the face of severe official discouragement, they turn out to be Catholics. The conversion of Sir Isaac Newton, shortly after James's victory in 1688, is as important a landmark within the realm of ideas as the conversion of Henri IV within the realm of politics.

It is striking how much of the strength of Catholicism was rooted in the rising commercial areas. In Venice, Florence, and Genoa, there was hardly a Protestant to be found. In Belgium, once it had reconquered its dissident Dutch provinces (which did not take it long after 1688), Catholicism was everywhere in the ascendant. In Italy, Belgium, France, and England, the Catholics, by the end of the seventeenth century, controlled most of the commercial wealth of Europe. Protestantism was driven back to the economically less advanced countries on the fringe of Europe, to Scotland, Sweden, Norway, and Denmark. In some way, it had clearly failed to adapt its doctrine to the new rising middle classes, and it paid the penalty. In these circumstances it is hard to avoid the feeling that, whatever had happened in 1688, its ultimate demise in England was something near inevitable.

Scotland, that remote Calvinist redoubt, marks James II's one important failure. Yet here too, it is hard to blame any short-term cause, since the writing on the wall had been plainly visible for so long. The Anglo-Scottish union of 1603 had, from the beginning, been unpopular on both sides of the border. James I's attempt to make it closer, at the beginning of his reign, had been met with determined opposition in both countries. The legacy of the 1640s had led both the Scots and the English to an increasing dislike of the other's interference in their national affairs. The first convenient opportunity to break the union was likely to be welcomed on both sides of the border.

By contrast, James's success cemented the union, which has endured to this day, between England and Ireland. It was always likely that this union would last, since it was based on a clear community of economic interest. England, that rising centre of commerce and manufacturing, desperately needed union with an agrarian country that was a source of cheap food. Ireland, an agricultural country, equally needed a regular outlet for its agrarian exports. The unity of England and Ireland was founded on such a strong economic base that it is difficult to suppose that unity of religion did more than cement a bond that would surely have lasted without.

That James II succeeded where Charles I failed is no doubt to his credit as a man. He was a formidable warrior, and no mean administrator, and he deserves the credit he is usually given for bringing England's armed forces to the peak of fighting fitness they had reached by his death. Yet, able though he was, he should not be given credit for bringing about results that were never in suspense. It is hard to believe that, even if Dutch William had succeeded in evading the Catholic Wind and landing in England, he would have found much welcome there. English xenophobia had always been strong, and the dislike of the Dutch was one of its most intense manifestations. The country that produced Andrew Marvell's *Satires on the Dutch* was not going to accept a Dutch king without considerable protest. A quick glance at the entry under 'Dutch' in the *Oxford Dictionary of Slang* will serve to underline the point: the images associated with a 'Dutch uncle' and with 'Dutch courage' are hardly kingly ones. The marvel is not that William failed: it is that he could ever have supposed he might succeed.

James II, then, was always on a winning wicket. His first and last Parliament, which voted him so much money that he never needed to call another, seems to have perceived this, and it showed sufficient intelligence to vote its own extinction. Whatever credit we may give James, it is a formidable task for those who are prepared to look for the deeper forces of history to deny that the first of the Enlightened Despots had time on his side. The Catholic Wind, no doubt, was a piece of good luck, yet it is a significant truism that luck favours the successful: those who have the luck are those who have the momentum. The Catholic Wind blew in 1688 because it had been blowing all across Europe for two generations and more. James benefited because he was in the right place at the right time, yet, whichever way the wind blew, his was undoubtedly the creed of the future. There is surely no historian so immune to the whole course of historical development as to maintain such an absurdity as that, if the wind had blown the other way, England might now be a Protestant country.

Index

Abbot, George, Archbishop of Canterbury xxiv, 22
'Absolute Monarchy', idea of xviii, 93-6, 98, 131
Agen, Syndic of 128
Alford, Edward 25, 43*n.*, 56, 64, 72
Alimony 117
Allegiance 184-8, 195-9
'Ancient Constitution' 1 and *n.*, 3*n.*, 122, 224
Antrim, Randall Macdonnell first Earl of 242 and *n.*, 274, 276 and *n.*
Apology of the Commons (1604) 78
Appropriation 37-8
Aragon, liberties of 101
Arminianism xxix-xxx, 51-2, 116, 201, 221-4, 235-6, 238, 249
Arundel, Thomas Howard 21st Earl of 112-3, 213, 255
Ashburnham, Jack 284, 285, 286, 287, 295
Ashurst, William 197
Astley, Sir Jacob 289, 298
Atheists 189, 193
Augustine of Hippo, St. 179*n.*, 180
Audley, Mervin Audley Lord 188

Bacon, Sir Nicholas, Lord Keeper 7, 23, 55
Bagshaw, Edward 185
Baillie, Robert 182, 236, 238, 239, 242, 243, 251, 298, 300
Balfour, Sir William 291, 292
Baronets 46
Barrington, Sir Thomas xii, 16, 54, 205
Bath, Henry Bourchier first Earl of 17
Barry, John 244, 269, 275
Bedford, Francis Russell second Earl of 149, 150
—, Francis Russell fourth Earl of 9, 34, 111, 209-10, 211
Berkeley, Sir John 285, 290 and *n.*
—, Sir Maurice 39
—, Sir Robert 139, 142
Bevill, Sir Robert 74
Billingsley, Capt. 291, 292
Bills, Parliamentary 9-10, 35, 69, 116
Black Rod, Gentleman Usher of 300
Bodin, Jean 139*n.*
Bond of Association (1584) 149, 216-7
Borlase, Sir John 265
Boroughbridge (Yorks.) 289
Brahe, Tycho 118
Bramston, Sir John 89, 137-44
Bristol, John Digby first Earl of 66-7, 239, 255, 257, 260, 265
Brooke, Robert Greville second Lord 113, 275
Browne, Henry 293
Buckingham, George Villiers first Duke of xiv, 52, 60, 72, 73, 81-2
—, Impeachment of 40-1, 48-9, 210, 223-4
Burges, Cornelius 239
Burghley, William Cecil first Lord 25, 49, 187-8

Calamy, Edmund 184*n.*, 185, 187, 190, 200*n.*, 203*n.*
Calvert, Sir George 60, 64, 68
Canons (of 1640) 112, 114
Carleton, Sir Dudley 201
Catalonia 122, 125, 126, 127, 128-9, 130
Chamberlain, John 79
Charles I, King 21, 28, 90*n.*, 165-77 *passim*, 183, 230-48 *passim*, 263-79, 281-302
Chudleigh, Capt. James 285, 288, 290, 295
Clanricarde, Ulick Burke fifth Earl of 266
Clientage xi-xii, 209-11
Clotworthy, Sir John 114, 273, 275
Coaches 148
Coal 160
Coke, Sir Edward 1 and *n.*, 5, 24, 25, 37, 43, 53, 55-6, 60, 61, 63, 64, 71, 74, 75, 81, 90, 94, 96, 102 and *n.*, 130, 185, 205, 218
—, Sir John xvii, 128, 133
Colles, John 148-9, 153-7, 159
Coin, alleged shortage of 125
Conquest, right of 98, 101*nn.*, 129, 224
—, in Ireland 267 and *n.*, 278*n.*
Conscience 191-5
Consent 6-7, 25-6, 128-9, 130-1, 134, 139*n.*, 226-7, 237
Contract, theories of 185, 224
Conyers, Sir John 282, 284, 289, 301
Cork, Richard Boyle first Earl of 267

Cottington, Francis Cottington first Lord 254
Counsel 8-9, 11-12, 48-50
'Court' and 'country' xxviii-xxix, 33*n*., 55-7, 67-8
Crawley, Francis 139*n*.
Crew, John 43, 61, 62, 63-4, 69, 74-5, 78, 81
Culpepper, Sir John 299
Custos Regni 116

Davenant, William 285, 286
Davenport, Sir Humphrey 137-144
Dearth 22, 125
Delbridge, John 42, 43-4, 56
Deposition 12, 20
Deputy Lieutenants 16, 47, 221
D'Ewes, Sir Symonds 193, 194, 239
Digby, Sir Kenelm 196*n*.
Digges, Sir Dudley 49, 50-2, 64, 67, 68, 69, 78, 81, 210
Dissolution, Act against (1641) 29, 300
Divine Right 4-5, 7, 61, 76, 94, 183-8, 195-7, 215 and *n*.
Dod, John 207*n*.
Dorset, Edward Sackville fourth Earl of 68, 77*n*., 254
Dyott, Richard 259

Edmondes, Sir Thomas 70
Edwards, Thomas 184, 185, 190, 191, 203
Elections 17, 19-20, 209
Elizabeth I 18, 49, 61
Eliot, Sir John 56, 182, 210
Essex, Robert Devereux third Earl of 112

Falkland, Lucius Carey second Viscount of 188, 250
Family, the 'decline' of xxii-xxiii, 184
Family of Love 149
Fasts 201*n*.
Favour, John 182
Featly, Daniel 179
Feudalism 126
Feudal tenures (in Ireland) 268-9
Fielding, Colonel 289
Fiennes, Nathaniel 97, 281
Fifteenths 43
Finch, Heneage 63, 75
—, Sir John 138*n*., 141, 257
Firearms 126
Five Members (1642) 105, 106
Fleetwood, Sir Miles 68
Forced Loan (1626-7) 125
Fortescue, Sir John (Chief Justice) 12, 27, 39
Free Speech 8, 76, 79
Fuller, Nicholas 39, 182
Fundamentals (in religion) 190

Galway, plantation of 266
Gauden, John 185, 197
General Assembly (of Kirk of Scotland) 237
Giles, Sir Edward 68
Glanville, John xvi, 69
Glyn, John 102-3, 259
God, alleged nationality of 182*n*.
Goring, Sir George, the elder 60, 71-2, 73, 76-7, 79
—, George, the younger 286, 287, 288, 290, 295, 296
Gormanston, Thomas Preston second Viscount of 267, 278
Gouge, William 183-4, 186
Graces, the (1626ff) 244-5, 268-72 *passim*
Great Chain of Being 106-7, 185-8
Great Contract (1610) 35
Grosvenor, Sir Richard 44
Gunpowder Plot (1605) 161*n*.

Hakewill, William 42, 81, 130
Hales, John 190
Hamilton, James Hamilton third Marquess of 242, 246, 247, 250
Harley, Brilliana 201
—, Sir Robert xvi, 3, 239
Hastings, Sir Francis 16, 18
—, Sir George 68
Hayman, Sir Peter 81, 86-7
Heath, Sir Robert 39, 41, 49-50, 71, 75-6
Henderson, Alexander 237
Henri IV, King of France 129
Henrietta Maria, Queen 285, 287, 290, 292-4, 296
Henry VIII 11, 117
Hesilrige, Sir Arthur 15
Hext, Sir Edward 17, 149-50, 161*n*.
Heylin, Peter 193, 198
High Commission, Court of 113, 117
Hobbes, Thomas 103-4, 106, 107, 185
Holland, Henry Rich first Earl of xvii, 294, 299
Holles, Denzil 259
—, Gevase 239
Hooke, John 160 and *n*.
Hooker, John 4-5
—, Richard 182, 183, 185, 188, 192, 195, 197, 202
Hooper, John, Bishop of Gloucester 198
Horsey, Sir Jerome 81

Hospitality 200
Hull (Yorks) 165
Husbands, divine right of 183-4, 193
Hutton, Sir Richard 142
Hyde, Edward 100

Impeachment and Parliamentary judicature 12, 37, 40-1, 48-9, 220-1, 242-3
Impositions 37, 39-40, 44, 46 and *n.*, 51, 52-3, 167
Inflation xviii-xxi, 124-5
Informers 56
Interregnum Bill (1584) 25
Ireland xxii, 98 29, 133, 233, 234, 240-5, 263-79, 294
—, alleged authority of English Parliament in 14, 245, 269-70, 272-4, 278
—, cost of 23, 271-2
—, Irish Army 270 and *nn.*, 274-5, 299
—, Irish Remonstrance 266, 267

James VI and I xiv, and *n.*, 1, 5, 7, 24, 35, 36, 38, 44, 46-7, 55, 59-79 *passim*, 130, 182, 194, 195, 248-9
Jermyn, Henry 282 and *n.*, 285, 286, 287, 288, 294-5, 297
Jewel, John, Bishop of Salisbury 203
Johnston of Wariston, Archibald 283
Jones, William 140
Justices of the Peace 7, 135

King's Servants 45-6
Knightley, Richard xii, 207 and *n.*
Knyvett, Sir Thomas 230

Languedoc, Estates of 128
Lanyon, John 291-2
Latin, harmlessness of 190-1
Laud, William, Archbishop of Canterbury xxii, 106, 180, 191-2, 194, 195, 228, 236, 237, 284, 255
Law, rule of 224-8
—, divine right of 185
Leicester, Robert Sidney second Earl of 3*n.*, 14, 26, 29
Lepton and Goldsmith, case of 81-8, 219
Lewkenor, Samuel 44
Licences to alienate 74
Localism xxviii-xxix, 17-20, 55-6
Lodgings 15, 16-17
Logwood 36
Lunsford, Thomas 295

McCarthy, Sir Donagh 266
Machiavelli, Niccolo 180-1
Magna Carta 12, 99
Mallory, William xvi, 71, 81-7 *passim*, 205
Manchester, Henry Montague first Earl of xvi, 15, 112-3
Mandeville, Edward Montague Viscount (courtesy) 112
Manwaring, Roger 98, 114, 183, 184, 187, 226
Manwood, Sir Roger 25
Marriage, royal 73-7, 82
—, mixed 194-5
Marshall, Stephen 186, 195, 201
Masters, divine right of 184
May, Sir Humphrey 47, 74
Maynard, John 100-1
Middlesex, Lionel Cranfield first Earl of 38, 45, 219-20
Mompesson, Sir Giles 213
Monopolies (*see also* patents) 21, 45, 166, 169-70
Montague of Boughton, Edward Montague first Lord 2, 15
Montrose, James Graham fifth Earl of 238, 283
Moore, Roger 264, 265, 277
More, Sir George 62, 68
Morton, Thomas, Bishop of Durham 185
Multiple Kingdoms 125, 132-3, 182, 230-231 *passim*, 263-79 *passim*

Nantes, Edict of (1598) 179
Navy, the xix-xx, 126, 128, 167, 168*n.*
Neale, William 70
Neville, Sir Henry 36
Newcastle, William Cavendish first Earl of 289
Newport, Mountjoy Blount first Earl of 288, 291*n.*, 292
Nicholas, Edward 45, 165-77 *passim*, 244*n.*, 263, 295
Nithsdale, Robert Maxwell first Earl of 247
Northumberland, Algernon Percy tenth Earl of 236, 258-9
Noy, William xvi, 75
Nutt, Elizabeth 291

Oaths 99, 183 and *n.*
Office, income from xxi, 163-4
Olivares, Conde Duque de 127, 130
O'Neill, Daniel 285, 294, 295, 298
—, Owen Roe 276 and *n.*
Ormond, James Butler twelfth Earl of 240
Osbaldeston, Lambert 111

Paget, William Paget fifth Lord 112, 113
Palmer, Julius 194
Palmes, Sir Guy xvi, 71
Parents, divine right of 184
Parker, Henry 137-8, 194
Parkhurst, John Bishop of Norwich 10, 15
Parliament, attachment to 253-5
—, and country 43-4
—, feared extinction of 39, 42, 96
—, power, extent of 33-43, 47-9
—, and war 27-8, 47
Parry, Sir Thomas 31
Parsons, Sir William 265, 268
Patents 44-6, 50
Pembroke, William Herbert third Earl of xxv, xxviii, 48-9, 67, 116
Percy, Henry 282, 284, 285, 286, 287, 288, 294, 295
Perkins, William 192, 195, 202-3
Perrott, Sir James 67, 81
Petition of Right (1628) 41-2, 224
Phelips, Sir Robert 17, 31-2, 37, 43, 52-3, 61-2, 63, 64, 67, 68, 71, 72-3, 81, 82-7, 128, 205, 218
Philip, Father Robert 293
Plague 263
Pollard, Hugh 285, 286, 287
Poll Tax 113, 130
Population growth 22, 125-6
Ponet, John, Bishop of Winchester 184
Poulett, Sir John 15-16
Poynings's Law 265, 270-1
Predestination xxiii, 150, 222 and *nn.*
Preston, John 52, 188, 200, 222
Privilege, Parliamentary 81-7, 217-8, 226
Protestation, the (May 1641) 243, 300-1
Prynne, William 92, 99, 190, 191
Purefoy, William 284
'Puritans' xi, xxiii-xxiv, 222-3, 236*n.*
Purveyance 169
Pye, Sir Robert 168 and *n.*
Pym, Alexander, the elder 147-50
—, Anne, née Hooke 160, 206
—, Charles 208-9
—, Dorothy 209
—, Erasmus 145-7
—, John xi, xv, xvi, xvii-xviii, xx-xxi, xxiii-xxiv, 15-16, 18-19, 34*n.*, 36-7, 43, 47-8, 54, 56, 74, 81, 90, 92-3, 97, 98, 104, 145-64 *passim*, 168, 184, 186*n.*, 197, 205-28 *passim*, 263, 272, 275, 296
—, Philippa 150, 152-3, 158-160
—, William 148, 156, 157 and *n.*, 158-9

Queries, the (1641) 268

Racing 208
Rates, Books of 167, 168
Recusants 45 and *n.*, 56, 74, 182, 194-5
Rich, Sir Nathaniel 71, 81
Richelieu, Cardinal 293
Roe, Sir Thomas 39, 299-300
Rous, Sir Anthony 159, 160, 161*n.*, 206
Rudyerd, Sir Benjamin xvi, 22, 42, 67, 91
Russell, John Russell first Lord 126
Rutherford, Samuel 190, 192 and *n.*, 200, 202

St. John, Oliver 95 and *n.*, 102, 106-7, 142
Salisbury, Robert Cecil first Earl of xx-xxi, 23, 124, 162
Saltpetre 127
Sandys, Edwin, the elder, Archbishop of York 179*n.*, 187, 197, 199, 200
—, Sir Edwin, the younger 13, 31-2, 35, 53, 84-8, 125, 134
Savill, Thomas Savill first Viscount 112
Saye and Sele, William Fiennes first Viscount xii, 81, 112, 113, 275
Sedition 97
Selden, John 35
Separation of powers 2, 122
Servants 184, 186-7 and *nn.*
Seymour, Sir Francis xv-xvi, 71, 81-2, 128
Shakespeare, William 8
Sherland, Christopher 223
Ship Money xxix, 27, 126-7, 137-44 *passim*, 258
Sibthorpe, Robert 196
Smart, Peter 235
Somerset, Edward Seymour first Duke of 126
Southampton, Henry Wriothesley third Earl of 35
Sovereignty 3*n.*
Spanish Armada (1588) 126
Spencer, Robert Spencer first Lord 91
Star Chamber 113, 152 and *n.*
Stewart, Henry 245, 273
Strafford, Earl of, *see* Wentworth, Sir Thomas
Strode, William 97
Subsidies, collection and assessment of 6, 17-20, 22, 42-4, 123, 125, 134-5
—, in Ireland 267, 271
Succession, doctrines of 25
Suckling, Sir John 285, 286, 288, 291, 297
Sully, Duc de 124
Supply, voting of xiv, xix, xxvii-xxviii, 21-2, 24, 35-48 *passim*, 67-72, 130

Tate, Zouch 15
Taylor, Jeremy 116, 189-90
Thirty Years' War 125, 132-3
Throckmorton, Baynham 301
—, Francis 151-2
Tonnage and Poundage 24, 39-40, 42-3, 53, 165, 177 *passim*, 225-6
Toleration 179, 216
Traquair, John Stuart first Earl of 246
Treason 84, 87, 89-109 *passim*
Triennial Act (1641) 29, 111, 243
Triplett, Thomas 239
Twysden, Sir Roger 27
Tyndale, William 190

Union of the Crowns (1603) 13-14, 35

Valuations xx-xxi, 151-7
Vane, Sir Henry the elder 26, 238, 242, 254, 255, 256, 261, 263, 284
Vaux of Harrowden, Edward Vaux Lord 186-7
Vavassor, Colonel 289

Waller, Sir Hardress 266
Wallington, Nehemiah 239
Wandesford, Sir Christopher 265
War xix-xx, 7-8, 21, 23-4, 40-1, 47, 124-9, 130-1, 131-3
Wardour, Sir Edward 168
Wardship xx-xxi, 145-62 *passim*
Warner, John, Bishop of Rochester 114-8 *passim*
Wentworth, Sir George 291
—, Peter 96
—, Sir Thomas, first Earl of Strafford xvi, 34, 38 and *n.*, 41-2, 65, 69, 79, 89-109 *passim*, 127, 129, 196, 198, 236, 257, 265-6, 267, 291, 292, 299
—, Mr. Thomas, Recorder of Oxford 39
Weston, Baron 139
—, Sir Richard 70
Wharton, Philip Wharton fourth Lord 112, 230
Whitelocke, Bulstrode 95, 99
—, James 39, 52
Whitgift, John, Archbishop of Canterbury 180, 184, 203
Widdrington, Sir William 239, 259
Wilde, John xvi, 70
Williams, John, Archbishop of York 66, 111, 114, 115, 189
Willmott, Henry 284, 286, 287, 294, 295
Windebank, Sir Francis 256-7
Winthrop, John 125
Winwood, Sir Ralph 49
Writs of Summons 4, 7, 60
Wyllys, George 254
Wynn, Sir Richard 295-6

Yelverton, Henry 184